INTERVENTIONS: NEW STUDIES IN MEDIEVAL CULTURE
Ethan Knapp, Series Editor

CHAUCER ON SCREEN

Absence, Presence, and
Adapting the *Canterbury Tales*

Edited by
KATHLEEN COYNE KELLY & TISON PUGH

Foreword by
TERRY JONES

THE OHIO STATE UNIVERSITY PRESS
COLUMBUS

Copyright © 2016 by The Ohio State University.
All rights reserved.

Library of Congress Cataloging-in-Publication Data
Names: Kelly, Kathleen Coyne, editor. | Pugh, Tison, editor. | Jones, Terry, 1942– writer of foreword.
Title: Chaucer on screen : absence, presence, and adapting the Canterbury tales / edited by Kathleen Coyne Kelly and Tison Pugh ; foreword by Terry Jones The Ohio State University Press.
Other titles: Interventions (Columbus, Ohio)
Description: Columbus : The Ohio State University Press, [2016] | Series: Interventions: new studies in medieval culture | Includes bibliographical references and index.
Identifiers: LCCN 2016031759 | ISBN 9780814253724 (cloth ; alk. paper) | ISBN 0814213170 (cloth ; alk. paper)
Subjects: LCSH: Chaucer, Geoffrey, –1400. Canterbury tales—Film adaptations. | Chaucer, Geoffrey, –1400. Canterbury tales—Television adaptations. | Tales, Medieval—History and criticism.
Classification: LCC PR1872 .C47 2016 | DDC 791.43/6—dc23
LC record available at https://lccn.loc.gov/2016031759

Cover design by Laurence J. Nozik
Text design by Juliet Williams
Type set in Adobe Minion Pro

∞ The paper used in this publication meets the minimum requirements of the American National Standard for Information Sciences—Permanence of Paper for Printed Library Materials. ANSI Z39.48–1992.

9 8 7 6 5 4 3 2 1

CONTENTS

List of Illustrations — ix

Foreword
    TERRY JONES — xi

INTRODUCTION Chaucer on Screen
    KATHLEEN COYNE KELLY AND TISON PUGH — 1

PART I THEORIZING ABSENCE

CHAPTER 1 Naked yet Invisible: Filming Chaucer's Narrator
    ELIZABETH SCALA — 19

CHAPTER 2 "The Play's the Thing": The Cinematic Fortunes of Chaucer and Shakespeare
    SUSAN ARONSTEIN AND PETER PAROLIN — 33

CHAPTER 3 Chaucer, Film, and the Desert of the Real; or, Why Geoffrey Chaucer Will Never Be Jane Austen
    LARRY SCANLON — 45

CHAPTER 4 Profit, Politics, and Prurience; or, Why Chaucer Is Bad Box Office
    KATHLEEN FORNI — 56

PART II LOST AND FOUND

CHAPTER 5 Chaucer and the Moving Image in Pre–World War II America
LYNN ARNER   69

CHAPTER 6 Lost Chaucer: Natalie Wood's "The Deadly Riddle" and the Golden Age of American Television
CANDACE BARRINGTON   88

PART III PRESENCE

CHAPTER 7 Chaucerian History and Cinematic Perversions in Michael Powell and Emeric Pressburger's *A Canterbury Tale*
TISON PUGH   111

CHAPTER 8 Idols of the Marketplace: Chaucer/Pasolini
KATHRYN L. LYNCH   130

CHAPTER 9 "Sorry, Chaucer": Mixed Feelings and Hyapatia Lee's *Ribald Tales of Canterbury*
GEORGE SHUFFELTON   149

CHAPTER 10 The Naked Truth: Chaucerian Spectacle in Brian Helgeland's *A Knight's Tale*
SIÂN ECHARD   167

PART IV THE BBC *CANTERBURY TALES* (2003)

CHAPTER 11 Putting the Second First: The BBC "Miller's Tale"
STEVE ELLIS   187

CHAPTER 12 Midlife Sex and the BBC "Wife of Bath"
SARAH STANBURY   196

CHAPTER 13 Serving Time: The BBC "Knight's Tale" in the Prison-House of Free Adaptation
LOUISE D'ARCENS   208

CHAPTER 14 The Color of Money: The BBC "Sea Captain's Tale"
KATHLEEN COYNE KELLY   218

CHAPTER 15 Sex, Plague, and Resonance: Reflections on the BBC
            "Pardoner's Tale"
                ARTHUR BAHR   230

CHAPTER 16 Time, Memory, and Desire in the BBC "Man of Law's Tale"
                KATHLEEN DAVIS   239

PART V ABSENT PRESENCE

CHAPTER 17 Marketing Chaucer: *Mad Men* and the Wife of Bath
                LAURIE FINKE AND MARTIN B. SHICHTMAN   251

List of Contributors   267
Selected Bibliography   271
Index   279

ILLUSTRATIONS

FIGURES 1.1A AND B	London scenes in (a) *Shakespeare in Love* and (b) *A Knight's Tale*	24
FIGURE 1.2	The stage in *Shakespeare in Love*	28
FIGURE 2.1	The *Troilus* frontispiece	34
FIGURE 2.2	The Swan Theatre, c. 1596, by Arnoldus Buchelius	35
FIGURE 5.1	Star Marc McDermott reading Chaucer on the set	72
FIGURE 5.2	Collage of "What Douglas Fairbanks Missed"	86
FIGURE 6.1	*Chicago Daily Tribune* display ad for the first broadcast of "The Deadly Riddle"	96
FIGURE 6.2	Public relations blurb for "The Deadly Riddle"	98
FIGURE 6.3	1956 Warner Bros. press photo of Jacques Sernas and Natalie Wood	99
FIGURES 7.1A AND B	*A Canterbury Tale* and Britain's timelessness	118
FIGURE 8.1	The friar in Pasolini's "Summoner's Tale"	141
FIGURE 8.2	January clutches May in Pasolini's "Merchant's Tale"	145
FIGURE 9.1	Cover image of *The Ribald Tales of Canterbury*	150

FIGURE 10.1	The Knight's Tale, from Mary Eliza Joy Haweis's *Chaucer for Children: A Golden Key*	173
FIGURE 10.2	The Knight's Tale, from Anne Anderson in Emily Underdown's *The Gateway to Chaucer*	173
FIGURE 10.3	Emily in the garden, from Janet Harvey Kelman's *Stories from Chaucer*	175
FIGURE 12.1	The BBC "Wife of Bath": Beth recuperates after surgery	199
FIGURE 12.2	The BBC "Wife of Bath": Beth rejuvenated	206
FIGURE 14.1	The BBC "Shipman's Tale": Meena's mallet	226
FIGURE 17.1	The rooster	257

FOREWORD

WHAT FUN! A Festival of Chaucer's works in the cinema or—more precisely—the lack of them!

This is an immensely varied collection of essays—from a detective story about tracking down a lost film about the Wife of Bath to a carefully considered analysis of *The Ribald Tales of Canterbury* (the 1985 pornographic film). There's lots of academic criticism here too: from why Shakespeare has so much more cinematic presence than Chaucer ("Chaucer was the property of a cultural elite," while "Shakespeare is box office because he has always been box office; Chaucer, on the other hand, is not and never has been") to an analysis of Pier Paulo Pasolini's *I racconti di Canterbury*, Brian Helgeland's *A Knight's Tale*, Powell and Pressburger's *A Canterbury Tale*, and the BBC's versions of the *Canterbury Tales*. Larry Scanlon compares Jane Austen and Chaucer, demonstrating why Jane Austen can so easily slip into drama while Chaucer cannot: "Chaucer's narrative is in the first person, while free indirect discourse in the novel is generally in the third."

Insights like these provide an illuminating discourse on why Chaucer has not had the impact on cinema that he should have had.

Terry Jones
April 2016

INTRODUCTION

CHAUCER ON SCREEN

KATHLEEN COYNE KELLY and TISON PUGH

FILMGOERS watch Geoffrey Chaucer walking naked down a hot dusty road; Chaucer's Wife of Bath (renamed Beth) is a BBC soap-opera star; Geoffrey Chaucer hath a blog and is on Facebook (houseoffame.blogspot.com); and high school and college students rap Chaucer on YouTube in endless variations on their class projects. Seeing—or being—Chaucer has never been easier. Yet who, or what, "Chaucer" has become remains an open question, as the history of adaptations of his corpus has demonstrated over the centuries, ranging from the fifteenth-century apocrypha to current adaptations beyond the Anglophone world.[1] This question excites, inspires, and sometimes frustrates Chaucer's readers, for it marks the ways that Chaucer's role in English literature is both foundational (the hoary, reverent image of Chaucer as "the Father of English Literature") and marginal (a benighted precursor to early modernity, forever in the shadow of Shakespeare).

Chaucer on Screen: Absence, Presence, and Adapting the Canterbury Tales investigates the various translations of Chaucer and his literature to film and television, pointing in particular to the disparate expectations of scholars in

---

1. For the Chaucerian apocrypha, see Kathleen Forni, *The Chaucerian Apocrypha: A Counterfeit Canon* (Gainesville: University of Florida Press, 2001); and *The Chaucerian Apocrypha: A Selection* (Kalamazoo: Medieval Institute Publications, 2005). For an online archive of post-1945, non-Anglophone Chauceriana, see Candace Barrington and Jonathan Hsy's "Global Chaucers" project at globalchaucers.wordpress.com.

the academy and of consumers of visual culture. It is a familiar gap, one discussed often in relation to class, education, and taste, but one that is closing as traditional distinctions between high and low culture fade in an increasingly globalized, digital culture. To argue for the categories "high" and "low" pays increasingly diminishing returns. We and the other contributors to *Chaucer on Screen* cannot offer definitive or final answers to the question of who Chaucer is and what and how he means (nor do we aspire to). Rather, we aim to foreground Chaucer's importance to any sustained discussion of medievalism and its cultural manifestations in which the Middle Ages is either characterized as the Dark Ages or reimagined as a lost Golden Age. In this light the practice of medievalism—that celebration of both the "dark" and the "golden"—accommodates a specialized genre of adaptation in which various artifacts in the vast store of medieval culture have always already been appropriated, borrowed, stolen, reproduced, remade, rethought, and repurposed from the moment authors and artists perceived or constructed a gap between themselves and the past, enabling them to imagine, as the Wife of Bath says, "th' olde dayes" (3.857).[2]

Medievalism bears its own rich literary legacy: as some scholars are fond of claiming, the first text of English medievalism, in its form as nostalgia for a medieval past (the thousand years spanning roughly 500 to 1500 CE), is *Beowulf*, the epic poem of a virtuoso adapter and syncretizer working sometime between the eighth century and the early eleventh. And, for another example at the end of this chronological range, consider Sir Thomas Malory, who mined the early thirteenth-century French Vulgate cycle to fashion an Arthurian legend for fifteenth-century England. At one point Malory's narrator looks backward, expressing sorrow that the "stabylyté" of love is a thing of the past—"than was love trouthe and faythfulnes ... in kynge Arthurs dayes."[3] Medievalism's roots lie in the Middle Ages as an era that was itself invested in the nostalgic meaning of yesteryear.

The aesthetic processes of medievalism have become increasingly important as a subject for academic inquiry, and the intersection of medievalism and film counts as a vibrant subsection of this area of analysis.[4] Although

---

2. Geoffrey Chaucer, *The Riverside Chaucer,* ed. Larry D. Benson, 3rd ed. (Boston: Houghton Mifflin, 1987).

3. Thomas Malory, *The Works of Sir Thomas Malory,* ed. Eugéne Vinaver, rev. P. J. C. Field, 3rd ed. (Oxford: Clarendon, 1990), 3.1120.

4. Foundational mongraphs in cinematic medievalism include John Aberth, *A Knight at the Movies: Medieval History on Film* (New York: Routledge, 2003); Nickolas Haydock, *Movie Medievalism: The Imaginary Middle Ages* (Jefferson, NC: McFarland, 2008); Laurie Finke and Martin B. Shichtman, *Cinematic Illuminations: The Middle Ages on Film* (Baltimore: Johns

often perceived as hopping behind medieval studies proper, critical inquiries into medievalism have been vigorously redefined and repositioned of late, as demonstrated by the ongoing success of such journals as *Studies in Medievalism* and *The Year's Work in Medievalism,* as well as in *postmedieval,* which recently featured a cluster on neomedievalisms and an issue devoted to comic medievalisms.[5] In the context of these debates, and according to Kathleen Biddick's account of a traumatic break in nineteenth-century medieval studies between high and low, professional and amateur, one might perceive Chaucer's literary achievements as having been stranded on the shores of the academy, while a good deal else of the medieval archive, for good or ill, depending on one's perspective, washed up on the opposite shore.[6]

Medievalisms and neomedievalisms thrive today as forms of artistic adaptation, ranging from the reverential and historical to the iconoclastic and ahistorical. Chaucer himself was an adapter par excellence of both form and content (and worked in both reverential and subversive modes), trying out many of the literary genres available to him as well as drawing on what he read and what he remembered—so goes the received narrative of Chaucer's relation to his sources and analogues. With Chaucer as an exemplar, and in addition to viewing adaptation and medievalism as related processes, the contributors to *Chaucer on Screen* often draw connections between source study and adaptation studies. What we call *first-wave* adaptation studies—that is, an approach that privileges a source text and judges adaptations on the basis of fidelity to that text—while not directly descended from historical and philological source studies, operate from a similar set of assumptions and practices. Stephen G. Nichols, in his introduction to the groundbreaking special issue of *Speculum* devoted to the New Philology in 1990, argues that philology, as traditionally understood and practiced by such scholars as Erich Auerbach and Leo Spitzer, "rejected . . . adaptation or *translatio,* the continual rewriting of past works in a variety of versions" in favor of "a preoccupation with scholarly exactitude" seeking "a fixed text as transparent as possible."[7] For the most part, first-wave adaptation critics analyze, often side-by-side, a known or posited precursor text and a "postcursor" text (or film), assuming a genealogical relation between the two, and hunting for variants not to be praised (to adapt

---

Hopkins University Press, 2010); and Bettina Bildhauer, *Filming the Middle Ages* (London: Reaktion, 2011).

    5. See especially *Studies in Medievalism* 17 (2009) through 20 (2011); "Medievalism Now," *The Year's Work in Medievalism* 28 (2013); and *postmedieval* 5.1 and 5.2 (2014).

    6. Kathleen Biddick, *The Shock of Medievalism* (Durham: Duke University Press, 1998).

    7. Stephen G. Nichols, "Introduction: Philology in a Manuscript Culture," *Speculum* 65 (1990): 1–10, 3.

Bernard Cerquiglini[8]) but to be condemned as corruptions. First-wave critics judge the aesthetic repercussions, as it were, that arise when a source text is transformed into another medium—a new story told slant, a film, a painting, a graphic novel, and so on.

Moreover, we suggest that this first-wave fidelity model in film studies strikingly resembles an epiphenomenon of source study in that the dependence of a particular film on its precursor serves as the primary object of interest. Historically, the majority of English and American Chaucerians has privileged Chaucer's works over his sources—and continues to privilege Chaucer's works over subsequent adaptations. For some, the continued practice of medievalism destabilizes periodicity and its boundaries by suggesting that the Middle Ages is not (yet) over. Additionally, cinematic and televisual adaptations of literary texts challenge the status of the book—what if *we* are over *it*? Early defenders of cinematic adaptations reproduce this sort of privilege by arguing for a taxonomy to distinguish texts and their effects from film. George Bluestone, in his pioneering 1957 study, *Novels into Film,* says that "changes are *inevitable* the moment one abandons the linguistic for the visual medium," further contending that "the end products of novel and film represent different aesthetic genera, as different from each other as ballet is from architecture."[9] Thomas Leitch describes Bluestone's approach as essentialist in that Bluestone assumes that the conventions of a written narrative cannot be translated to the screen (large or small, we would add), and vice versa.[10] Indeed, we can point to any number of texts that, postfilm, we might describe as *cinematic.* In his cross-temporal reading of Paul Wegener's *Der Golem* (1920) and Chaucer's Knight's Tale, James J. Paxson offers a particularly apt exploration of the cinematic literary, using Chaucer's tale to imagine "the prefiguration of cinematographic expression in medieval literature."[11] Moreover, when Deborah Cartmell and Imelda Whelehan declare that "an adaptation on screen can re-envision a well-worn narrative for a new audience inhabiting a different

---

8. Bernard Cerquiglini incites: "Philology is a bourgeois, paternalist, and hygienist system of thought about the family; it cherishes filiation, tracks down adulterers, and is afraid of contamination. Its thought is based on what is wrong (the variant being a form of deviant behaviour)" (*Elogue de la variante: Histoire critique de la philology,* translated by Betsy Wing as *In Praise of the Variant: A Critical History of Philology* [1989; Baltimore: Parallax, 1999], 111).

9. George Bluestone, *Novels into Film* (1957; Baltimore: Johns Hopkins University Press, 2003), 5; italics in original.

10. Thomas M. Leitch, "Twelve Fallacies in Contemporary Adaptation Theory," *Criticism* 45.2 (2003): 149–71, 150–54.

11. James J. Paxson, "The Anachronism of Imagining Film in the Middle Ages: Wegener's *Der Golem* and Chaucer's *Knight's Tale,*" *Exemplaria* 19.2 (2007): 290–309.

cultural environment, and their relationship to the 'origin' may itself change enormously," they, unlike Paxson, tacitly privilege the book.[12]

It is enormously difficult to resist Bluestone's and Cartmell and Whelehan's characterizations of the relationship between film/television and text because our pedagogy often depends on such arguments, in that instructors justify assigning a film or television adaptation in class because we have discovered added value in discussing film and film theory (which simultaneously decenters and valorizes the book). Moreover, film also serves as a crucial avenue into medieval literature for millennial students. Amy Kaufman argues eloquently that

> students . . . need bridges, particularly today's students who are taught that anything not immediately relevant to their financial success, or to the great technological vacuum into which they inevitably will be sucked, is a waste of their time and tuition money. These students are pressed to forget the past and look toward the future, toward STEM majors and Wall Street and cell phones and cubicles and away from the quiet musings of a writer with the time, space, and leisure to contemplate the essence of the human condition.[13]

Thus we are not criticizing: we are describing our own teaching practices. Still, we would like to advance another argument about adaptation: perhaps it is simply the wrong premise upon which to base a critical and aesthetic judgment of Chaucer's works on screen. Thomas Leitch advocates seeing cinematic adaptations as a distinct genre freed from their literary roots: "Only adaptation study, whether or not it uses the source text as a touchstone, remains obsessed with asking whether a given film is any good as a preliminary, a precondition, or a substitute for asking how it works."[14] What would happen, then, if we began asking, not whether *A Canterbury Tale, The Ribald Tales of Canterbury, I racconti di Canterbury, A Knight's Tale,* the BBC *Canterbury Tales,* and other examples of *Cinema Chauceriana* are any good, but how do they work?[15]

Besides the pressures of the classroom, we can identify another obstacle to jettisoning the comparative mode when analyzing adaptations. Linda

---

12. Deborah Cartmell and Imelda Whelehan, *Screen Adaptation: Impure Cinema* (Basingstoke, Hampshire: Palgrave Macmillan, 2010), 23.

13. Amy S. Kaufman, "Lowering the Drawbridge," *The Year's Work in Medievalism* 28 (2013): 2–8, 2.

14. Leitch, "Twelve Fallacies," 149–71, 162.

15. We use the term *Cinema Chauceriana* in homage to Kevin Harty's classic *Cinema Arthuriana: Twenty Essays,* rev. ed. (2002; Jefferson, NC: McFarland, 2010), acknowledging, along with Harty, the fustiness and fussiness of such a term.

Hutcheon writes of the "palimpsestuousness" of adaptation; that is, the "oscillation between a past image and a present one" that an audience in the know, and only an audience in the know, experiences.[16] For Hutcheon, "adaptation *as adaptation* involves . . . a conceptual flipping back and forth between the work we know and the work we are experiencing."[17] This volume exists because we contributors are in the know, and we cannot *unknow*. It should be noted that while those not in the know cannot bring this double vision to a cinematic or televisual adaptation of Chaucer's *Canterbury Tales* or other works, that does not mean that such viewers cannot discern the cinematic equivalents of what Michael Riffaterre calls "ungrammaticalities" in a text, which he describes as lexical deviations, such as solecisms and nonsense words; seemingly inappropriate phrases and details; sudden shifts in viewpoint, style, or voice; and so on.[18] Cinematic ungrammaticalities—discontinuities in camera work, dialogue that sounds out of place or time, elements of the *mise-en-scène* that clash with or signify outside of the logic of the film, and self-conscious acting—may very well register for viewers as puzzles without necessarily leading to sources. A cinematic ungrammaticality may simply raise the possibility that another, previous narrative exists.[19] And even if those not in the know never discover a source text, their appreciation and enjoyment of a given adaptation is not necessarily diminished. How many music fans of a certain generation happily listened to Janis Joplin's "Piece of My Heart" before discovering that it was a cover of Erma Franklin's original? There are pleasures, and there are palimpsestuous pleasures.

Chaucer on Screen is intended as an intervention into traditional attitudes toward Chaucer and his cinematic and televisual adaptations, and in the way that Francesco Casetti describes when he argues that

> film and literature can also be considered as *sites of production and the circulation of discourses*; that is, as symbolic constructions that refer to a cluster of meanings that a society considers possible (thinkable) and feasible (legitimate). . . . Within this perspective adaptation is no longer seen as a work

---

16. Linda Hutcheon, *A Theory of Adaptation*, 2nd ed. (London: Routledge, 2006), 172.
17. Hutcheon, *Theory*, 139.
18. Michael Riffaterre, "Syllepsis," *Critical Inquiry* 6 (1980): 625–38.
19. As Leitch argues, "The single trait most likely to encourage a film to be watched as an adaptation is . . . a period setting. . . . Adaptations that wish to announce their status as adaptations are adorned with period music" and are obsessed "with authors, books, and words. . . . The intertitles of avowed adaptations are utterly distinctive" ("Adaptation: the Genre," *Adaptation* 1.2 [2008]: 106–20, 111–17). We prefer to give viewers more credit for their experiences of an adaptation as a genre.

repeating another work.... We are no longer confronted with a re-reading or a re-writing: rather, what we are dealing with is the *reappearance, in another discursive field, of an element (a plot, a theme, a character, etc.) that has previously appeared elsewhere.*[20]

In the abstract, there is nothing particularly provocative about this reformulation of the relationship between source and text: seniority, or chronology, loses its privilege (Bakhtin); the author is repositioned as an author-function (Barthes, Foucault); and narrative itself takes on a kind of replicating agency (Derrida, Miller). Such concepts emphasize the fluidity among source texts, authors, adaptations, and their (re)animators, usefully allowing readers and viewers to see anew, and to question, temporal causality.

For some, however, it is quite another matter to think through these ideas in regard to Chaucer and his sources. At the 2004 New Chaucer Society meeting, a handful of Chaucerians, partly in response to the 2002 publication of the first volume of the revised edition of *Sources and Analogues of the* Canterbury Tales, did just that, in a session titled "The Afterlife of Origins."[21] One of the participants, Nancy Bradbury, summarized the range of current approaches to source study as "at one extreme, privileging of empirically demonstrable 'hard sources' over all other kinds of textual relations, and, at the other, the rejection of traditional source studies study altogether on the postmodernist grounds that one vast intertext connects all texts equally."[22] A "hard source" is, in Peter Beidler's words, "a specific work for which we have an extant copy and that we know, from verbal similarities, character names, and plot sequences, that Chaucer used."[23] At the other end of the spectrum is the "lost" source. While all sources, adamantine or squishy, can be interrogated with respect to their status qua source, it is, not surprisingly, so-called soft sources that generate the most heated discussion.

---

20. Francesco Casetti, "Adaptation and Mis-adaptations: Film, Literature, and Social Discourses," *A Companion to Literature and Film*, ed. Robert Stam and Alessandra Raengo (Oxford: Blackwell, 2004), 81–91, 82; italics in original.

21. Robert M. Correale and Mary Hamel, eds., *Sources and Analogues of the* Canterbury Tales (Cambridge: Brewer, 2002). Volume 2 was published in 2005. The papers from "The Afterlife of Origins" session were published under the heading "Colloquium: The Afterlife of Origins," *Studies in the Age of Chaucer* 28 (2006): 217–70. All italics are original.

22. Nancy Bradbury, "Proverb Tradition as a Soft Source for the *Canterbury Tales*," "Colloquium: The Afterlife of Origins," *Studies in the Age of Chaucer* 28 (2006): 237–42, 237.

23. Peter Beidler, "New Terminology for Sources and Analogues: Or, Let's Forget the Lost French Source for The Miller's Tale," "Colloquium," *Studies in the Age of Chaucer* 28 (2006): 225–30, 226.

By comparison, adaptation study as a whole generates stances that are less combative because in most instances, the source text under discussion is unequivocally known—the film title, for example, often reproduces the title of the book. And these days, as promotional paratexts accompanying films proliferate, spectators are given unprecedented access to the genesis of any film that they may choose to explore. In fact, when making and then marketing an adaptation, most film studios hope to exploit the cultural capital that the precursor text has accrued. We know of no adaptation of the *Canterbury Tales* of which this is not true. For instance, while Brian Helgeland's *A Knight's Tale* (2001), a loose, enjoyable romp with little debt to Chaucerian texts, ignored Chaucer in its initial promotional materials, it is now described on the Internet Movie Database as "inspired by the *Canterbury Tales*, as well as the story of Ulrich von Lichtenstein."[24] Indeed, should we even consider *A Knight's Tale* an adaptation? Perhaps it is more accurate to speak of it as an extensive allusion. Some allusions hardly need Chaucer at all, such as when in David Fincher's *Se7en* (1995) the detectives Somerset (Morgan Freeman) and Mills (Brad Pitt) study Chaucer's Parson's Tale while tracking down a serial killer. John Ford's *The Treasure of the Sierra Madre* (1948) and Sam Raimi's *A Simple Plan* (1998) share with Chaucer's Pardoner's Tale the folkloric motif of three men seeking their fortune but finding death instead. Given the extensive range of this topos, it is challenging to ascertain whether these parallels constitute allusions, analogues, or simply coincidences among storylines over a six-hundred-year timeline.

In any event, we are suggesting that there are precedents, and good reasons, for including film and television adaptations of Chaucer's texts in studies of his sources and analogues. We'd like to disrupt chronological thinking that positions Chaucer as the privileged ur-storyteller, requiring a definition of analogues as those tales that exist prior to or contemporary with Chaucer. Additionally, we'd like to acknowledge as analogues those tales (whatever the medium) that come "after" Chaucer. We thus stand within those "postmodernist grounds" that Nancy Bradbury describes, in which "one vast intertext connects all texts equally." Carolyn P. Collette aligns herself with this end of the spectrum when she invokes Deleuze's metaphor of the rhizome as a way to understand relations among texts: "Synchronic models of 'source study' [as well as] . . . identify[ing] the *sociolect* of a group or subculture may be much more useful than the more diachronically-based models of originary

---

24. This phenomenon confirms Leitch's point that marketing adaptations as adaptations enhances a film's profitability ("Adaptation," 116).

paradigms."[25] The current interest in identifying and tracking memes—ideas or behaviors or words, even styles or tones or attitudes, that arise, circulate, and often "mutate" in culture—comes to mind, especially given debates over the term and the understanding of memes as somehow replicating "genetically." Memetics, it might be argued, is source study scientized: consider the almost obsessive drive to pin down the source of a meme, an endeavor made relatively easy these days through tracking its genealogy, gestation, and promulgation across searchable print and digital media. (And now that the meme has achieved traction in the popular imagination, the very idea of the meme begets new and mutated definitions and practices of memes.)

Controversies aside, the construct of the meme permits us to see sources and analogues as the privileged textual phenomena that they are while acknowledging that culture often expresses itself through phenomena never captured by the archive. We might understand such medieval sources as "floating"; that is, references so diffused throughout the cultural landscape of fourteenth-century England that they cannot be definitively pinned down to a particular text, author, or language. Understanding that Chaucer drew on the memes of his day that are not preserved and never could have been preserved in the historical record gives us some leeway to shift from a diachronic approach to sources to a synchronic approach. Such a perspective, suggests Collette,

> constructs a Chaucer quite different from the figure who has dominated Chaucer studies for the last hundred years. No longer the isolated genius, the seminal father-figure who saw further and more clearly than any of his contemporaries the potential of the English language, he emerges as less solitary in his genius, more social, communal, shaped by and shaping the cultural paradigms of his time and later.... In addition to the conversation an author may have with his sources and his readers, we [must] add the conversation he is part of in the intellectual world he inhabits.[26]

The Romantic construct of Chaucer as isolated genius may well hold an allure for those who see themselves as similarly sequestered in the university. In this volume, however, the contributors opt for a "social, communal" Chaucer, demonstrating that the intellectual world that we inhabit is not a world confined to the university but one that is capacious enough for another pass at

---

25. Carolyn P. Collette, "The Alchemy of Imagination and the Labyrinth of Meaning: Some Caveats about the Afterlife of Sources," "Colloquium," *Studies in the Age of Chaucer* 28 (2006): 243–48, 245.

26. Collette, "Alchemy," 247.

determining what of Boccaccio's *Decameron* Chaucer knew, as well as for the image of a charismatic Chaucer trudging naked down a dusty road.

While the majority of adaptation studies takes the cinema as the default medium, the contributors to *Chaucer on Screen* include television as well as film in their purview and often apply the observations and arguments about film adaptation to television. However, we are mindful that film and television are two distinct media with separate—but entangled—histories. Just as cinema in its early days often reproduced, or remediated, the conventions of the stage, early television remediated not only stage conventions but film conventions as well.[27] However, over time, film and television developed their own aesthetics, production values, and conventions, partly in response to the physical and material context in which audiences experience each medium. Leaving home for the theater is an event, and viewing is experienced publicly and communally. (Family and friends are optional, but strangers are not.) Filmgoers expect visual effects that only the big screen can deliver, which spurred such innovations as Cinemascope and 3D and the reliance on the panoramic shot and crane shot. In contrast, audiences usually watch television privately amid the comforts of home—with or without kith and kin. Television directors must accommodate the small screen and eschew panoramic vistas for close-ups. Yet many arguments about the aesthetic and generic differences between film and television have collapsed, unless one is explicitly discussing the two media before the advent of Betamax or, perhaps, even the TV movie-of-the-week. New technologies and changes in taste have resulted in cinematic television and televisual film. These days, our experiences of the two media include watching movies at home according to our own schedules and binge-viewing television serials as if they were mammoth films.

Furthermore, even distinctions between stand-alone films and TV series are blurring, as studios produce sequel after sequel, and many television series are intended to have a clear ending, such as the BBC *Canterbury Tales* (2003), discussed in this volume. Another case in point is Jonathan Myerson's much-celebrated *The Canterbury Tales* (1998–2000), with its frame narrative dramatized with claymation characters (by Aida Zyablikova, Christmas Films, Moscow) and each episode animated by a different director.[28] Using stop-mo-

---

27. See Jay David Bolter and Richard Grusin, *Remediation: Understanding New Media* (Cambridge: MIT Press, 1998).

28. For critical discussions of the animated series, see Steve Ellis, *Chaucer at Large: The Poet in the Modern Imagination* (Minneapolis: University of Minnesota Press, 2000), 139–40; Kathleen Forni, *Chaucer's Afterlife: Adaptations in Recent Popular Culture* (Jefferson, NC: McFarland, 2013), 96–104; and Peter Beidler, *The Lives of* The Miller's Tale: *The Roots, Composition, and Retellings of Chaucer's Bawdy Story* (Jefferson, NC: McFarland, 2013). For masterful

tion figures to represent Chaucer and his fellow pilgrims and animation to retell a handful of Chaucer's tales modifies yet again one's vision of Chaucer on screen: the so-called juvenility of animation sharply contrasts with the "adult-themed" nature of Chaucer's tales. Animated shorts and feature films have long been a part of cinema, and cartoons found a congenial niche early in the advent of television (and, in fact, many of the cartoons shown in theaters were recycled on television). Myerson, in his discussion of his animated adaptation, is quite conscious of his medium. In praise of television, he says that "the tales have never managed to find a foothold on the screen. The theatre allows for metaphor but film is horribly realistic . . . I knew animation could be the key."[29] The BBC, in its longstanding commitment to promoting British heritage, has often used television for educational purposes. Myerson's Chaucerian project is part pedagogical, aiming to reach the masses and thus improve them—as Myerson says, to "get more people interested in Chaucer."[30]

The animated *Canterbury Tales* reminds us that adaptation can often be a radical practice. Chaucer is a bulbous-nosed, gentle soul who speaks directly into the camera as he introduces his fellow pilgrims. Echoing in prose The General Prologue's masterful opening lines, this Chaucer speaks of spring: "When April's soft showers have cracked the March drought, when the warm west wind has breathed his sweet breeze through tender buds, that's when people get the itch to go on pilgrimages." Surely some viewers might lament the loss of the historical Chaucer's poetry—that "itch" may grate—as well as wince at Myerson's comment, "I don't believe in venerating old texts."[31] However, to look into the mobile face of Chaucer and to listen to his worldly-wise commentary may well disarm tendentious criticisms of fidelity. At one point, in a winsome moment of metanarrative play, the Merchant snipes: "Chaucer—he ain't got no sense of rhythm." Of course, the historical Chaucer played masterfully with the rhythms and rhymes of language, and so the film gently

---

introductions to animation, see Paul Wells, *Understanding Animation* (London: Routledge, 1998) and *The Animated Bestiary: Animals, Cartoons, and Culture* (New Brunswick: Rutgers University Press, 2009).

29. Jonathan Myerson, "Inside Stories: Pilgrim's Progress—How Chaucer Moved from Page to Animated Film," *Broadcast* (11 Dec. 1998): 12–13.

30. Myerson, as quoted in Carol Midgley, "Chaucer? Not a Lot of People Know That," *The Times*, 23 Nov. 1998. For a brief overview of the BBC and its educational mission, see Kathleen Coyne Kelly, "The BBC *Canterbury Tales* (2003)," *Medieval Afterlives in Contemporary Culture*, ed. Gail Ashton (London: Bloomsbury Academic, 2015), 134–43. For the full "BBC Tale," see Asa Brigg's monumental five-volume *The History of Broadcasting in the United Kingdom* (Oxford: Oxford University Press, 1995), which covers the BBC through the 1970s. Also see Margaret Rogerson, "Prime-Time Drama: *Canterbury Tales* for the Small Screen," *Sydney Studies in English* 32 (2006): 45–63.

31. "The Animator's Tale," *BBC News* (17 Mar. 1999); web.

pillories him for that which it strips from him. Yet this modernization closely parallels Chaucer's text in numerous other motifs in such a way that Chaucer may be said to serve both as the foundation of this narrative and as its grace notes. Moreover, the visual, not the verbal, establishes Myerson's adaptations of Chaucer's characters, with "Chaucer's" words echoing Chaucer's *Canterbury Tales*. "This is Harry Bailly, the innkeeper here—not the type to hide his light," he proceeds. He then comments on the Prioress: "And her table manners!" We may miss Chaucer's lively verbal portraits, yet the appealing images compensate for such an inevitable shift.

When Myerson's pilgrims arrive at Canterbury, these animated *Canterbury Tales* diverge notably from their unfinished source text, yet here viewers realize the playful potential of adaptation to rewrite its foundational scripts. Chaucer reverently intones, "Canterbury: shrine of the martyr"; this adaptation then ends with his cheeky admonition, "But whatever you do, don't take me too literally." These words make little sense on the cartoon's narrative level—there is no reason to doubt Chaucer's identification of Canterbury or to distrust his words—yet they dramatize every adapter's challenge with respect to reception: that the audience may well take her or his creation "literally" from the letter, the precursor text, rather than from its newly visual incarnation. A Chaucer whom we cannot take literally: this is the equivocal gift of Myerson's *Canterbury Tales*.

•

Chaucer on Screen's first part, titled "Theorizing Absence," contains essays by scholars who explicitly theorize the relative lack of cinematic and televisual representations of Chaucer in comparison to other narrative artists of the English literary tradition, such as William Shakespeare, Charles Dickens, Jane Austen, Charlotte and Emily Brontë, and Henry James. The four essays in part I function as a series of short provocations, presenting varying points of view with respect to how Chaucer's language and narrative positioning obstruct modern readings. Elizabeth Scala, in "Naked yet Invisible: Filming Chaucer's Narrator," explores the different ways in which Chaucer and Shakespeare inhabit their respective works, suggesting particularly that Chaucer's various narrative personae—as Pilgrim, as *Troilus*-narrator, as naive dreamer—create fictional frames that, ironically, given their jovial stance, distance him from audiences. Shakespeare, in contrast, is repeatedly reimagined by audiences as an active participant in his plays, not merely as the scribe behind them. Susan Aronstein and Peter Parolin reframe the question of Chaucer's and Shakespeare's varying fates on film in "'The Play's the Thing': The Cinematic

Fortunes of Chaucer and Shakespeare," in which Shakespeare's audiences are conceived as collaborators in the creation of his meaning, in contrast to Chaucer's. As they argue, audiences expect Chaucer's tales to be reductively reproduced, while assuming that Shakespeare's plays will be continually renewed through the process of adaptation.

Larry Scanlon examines the meaning of medieval conceptions of reality *contra* modern theory's sense of the Real for Jean Baudrillard and Slavoj Žižek. Throughout "Chaucer, Film, and the Desert of the Real; or, Why Geoffrey Chaucer Will Never Be Jane Austen," Scanlon links these contrasting notions of the Real to Jane Austen's use of free indirect discourse (Pasolini's favored mode), contemplating how its deployment creates a fictional reality conducive to cinematic technologies, whereas Chaucer's famed irony does not. Surveying the field of Chaucerian adaptations—or, rather, the lack thereof—Kathleen Forni, in "Profit, Politics, and Prurience; or, Why Chaucer Is Bad Box Office," turns her attention to Hollywood's hit-making complex and its apparently steely determination to overlook Chaucer, examining the corporate assumptions behind producers' decisions to green-light some projects and reject others.

Part II, "Lost and Found," features two essays that address early Hollywood and television history, piecing together tantalizing hints of lost Chaucerian productions that are extant only in piecemeal fashion as archival relics. In "Chaucer and the Moving Image in Pre–World War II America," Lynn Arner makes a foray into the Hollywood archives of early cinema to trace how Chaucer surfaces, is repressed, and surfaces again and again, never achieving the fame or popular acclaim of Robin Hood or King Arthur. Candace Barrington, in "Lost Chaucer: Natalie Wood's 'The Deadly Riddle' and the Golden Age of American Television," writes a scholarly detective story of sorts, investigating the circumstances surrounding the creation and apparent loss of a Chaucerian film from television's Golden Age, based on The Wife of Bath's Tale and starring Natalie Wood.

The next section, Part III, titled "Presence," includes with four explorations of Cinema Chauceriana, some familiar to medievalists and others less so: Michael Powell and Emeric Pressburger's *A Canterbury Tale* (1944); Pier Paolo Pasolini's still-controversial *I racconti di Canterbury* (1972); Bud Lee's soft-core *The Ribald Tales of Canterbury* (1985); and Brian Helgeland's *A Knight's Tale* (2001), which so famously features a naked Chaucer. Tison Pugh, in "Chaucerian History and Cinematic Perversions in Michael Powell and Emeric Pressburger's *A Canterbury Tale*," theorizes the potential of perversity to arise in trans-temporal adaptations, underscoring how Powell and Pressburger's homage to Chaucer and England's idyllic past condemns the cinematic technologies through which they tell their story. In this light, perversity becomes the defining feature of Chaucer and, indeed, of England—yet it is a perversity worth dying for, given the film's investment in the "why we fight" tradition of filmmaking during the years of World War II. In "Idols of the Marketplace: Chaucer/Pasolini," Kathryn L. Lynch refutes criticisms of Pasolini's film that dismiss it as insufficiently engaged with the Middle Ages and Chaucer's literature, demonstrating instead how it tangles with the past through a medium of artistic self-consciousness, most evident in Pasolini's performance as Chaucer but also in numerous narrative moments that express a certain kind of fidelity to the *Canterbury Tales* while also reconstructing their meaning for a cinematic medium.

George Shuffelton, in "'Sorry, Chaucer': Mixed Feelings and *The Ribald Tales of Canterbury*," examines how porn star Hyapatia Lee rewrote Chaucer's text in ways friendly to women. In her role as the Hostess, Lee displaces both Harry Bailly and Chaucer and replaces their male authority with her own. The film fails to meet these goals, Shuffelton demonstrates, in part because the conventions of pornography prove more difficult to overcome than Chaucer's authority. The film's failure exposes a widely shared modern ambivalence about Chaucer (a mixture of desire, fear, admiration, and revulsion); moreover, bringing out the latent pornographic potential of the *Canterbury Tales* elicits a number of other, even more unsettling, possibilities. In "The Naked Truth: Chaucerian Spectacle in Brian Helgeland's *A Knight's Tale*," Siân Echard explores what she sees as unexpected points of contact between the spectacle of tale and film, suggesting that despite the obvious gaps between Chaucer's and Helgeland's narratives, resonances and affinities establish profitable crosscurrents between them. By examining illustrated adaptations of The Knight's Tale aimed at children, Echard offers a way to attend to the many formal, thematic, and readerly interplays linking Chaucer and his many audiences. Chaucer—despite Geoff's nudity in the film—is not exactly on display in *A Knight's Tale,* and yet reading *one* Chaucer while watching the *other* proves to be an unexpectedly rewarding experience.

Part IV, titled "The BBC *Canterbury Tales* (2003)," presents a cluster of short essays devoted to the BBC *Canterbury Tales* (2003). In "Putting the Second First: The BBC 'Miller's Tale,'" Steve Ellis shows how Chaucer's Nicholas, a *hende* clerk in search of a sexual dalliance, is transformed into a trickster figure who mercilessly arranges the downfall of the other protagonists, not only of John but also of Danny Absolon, Alison herself (who goes unpunished in Chaucer's tale), and other characters who do not figure in Chaucer's original narrative. The BBC "Miller's Tale" is arguably a darker and more disturbing satire on human credulity than the laughter-provoking, carnivalesque inversions of Chaucer's original. Sarah Stanbury, in "Midlife Sex and the BBC 'Wife of Bath,'" examines how the program turns Chaucer's Wife of Bath's Prologue and Tale into a single interpellated fable about age, desire, and the public, tapping into the ethical calibrations of media and celebrity culture in which sexualized older women get notably little airtime, as well as the desires of the BBC's midlife viewers for a potent midlife diva. Louise D'Arcens, in "Serving Time: The BBC 'Knight's Tale' in the Prison-House of Free Adaptation," considers how the concept of a "free" adaptation underpins this version of Chaucer's tale in which class, gender, and racial politics have been radically reimagined. Moreover, she argues that the staging of Emily's pedagogic relationship to Ace and Paul dramatizes screenwriter Tony Marchant's and the BBC's cultural mission of using free adaptation to liberate British audiences from their ignorance of a celebrated originary text in their literary tradition.

In "The Color of Money: The BBC 'Sea Captain's Tale,'" Kathleen Coyne Kelly explores how ethnicity and race matter in this adaptation set in a South Asian enclave in Gravesend. Moreover, by considering the "origin" of The Shipman's Tale—that is, a tale from the Śukasaptati (*Seventy Tales of the Parrot*), compiled sometime in the sixth century and preserved in Sanskrit by the twelfth century—Kelly dramatizes circulation itself as we return to Chaucer's tale, a story about the exchange and transmission of money, bodies, and language. In this adaptation, what goes around comes around, from India to England and back again. In "Sex, Plague, and Resonance: Reflections on the BBC 'Pardoner's Tale,'" Arthur Bahr, in a meditative mode, considers the BBC's decision to introduce a sustained focus on gender and sexual violence notably absent from Chaucer's tale, in spite of—or, arguably, because of—the Pardoner's historically contested gender identity. These changes, Bahr argues, make sense as an attempt to fuse The Pardoner's Prologue with The Pardoner's Tale and to translate the sins depicted in the original into terms viscerally sensible to contemporary audiences. But they also de-queer Chaucer's Pardoner, making straightforwardly legible (albeit repugnant) that which the medieval text leaves occluded and strange. Kathleen Davis, in "Time, Memory, and Desire in the BBC 'Man of Law's Tale,'" analyzes the BBC production's delicate response to The Man of Law's Tale's complex and much-studied position in the historical nexus of religion, race, and colonialism, including the economies of world trade so central to Chaucer's texts, to colonial practice, and to political/religious strife today. Key to this analysis, Davis argues, is the BBC production's focus on religious extremism and the relation of such extremism to the logic of colonialism, sexual desire, and law. There is no such thing as "safe religion," as evident when Constance tells Alan, "My God is a jealous God."

The consequent question of the inevitability of violence connects these two versions of Constance and her always-unsettling tale.

The final essay of the volume, Laurie Finke and Martin B. Shichtman's "Marketing Chaucer: *Mad Men* and the Wife of Bath," stands alone under the part V heading of "Absent Presence." It addresses the spectral presence of the Wife of Bath in a particular thread in the television series *Mad Men*, theorizing the ways in which Chaucerian allusions circulate in popular culture while concomitantly disavowing the connection. At its heart, then, Finke and Shichtman's essay probes the very meaning of allusion and adaptation, provocatively undermining the possibility of sustained adaptation studies when the source text stands as one's fetishistic premise of analysis.

In sum, the contributors to *Chaucer on Screen* trace out the legacies of a fourteenth-century English poet with an uneven film and television career. They savor the pleasures and explore the challenges that screen adaptations present to modern readers and filmgoers (both those who are familiar with Chaucer's works and those who are not), while acknowledging the flaws of cinematic and televisual retellings and interpretations of the *Canterbury Tales*. In every instance, contributors engage with Chaucer/"Chaucer" and how he figures in his continual—if only occasional—rebirth into the modern media of film and television. *Chaucer on Screen* aims to erase the ideological lines between textual sources and visual reimaginings, for we are certain that many pleasures, scholarly and otherwise, can found in multiple media across disparate eras.

PART I
THEORIZING ABSENCE

CHAPTER 1

NAKED YET INVISIBLE
Filming Chaucer's Narrator

ELIZABETH SCALA

IT IS NEARLY impossible to argue, from the negative evidence we have, about Chaucerian film—the lack of film, really—for little of Chaucer's works has made it to the silver screen.[1] This absence begs for explanation (even as it must be satisfied with a surmise) in a culture otherwise fascinated with recreating, visualizing, and acting out the Middle Ages. On screens both large and small, imaginative reconstructions of medievalized worlds are a thriving industry and big business: *Harry Potter, The Lord of the Rings, Game of Thrones.* Each vies with the other in mass appeal. Despite our fascination with swords and armor, the popularity of costume drama, and the visual potentialities of computer-generated historical reconstruction, Chaucer and Chaucerian stories have made startling few appearances in cinema. Shakespeare, by contrast, is everywhere—recently in Justin Kurzel's *Macbeth* (2015) and Joss Whedon's *Much Ado about Nothing* (2013), the latter of which had already been filmed to much acclaim by Kenneth Branagh in 1993. But even the playwright's life and time fascinate our historical imagination. Both *Shakespeare in Love* (dir.

---

1. Recent popularizations of Chaucer on television are the subjects of various essays in this collection. The single feature-length film adaptation of the *Canterbury Tales* remains Pier Paolo Pasolini's well-known and somewhat scandalous 1972 film, *I racconti di Canterbury.* Given the broad parameters of adaptation, one can also read Powell and Pressburger's *A Canterbury Tale* (1944) in these terms. See Nickolas Haydock's discussion of the film as such in *Movie Medievalism: The Imaginary Middle Ages* (Jefferson, NC: McFarland, 2008), 20–24.

John Madden, 1998) and the more recent *Anonymous* (dir. Roland Emmerich, 2011) have claimed our attention. Chaucer, by contrast, is virtually nowhere, and that contrast is striking. It is the basis of my thinking about the absence of Chaucerian film. The fact that Shakespeare endures not only endless theatrical making but continual cinematic remaking renders the never-attempted screenplay of Chaucer's dramatic romances, *Troilus and Criseyde* and The Knight's Tale, all the more surprising for a modern consumer culture obsessed with novelty and always looking for a new story—even if the story winds up being very old. How is it that Shakespeare is omnipresent, even repetitively so, while Chaucer has disappeared, unseen and unheard of beyond Paul Bettany's naked performance in Brian Helgeland's *A Knight's Tale* (2001)?

This essay will treat its subject—Chaucer's absence on film—largely by asking why and especially how it is that Shakespeare is everywhere and Chaucer nowhere. It is not, or not merely, that Shakespeare is alive in stage performances around the globe and thus inhabiting the world beyond the printed texts of his plays.[2] Shakespeare, I want to argue, inhabits his works and his characters in ways Chaucer does not. And this difference affects the ways we think about and approach what might otherwise be considered similar, historically distant, and linguistically difficult properties. An actor on the stage before becoming the premier dramaturge for the theater in which he was a sharer, Shakespeare played (sometimes literally) many of the parts he wrote.[3] In some sense he is every character. Like the "Bankside poet and player" portrayed by Joseph Fiennes in *Shakespeare in Love,* the playwright can easily step into any role. One way or another, he inhabits all the characters before he ever puts them on the stage.

By contrast as well as by design, Chaucer is *none* of his characters. He assiduously avoids playing the parts he writes and withdraws from his fictional figures in a continually mediated narrative frame. This mediation, in essence, has become his authorial signature. The effect of Chaucer's withdrawal places him elsewhere, leaving his poems to the ministrations of surrogates—Chaucer the Pilgrim; the *Troilus* narrator; the reluctant dreamer; the reader without any personal experience in love. That condition gives authority to fallible figures, like Pandarus, or leaves matters to the hands of an Adam Scriveyn and their deprivations. Sharing an oblique relation to the writer who stands behind them, these figures help him keep his distance from the story, and from us, by

---

2. This distinction between the closed Chaucerian text and the open, more easily adaptable and revisable work of Shakespeare, rooted in its origins as cooperative performance, is the subject of Aronstein and Parolin's essay in this volume.

3. On Shakespeare's role as a sharer in the theater see, most recently, Bart van Es, *Shakespeare in Company* (Oxford: Oxford University Press, 2013).

taking responsibility for its partial, variant, and sometimes unfinished form. His remoteness is what makes Chaucer appear modern, skeptical of the fictions he helps narrate and unsure of their ultimate significance. But it also, I would argue, positions him beyond our reach and has kept him out of view, distancing his works in the cultural imaginary despite their rather adaptable plots.

These considerations could be pursued at length through a detailed study of each poet's canon, but that kind of work is impractical here. Instead, I will turn to the two popular representations of Chaucer and Shakespeare "at work" just mentioned, each of which reveals a sophisticated historical awareness of the circumstances surrounding these writers in the midst of more imaginative speculations and fantasies about them. *A Knight's Tale* and *Shakespeare in Love* are each fanciful yet clever constructions of the early careers of these two literary giants. Neither film is historically faithful in the narrow sense, but both are deeply invested in the past.[4] By comparing the two films, both of which imagine the personal experiences accounting for the genesis of each author's work, I show how Chaucer's oblique and self-conscious relation to his own writing helps to explain its limited appearance on screen.

●

The theater is a crucial factor linking, and ultimately separating, Chaucer and Shakespeare. The similarities and analogies between the two writers have long been noted in terms of theatricality. Well before secular dramatics were the principal entertainment of English society in purpose-built playhouses, Chaucer's *Canterbury Tales* positioned its narrating figures as dramatis personae on a staged journey in which each is called to perform a story for an internal audience. Chaucer describes his "cast" of characters in The General Prologue, which both sets up and retroactively accounts for, to greater and lesser degrees, the figures speaking his collection's different "parts." Such connections led George Lyman Kittredge, a scholar of both Chaucer and Shakespeare,

---

4. Anachronism is mentioned throughout the critical reception of both films. For *A Knight's Tale*, see especially Kathleen Forni, "Reinventing Chaucer: Helgeland's *A Knight's Tale*," *Chaucer Review* 37 (2003): 253–64; and David Matthews, "What the Trumpet Solo Tells Us: A Response," *Parergon* 25 (2008): 119–27. On the anachronism in *Shakespeare in Love*, see Elizabeth Klett, "*Shakespeare in Love* and the End(s) of History," *Retrovisions: Reinventing the Past in Film and Fiction*, ed. Deborah Cartmell and I. Q. Hunter (London: Pluto, 2001), 25–40. Richard Burt also treats anachronism in the film as part of the way it peddles a dated form of scholarship; see "*Shakespeare in Love* and the End of the Shakespearean: Academic and Mass Culture Constructions of Literary Authorship," *Shakespeare, Film, Fin de Siècle*, ed. Mark Thornton Burnett and Ramona Wray (New York: St. Martin's, 2000), 203–31.

to formulate the "dramatic principle" by which generations have read the correlation between The General Prologue and individual stories in theatrical terms.[5] Following, modifying, or refuting this dramatic principle has governed studies of the *Canterbury Tales,* in one way or another, ever since.

Another reason we can easily form analogies between the two writers is that Shakespeare read Chaucer and used a number of his works in fashioning his plays. But Shakespeare rarely turns to Chaucer for plot. Even when using Chaucer most directly, as in *Troilus and Cressida* or *A Midsummer Night's Dream,* Shakespeare is attracted to Chaucer for something other than the main storyline. (Only *The Two Noble Kinsmen,* a collaboration with John Fletcher, follows the plot of its Chaucerian precursor, The Knight's Tale, even closely.) It is, rather, an intense focus on character that more pervasively links the two poets. And even the title of *Kinsmen* turns the story of its narrator (the Knight) and the assumptions of noble aristocracy into one about its characters and their relation to one another, making it a play about relationality itself.[6] Shakespeare's interest in Chaucer, and his attraction to Chaucer as a source of some of his dramatic characters, perhaps traces to Chaucer's own interest in character, which is manifested in a dramatic genre that is very different from Shakespeare's and whose naive yet revealing narrator is one of its most distinctive parts.[7] But here the two writers part company. Despite the dramatic similarities between the two, Chaucer removes himself from the stage he sets for his fictions, whereas Shakespeare more masterfully "struts and frets his hour upon the stage" with them (*Macbeth* 5.5.25).[8]

Theatricality also ties *A Knight's Tale* to *Shakespeare in Love,* as Chaucer takes up a charismatic performative persona, unlike any he occupies within his poems, in the film's plot. Bettany's Chaucer appears "onstage" parading

---

5. See George Lyman Kittredge, *Chaucer and His Poetry* (Cambridge: Harvard University Press, 1915); C. David Benson, *Chaucer's Drama of Style: Poetic Variety and Contrast in the Canterbury Tales* (Chapel Hill: University of North Carolina Press, 1988); and John Ganim, *Chaucerian Theatricality* (Princeton: Princeton University Press, 1990).

6. Such a reading of *Two Noble Kinsmen* would be "to long to heere," to quote Chaucer's Knight (1.875). Think merely of the relations beyond literal "kin" that occupy the play: Flavina's friendship with Emilia, and the Jailer's Daughter's attraction to Palamon, among others. All quotations of Chaucer's works in this essay come from *The Riverside Chaucer,* ed. Larry D. Benson, 3rd ed. (Boston: Houghton Mifflin, 1987) and are referenced by line numbers.

7. Additionally, both poets are metatextual in that they are aware of the genres they write and comment on them specifically within their texts. Shakespeare alludes in various ways to the conditions of a play's performance; Chaucer routinely ponders the vagaries of his narrative and its vulnerable form (Meredith Anne Skura, *Shakespeare the Actor and the Purposes of Playing* [Chicago: University of Chicago Press, 1993], 5).

8. Quotation from *Macbeth* is taken from *The Riverside Shakespeare,* ed. G. Blakemore Evans and John Tobin, 2nd ed. (Boston: Houghton Mifflin, 1997).

himself in the field and mounting the lists in his introduction of the eponymous knight the film is about.⁹ Unsurprisingly, the theater is a central focus in *Shakespeare in Love*. With a script that recreates the London theater scene in 1593, the film constructs an imagined early career in England's bustling capital for the playwright and erstwhile actor in the years for which we have no biographical information about Shakespeare's life. These efforts to recreate the environment of the early Elizabethan playhouses are met by the more fanciful presentation of a tournament "circuit" in *A Knight's Tale*, with its overt analogies to modern sporting events. Yet each film thereby offers some of its most stunning historical spectacle in its surround. The neighborhood of the theater is among *Shakespeare in Love*'s most intriguing visual splendors and forms the main setting for most of the film's scenes (see figure 1.1a), much of which occurs inside, onstage, and in the taverns about the playhouse. A slow pan across the interior of a recreation of the Rose Theater opens the film, and this loving sweep from the galleries down to the bare floor orients the viewer and grounds our perspective. That camera movement sets in motion a visual absorption in the film's historically reconstructed atmosphere. Tracking down from sky seen above the playhouse's open roof, across the stalls to the pit, our gaze alights on a playbill strewn on the dirt floor, an advertisement for a fictional version of the scene we are about to watch: "The Lamentable Tragedie of the Moneylender Reveng'd," revealing the truth of the theater—what the theater truthfully represents as well as a truthful representation of what happens in the theater itself—as the main interest of the film. Indeed much of the film's 123 minutes occur in and around a playhouse—the Rose, the Curtain, and a stage set up at Whitehall. Similarly, as Sîan Echard notes in her essay in this volume, the entry of knights into the city across London Bridge, with its shops and timbered houses, offers some of the best scenery *A Knight's Tale* offers (see figure 1.1b). These panoramas situate both writers in a London milieu that would insert history as well as "real life" into the *mise-en-scene*.

The complexity and intimacy of Shakespeare's life in the theater are important to the film narrative; it is no mere location. *Shakespeare in Love* plays upon the dramatic character of theater itself in Elizabethan England, not just the dramas performed in those spaces. Getting the play on—financing it; casting and rehearsing it; weathering the closings and reopenings of the playhouses; and, above all, writing it—provides as much of the film's

---

9. See Haydock on the scholarly source of Helgeland's heraldry narrative—Maurice Keen's account of William Marshall's herald, in *Chivalry* (New Haven, CT: Yale University Press, 1984), 134–64—in his essay "Arthurian Melodrama, Chaucerian Spectacle, and the Waywardness of Cinematic Pastiche in *First Knight* and *A Knight's Tale*," *Studies in Medievalism* 12 (2002): 3–39, 27.

FIGURES 1.1A AND B. The London scenes in (a) *Shakespeare in Love* and (b) *A Knight's Tale*.

dramatic action as the star-crossed love stories it tells, which analogizes Will's romance with Viola to *Romeo and Juliet.* Will writes scene by scene almost up to the minute of performance, settling the play's genre only at its end, when the final outcome of the external forces driving the play's romance become apparent. The play itself is beset by problems throughout the film—up to the very moment it opens when the boy actor playing Juliet suddenly drops two octaves, his voice cracking as he attempts to read lines behind stage. This, of course, sends his real "Juliet," to and about whom Will has been writing all along, to take the boy-actor's place on stage.

Throughout the film, life in the theater rivals Shakespeare's "own" story as its main focus. Indeed, at times the theater *is* Shakespeare's own story. Marc

Norman and Tom Stoppard's clever screenplay entwines the story of Romeo and Juliet (and *Romeo and Juliet*) with Will and Viola in a recursively postmodern narrative.[10] The film's fictional romance "produces" the narrative of the play in deflected form. Not only does Will write about Viola when he composes Romeo's lines to Juliet, he also rewrites more comic episodes (the film's nearly slapstick balcony scene) into the better-known scenes of Shakespeare's tragic love story. But, as we know, the play has produced the film. In the style of postmodern pastiche, *Shakespeare in Love* shows viewers a past explaining the future they already know, even as it leaves intact many of the uncertainties we have about Shakespeare rather than ironing them out.

In one of its more historically bizarre scenes, Shakespeare visits a proto-psychiatrist, Dr. Moth, to cure his writer's block. His writing ability is psychologically related to his erotic life (what might be a curious fact for the writer of *Titus Andronicus*, an early and gruesome tragedy of Shakespeare's mentioned several times in the film). It seems he cannot write without a muse. Yet true to its pastiche historical form, his writing is also derivative; it is not merely the original product of his creative imagination. The film begins with the playwright, at the behest of Phillip Henslowe, working on the script of "Romeo and Ethel, the Pirate's Daughter," a comedy that will contain both a shipwreck and "a bit with a dog." And even when trying to follow Henslowe's instructions, Will can begin writing in earnest only once Kit Marlowe feeds him the idea for *Romeo*: an Italian "always in and out of love" until he meets "the daughter of his enemy. His best friend is killed in a duel with Ethel's brother. Or something. His name is Mercutio." But not everything is handed to the playwright from a superior artist or for a fee. He also culls from the streets just outside the playhouse lines and phrases he will transform into art: "A plague on both your houses." Mercutio's mighty line originates as the condemnation of a puritan ranting about the theaters and their portrayal of vice. These inspirational threads make the origin of Shakespeare's play a personal affair that happens in and around the theater (even as they also reveal in good New Historicist fashion the local social influences on the playwright's quasi-Romantic genius). Shakespeare and the theater are inhabited by each other.[11]

---

10. On the film's postmodernism, see Todd Davis and Kenneth Womack, "Reading (and Writing) the Ethics of Authorship: *Shakespeare in Love* as Postmodern Metanarrative," *Literature/Film Quarterly* 32 (2004): 153–62. Haydock's "Arthurian Melodrama" urges us to see *A Knight's Tale* in similarly pastiche terms.

11. What has to go unrecognized, of course, are the many books and earlier plays upon which Shakespeare's are based. For discussion see Jane Kingsley-Smith, "Shakespearean Authorship in Popular British Cinema," *Literature/Film Quarterly* 30 (2002): 158–65, 161.

But the theater—its spectacle, costumes, and finances—is nowhere better represented than in the body of the actor. Among the various stories that it tells, *Shakespeare in Love* is about a "secret" love of acting and performance amid the disdain for the player common in Elizabethan England.[12] The film's "historical" narrative is teeming with erstwhile actors, which is part of its comedy. As one early scene shows, the tavern is full of men waiting for their chance "to be known" when Henslowe announces auditions (since his own company is out touring the inn yards while the theaters are closed because of the plague). Parts are handed out as tips to tavern workers. And despite a severe stutter, Mr. Wabash, Henslowe's tailor, is cast as The Prologue. Wabash "wants to be an actor," and Henslowe has "a few debts here and there." The play is thus currency and sometimes collateral, as Henslowe's initial debt to the moneylender, Mr. Fennyman, is paid by making him a partner in the production of "Romeo and Ethel," whose profits Fennyman calculates with exactitude. But this mere financier's role only lasts for so long as even he is eventually given a proper part, cast as *Romeo*'s apothecary, as both film and play reach their end. Fennyman's journey from mercenary capitalist to theater lover is the narrative of the film writ large, figuring its modern consumerist audience in relation to Shakespeare's works.

Accused of being "vagrants and peddlers of bombast," the players find their status throughout the film to be a lowly one. Everyone, it seems, enjoys their entertainments but accords actors little respect. Paradigmatically, when Shakespeare sneaks into a party at the de Lesseps estate with the hired musicians, he nicks a bit of food from a passing servant, who scolds, "No food for the players, master's orders." And throughout the film we see a similar begrudging attitude toward such men. Admired for their talent yet disdained as mere beggars for public attention, according to Meredith Skura, such ambivalence characterizes the attitude toward actors. Will is trying to escape these humiliating conditions, looking to buy a share in the Lord Chamberlain's Men for which he needs fifty pounds. But it is Shakespeare's status as an actor (rather than writer) that is initially recognized by everyone, down to the man who ferries him across the Thames. Acting places him inside his plays rather than beyond them.

The ease with which disdain turns to admiration for the actor and his magical self-transformation is on display when Henslowe's company returns. Fennyman, now a partner in the production, takes over rehearsal and looks to manage the players with his usual threats. As Will hands out roles and

---

12. On the ambivalent status of actors in Renaissance England, see Skura, *Shakespeare the Actor*, 30–46.

describes the story he has begun to set in motion—"Gentlemen, today we embark on a great voyage"—Fennyman whispers to Henslowe:

FENNYMAN: Who is that?
HENSLOWE: Nobody, sir. The author.

Neither author nor players matter to the man looking to extract the most money from the play as he can. Fennyman interrupts in his typically brusque way, "Listen to me, you dregs. Actors are ten a penny." But before he can pronounce in even more derisive language how easily replaceable players are, the camera shifts to the explosive entrance of Ned Alleyn: "Huzzah: the Admiral's Men are returned to the House!" Henslowe's principal dramatic actor commands a kind of attention different from Fennyman's and from the audience at large. At first, Fennyman is dumbfounded, asking Henslowe, "Who is he?" But Ned answers himself, freezing Fennyman into awed submission: "Silence, you dog! I am Hieronymo. I am Tamburlaine. I am Faustus. I am Barabas, the Jew of Malta. Oh yes, Master Will, I am Henry the Sixth.... Pay attention. You will see how genius creates a legend." This over-the-top performance by Ben Affleck has been noticed as part of the film's self-aware citation of Hollywood celebrity. Yet from this point on, Fennyman, like everyone else, becomes a fascinated spectator of the play and its actors, with the talented Alleyn as Mercutio and the equally mesmerizing Thomas Kent (Gwyneth Paltrow as Viola, in disguise) as Romeo. The effect is captured by a receding camera that moves backward from the point of view of the onstage actors looking out at the audience, here principally Mr. Fennyman, watching them rehearse, and continuing its withdrawal back through doorways to behind-the-scenes scenes of sword-fighting rehearsal and juggling practice (see figure 1.2).

Fascinated spectators are what the film and its actors, like Shakespeare himself, create. In fact, their creation culminates in the attentions of Queen Elizabeth: "next time you come to Greenwich, Master Shakespeare, come as yourself." She has fully recognized the talents of Shakespeare in *Romeo and Juliet* (just as she recognizes him as the figure disguised as Viola's lady-in-waiting earlier). The film also originates in the same fascination it purports to create, as we watch this young gentlewoman watching (and clearly not for the first time) a Whitehall production of *Two Gentlemen of Verona*. Viola has recognized early on what the film seeks to explain to everyone else: that Shakespeare is a "writer that commands the heart of every player." And since the film also suggests that a player lives in almost everyone, it means he commands *all* hearts. Viola's love of poetry, and of Shakespeare's poetry particularly, emerges in the film narrative as the desire to act. As she tells her nurse,

FIGURE 1.2. The "truth" revealed by theater in *Shakespeare in Love*.

"I would stay asleep my whole life if I could dream myself in a company of players." Their conversation moves from a bedtime review of *Two Gentlemen* to her own desire for "poetry, and adventure, and love above all." Viola wants "love as there has never been in a play" even as she winds up enacting "the very truth and nature of love" in Will's new play. "Stage love" becomes "true love" under the hand of the poet, especially once Viola displaces the "pip-squeak boys in petticoats" playing the heroine's part and the playwright himself steps into Romeo's role.

Time and again the player's the thing. Not only does a "real" woman wind up playing one of Shakespeare's heroines, Shakespeare's heroines, by this logic, speak and feel like real women. *Shakespeare in Love* interprets the feeling expressiveness of Shakespeare's works and characters, their individuating voices, by showing us that "real": the emotional experiences of Will and Viola that lie behind the poetic words in *Romeo and Juliet*.[13] But even more, the film seeks to show us that Will lies behind and within Shakespeare's writing. From the film's very beginning, Will is the imaginary actor of his plays, even as his characters embody versions of his experience. He is inside his writing and his plays, as he transcribes and translates his words to Viola into the sonnets Romeo and Juliet speak to and with each other, which mime the way Will

---

13. On the very problematic of the Real and reality in *Shakespeare in Love*, see Ayanna Thompson, "Rewriting the 'Real': Popular Shakespeare in the 1990s," *Journal of Popular Culture* 40 (2007): 1052–72.

sends Sonnet 18 to Viola in a letter "by the hand of Thomas Kent."[14] The film thus traces and interweaves two stories of star-crossed lovers. In one narrative, Viola plays "Juliet" to Shakespeare's "Romeo," and their romance effectively writes the play to be performed in the theater. Onstage, however, Viola (as Kent) plays Romeo for Shakespeare's company until she is discovered and the theater closed for public indecency. The narratives interpenetrate when Kent is thus revealed, and Will himself must step into the role he has otherwise been playing offstage all along. Shakespeare's real life and his stage life are one, and his status as an actor, a "Bankside poet and player," becomes the source of his ability to reveal "the very truth and nature of love"—a wager that earns him those fifty pounds and thus his share in the Lord Chamberlain's Men. For all the historical narratives that *Shakespeare in Love* strives to tell, it primarily tells us that Shakespeare, actor and poet, resides within his own works.

Not so for Chaucer. The structure of *A Knight's Tale* renders visible the difficulty of translating Chaucerian narratives, and especially Chaucer's relation to his narratives, to the screen. As its commentators have recognized, despite its reference to one of the stories of the *Canterbury Tales*, Helgeland's film "fails to engage Chaucer's tale on any thematic or aesthetic level." Instead, the film can only attempt a "consider[ation of] the history of the Chaucerian persona and how Chaucer is constructed in the popular imagination."[15] Chaucer's tales are not stories with which one engages in direct relation to the characters, as in Shakespeare's plays and their monologues. They are, by contrast, highly mediated fictions whose distancing narrative voices are difficult to ignore.

A Knight's Tale finds an ingenious way to make Chaucer's narration a part of its story and to make a writer necessary to its Hollywood version of medieval romance. Working as a "herald," Chaucer introduces, in the style of a modern-day wrestling announcer, the figure he has created by an act of forgery. The film's plot incorporates his writing, literally, as he fashions "patents of nobility" for the knight he brings into being and whose adventure comprises the main storyline. Chaucer's story, as a struggling writer whose allegorical *Book of the Duchess* no one has heard of, is fantastically augmented by his portrayal as a degenerate gambler who has lost the shirt off his back (indeed all of his clothes) when he enters the film. This psychological narrative of addiction and dependency only marginally competes with the narrative he creates for William Thatcher, which turns a Cheapside roofer's son into Sir

---

14. The lack of biography we have for Shakespeare lies behind and is answered by film. For further discussion see Thompson, "Rewriting," 64–66; and Burt, "*Shakespeare*," 219–21.

15. Forni, "Reinventing," 255, 254.

Ulrich von Lichtenstein of Gelderland (an identity that somehow makes this manufactured knight English).[16] Ministering behind the scenes and later in front of the cheering crowd, Chaucer reveals himself as a pitiful rogue whose losses to Peter the Pardoner and Simon the Summoner can be fully paid only at a later date: "I will eviscerate you in fiction. . . . I was naked for a day; you will be naked for all eternity." Those in the know—the few already familiar with the *Book of the Duchess*—recognize the proleptic allusion to the *Canterbury Tales*. The poet's depiction of the close friendship of these two men will later appear as Chaucer's subtle intimation of their sodomitical pairing amid his outright declaration of the nature of their thievery in The General Prologue (1.669–72).[17]

Where Chaucer typically appears hapless within his poems, that haplessness is explained and rationalized, indeed psychologized, by *A Knight's Tale*, in which Chaucer is completely down and out in Rouen and London. Figured as both gambling addiction and the continual losses that addiction incurs, his haplessness "nakedly" characterizes his abject position in the film and ultimately functions as the source and inspiration of his great storytelling collection.[18] By the film's end, we have a writer newly aware of what might be the future subjects of his poetry, the more humble and everyday fellows (makeshift squires, ambitious blacksmiths, nervy women) beyond the aristocrats and aristocratic life he "typically" depicts. We have here both an accurate portrayal of Chaucer and an entirely modern democratization of his fiction writing. Miming the ending that many of his poems state or imply, the film ends with Chaucer's intent to remember and implicitly to reframe his odd experience. He characteristically muses at the close to the *Book of the Duchess* itself:

> Thys ys so queynt a sweven
> That I wol, be processe of tyme,
> Fonde to put this sweven in ryme
> As I kan best, and that anoon. (1330–33)

Similarly, the dream that comprises the *House of Fame* is a response to the poet's search for love "tydynges" (2143). Both the reading that inspires the

---

16. Indeed, it is much like the fiction of Shakespeare's writer's block (and impotency) that sends him to Dr. Moth. Both films imagine distinctly psychological conditions for these writers in need of therapy.

17. On this insinuation and its effects, see my "Yeoman Services: Chaucer's Knight, His Critics, and the Pleasures of Historicism," *Chaucer Review* 45 (2010): 194–221.

18. On the naked entrance of Chaucer in the film and what that nakedness means, see George Edmondson, "Naked Chaucer," *The Post-Historical Middle Ages*, ed. Elizabeth Scala and Sylvia Federico (New York: Palgrave Macmillan, 2009), 139–60.

dreams and implicitly the dreams themselves are the fodder for Chaucer's books. *A Knight's Tale* participates in these self-same gestures, ending with the scene of Chaucer's "discovery" of the idea behind the *Canterbury Tales*. Watching William's success both in tournament and in love, he claims to the others, "I think I'm going to have to write some of this story down." Not merely "the part about the prince and the knights," as Wat suggests, but "all of it." Chaucer, it seems, has finally been freed from the constraints of allegory. Thus the book he will write promises to be *different* from the film we have just seen and somehow inspired by it. As in *Shakespeare in Love,* the film sustains the fantasy that Chaucer's work has a "real" origin, a personal and psychological one at that. He was not merely writing for the sake of curiosity or social satire, or just making it up or recasting a story that had been told before. "I'm a writer," Chaucer says in the film. "I give the truth scope." As the dream poems fictionalize Chaucer's experiences, Helgeland argues that so too does the *Canterbury Tales,* which has to be true even if not in the direct terms the film imagines and fabricates.

But unlike Will in *Shakespeare in Love,* Chaucer cannot step into and fully inhabit the fiction he creates in *A Knight's Tale*. When Ulrich's nemesis Adhemar follows him back to Cheapside and sees his bedraggled (and now blind) father, he has the knight's papers inspected and his identity challenged. Jocelyn warns William of his impending arrest and urges him to run. He refuses: "I cannot run. I am a knight. And I will put myself to the hazard." Chaucer, like the rest of William's friends, forsakes the fiction of nobility and responds with cold, detached pragmatism, urging him to flee. This writer gives up on the story he has written; he cannot step into or help sustain the fiction. But William resists and, to the group's collective chagrin, ends up in the stocks. In a most un-Chaucerian ending to the story, William is released and knighted by Edward the Black Prince, whom Ulrich had met in the field as Sir Thomas Colville. Ulrich allowed the injured Colville to finish in the Rouen tournament (where others withdrew after they recognized his royal colors). The two knights nod as they pass each other, making for a draw, which allows William to win without unhorsing Colville. William only recognizes Colville as the Black Prince from the stocks, making his gesture toward his opponent all the more "noble." Edward's gesture shifts the narrative to a romance of the fair unknown and removes all doubt and uncertainty about the inherent nobility of William's character.[19] His royal historians having

---

19. In the narrative of knightly self-fashioning and innate nobility that *A Knight's Tale* seeks to tell, William and Edward recognize themselves as versions of each other. Knowing Edward's identity (and his wound) makes men like Adhemar withdraw. They know no way to let anyone save face. But William, who is similarly disguised in order to enter the lists, comes

discovered that William comes from an "ancient royal line," Edward proclaims, "This is my word and as such is beyond contestation." No Chaucerian narrative has ever ended with such declarative assurance or such certainty about its own interpretation. *A Knight's Tale* withdraws from Chaucer and Chaucerian fictions of ambiguity almost as much as Chaucer withdraws from the characters and the fictions he writes in the film's storyline.

Satisfying their modern audiences who already know these writers' future works, both *Shakespeare in Love* and *A Knight's Tale* conclude with the promise of more fiction. Impressed with *Romeo and Juliet*, Queen Elizabeth asks for "something more cheerful next time, for Twelfth Night." We have already seen Will's creative imagination take off in that direction as he and Viola discuss her impending voyage to Virginia after the marriage to Lord Wessex that her father has arranged. It is the fact that shapes the ending of *Romeo*, finally turning Henslowe's desired comedy into tragedy. Similarly, Chaucer stands at the end of *A Knight's Tale* ready to transform "all of it" into fiction, everything but the kind of story we have just witnessed. To tell the stories of the less-than-noble classes, those whom he earlier called "all of you not sitting on cushions," he will have to refrain from telling the kind of idealizing narrative Helgeland has crafted. To become Chaucer, he will have to exit rather than immerse himself in the story the film has written for him, a retreat he already urged on William when he told him to run.

A Knight's Tale and *Shakespeare in Love* are imaginative fantasies about two of our most historically important poets. Neither pretends to be a fully historical account of anything. And yet the differences in these fanciful depictions of Chaucer and Shakespeare, herald and player, tell us more than they realize. Shakespeare's theatrical life has meant we can easily draw connections between him and his characters. Their words are always Shakespeare's. The fact that Chaucer keeps his distance and remains in a shadowy background apart from his fictionalized narrator has meant that his stories will always belong to someone else.

---

to understand Edward's desire to test himself in the field, to experience and to earn his identity with his deeds. Malory's Lancelot similarly disguised himself to enter tournaments and experience his identity. For fuller discussion of this phenomenon, see my essay, "Disarming Lancelot," *Studies in Philology* 99 (2002): 380–403.

CHAPTER 2

"THE PLAY'S THE THING"

The Cinematic Fortunes of Chaucer and Shakespeare

SUSAN ARONSTEIN and PETER PAROLIN

WE BEGIN our consideration of the very different cinematic fortunes of Chaucer and Shakespeare with two well-known images. The first comes from an early manuscript edition of *Troilus and Criseyde* (see figure 2.1). In it, Chaucer, encased in a medieval lectern, reads his work to Richard II's attentive court. He stands above his aristocratic audience, finger raised, *auctor* and *auctorite*, surrounded by indicators of wealth and status: rich clothing, groomed landscapes, a castle in the distance. Only someone similarly wealthy and privileged could have commissioned and owned this manuscript—a masterpiece in its own right, expensively and lavishly illustrated, its written words accessible only to those with the status and funds to receive an education. Here, from the very beginning of Chaucer's reception, we have an image that enshrines the author and his works, that fixes them both and marks them out as the property of a cultural elite.

In contrast to the *Troilus* frontispiece's veneration of the author, Swiss traveler Johannes de Witt's 1596 sketch of London's Swan Theatre depicts a space in which the figure of the author is decidedly absent (see figure 2.2). The scene here is popular and performative: boys playing women are greeted by a chamberlain; a spectator watches the action from a gallery above the stage. A flag flies above the theater, but far from being a royal standard, it represents, in the image of a swan, the playhouse itself. As de Witt observes, "The most outstanding of all the theatres . . . is that whose sign is the swan

FIGURE 2.1. The *Troilus* frontispiece, with Chaucer reading his work to Richard II's court. By permission of the Master and Fellows of Corpus Christi College, Oxford.

(in the vernacular, the theatre of the swan), as it seats 3000 people."[1] In the vernacular, with three thousand people—de Witt imagines the theater as a shared social space, the locus of public pleasure and commercial enterprise. The business of putting on early modern plays, this drawing tells us, is the collaborative business of public performance and collective experience, not the solitary business of a privileged writer asserting textual authority and ownership.

These images can help us understand why the works of Chaucer and Shakespeare have been treated so differently by the film and television industries. Chaucer's privileged place in English literary history positions him within what Peter Walsh calls the "expert paradigm," making him the property of "the people who know things." As the products of an *auctor*, his works constitute a canon, "a bounded body of knowledge which an individual can master."[2]

---

1. "Swan Elizabethan Theatre," elizabethan-era.org.uk, Web, accessed 1 May 2016.

2. Peter Walsh, "That Withered Paradigm: The Web, the Expert, and the Information Hegemony," *Democracy and the New Media*, ed. Henry Jenkins and David Thorburn (Cambridge,

FIGURE 2.2. Sketch of the Swan Theatre, c. 1596.
By Arnoldus Buchelius, after the sketch sent to him by his friend
Johannes de Witt. Utrecht University Library, Ms. 842, f. 132r.

Readers consume, not produce, canons. A subject to be mastered, guarded by experts, "Chaucer" leaves few openings for the play of remediation necessary for a successful film; his tales available for *reproduction*, the faithful replication of the original, but not *adaptation*, defined by Linda Hutcheon as "repetition

---

MA: MIT Press, 2003), 365-72, at 365. Qtd. in Henry Jenkins, *Convergence Culture: Where Old and New Media Collide* (New York: New York University Press, 2008), 52.

without replication," "with a difference."³ "Shakespeare," on the other hand, has always belonged to what Henry Jenkins, writing about fan fiction in the age of new media, calls "convergence culture." Convergence culture privileges the collaboration of the collective intelligence, encouraging consumers "to participate in the production and consumption of cultural goods—on their own terms."⁴ Shakespeare's plays were never meant to be passively consumed. From the very beginning of their cultural life, theatrical productions work against "the idea of a definitive version produced, authorized and regulated" by the Author.⁵ To adapt Jenkins's discussion of fan fiction, Shakespeare has never been a "limited good" but rather "shareware" that "accrues value as it moves across different contexts, gets retold in various ways, attracts multiple audiences, and opens itself up to a proliferation of meanings."⁶

Chaucer's works, conversely, were almost immediately perceived as a "limited good" to be verified, codified, and collected, a process that diminished rather than expanded his canon. Beginning in the nineteenth century with the founding of the Chaucer Society, the expert culture focused on uncovering the "original" text, stripping away early modern "fan fictions" such as *The Plowman's Tale* and *The Tale of Beryn* and determining authorial intent. With each successive edition, "Chaucer" became more scholarly, fixed on the page, surrounded by an extensive critical apparatus: background introductions, manuscript histories, editorial and interpretive notes, and glossaries. This is not to say that access to Chaucer has been limited to the academy; more "popular" versions of Chaucer's works, seeking to make "the Father of English Literature" available to nonspecialists, have, since the nineteenth century, existed alongside scholarly editions. However, instead of the public free-for-all in which Shakespearean stage and film adaptations coexist with the Norton, Riverside, and Arden editions of the plays, Chaucer is most often offered to the general reader in the form of translations (both cheap paperback versions or lavishly illustrated coffee table books) and children's picture books.

There have been similar attempts—from the First Folio, with its engraving of Shakespeare as the great author in isolation, to scholarly editions of his plays—to "fix" and authorize the Shakespearean canon.⁷ The ongoing reproduction of Shakespeare as the cornerstone of Anglo-American high culture and the ongoing textual transmission of his plays, however, have always existed alongside the performance of those plays. Beyond being experienced

---

3. Linda Hutcheon, *A Theory of Adaptation*, 2nd ed. (London: Routledge, 2006), 7, 9.
4. Jenkins, *Convergence Culture*, 137.
5. Jenkins, *Convergence Culture*, 266.
6. Jenkins, *Convergence Culture*, 266.
7. See John Jowett, *Shakespeare and Text* (Oxford: Oxford University Press, 2007).

as book, Shakespeare has always been understood as performance; in Hutcheon's terms, Shakespeare's plays engage audiences by *showing* stories rather than *telling* them.⁸ But since any performance of a play is also necessarily a transformation of that play (from script to embodied production, from one interpretation to another, from one performance space to another), each production turns a Shakespearean story into something other than it has previously been. Performing Shakespeare entails a process of negotiation between convention and innovation and between practical constraints and the creative play of actors and directors, designers and technicians; in short, each production requires and responds to a collaborative process, unleashing the active participation of artists and viewers. Shakespeare's works are both text and performance, edition and adaptation. Indeed, we might say that adaptation and remediation are the conditions of Shakespeare's existence.

Whereas Chaucer's canon remains fixed in the academy, performance breeds performance and adaptation breeds adaptation in an ever-expanding Shakespearean archive. And, indeed, we propose that this distinction between a closed canon and an expanding archive provides a framework for thinking about the cinematic fortunes of these two authors. Adaptations and remediations based on a closed canon, such as Chaucer's, are often viewed by the experts who guard them in terms of what Hutcheon calls *fidelity criticism*. Fidelity critics see the movement from origin to adaptation as strictly linear: adaptations—even good ones—are *later* and *secondary*, derivative, appropriative, or downright exploitative.⁹ On the other hand, Shakespeare's works can be seen as what Abigail Derecho, adapting Derrida, defines as archontic literature. The Shakespearean archive does not "possess definite borders that can be transgressed"; rather, it encourages "enlargement and accretion," inviting readers, authors, and other creative artists "to enter . . . make new artifacts . . . and deposit the newly made work back into the archive."¹⁰ Archives ideally eschew hierarchy and linearity; each artifact within them contributes to and celebrates an ever-expanding repository. And, despite the occasional dismayed protest from an academy that would like to assert the primacy of the Shakespearean original, "Shakespeare" is an archive that readers can enter at any point in the adaptive chain. Readers can first encounter Shakespeare through

---

8. Throughout her study Hutcheon discusses showing versus telling, which are two of the three modes of textual engagement she uses to frame her theory. The third mode is interaction.

9. See Hutcheon's first chapter, "Beginning to Theorize Adaptation," *Adaptation*, 1–32.

10. Abigail Derecho, "Archontic Literature: A Definition, a History, and Several Theories of Fan Fiction," *Fan Fiction and Fan Communities in the Age of the Internet: New Essays*, ed. Karem Hellekson and Kristian Busse (Jefferson, NC: McFarland, 2006), 51–78, 65.

Baz Luhrmann or Franco Zeffirelli just as easily as through the First Folio or the Norton Anthology.

The multitude of texts in the rich Shakespearean archive rightly demands attention as autonomous cultural artifacts even as they contribute to the Shakespeare industry and to ideas about what constitutes Shakespeare. Filmic adaptations of Shakespeare carry not just the aura of Shakespeare but their own auras as well. In dialogue both with Shakespeare and with each other, they are, in Hutcheon's term, palimpsestuous, both containing and actively engaging their filmic precursors: for instance, Zeffirelli cast action star Mel Gibson as *Hamlet* (1990), effectively challenging Laurence Olivier's interpretation of the play as "the tragedy of a man who could not make up his mind," while Michael Almereyda (2000) set Hamlet's "to be or not to be" speech in the action section of a video store, possibly glancing at Gibson's performance a decade earlier and ironizing the entire performance tradition of the psychologically stunted prince of Denmark.[11] These multiple *Hamlet*s can be taken together to undermine the increasingly outmoded idea that the analysis of Shakespeare films should measure the degree to which an "original" "Shakespearean" text has been captured cinematically, insisting instead on each new film as a deposit to the ever-expanding archive, an addition that reveals intertextual play and that may retrospectively alter the meaning of previous entries. As Hutcheon notes, "Palimpsests make for permanent change."[12]

Of course, even in the archive, adapters of Shakespeare are keenly aware of "Shakespeare" the high culture icon. Hutcheon suggests that adaptations can be motivated by the desire either to enshrine or to topple their source material, and this is especially the case with Shakespearean adaptations, which often grapple with the authority of the Shakespearean text, explore their own relationship to that text, and assert their own aspirations as independent entities. Zeffirelli's *Romeo and Juliet* (1968), for example, enshrines. Shot on location in Verona, the film aligns itself with the play's textual authority by bringing the story to lush visual life and luxuriating in Shakespeare's language as spoken by an international cast of distinguished theater actors. Gus Van Sant's *My Own Private Idaho* (1991), on the other hand, adapts the *Henry IV* plays by using them as the deep structure for a subversive story about two hustlers and their search for love and family in contemporary Portland and Italy. The film's actors are not primarily trained Shakespeareans; furthermore, Van Sant's occasional use of lines from the play (acknowledged in the credits as "additional

---

11. Olivier's interpretive phrase is delivered in voice-over at the beginning of his 1948 *Hamlet*.

12. Hutcheon, *Adaptation*, 29.

dialogue by William Shakespeare") only underscores the primacy of Van Sant's role and the subordinate status accorded to Shakespeare. Adaptations may also challenge notions that Shakespeare guarantees national or cultural purity by cross-casting actors of different nationalities, as in Branagh's Shakespeare films, or by juxtaposing actors known for radically different kinds of cultural work, as in Kelly Asbury's 2011 *Gnomeo and Juliet,* a computer-animated adaptation of *Romeo and Juliet,* where the voices of Maggie Smith and Patrick Stewart feature alongside those of Hulk Hogan, Ozzy Osborne, and Dolly Parton.

The Shakespearean archive is open, ongoing, porous, and heterogeneous. Even an artifact that might aspire to close its boundaries to the "non-Shakespearean" is inevitably implicated in this porous heterogeneity, becoming part of a chain of adaptations that comment on each other and that, by their very multiplicity, attest to Shakespeare's seemingly endless potential for adaptation. Indeed, as Hutcheon's biological model of textual adaptation suggests, Shakespeare survives and thrives by virtue of adaptation, by being "made suitable," evolving "to fit new times and different places."[13] Throughout the twentieth and twenty-first centuries, one of the primary ways in which old stories survive has been through successful remediation from page to screen. Shakespeare has made this transition since the inception of the film industry, when he was considered a fit subject for appropriation by the new medium precisely because there was already a widespread cultural understanding that his plays were available to be adapted through performance. Additionally, adapting Shakespeare gave the nascent film industry the cultural cachet by which it could legitimize itself. Shakespeare conferred his prestige on film while film conferred new relevance on Shakespeare through the opportunity to enter an undiscovered country in which he could be adapted and kept vital yet again, this time through a dazzling new means of remediation that made his works available to a wider and more popular audience.

As an exemplar of high culture who simultaneously lives in the popular domain, Shakespeare has consistently offered both prestige and possibility to the film industry as a whole and to individual artists. Directors like Olivier, Branagh, Akira Kurosawa, Orson Welles, and Julie Taymor have asserted *auteur* status through their multiple adaptations of Shakespeare; other directors, from Max Reinhardt to Joss Whedon, have engaged with Shakespeare in high-profile one-offs. In addition, several of the most prominent Shakespeare directors have also played leading roles in their Shakespeare films, sometimes

---

13. Hutcheon, *Adaptation,* 31.

earning Oscar nominations along the way.[14] Other actors have built well-known bodies of work around Shakespeare. In a period of three years, Julia Stiles became the turn-of-the-century teen-queen of Shakespeare, appearing in Gil Junger's *10 Things I Hate about You* (1999), Almereyda's *Hamlet* (2000), and Tim Blake Nelson's *O* (2001). Joseph Fiennes played Shakespeare in John Madden's *Shakespeare in Love* (1998) before taking on Bassanio in Michael Radford's *Merchant of Venice* (2004). Al Pacino, deep into a career as a successful movie star, engaged with Shakespeare as actor and director of *Looking for Richard* (1996) and returned to him to play Shylock in Radford's *Merchant*.

While "Shakespeare" lends his prestige to the medium, its directors, and its stars, film keeps Shakespeare historically relevant. Cinematic Shakespeares are open to history, taking their shape from the pressure of historical events and historical strands of thought. Olivier's *Henry V* (1944) is partly a propaganda piece, telling a story of English heroism to inspire the British in the midst of World War II; Branagh, by contrast, saw his *Henry V* (1989) as an antiwar rejoinder to the conflict in the Falkland Islands. Furthermore, because Shakespeare's works are open to history, the repeated filmic reworking of his plays becomes a means for negotiating unfinished, or emergent, cultural business. In *Prospero's Books* (1991), Peter Greenaway plumbs the relationship between textuality and creativity, even as his film pioneers the use of digital technology in reimagining Shakespeare's story. Julie Taymor's *Tempest* (2010), starring Helen Mirren as Prospera, explores the relationship of both early modern and contemporary women to positions of political and theatrical power, even as it recasts the central father-daughter relationship as a mother-daughter tale.

As Shakespeare films have absorbed the historical and cultural concerns of the twenty and twenty-first centuries, they have also evolved alongside the medium itself: the use of sound, color, and computer animation, and the changing conventions of cinematography and film editing, have all made their mark on Shakespeare films and what directors understand they can accomplish with Shakespeare on screen. Genre, too, has made its mark: Shakespeare films not only comprise a genre of their own; they also play with classic Hollywood genres: *10 Things I Hate about You* is romantic comedy; Branagh's *A Midwinter's Tale* (1995) is backstage drama; his *Love's Labour's Lost* is Hollywood musical; and Kurosawa's *Ran* (1985) is Noh-style warrior epic. Adapting Shakespeare thus permits directors the freedom of engaging with their cinematic

---

14. Olivier won the Best Actor Oscar for *Hamlet*; Branagh was nominated for both Best Actor and Best Director for *Henry V.*

medium in multiple ways, performing metacommentary on their industry by translating the early modern text into the generic conventions and symbolic vocabulary of the cinematic medium, "making (Shakespeare) suitable," by reimagining his plays as *films,* allowing them to evolve, to adapt to their new context, and to make them accessible to a nonspecialist audience.

In stark contrast to Shakespeare's persistent cinematic presence, Chaucer is, as the essays in the first part of this collection demonstrate, strangely absent. While Shakespeare's works, with their history of performance and adaptation, were an obvious fit for the new industry, Chaucer's works, primarily associated with the schoolroom, were not. Chaucer has seldom been used to lend his prestige to the industry; few filmmakers have sought to enshrine or topple him, and there is no independent tradition of Chaucerian films— few autonomous cultural artifacts "open to history" and no dialogue between the original text and an evolving popular tradition. A century of mainstream Shakespeare films has at this point primed popular audiences for continuous additions to his cinematic canon. Because of its successful remediation to film, Shakespeare's work has a place in the "common memory"; even if someone has never actually seen or read a Shakespearean play, chances are they "know" one or more of his most canonical works—*Romeo and Juliet, Hamlet, Lear.* Chaucer, on the other hand, may be the Father of English Literature, but at the cinema he is a mainly missing one.

Ironically, the fact that Chaucer's works were relegated to the schoolroom rather than kept alive in the new popular medium of film may have in turn damaged their fortunes in the schoolroom, progressively narrowing the audience that encounters these works. Chaucer is no longer part of the required high school curriculum in the United States, and most university students will not study him unless they are English majors (and not even all English majors still read Chaucer). Thus, while people may have an inkling that Chaucer wrote in "old" English and the title the *Canterbury Tales* may ring a bell, very few of them have any actual familiarity with his works. On the other hand, Shakespeare's centrality in the Anglo-American school curriculum—bolstered by his cinematic presence—ensures a ready-made audience, familiar with his stories, curious to experience how they might be realized, and eager to see what a famous actor might make of a certain role. Viewers can revel in their ability to read one adaptation in relation to another: how do Branagh and Whedon conceptualize *Much Ado about Nothing,* for example; and which of their films is the more interesting/surprising/successful treatment of the play? When the creators of the website for the PBS series "In Search of Shakespeare" included a lesson plan "for educators" comparing different film adaptations of *Hamlet,* they suggested five different film versions students might use to complete the assigned activities.[15] This interplay between cinema and classroom produces a synergy in which new films ensure Shakespeare's continued accessibility and relevance, and Shakespeare's assured place in the curriculum guarantees that these films will automatically have a life within the educational mainstream at the high school and college levels.

Marketability is key. As Hutcheon reminds us, stories do not just spontaneously adapt themselves to new environments and new mediums. Instead, adaptation takes place within a context of producers, consumers, and medium. No story gets adapted to film unless there is something in it for the producers/studios paying for that adaptation, and while a text's "cultural capital" will occasionally compensate for less-than-stellar box-office potential, in general, "the money" wants to make more money; a tale is considered fit for adaptation only if it has the potential both to deliver a preexisting audience and to attract a new one. Thus, "hot books," such as the *Harry Potter* and *Hunger Games* series, are snapped up by the industry, endowed with astronomical budgets, and rushed to the big screen; "literary" books—preferably in the public domain—are chosen for their "prestige" factor, their appeal to a niche audience, and their place in the school curriculum with its potential pedagogical afterlife.

Chaucer in the twenty-first century may well fail all these tests of marketability. A Chaucer film has only a limited (and shrinking) preexisting audience. Furthermore, perceptions (perhaps misperceptions) about the nature of this preexisting audience have in many ways dictated the ways in which Chaucer's works have been adapted to the screen. While Shakespeare has been freely and irreverently adapted to new genres and settings, modernized and musicalized, moved from Verona to Los Angeles and back again, made into a spaghetti western, and set in a brewery, adaptations of Chaucer for the general (as opposed to the NC-17) audience have, on the whole, seemed always to have one eye on the academics and the classroom—on being a fit tribute to, in Robert Henryson's phrase, "worthie Chaucer glorious."[16] Thus, these adaptations—even those like the BBC *Canterbury Tales* that transpose the text to contemporary times—have valued not play but "faithfulness" to

---

15. For the PBS lesson plan, see Tom Fitzgerald, "In Search of Shakespeare: Comparing Film Adaptations," pbs.org, Web, accessed 1 November 2015.

16. Robert Henryson, *The Poems of Robert Henryson,* ed. Denton Fox (Oxford: Clarendon, 1981), 112, line 41. Furthermore, Chaucer adaptations have, on the whole, been confined to the small screen and produced under the auspices of the BBC, with its government funding (and thus no need to sell tickets or advertising) and its mandate to preserve cultural heritage. For an insightful discussion of the BBC and cultural heritage, see Kathleen Coyne Kelly, "The BBC *Canterbury Tales* (2003)," in *Medieval Afterlives in Contemporary Culture,* ed. Gail Ashton (London: Bloomsbury Academic, 2015), 134–43.

the original—or at least the spirit of it. This emphasis on faithfulness often impedes the text's remediation; rather than adapting the tale to a genre suited to the new medium—a sitcom, a romantic comedy, an action film—these programs place the medium in the service of the original. A faithful adaptation of a literary text does not necessarily a good (or commercially successful) film make; to make the transition from the page to the screen a text must make the move from the "telling" mode to the "showing" mode. Adaptations that seek to replicate their literary original without reimagining it as a *film* rarely succeed as an *adaptation,* an act of "making suitable"; rather, these dutiful and often stilted productions emphasize their originary text's *failure* to evolve. Take, for instance, the BBC animated *Canterbury Tales*. This production mostly "sticks to the text," imposing a voice-over narration of Chaucer's (translated) words onto an animated visual. While the knowing audience can get pleasure by figuring out what has been changed—the reordering of the stories (we begin with "The Nun's Priest's Tale"), how lines have been moved around (Theseus's Prime Mover speech frames "The Knight's Tale"), what has been left out (the storylines of Theseus and Hippolyta), and what has been added (the eerie glimpse of the beautiful wife morphing back into the hag)—the stories have not been rethought as *animated films*. Instead, animation functions as a visual aid for Chaucer's words, and even the animation feels stilted: story-boarded with limited backgrounds and movement, it calls attention to itself as "art." This series may have won critical acclaim—and the approval of the experts—but it does not truly adapt Chaucer in the evolutionary sense of making it suitable for an audience that grew up on Disney and Nickelodeon. Its image of Chaucer, a visual adaptation of the Ellesmere portrait, is that of the ironic spectator, the author, the authority—observing, commenting, memorializing.

We end with another image of Chaucer, not the static image of an *auctor* who is the property of experts (English majors, graduate students and professors) but the naked, playful Chaucer—the one with a gambling addiction and a way with words—of Brian Helgeland's box-office hit, *A Knight's Tale*. Ironically, but perhaps not surprisingly, it is Helgeland's irreverent and thoroughly adapted Chaucer, celebrity promoter and publicist, that has made "Chaucer" suitable for a twenty-first-century audience and generated an archive, inspiring a fanfic site featuring such tales as "A Knight in Not-So-Shining Armor" and "Because Geoff Loved Kate."[17] Here indeed is a Chaucer liberated from the experts and the page, an answer to a closed canon bound by authorial intent and academic tradition. The fact that Chaucer was absent from the film's initial marketing materials—which focus on William Thatcher's medievalized

---

17. "*A Knight's Tale* Slash Archive," www.fanfiction.net; Web, accessed 1 May 2016.

American success story, his rise from rags to riches through the world of sports—points to the consequences of fixing Chaucer on the page and in the ivory tower. *Shakespeare in Love* was playfully able to market Shakespeare to win critical acclaim, box-office dollars, and seven Academy Awards, but the promoters of *A Knight's Tale* clearly felt that attaching Chaucer's name to a film was more likely to put audiences off than bring them in. The Chaucer of dutiful school projects and difficult translation exercises points to the past; the living, *playful* Chaucer of Helgeland's film points to the future, exemplifying Jacques Derrida's ideal, always-open archive: "much and more than a thing of the past . . . the archive should call into question the coming of the future. . . . It is a question of a future . . . of a promise and of responsibility for tomorrow."[18] Rather than deploring Chaucerian play, we should embrace it. It is such play that will keep Chaucer alive, part of the common memory, guaranteeing an archive, "a pledge, and like every pledge [gage], a token of the future. . . . What is no longer archived in the same way is no longer lived in the same way."[19]

---

18. Jacques Derrida, "Archive Fever: A Freudian Impression," trans. Eric Prenowitz, *Diacritics* 25 (1995): 9–63, 34 and 36.

19. Derrida, "Archive," 18.

CHAPTER 3

CHAUCER, FILM, AND THE DESERT OF THE REAL; OR, WHY GEOFFREY CHAUCER WILL NEVER BE JANE AUSTEN

LARRY SCANLON

IT IS NO particular stricture on Jean Baudrillard or Slavoj Žižek to suspect that neither has spent much time with Chaucer's *House of Fame* or that neither realizes that in this poem Chaucer anticipated by some six centuries their arresting, metonymic figure of "the desert of the [R]eal." A dreaming Chaucer leaves the Temple of Glass and its depictions of the *Aeneid* only to find himself in a "large feld" consisting of nothing for as far as the eye can see but sand as fine-grained as that of "the desert of Lybye" (1.482, 488).[1] Like its postmodern counterparts, Chaucer's desert constitutes the indefinite ground for a more or less self-contained universe of signification. Both Baudrillard and Žižek treat the metonym of the desert as the dystopic revelation of modern culture, but in terms that are nearly antithetical. For Baudrillard, the desert of the real describes those scraps of social reality not already colonized by a postmodern economy of simulation and its production of the hyperreal.[2] (Among other metonyms, he offers Disneyland—that demotic, commodified House of Fame—as a model of the hyperreal.) Žižek takes up the metonym in his response to 9/11, *Welcome to the Desert of the Real*. He never mentions Baudrillard by name, but it is clear he completely repurposes the metonym. For

---

1. Citations of Chaucer are taken from *The Riverside Chaucer*, ed. Larry D. Benson, 3rd ed. (Boston: Houghton Mifflin, 1987).

2. Jean Baudrillard, "Simulacra and Simulations," *Selected Writings*, ed. Mark Poster (Stanford: Stanford University Press, 1998), 166–67.

him, the desert of the real exposes the simulacrum, the hyperreal, and similar postmodern heuristics as themselves illusory. The preliminary significance of 9/11 is the breach it opens in "the border which separates the digitalized First World from the Third World 'desert of the real.'"[3] Yet that breach constitutes no more than Žižek's point of departure. Savagely rejecting the temporal privilege assumed by conservative columnist George Will's fatuous proclamation of the end of the American "holiday from history," Žižek concerns himself more crucially with the illusory vanguardism "of our 'postmodern' time, with its freedom to deconstruct, doubt and distanciate oneself."[4] From his perspective, one can assign no particular epochal significance to 9/11 beyond the additional pressure it puts on an already compromised intellectual left, paralyzed by "the postmodern disdain for great ideological Causes."[5] As a rhetorical figure, *the desert of the real* thus straddles a familiar divide between modernist and postmodernist politics: between positions that locate the temporal privilege of the modern with Marxism and other classic modern positions and those that locate it in postmodern critiques. Moreover, the very contention to which the figure gives rise reinforces its essential modernity.

That leaves the *House of Fame*'s prefiguration of the figure in a curious position. I begin here to link Chaucer's absence in the cinema to a broader historiographical problem. From its retelling of Book 1 of the *Aeneid*, to its recreation of Dido's lament, to its parodic engagement with Dante's *Paradiso*, to its many conceits of transparency, to its House of Rumor, the *House of Fame* concerns itself with simulation and mimesis—that is, with the Real and its relation to fictional, poetic, and narrative representation. Both Baudrillard and Žižek take the quest for a reality lying beyond all representation to be characteristically a modern one. The *House of Fame* treats the problem in terms that belong recognizably to the later Middle Ages. Yet the poem also strongly suggests that the problem is not so much period-bound as endemic to the mimetic impulse itself. Chaucer the Dreamer's first encounter recreates the famous ekphrasis from the opening book of the *Aeneid*, where Aeneas finds himself face to face with paintings of the fall of Troy in a Carthaginian Temple of Hera. Vergil's episode is itself a rewriting of Book 8 of the *Odyssey*, in which Odysseus, to this point unknown to his hosts, breaks down while listening to a poet sing of his wanderings. Like Homer, Vergil places his protagonist in the presence of the narrative that defines him—that is, he puts the referent

---

3. Slavoj Žižek, *Welcome to the Desert of the Real: Five Essays on September 11 and Related Dates* (London: Verso, 2012), 41.
4. Žižek, *Desert*, 3.
5. Žižek, *Desert*, 107.

in the presence of its sign. Unlike Homer, Vergil makes the sign visual rather than aural. He gives the sign a material, a-linguistic tactility to rival that of the referent—Aeneas—himself. Chaucer amplifies this tendency by making Vergil's ekphrasis the focal point of the Temple of Glass. Chaucer consecrates this temple not to a deity but to narrative, and more specifically to narrative's creative, constructive, plastic capacity to simulate the Real. He then displaces the encounter between referent and sign from Aeneas to Dido, the remainder of Book 1 of the *House of Fame* dominated by her lament that literary tradition has treated her unfairly. This displacement demonstrates a fascination with female subjectivity that constitutes one of the hallmarks of Chaucer's entire career, but it also rewrites the sign/referent encounter in starker terms. For both Odysseus and Aeneas, the traumatic confrontation with their poetic biographies constitutes a trial, a setback, another obstacle, but only one in a series. Within that series it is not the most significant, and the series itself leads to ultimate triumph. Dido's complaint is that this encounter now defines her character, that her identity has been engulfed in a narrative signifying nothing but loss. The complaint thus presages another of Chaucer's career-long preoccupations: the futile but irresistible quest to capture those aspects of historical reality and human experience that elude the grasp of poetic signification. In a more immediate sense Dido's complaint presages the featureless desert where Book 1 ends. Chaucer the Dreamer finds the profound, inexhaustible matrix of poetic significance that constitutes the temple surrounded by a reality that defies any form of articulation and is devoid of all signifying structures.

There is an obvious objection to the continuity I am proposing. Late medieval culture was Christocentric. Postmodernity is not. One might therefore plausibly argue that Chaucer's desert is more delimited than the postmodern counterparts of Baudrillard and Žižek. Chaucer's desert figures only the postlapsarian world of a fallen humanity; the temple of poetic plenitude against which Chaucer sets his desert is equally fallen. As deployed by Baudrillard and Žižek, *the desert of the real* is no less metonymic, but now the trope figures reality in its ontological totality. Indeed, Chaucer explicitly acknowledges the Christian cast of his desert. His immediate response to this expansive void is prayer: "'O Crist,' thoughte I, 'that art in blysse, / Fro fantome and illusion / Me save!'" (1.492–94). He then espies the eagle, the poem's parodic vision of Dante, who will carry him into the next book. However, on closer inspection, this objection does not so much invalidate the continuity as give it a deeper, more dynamic character. What initially appeared to be a neglected correspondence now becomes a return of the repressed (bearing in mind Lacan's stricture that the repressed never actually goes anywhere). To repeat:

the desert of the Real is a metonym. Both Baudrillard and Žižek use it as shorthand for the dystopic, disenchanted outlook that separates modernity from the mystified idealizations of the premodern past. But if this metonym of disenchantment merely repeats Christianity's notion of humanity's postlapsarian condition, then what happens to the epistemological privilege that the figure also assumes? What are we to make of this drive to disenchant that expresses itself in the terms of the very system it seeks to transcend?

In case this possibility still seems largely random, it is worth remembering that the term *Real* itself is a late medieval development. *Realis,* an adjective derived from *res* (thing), emerged in late antiquity as a grammatical term designating forms referring to actual states. By the later Middle Ages it had come to designate any form of actuality. The *Oxford English Dictionary* notes that the Latin word is common in British sources from the twelfth century onward and stresses its use in legal contexts in Latin, French, and Anglo-Norman to refer to things as opposed to people. Strikingly, the term would play an important role in scholastic discussions of the Eucharist and transubstantiation, ultimately to be enshrined in the dogmatic phrase "the Real Presence." For a *locus classicus,* we can cite Aquinas in Part III, Question 76 of the *Summa Theologiae.* Here he does not speak of the Real Presence but of "real concomitance" (*ex reali concomitantia*). That difference is itself noteworthy, for Aquinas is insisting that the presence of Christ's body in the Eucharist comes not simply from "the power of the sacrament" but also as a matter of natural fact. Transubstantiation brings the "entire Christ" into the sacrament, his body as well as his divinity, because the two are naturally united:

> Ex naturali autem concomitantia est in hoc sacramento illud quod realiter est conjunctum ei in quod praedicta conversio terminatur. Si enim aliqua duo sunt realiter conjuncta, ubicumque est unum realiter, oportet et aliud esse: sola enim operatione animae discernuntur quae realiter sunt conjuncta.

> And by a natural concomitance there is also in this sacrament that which is really united with that thing wherein the aforesaid conversion is terminated. For if any two things be really united, then wherever the one is really, there must the other also be: it is only by an operation of the mind that things are distinguished which in reality are conjoined.[6]

---

6. St. Thomas Aquinas, *Summa Theologiae* (London: Blackfriars, 1963), vol. 58, 94. The translation is my own.

The earliest citation for the adjective in English is also Eucharistic, from 1400. It occurs in *Meditations on the Supper of Our Lord and the Hours of the Passion*, a Middle English version of Bonaventure's *Meditationes Vitae Christi*:

> Þys soper was real, as þou mayst here;
> Foure real þynges cryst made þere.
> Þe fyrst ys a bodly fedyng;
> Þe secunde ys hys dycyples fete wasshyng;
> Þe þred, yn brede hym self takyng;
> Þe fourþe, a sermoun of feyre makyng.[7]

Obviously, we cannot draw a single line from such densely theological applications to the modern notion of the Real. But it seems even more unlikely there is no influence at all. Modernity's romance with the Real—both in its negative sense, as a principle of disenchantment, and in its more positive plenitudes—repurposes a transcendent ontology of precisely the sort that modernity is supposed to replace. And without accounting for all of the intermediate steps, it seems clear that modernity's break with the past—its defining feature—depends on repressing continuities when launching new departures.

These repressive tendencies in modernity help explain not only why the scarcity of film adaptations of Chaucer is noteworthy but also why it is unlikely to change. What follows is an argument from absence. It is highly speculative as all such arguments necessarily are.[8] In my consideration of Chaucer's relative absence from film and video, I will set aside the issue of Shakespeare. Shakespeare was a dramatist and the one author in the Anglophone canon who can clearly claim to be more monumental than Chaucer. Instead I propose Jane Austen as the standard of comparison. Like Chaucer, Austen is a major canonical figure. Like Chaucer, she is a master ironist. Like him, she is fascinated by the problem of marriage, female subjectivity, and the relation between narrative and moral discourse that the combination of the first two seems inevitably to foreground. Unlike Chaucer, however, Austen has enjoyed an abundance of adaptations on film and video. The filmography on the Jane Austen.org website contains sixty-eight entries, including a handful of dramatizations of Austen's life.[9] What has Austen got that Chaucer hasn't?

---

7. *Meditations on the Supper of Our Lord, and the Hours of the Passion*, ed. J. Meadows Cowper (London: Early English Text Society, 1875), 2.

8. But not for that reason necessarily useless or invalid. See John Lange, "The Argument from Silence," *History and Theory* 5 (1966): 288–301.

9. As Renee Warren avers, "Despite completing just six novels, Jane Austen's work has appeared in countless movie and television presentations" ("Jane Austen: Movie and Television Shows," www.janeausten.org, 20 Feb. 2014).

My answer: free indirect discourse and two misrecognitions centered on it. The first misrecognition is that free indirect discourse is an invention of the novel. The second concerns the mimetic, "realistic" effects that free indirect discourse produces. There is a dominant current in modern literary thought that has always considered these effects as visual, objective, even scientific, and it continues so to do. In fact, these effects are irreducibly linguistic—as indeed are their conventional definitions as visual and objective. The first modern theories of narrative began with the opposition between *showing* and *telling*—an opposition as empirically compelling as it is philosophically incoherent. The opposition underwrites an evolutionary, progressivist view of literary history. Free indirect discourse enables the novel to achieve an impartial objectivity—enables it to float free of the ideology-ridden didacticism of previous forms. This view traditionally cites Flaubert as constituting the definitive break, but it can cite Austen as well. It has proven extremely resilient: Frances Ferguson recently suggested that "free indirect style is the novel's one and only formal contribution to literature." She then argues that Austen's use of the narrative mode in *Emma* produces an ideal of a "sociological knowledge that can only be used experimentally."[10] It is true that Ferguson stops well short of claiming that Austen's narrative is scientific. But it is just as true that her initial claim badly needs some empirical qualification. She justifies it by comparing Austen's narrative style to that of Richardson and the epistolary novel on the one hand and that of drama on the other. That it never occurs to her to look further backward I take less as reflection on her than as an instance of the epistemic dilemma that I have been discussing throughout this essay.

Free indirect discourse cannot begin with the novel because it is already a characteristic resource of Chaucerian irony. We need look no further than this instance from the Monk's portrait in The General Prologue, which E. Talbot Donaldson made famous in his 1954 essay "Chaucer the Pilgrim":

> And I seyde his opinion was good.
> What sholde he studie and make hymselven wood,
> Upon a book in cloystre alwey to poure,
> Or swynken with his handes, and laboure,
> As Austyn bit? How shal the world be served?
> Lat Austyn have his swynk to hym reserved! (1.183–88)[11]

---

10. Frances Ferguson, "Jane Austen, *Emma*, and the Impact of Form," *Reading for Form*, ed. Susan J. Wolfson and Marshall Brown (Seattle: University of Washington Press, 2006), 231–55, 233, 246.

11. For Donaldson's essay, see *PMLA* 69.4 (1954): 928–36.

These lines are a textbook instance of free indirect discourse. We might compare them briefly to Mieke Bal's discussion in *Narratology: Introduction to the Theory of Narrative*. Bal defines free indirect discourse as a "mixture of narrative levels," or as "interference" between the text of the narrator and the text of a character. She offers this sentence as an illustration: "Elizabeth would be damned if she'd go on living like this."[12] Line 184 from The General Prologue displays exactly the same interference in the narratorial voice: "What sholde he studie and make hymselven wood." I should note here a qualification, especially as it is one that will quickly return us to my larger point: Chaucer's narrative is in the first person, while free indirect discourse in the novel is generally in the third. (There are also third-person instances in Chaucer—e.g., The Pardoner's Tale 7.708–10). Yet even this difference does not deliver the clean distinction the evolutionary model claims. It is certainly possible to read Chaucer's narratorial endorsement—"And I seyde his opinion was good"—as a parodic confirmation of an intent that is ultimately didactic. (That is the tack Donaldson himself takes. Chaucer the Author intends the bumblings of Chaucer the Pilgrim to lead the reader to the appropriate moral judgments about the character flaws the bumblings inadvertently disclose.)[13] But it is just as possible to read Chaucer's use of the first person more deconstructively. That is, he is reminding his readers that an entirely objective narratorial viewpoint is impossible. In that case, Chaucer would be anticipating postmodern critiques of the more positivist excesses of modern realism.

Advocates for the newness of the novel could point to other differences between Chaucer's use of free indirect style and that of the novel. But my purpose is not to eliminate the historical distinction between modern prose fiction and late medieval poetic narrative. On the contrary, I wish to introduce a historical distinction somewhere else, that is, in the modes of imagining the Real. The Real may or may not have a history, but even those who take reality to be a modern discovery need to concede that the discovery itself is historically conditioned. In spite of the large differences among them, Baudrillard, Žižek, and Ferguson are all alike in imagining the Real as a scientific fact. This correlation is not the simple tautology it may seem. To equate the Real with science is not simply to ground it in universal skepticism or the principle of falsifiability. It is also to assign the Real a positive content. It is to assign the Real with the positive content of scientific knowledge—paradoxically enough, to treat scientific truths as infallible revelations rather than

---

12. Mieke Bal, *Narratology: Introduction to the Theory of Narrative*, 2nd ed. (Toronto: University of Toronto Press, 1997), 47.

13. E. Talbot Donaldson, *Speaking of Chaucer* (New York: Norton, 1970), 1–32.

provisional—albeit well-tested—propositions. I take this tendency to underlie Feguson's approving equation of Austen's narrative with "sociological knowledge" and the experimental method. Without in any way linking Ferguson herself or this particular reading to the current vogue for Austen adaptations, I want to suggest that the vogue nevertheless shares Ferguson's conflation of scienticity with free indirect style. I want also to suggest that the adaptations take things a step further by associating this formal feature with the Real.

Convictions about the preeminent truth-value of modern realism serve a crucial role in film and television adaptations. In *The Craft of Fiction,* the 1921 study that enshrined the opposition between showing and telling into modern critical consciousness, Percy Lubbock begins his discussion of Flaubert by asserting that

> the art of fiction does not begin until the novelist thinks of his story as a matter to be *shown,* to be so exhibited that it will tell itself. . . . The book is not a row of facts; it is a single image. . . . Narrative—like the tales of Defoe for example—must look elsewhere for support; Defoe produced it by the assertion of the historic truthfulness of his stories. But in a novel, strictly so called, attestation of this kind is, of course, quite irrelevant; the thing has to *look* true, and that is all.[14]

By the end of this brief and elegant exposition, the novel has become a "thing": not only something not to be told but also not really an assemblage of words at all. As Lubbock makes clear a few pages later, the novelist achieves the look of truth through the conflation of narrative viewpoints: "It is a matter of method. Sometimes the author is talking with his own voice, sometimes he is talking *through* one of people in the book—in this book for the most part Emma herself."[15] (Lubbock does not use the terms *free indirect discourse* or *free indirect style*. The phrase *style indirect libre* seems to have been coined by Charles Bally in 1912. It is not clear Lubbock knew Bally's work. But there is little doubt they are both describing the same formal characteristic.) The category of the visual has an intriguing and complex function in this argument. On the one hand, Lubbock's notion of realism remains uncannily close to the term's etymology: the true nature of reality is thing-like. Any literary presentation of the Real that emphasizes its "thingness" will look true, will bear a more convincing resemblance to the truth. On the other hand, Lubbock's repeated

---

14. Percy Lubbock, *The Craft of Fiction* (1921; New York: Peter Smith, 1945), 62; emphasis in original.

15. Lubbock, *Craft,* 68.

recourse to visual metaphors seems to work precisely because they are metaphors. It is not just that metaphor is a linguistic relation *par excellence*. It is also that in metaphorically shifting the mode of apprehension of the Real from language to sight, Lubbock can claim more of the material solidity of the *res*, all the while somewhat surreptitiously retaining the *signum*. Through free indirect discourse, story becomes "a matter to be shown," *shown* in this case amounting to a story "so exhibited that it will tell itself." Lubbock associates this manner of *ipse dixit* with scientific truth. However, is this self-narrating object not closer to the language of revelation? Indeed, as a semiotic structure, does it not bear a slightly uncanny resemblance to the material sign that is the medieval sacrament?

There is not much philosophical distance between Lubbock's "look of truth" and the practical aesthetic of film and TV adaptation. Allow me to cite the first sentence of the container copy for the DVD of the 1980 BBC adaptation of *Pride and Prejudice,* dramatized by Fay Weldon and directed by Cyril Coke:

> Shot on location in the beautiful English countryside, this flurry of romantic courtships full of injured pride and unfounded prejudice springs vividly to life in this remastered production of Jane Austen's most famous novel *Pride and Prejudice*.[16]

The opening participle wonderfully suggests a causality without actually taking responsibility for it. *Pride and Prejudice* "springs vividly to life"—its vitality doubly attested in Latinate and Anglo-Saxon terms—because the scenic backdrop has now been filled in. The objecthood to which the story aspires has been more fully realized. What I found most revealing about this blurb is the way it deals with what is actually a lack. Austen's use of free indirect discourse can never be brought to the screen. Yet the blurb compensates for that lack by embracing the visual ideal by which traditional narrative theory has misrecognized as the effect of that technique. Traditional narrative theory has redefined the irreducibly linguistic structure of free indirect discourse as a magical visuality—*the look of truth*; thus, filmic adaptations can dispense with the language and concentrate on the look.

Or perhaps I should say "almost dispense with." So much of the action in an Austen novel takes place in her use of free indirect discourse that film and video adaptations cannot entirely ignore it. Strikingly, the adaptations

---

16. *Jane Austen's "Pride and Prejudice"* (BBC Miniseries, 1980; New York: BBC Worldwide Americas, 2004), DVD cover note.

often fill in the gap by recourse to a staple of filmic narration analogous in crucial respects to free indirect discourse: shot/reverse shot. Adapters will typically appropriate particularly memorable fragments of Austen's dialogue. Then, when they are necessarily obliged to leave out the long stretches of free indirect discourse with which Austen frames her dialogic exchanges, they substitute sequences of shot/reverse shot. In David Bordwell's description, shot/reverse shot describes

> a pair of shots depicting complementary areas of space. The clearest case follows this pattern:
>
> 1. A character looks offscreen.
> 2. A second character looks offscreen in the opposite direction.[17]

Like free indirect discourse, this "stylistic figure" seeks an "ideal positionality." Like free indirect discourse, it seeks that positionality by moving in and out of particular narrative viewpoints. And, as in free indirect discourse, this movement produces a positionality that is, strictly speaking, logically impossible. As Bordwell explains, in a shot/reverse shot, characters rarely face the camera directly and thus never reproduce one half of the possible visual that follows the other half "exactly opposed to it." Instead, the camera angles are always oblique, suggesting an opposition but not directly portraying one. The figure "does *not* represent either character from the other's optical standpoint."[18] Like free indirect discourse, shot/reverse shot is a mode of narration that manages to produce verisimilitude out of an irreducible semantic indeterminacy. Indeed, while the shot/reverse shot is obviously more visual than free indirect discourse, it repeats the same repression. The shot/reverse shot is essentially iterative. To that extent, it is linguistic or at least discursive rather than purely visual in some immediate sense, and to the same extent it constitutes a showing that is actually a form of telling. No one disputes that Hollywood cinema inherits most of its canons of verisimilitude from the realist novel. The congruence between these two modes of narration may well be a specific point of formal transmission. Nevertheless, even if the congruence is sheer coincidence it still has the effect of tightening the connections between the novel and the commercial aesthetic of television and film. That aesthetic generally seeks its pleasure in the plenitude of the Real. Literary adaptations returning to the

---

17. David Bordwell, *Narration in the Fiction Film* (Madison: University of Wisconsin Press, 1985), 110.

18. Bordwell, *Narration*, 110. Bordwell is not concerned with television, but video narration uses this technique as well.

source of that aesthetic will almost by definition seek to intensify this pleasure in plenitude. They will find their look of truth in the stately home rather than the desert. When even such rigorous modern skeptics as Baudrillard and Žižek seek to preserve some measure of the same pleasure by overstating the novelty of modern disenchantment, is there much reason to expect a warmer filmic reception for medieval literature's greatest ironist?

CHAPTER 4

PROFIT, POLITICS, AND PRURIENCE; OR, WHY CHAUCER IS BAD BOX OFFICE

KATHLEEN FORNI

> The question that really bothered me was this: If Chaucer is dubbed, however inaccurately, "the Father of English poetry," why was he, at the millennium, relatively ignored? Why wasn't he being considered for the kinds of adaptations that would make him as current, viable, and available as Shakespeare and Austen?
> —Sheila Fisher[1]

> Clearly, film is a product, and entertainment is a business.
> —Bastion Cleve[2]

THE SHORT ANSWER to the paucity of wide-release cinema Chauceriana is that the *Canterbury Tales* is simply not perceived to be a profitable commercial property. In other words, the Chaucer brand is not good box office. The more difficult question to answer is why this is, or is perceived to be, the case. No doubt, translating the *Canterbury Tales* into a visual medium poses a number of aesthetic and technical difficulties. But as Chaucer's existing visual oeuvre

---

1. Sheila Fisher, *The Selected Canterbury Tales: A New Verse Translation* (New York: Norton, 2012), xvi.
2. Bastion Cleve, *Film Production and Management*, 3rd ed. (Burlington, MA: Focal Press, 2006), 11.

attests, the artistic and institutional challenges posed by his capacious poem have inspired a range of remarkably creative responses, arguably sensitive to the spirit of Chaucer's text and, more importantly, capturing some critical acclaim and commercial success within their niche markets. A brief examination of the techniques used by three extant formal adaptations—Pier Paolo Pasolini's *I racconti di Canterbury* (1972), *Animated Epics: The Canterbury Tales* (1998–2000), and the BBC1 *Canterbury Tales* (2003)—to address industrial constraints involved in translating the *Canterbury Tales* to video/film can shed light on how producers have brought Chaucer to the screen and why Chaucer has yet to see a major-studio theatrical release. But while material concerns certainly predominate, one would be remiss to simply dismiss ideological and cultural considerations in explaining why the *Canterbury Tales* is not considered a marketable commodity by Hollywood. Pasolini might be charged, for instance, with associating the poem with the unpromising genre of avante-garde pornography. Adaptations of the *Canterbury Tales* also tend to embody a conservative pessimism that emphasizes the limitations on human aspirations at odds with a popular culture ethic of optimistic egalitarianism. But the taint of salacity and eschewing the "feel good" ending are not enough to sink a creative property. I can only surmise that the *Canterbury Tales* title does not have the leverage of a presold property (i.e., a film whose title or author enjoys broad name recognition) because it lacks the cultural capital in the United States that it carries in the United Kingdom and Chaucer's medievalism is discordant with popular culture conventions that reimagine the Middle Ages within the adventure and romance genres. Brian Helgeland's *A Knight's Tale* (2001) demonstrates, however, that it takes only one commercially savvy creator to profitably repackage one of Chaucer's tales for mass consumption. This film also attests to the fact that Chaucer himself can be a bankable icon, representing both the social mobility and faith in self-fashioning embodied in the American Dream.

As a caveat, it is difficult to account for a negative—that is, Chaucer's absence from film—and my first impulse is to suggest that the perceived neglect is perhaps owing in part not only to a sense of professional rivalry (when faced with the scores of Shakespeare film adaptations) but also to a sense of disparity between Chaucer's canonical profile and his popular-culture presence. Chaucer's perceived attenuated cinematic presence also suggests a latent desire for more cinema Chauceriana, since promoting the poet to the culture at large might presumably be advantageous to medievalists in marketing our own academic product. Many Chaucerians likely sympathize with Steve Ellis's contention that Chaucer, "whose work (at least in the *Canterbury Tales*) is regarded as accessible, cheerfully realist, and 'English,'" should be a "popularizer's dream."³ One might add that from a commercial standpoint, his work is in the public domain and comes with some built-in name recognition thanks to his continuing, if diminishing, presence in the educational curriculum. In other words, there would seem to be some potential profit (material benefit or financial gain) for film producers. But in addition to the "difficulties of language and unfamiliar historical context" that Ellis suggests separate Chaucer from a general audience, the poem poses a number of artistic challenges for the visual adapter, not posed, for instance, when making the transition from stage to screen. The seventeen-thousand-line *Canterbury Tales* is episodic and unfinished, a loosely related series of self-contained, versified short stories in a sparsely sketched and unfinished framework. There is no Aristotelian plot (beginning, middle, end), no three-act structure, no central conflict, no primary protagonist, and very little realistic character motivation. The General Prologue is heavily diegetic, featuring a long series of static descriptive portraits. And while many of Chaucer's thematic concerns are broadly transhistorical (the miseries of marriage, clerical malfeasance, temporal justice), they are articulated through the prism of the culturally topical (glossing, pardons, chivalry). And, of course, it's in Middle English.

One might agree with James Welsh that "everything is adaptable" given the "right imaginative initiative."⁴ While substantial, none of these obstacles is insurmountable given cinema's temporal and spatial fluidity and its facility in translating lengthy verbal descriptions into compact visual images. And as both the hundreds of amateur vignettes on YouTube and Chaucer's extant adaptations attest, the artistic and technical challenges posed by his poem have inspired a range of remarkably creative responses. It takes more than imaginative initiative to produce a movie, however, and what is insurmountable is the primary institutional contingency of a wide-release film—namely, the desire to turn a financial profit. Indeed, Simone Murray maintains that "of all filmmaking, economic motivations are often most readily evident in relation to adaptation."⁵

Understandably, film producers tend to prefer adaptations with previous box-office successes, operating under the assumption that the remake

---

3. Steve Ellis, *Chaucer at Large: The Poet in the Modern Imagination* (Minneapolis: University of Minnesota Press, 2000), 19.

4. James Welsh, "Issues of Screen Adaptation: What Is Truth?" *The Literature/Film Reader: Issues of Adaptation,* ed. James Welsh and Peter Lev (Lanham, MD: Scarecrow, 2007), xiii–xxviiii, xv.

5. Simone Murray, "The Business of Adaptation: Reading the Market," *A Companion to Literature, Film, and Adaptation,* ed. Deborah Cartmell (Chichester: Blackwell, 2012), 122–39, 137.

will appeal to the generic expectations of audiences. Since film adaptations of literary texts are often viewed as "safe bets with a ready audience," one would assume that Chaucer might enjoy some profit (advantage or benefit) as a presold property.[6] That Chaucer has no conventional commercial track record and an unconventional generic affiliation might be laid at Pasolini's door for associating the Chaucerian with pornography. *I racconti di Canterbury* remains the only cinematic adaptation of the poem and appears to have served as a cautionary example to subsequent filmmakers. The film is auteurist, neorealist, rated X, poorly dubbed, elliptical, and disjointed and features amateur actors—violating (purposefully) almost every precept of mainstream feature-film production.[7] Pasolini, for whom sexuality is always a political expression and who turns to the Middle Ages as a time of precapitalist libidinal licentiousness, famously focuses on Chaucer's fabliau sensibility. All of the tales take as their subject transgressive sexuality and/or the symbiosis of sexuality with deception and greed. The mock "Retraction" proclaims that the tales have been told "for sheer pleasure," and while for some the net effect is to suggest an unfettered "celebration of bodies,"[8] non-normative sexuality is consistently, and painfully, punished. Rather than turning to the Middle Ages as a precapitalist idyll of ebullient eroticism (as he arguably does in *Il Decameron*, the first installment of his *Trilogia della vita*), Pasolini's *I racconti di Canterbury* seems to be both a pessimistic commentary on his contemporary political and cultural climate and a lesson in authoritarian repression, casting Chaucer as a fantasist of cruel ecclesiastical sanctions against violations of heterosexual monogamy. The film did, however, create a franchise of sorts, inspiring a number of imitators who associated the *Canterbury Tales*, or Chaucer, or both, with pornography, as Cathal Tohill and Pete Tombs observe:

> Following the huge local success of Pasolini's *Decameron*, his 1971 film of the *Canterbury Tales* was being imitated in anticipation of its expected success even *before* it had been released. Unfortunately, somebody didn't do their homework properly, and several of the resulting films laboured under the misapprehension that Canterbury was the author of the tales in question, which lead to some strange titlings, as well as peculiar hybrids like *The*

---

6. Linda Hutcheon, *A Theory of Adaptation*, 2nd ed. (Abingdon: Routledge, 2013), 87.

7. See John Robert Marlow, *Make Your Story a Movie* (New York: St. Martins, 2012), 37–40.

8. Sam Rohdie, *The Passion of Pier Paolo Pasolini* (Indianapolis: Indiana University Press, 1995), 79.

Sexbury Tales (1971), *The Lusty Wives of Canterbury* (1972) and *The Other Canterbury Tales* (1972).⁹

Bud Lee's *The Ribald Tales of Canterbury* (1985), "the second-most expensive X-rated film of all time," perhaps represents the culmination of Pasolini's legacy, but no mainstream filmmakers have repeated the experiment.¹⁰

Pasolini's turn to Chaucer was an anomaly, inspired both by the English poet's association with Boccaccio (whom Chaucer is depicted as plagiarizing in the film) and by his desire in the *Trilogia della vita* to represent an "authentic," preindustrial pastoral unburdened by bourgeois bad consciousness and middle-class sexual mores. It is not surprising, however, that the two most recent adaptations, *Animated Epics: The Canterbury Tales* (S4C in association with BBC Education, BBC Wales, and HBO) and the BBC1 *Canterbury Tales,* originated in the United Kingdom where Chaucer has had a long small-screen presence, partly, no doubt, because "the English literary tradition [has] long been a rallying point of national superiority" and because of Chaucer's totemic association with British linguistic and cultural heritage.¹¹ The BBC's investment in Chaucer is partly the result of the "unifying myth" of Reithian public service broadcasting (named for Lord John Reith, BBC's first director general). Beyond the remit "to educate, inform, and entertain," the BBC's cultural paradigm includes defending "a great heritage" ("We are custodians of unique and important heritage") and serving to "both reflect and help define national identity."¹² British public television is also somewhat shielded from market-driven considerations, amenable to a serial format and flexible programming, and produced at a far lower cost than film productions. Both shows have extended their shelf life (and profits) by video/DVD sales to the educational market.

Emma French argues that Shakespeare adaptations of the past few decades have employed a highly effective "rhetoric of veneration and irreverence in an effort to secure an effective hybrid balance between . . . 'high' and 'low'

---

9. Cathal Tohill and Pete Tombs, *Immoral Tales: European Sex and Horror Movies, 1956–1984* (New York: St. Martins, 1995), 197.

10. Daniel Comiskey, "The Naked Truth," *Indianapolis Monthly,* Mar. 2008, 127. On the potential exaggeration in claims concerning production costs of *The Ribald Tales of Canterbury,* see George Shuffelton's essay in this collection.

11. Lynda Boose and Richard Burt, "Totally Clueless? Shakespeare Goes Hollywood in the 1990s," *Shakespeare, the Movie: Popularizing the Plays on Film, TV, and Video,* ed. Lynda Boose and Richard Burt (London: Routledge, 1997), 8–22, 12.

12. Lucy Kung-Shankleman, *Inside the BBC and CNN: Managing Media Organizations* (London: Routledge, 2000), 133, 142.

in the marketing of Shakespeare on film" to mass audiences.[13] *I racconti di Canterbury* clearly fails to achieve this successful marketing paradigm, for its cinematic style is too high and its content too low. But both writer Jonathan Myerson's *Animated Epics: The Canterbury Tales* and the BBC live-action *Canterbury Tales* episodes more clearly strike that balance between artistic innovation and popular culture genres. The animated *Canterbury Tales* trilogy turns to animation in a strategic and aesthetic effort, according to Myerson, to make "Chaucer accessible."[14] Associated with imaginary fantasy and a fabricated world, animation provides the distancing that makes Chaucer's adult subject matter (rape, adultery, murder) more palatable to a young audience. Chaucer is made accessible both by the use of colloquial English and by the extraordinary abridgement and compression characteristic of commercial adaptations. Appropriating a range of animation styles and techniques, from the relatively realistic look of stop-motion 3-D to highly stylized 2-D drawings, the production foregrounds Chaucer's variety of genres and philosophical moods, ranging here from flatulence to fatalism. The inherent fluidity of the animated image underscores both the comic and the chimerical aspects of Chaucer's poetry. Add to this an anti-elitist spirit, a consistent exposure of hypocrisy, and a mockery of adult pretensions—social, religious, intellectual—and you have a winning formula: "Leaving London" was nominated for Best Animated Short Film at the 1999 Academy Awards.

While the different animation styles by several teams of animators accentuate Chaucer's generic diversity, animation as a genre tends to be pigeonholed as children's or juvenile entertainment. The problem is that since Chaucer often deals with sexual malfeasance (adultery, rape, spousal abuse), the *Canterbury Tales* is, or is perceived to be, inappropriate for children. It is quite telling that even with its Academy Award nomination, HBO did not air the third segment of the animated series ("The Journey Back") featuring the Miller's and the Reeve's tales. According to a *Variety* contributor, "even though it's somewhat toned down, the *Canterbury Tales* may still be too bawdy for the uninitiated."[15] A review in the *Los Angeles Times* prior to HBO's airing of the first two episodes (which were given a TV-14 rating) is certainly cautionary: "Don't let the family hour air times deceive you. This wizardry of stop-motion puppetry and gorgeous cel animation is not for children."[16] Similarly, Michael

---

13. Emma French, *Selling Shakespeare to Hollywood* (Hatfield: University of Hertfordshire, 2006), 2.
14. "The Animator's Tale," *BBC News Online*, news.bbbc.co.uk, 17 Mar. 1999.
15. Laura Fries, Review of *Animated Epics: The Canterbury Tales*, *Variety*, 26 May 1999.
16. Lynne Heffley, Review of *Animated Epics: The Canterbury Tales*, *Los Angeles Times*, 26 May 1999.

Salda suggests that in spite of Joanna Quinn's BAFTA and Emmy awards for her contribution, "some educators may find the 'Wife of Bath's Tale' too raw for all but high school and college audiences":

> Like its source in the *Canterbury Tales,* this animated version pushes beyond the boundaries of what many school districts deem acceptable. The film's depiction of the hag's pendulous breasts and the intercourse enjoyed by the knight and hag—as her form fluctuates between aged crone and young beauty—may well disturb some viewers. Likewise the rape scene . . . even though it's handled discreetly . . . makes this adaptation perhaps suitable only for older students.[17]

These kinds of reviews can be poison, especially for those who aspire to some return on their investment in the education market.

The BBC overcomes the problems of fitting the *Canterbury Tales* into conventional generic classification and of capturing a wider audience by offering six independent dramatic one-offs. Chaucer's tales are transformed into contemporary genres (noir, romance, the con) reflecting contemporary concerns (socioeconomic inequality, immigration, racism, and crime). The intention was not necessarily to reflect Chaucer's rich generic diversity but, according to Laura Mackie (the executive producer), to cast a wide generic net in order to capture audience share: "The six films offer very different viewing experiences. . . . Some will appeal to audiences who like comedy drama while others will appeal to an audience who want a more challenging narrative. Hopefully, the audience will be drawn to one for a particular piece of casting or storyline and come back for more."[18] As for the problem of fidelity, the intention was to move beyond the provincial demographic of Chaucer aficionados. According to the producer, Kate Bartlett, the episodes "had to appeal to those more familiar with Chaucer but also work in their own right as single films, to an audience unfamiliar with Chaucer—and this was important to all of us."[19] This strategy can also backfire, however, for while professional reviews were largely laudatory, the bogey of infidelity infiltrated several critical appraisals.[20] The

---

17. Michael N. Salda, *Arthurian Animation* (Jefferson, NC: McFarland, 2013), 127.
18. "BBC1 *Canterbury Tales* (brief pack)," bbc.co.uk/pressoffice, 8 Aug. 2003.
19. "BBC1 *Canterbury Tales* (brief pack)."
20. See, for instance, Nancy Banks-Smith (*The Guardian*): "*The Canterbury Tales* contain as little Chaucer as is permissible under the Sales of Goods Act. . . . The stories have been detached from their gold setting like old jewelry broken into pieces, and we were left with half-a-dozen modern one-act plays. Python and scholar Terry Jones, who shed a new and blinding light on The Knight's Tale, believes Chaucer was murdered. I see what he means." Thomas Sutcliffe (*The Independent*) agrees: "the BBC's *Canterbury Tales* isn't Chaucer, it's Chaucer

most glaring omission (from a Chaucerian's point of view) is the pilgrimage frame and the links between the tales, negating both the theme of the journey and the stories as impersonated art. While the atavistic critical impulse is to read the omission as a commentary on cultural dislocation and communal fragmentation, the decision was dictated by industrial constraints, namely, the need for flexible programming (order of episodes), the impossibility of assembling the large cast for the shoot, and the desire to get the audience "hooked in the first three minutes."[21]

I am mindful of Murray's caveat that material considerations are "frequently introduced as a preliminary framing device to set up the ensuing textual analysis, rather than being presented as any form of challenge" to cultural or aesthetic evaluation.[22] But while industry interests dictate the production and distribution of popular culture products, consumption is also obviously an important factor, and shows are not made, or remade, unless they are consumed. In the past I've argued that Chaucer's film oeuvre is fundamentally conservative, presumably a bad fit for a mass cultural product such as film. John Fiske maintains that popular discrimination demands pleasure and relevance.[23] Both derive, in part, from products that appear resistant or oppositional to dominant interests (conservative, capitalist, patriarchal) but also that facilitate the projection of social interests and social identities, particularly of disempowered or marginalized groups. Notwithstanding a veneer of dissent in the three extant formal adaptations, one finds both a consistent assertion of normative politics and a conservative pessimism at odds with the optimistic "egalitarian ethic" dear to American popular culture.[24] Pasolini

---

Flavouring." These reviews and others are available at *"The Canterbury Tales," The Guardian*, theguardian.com, 12 Sept. 2003.

21. See James Hamilton, "Chaucer on the Road Again," *Televisual* (Jun. 2003): 20–22. The original plan was to "link the stories as Chaucer does with six of the characters meeting up in a traffic jam on the M2 as they were making their way to Canterbury . . . but the logistics of getting such a large cast together proved too much" (22). See also Jonathan Myerson: "[The producer, Kate Bartlett] says she toyed with a linking device, echoing the role of the pilgrims, but was eventually forced to abandon the idea: 'I would have had to cut five minutes from already perfectly balanced 60-minute pieces.' And, as she also admits, 'If the audience aren't hooked in the first three minutes, they're off to ITV'" ("Tales of the Unexpected," *The Observer*, theguardian.com/theosbserver, 30 Aug. 2003).

22. Murray, "Business of Adaptation," 128.

23. See John Fiske, "Popular Discrimination," *Modernity and Mass Culture*, ed. James Naremore and Patrick Brantlinger (Indianapolis: Indiana University Press, 1991), 103–16. See also Tony Bennett, "The Politics of 'the Popular' and Popular Culture," *Popular Culture and Social Relations*, ed. Tony Bennett, Colin Mercer, and Janet Woollacott (Philadelphia: Open University Press, 1986), 6–21.

24. Lane Crothers, *Globalization and American Culture*, 3rd ed. (Plymouth: Rowman & Littlefield, 2013), 41: "Issues of social and economic class . . . are largely absent from American

presents the *Canterbury Tales* not as a celebration of the carnivalesque but as a lesson in authoritarianism and ecclesiastical domination, with perversity lying less in the sexual act than in the desire to transgress. The animated *Tales,* bringing out the "dark and disturbing undertones" of Chaucer's poem,[25] emphasize the limitations on human determination and agency and the transient nature of happiness. And the BBC's domestic melodramas consistently represent broken relationships and individual dysfunction less as products of larger social and institutional forces at work in "life in the new century" (e.g., racism, socioeconomic inequality, poverty) than as individual failings (e.g., insanity, criminality) best ameliorated through the transformative power of romantic love.

Of course, this kind of academic analysis of popular culture only goes so far since any number of box-office successes are littered with conservative or defeatist tropes addressing the limitations on human potential. Thus, the question remains: if television has proved an appropriate production and distribution format in the United Kingdom, then why not in the United States? Why is there no HBO or AMC *Canterbury Tales* targeted at either adults or children? Sheila Fisher's answer to her query about the dearth of adaptations in my epigraph is that Chaucer's absence from American cinema "might well lie in the language in which Chaucer originally wrote: his Middle English."[26] But there is very little of even translated Middle English in any of the adaptations, and so there must be something more than the problem of linguistic alterity.

Chaucer's absence from the (American) wide screen must reflect both his relatively low cultural profile in the United States and his unconventional medievalism. Adaptations of the *Canterbury Tales* are almost exclusively an Anglo phenomenon in part because Chaucer, like Shakespeare, is a "signifier for British cultural superiority"[27] and, perhaps even more than Shakespeare, is associated with British linguistic and literary nationalism.[28] Chaucer's medievalism is also discordant with popular filmic convention that shoehorns

---

programming (even if they certainly exist in American life).... The characters in American programs rarely, if ever, link their social and economic status to political or financial factors beyond their control, even if the shows focus on middle-class families or characters. Likewise, better-off characters ... are usually seen to have achieved their status by their own hard work, not as the result of some racial, ethnic, gender, or class bias."

25. Ellis, *Chaucer at Large,* 139.
26. Fisher, *Selected Canterbury Tales,* xvi.
27. Boose and Burt, "Totally Clueless?" 13.
28. On Chaucer's association with British nationalism, see Christopher Cannon, *The Making of Chaucer's English: A Study of Words* (Cambridge: Cambridge University Press, 1998), 48–55.

courtly love and chivalry into the romance and adventure genres. His Arthurian knight is on a quest to atone for his rape of a maiden; Emily does not need rescuing and is forced into a feudal marriage; Griselda's Cinderella story devolves into perverse psychological abuse; and Criseyde jilts Troilus. Such idiosyncratic genre-bending is appealing to a postmodern critical sensibility but not to popular discrimination, which prefers the play of meaning that can be projected onto the conventional formula.[29]

With a visual legacy associating the title with avant-garde erotica, juvenile entertainment, and British cultural identity, the *Canterbury Tales* labors (at least in the United States) under the paradoxical stigma of being both too high and too low, or, as a colleague suggested, too sexy and not sexy enough. One might add that however well the irony of a work that tempers high-minded philosophy and scatological humor might appeal to a British sensibility, the conceptual conjunction is perceived to be untenable for mass American consumption. That said, however, as Helgeland's *A Knight's Tale* attests, it only takes the imaginative initiative of a former English major, and a few "hooks"—namely, a critically acclaimed director, celebrity actors, a popular genre, and an exotic location—to successfully produce and distribute a loose modern analogue of a Canterbury tale. And this film demonstrates as well that if the *Canterbury Tales* brand is hard to market to the masses, Chaucer "the man" (as Donald Howard would say) surely is not.[30] Chaucer's historical figure as reinvented in the popular (and the critical) imagination appears to be a signifier for social possibility and the fluidity of social class at the heart of the American dream. Helgeland's silver-tongued, ne'er-do-well Chaucer exists outside, or above, a rigid class hierarchy, occupying a curiously ambiguous social position, equally at home penning sentiments of *fin amors* or competing in a farting contest. In short, he is a master of self-fashioning. Even better, he is genial and modest, content with his own subservient position while putting his poetic talents (here, equated with literacy) to use in defeating class-demarcating aristocrats.

I put the question of Chaucer's absence from mainstream cinema to my premodern colleagues. Their well-intentioned response was to ask how the *Canterbury Tales* would profit from being translated to film. In other words, how does the poem, or professional Chaucerians, or the public benefit from film adaptation? The assumption, I think, is that the aesthetic object is a delicate exotic fruit easily damaged, or perhaps contaminated, with untutored

---

29. On popular discrimination, see Fiske, "Popular," esp. 106–9.
30. Donald Howard, "Chaucer the Man," *PMLA* 80.4 (1965): 337–43, and see also Howard's magisterial biography, *Chaucer: His Life, His Works, His World* (New York: Dutton, 1987).

tampering. One might suggest, however, as do adaptation theorists who invoke an evolutionary metaphor, that film adaptation accommodates the literary text to a changing cultural environment.[31] The survival of the *Canterbury Tales* is not necessarily predicated on its fitness for popular consumption, but this form of variation certainly cannot hurt. Concluding his history of Shakespeare visual adaptations, Kenneth Rothwell suggests that "Shakespeare remains incarnate in the trinity of page, stage, and screen, each offering its own unique insights into his mind and art from the muses of literature, theatre, and mass entertainment. Thrice armed, he is unlikely to go away."[32] Whether the film adaptation leads audiences to seek out the original remains dubious. But at the very least a wide-release *Canterbury Tales* would foster brand recognition, perhaps making our students—and the culture at large—more amenable to, and appreciative of, our academic product.

---

31. Hutcheon, *Adaptation*, 31–32.

32. Kenneth Rothwell, *A History of Shakespeare on Film: A Century of Film and Television*, 2nd ed. (Cambridge: Cambridge University Press, 2004), 274.

PART II
LOST AND FOUND

CHAPTER 5

CHAUCER AND THE MOVING IMAGE IN PRE-WORLD WAR II AMERICA

LYNN ARNER

IN 1929 the Academy of Motion Picture Arts and Sciences offered public schools and state universities a recycled version of *Douglas Fairbanks in Robin Hood* (U.S., Douglas Fairbanks Pictures Corporation, 1923), to aid in the study of medieval literature and history. This offer constituted the Academy's initial foray into exploring the educational value of "old negatives" after "all the theatrical potentialities" of these films had been exhausted.[1] Actor and producer Douglas Fairbanks, the Academy's first president, donated use of the original negative of *Douglas Fairbanks in Robin Hood* for the experiment. If the experiment proved successful, the Academy expected schools thereafter to lease prints made from other old negatives, a plan the film industry promoted as "an investment in good will."[2] Cut from eight reels to one, *Douglas Fairbanks in Robin Hood* was reincarnated as *In the Days of Chivalry* (U.S., Motion Picture Academy of Arts and Sciences, 1929). This reincarnation excised the romantic coupling of Robin and Marion, centered disproportionately on the opening tournament, and included brief scenes depicting the

---

1. Charles Roach, "Theatrical Motion Pictures for the Educational Field," *The Educational Screen* 9.2 (Feb. 1930): 36–38, at 37.

2. Roach, "Theatrical," 37–38. See also "Teaching Aids to Accompany the Film *In the Days of Chivalry*" (Hollywood: Academy of Motion Picture Arts and Sciences, 1929), 1–2; and "Classroom Films" (Hollywood: Academy of Motion Picture Arts and Sciences, 15 Jul. 1930), 7–8.

medieval castle, the knights' departure for the Holy Land, and the exploitation of peasants.[3] The Academy explained that local educators had helped with the project, and indeed, in *The Educational Screen* in 1926, two teachers from the Visual Education Department of the Los Angeles City Schools had provided a "Robin Hood" lesson plan for studying medieval life, an exercise based on Fairbanks's film.[4] To assist educators, the Academy issued a twenty-page teaching aid to accompany *In the Days of Chivalry*. This aid explains that the film will "introduce vitality into the study of *Ivanhoe,* Chaucer, and *The Idylls of the King.*"[5] Chaucer's name subsequently appears in the guide: his knight and squire constitute two of twenty-eight proposed discussion topics, and his writings are said to provide a good record of medieval armor.[6] Shortly after issuing this teaching aid, the Academy boasted that its school experiment was a success and that it had donated thirty-two prints of *In the Days of Chivalry* to twenty public schools and state university visual education departments throughout the United States.[7]

It is unlikely that the Academy, or the larger film industry, possessed any sincere interest in encouraging the study of Chaucer. In fact, the Academy's circumlocutory promotion of Chaucer via a warmed-over Robin Hood movie foregrounds the dearth of Chaucerian films in the silent era. This chapter investigates the scarcity of Chaucer-themed moving images in the United States before World War II. This piece begins by sketching the scant traces of Chaucerian motion pictures from the 1890s to 1939 and by explaining why this lack is unusual when considered alongside films with seemingly comparable subjects. Engaged with social and cultural histories of American cinema, the bulk of the essay outlines key reasons why Chaucer was an unlikely subject of the moving image in pre–WW II America. In the process, this chapter considers the simultaneous presence of Chaucer in the larger American film culture at the time.

Although English and European films were frequently exhibited in the United States prior to WW I, international cinema offers few traces of Chaucer before WW II. In 1909 *Il Conte Ugolino* (Italy, Itala Film, 1909) featured a title character that appears in The Monk's Tale and Dante's *Inferno,* although

---

3. "School Film Experiment Success," *Bulletin* 36 (1 Nov. 1930): 6; and "Teaching Aids," 4.

4. Ercel C. McAteer and Marian Evans, "'Robin Hood'—A Film Lesson," *The Educational Screen* 5.1 (Jan. 1926): 11–13, 59.

5. "Teaching Aids," 3.

6. "Teaching Aids," 9, 14.

7. "School Film Experiment Success," 6; and *Annual Report* (Hollywood: Academy of Motion Picture Arts and Sciences, 1930), 25. See also *The Educational Screen* 10.1 (Jan. 1931): 12.

Dante is credited as the source.[8] The 1910s generated two films titled *Griséldis* (France, Pathé Frères, 1912; and Austria, Wiener Kunstfilm, 1919), but it is unlikely that either film was based specifically on Chaucer's Griselda since Griselda was a recurrent figure in European literature and opera.[9] One might think that Chaucer enjoyed a place of honor among British spectators, and indeed two British titles evoke the *Canterbury Tales: A Pilgrimage to Canterbury* (U.K., Gaumont Co., 1927) and *Canterbury Pilgrimage* (U.K., Religious Films, 1937). However, the first is a travelogue, while the second centers on Thomas Becket.

One Hollywood film claimed to be derived from Chaucer. The opening title of *On Borrowed Time* (U.S., MGM, 1939) reads:

We tell you a tale of everyday people in a little town of present-day America. It is an absurd, charming and stupendous story—but it is not a new one. Gossip of a similar amazing occurrence was whispered in the days when old Chaucer was writing his "Canterbury Tales."

Mr. Chaucer liked the story and believed it—and so do we. If, perchance, *you* don't believe it, we respectfully insist that we [and Mr. Chaucer] must be right. Because faith still performs miracles and a good deed does find its just reward.

The program notes for the preview of *On Borrowed Time* at the Westwood Village Theatre in Los Angeles contain the above passage and explain that Lawrence Edward Watkin, English instructor at Washington and Lee University, generated the story after hearing, in a Chaucer class, a tale about an old woman who was allowed to detain Death in her apple tree until the townsfolk, finding Death essential, made her free him. Watkin adapted this tale, substituting an old man for the old woman.[10] *Variety* confirms that Watkin "took the story from a legend in Chaucer."[11] The film appears to claim some basis in The Pardoner's Tale, but it is difficult to discern connections, apart from the presence of both an allegorical male character and a tree associated with

---

8. Pierre Leprohon, *The Italian Cinema* (London: Praeger, 1972), 20–21.

9. *Bioscope* (29 Feb. 1912), supplement iii, summarizes Pathé's *Griséldis*. Kevin J. Harty, *The Reel Middle Ages* (Jefferson, NC: McFarland, 2006), 218, believes the film is based on Charles Perrault's *La Marquise de Salusses, ou la patience de Griseldis*.

10. Program notes, *On Borrowed Time*, Westwood Village Theatre, Los Angeles, 29 Jun. 1939.

11. "Inside Stuff-Legit," *Variety* 129.9 (9 Feb. 1938), 57. See also Review, *On Borrowed Time*, *Variety* 135.4 (5 Jul. 1939): 14.

FIGURE 5.1. As part of its promotion of *The Taxi Dancer* (U.S., 1927), MGM touted star Marc McDermott as so discerning that he found and perused John Urry's edition of Chaucer on the set. As the blocking of the publicity photo indicates, however, a local exhibitor or newspaper decided that both the film and the celebrity were more marketable without Chaucer. Photo by International Newsreel, 1926. Author's collection.

death. Despite such rare gestures toward Chaucer, the poet seemed to have been all but banished from the American screen before WW II (see figure 5.1).

The dearth of Chaucerian motion pictures is striking when one considers the plethora of seemingly similar films. Scripts based on canonical literature abound in the early decades of American cinema. From the 1890s through the early 1910s, filmmakers in the United States (and in Britain and Europe) frequently drew upon literature, fables, and myths, and, as Lea Jacobs explains, after 1914 the adaptation of well-known plays and novels for the American screen became a mainstay in an industry seeking greater cultural respectability.[12] Shakespearean films, especially before the 1920s, were so commonplace that, as William Uricchio and Roberta E. Pearson point out, from 1908 to 1913 the American film industry produced at least thirty-six fifteen-minute

---

12. Lea Jacobs, *The Decline of Sentiment: American Film in the 1920s* (Berkeley: University of California Press, 2008), 16.

Shakespearean films.[13] Given the importance of canonical literature in the first decades of American cinema, Chaucer would seem an obvious choice.

Moreover, medieval themes thrived in the first several decades of American film production. Recurrent topics included Robin Hood,[14] the crusades,[15] King Arthur's court,[16] and the life of François Villon,[17] each enjoying multiple incarnations by 1939. Pictures heavily grounded in medieval history were not uncommon, including *Becket* (U.S., Vitagraph Co. of America, 1910); *The Death of King Edward III* (U.S., Vitagraph Co. of America, 1911); and *Joan the Woman* (U.S., Cardinal Film, 1916). Films based on medieval literature enjoyed a sizable presence, such as *Everyman* (U.S., Crawley-Maude Features, 1913); *The Adventures of Marco Polo* (U.S., Samuel Goldwyn, 1938); and *In the Days of Chivalry* or *Aucassin and Nicolette* (U.S., Edison Manufacturing Co., 1911), starring Marc McDermott. With the number of movies rooted in the Middle Ages, Chaucer's absence is glaring.

This absence is even more surprising when one considers the presence of motion pictures based on the works of Dante and Boccaccio. Before 1939 several pictures grounded in Dante's writings were either produced or circulated in the United States: *Francesca da Rimini; or, The Two Brothers* (U.S., Vitagraph Co. of America, 1908) and *Francesca da Rimini* (U.S., Vitagraph Co. of America, 1910), a tale told by both Dante and Boccaccio; *L'Inferno,* or *Dante's Inferno* (Italy, Milano Films, 1909) and *L'Inferno,* or *Dante's Inferno* (Italy, Helios, 1911);[18] and seeming biopics *Dante e Beatrice* or *The Life of Dante* (Italy, Socièta Anonima Ambrosio, 1913) and *The Life of Dante* (Express Films, 1924).[19] Two Hollywood studio films, *Dante's Inferno* (U.S., Fox Film, 1924) and *Dante's Inferno* (U.S., Fox Film, 1935), engaged with Dante's writings but

---

13. William Uricchio and Roberta E. Pearson, *Reframing Culture: The Case of the Vitagraph Quality Films* (Princeton: Princeton University Press, 1993), 68.

14. Examples: *Robin Hood* (U.S., Kalem Co., 1908); *Robin Hood* (U.S., Thanhouser Film, 1913); *Douglas Fairbanks in Robin Hood* (U.S., Douglas Fairbanks Pictures, 1923); *Robin Hood, Jr.* (U.S., Ambassador Pictures, 1936); and *The Adventures of Robin Hood* (U.S., Warner Brothers Pictures, 1938).

15. Examples: *A Tale of the Crusades* (U.S., Vitagraph Co. of America, 1908); *Richard, the Lion-Hearted* (U.S., Associated Authors, 1923); and *The Crusades* (U.S., Paramount Productions, 1935).

16. Examples: *Launcelot and Elaine* (U.S., Vitagraph Co. of America, 1909); *Parsifal* (U.S., Edison Manufacturing Co., 1904); *A Connecticut Yankee at King Arthur's Court* (U.S., Fox Film, 1921); and *A Connecticut Yankee* (U.S., Fox Film, 1931).

17. Examples: *Poet of the People* (U.S., Thanhouser Films, 1911); *If I Were King* (U.S., Fox Film, 1920); *The Beloved Rogue* (U.S., Feature Productions, 1927); *The Vagabond King* (U.S., Paramount Publix, 1930); and *If I Were King* (U.S., Paramount Pictures, 1938).

18. *The New York Dramatic Mirror,* 2 Aug. 1911, 21, 25.

19. *Moving Picture World* 15.12 (22 Mar. 1913): 1202; and *The Film Daily* 28.41 (18 May 1924): 11. Express Film Co. seems German.

focused primarily on modern stories, a common strategy in many American films rooted in medieval topics. Boccaccio's *Decameron* was a source for several films exhibited in the United States: *The Golden Supper* (U.S., Biograph Co., 1910), based on Tennyson's rendition of Boccaccio's tale of Messer Gentil de' Carisendi; *For Women's Favor* (U.S., Lund Productions, 1924), a modern rewriting of the tale of the falcon of Count Federigo degli Alberighi; and the musical *Liebesgeschichten von Boccaccio* (Germany, UFA, 1936), or *Love Tales of Boccaccio*.[20] Clearly, being a medieval poet did not automatically bar Chaucer from the screen. Furthermore, the production and circulation of Boccaccio and Dante films in the United States indicate that Chaucer's Catholicism was not likely much of an issue, especially since his associations with Catholicism had been largely exorcised by late nineteenth- and early twentieth-century Protestant retellers of his tales, as Velma Bourgeois Richmond and Candace Barrington point out.[21] Also, motion pictures based on specific tales by Dante and Boccaccio attest that the unwieldy format of the *Canterbury Tales* does not explain the inattention to Chaucer, since a single story could be excerpted from a medieval compendium. Given the cornucopia of films based on canonical literature or rooted in the Middle Ages, including pictures about the lives and writings of other medieval poets such as Villon, Dante, and Boccaccio, why was Chaucer all but absent?

Several historical and cultural reasons rendered Chaucer an unlikely subject in American moving images before WW II. First, the Americanization of film was one factor (Dante's exceptionalism will be discussed later). In the 1890s and the nickelodeon era (circa 1905–11), American films were typically exhibited alongside European and English productions. However, as Richard Abel explains, as early as 1908 through 1910, in part because of anxieties about the influx of immigrants and the insistence on Americanizing these immigrants, various practices of excluding "foreign film product" from the U.S. market developed. A simultaneous push for a national product fostered pictures that featured American actors, subjects, modes of storytelling, and aesthetics, especially aesthetics influenced in part by realism.[22] The

---

20. Frank S. Nugent, "The Screen: The Roxy Presents 'The Woman Alone,' A New Melodrama by Alfred Hitchcock—Two From Abroad," *The New York Times*, 27 Feb. 1937. See also Review of "*Liebesgeschichten von Boccaccio,*" *Variety* 125.12 (3 Mar. 1937): 15; and Review of "*Liebesgeschichten von Boccaccio,*" *Variety* (16 Sept. 1936): 17.

21. Velma Bourgeois Richmond, *Chaucer as Children's Literature* (Jefferson, NC: McFarland, 2004), 21, 45–46, 54, 88, 151, 153, 205–6; and Candace Barrington, "'Forget What You Have Learned': The Mistick Krewe's 1914 Mardi Gras Chaucer," *American Literary History* 22.4 (2010): 806–30, at 810.

22. Richard Abel, *The Red Rooster Scare: Making Cinema American, 1900–1910* (Berkeley: University of California Press, 1999), chaps. 5 and 6, esp. 152.

Americanization of film, Abel explains, continued into the 1910s, although ultimately it was the outbreak of WW I that nearly eliminated foreign films from the American market.[23] Similarly, Jacobs argues that in the 1920s changes in American literary tastes affected changes in tastes regarding the cinema. Literary tastes for naturalism helped to produce protonaturalist and naturalist aesthetics in some Hollywood films, aesthetics that included attempts to create, even at the literal level of speech on title cards, an American vernacular and that typically established a taste for simple stories about ordinary people, preferences that, Jacobs explains, had an impact on various genres at the time.[24]

Given this expansive Americanization of the cinema, the chances of Chaucer's writings appearing on film decreased as early as the late nickelodeon period because of an intersecting nexus of issues that might loosely be understood as cinematic nationalism. Chaucer may have been known as the Father of the English language, but Middle English was a vast distance from American vernacular speech, and modern audiences, even Brits, felt emphatically more comfortable with the neologisms and slang in Hollywood films than with Chaucer's English, the *New York Times* and film magazines intermittently declared.[25] Hollywood fan magazines routinely acknowledged Chaucer as the Father of English Literature,[26] but English literature was not American literature, especially amid efforts to Americanize the cinema through such conventions as homegrown models for storytelling and the valorization of realism and naturalism, aesthetic tastes against which Chaucer's poetry would not fare well. Moreover, most Chaucerian narratives revolve around kings, princes, dukes, knights, ladies, and other members of the ruling classes, not the classes who enjoyed center stage in scripts about the lives of ordinary people, and not characters with whom American viewers from the working classes would easily identify. Likewise, Chaucer's tales do not fit comfortably

---

23. Richard Abel, *Americanizing the Movies and "Movie-Mad" Audiences, 1910–1914* (Berkeley: University of California Press, 2006), esp. 6.

24. Jacobs, *Decline*, chaps. 1 and 2.

25. Examples: Ernest Marshall, "Screen News from London Town: British Critics Find That Public Is Not So Patriotic Regarding Entertainment," *The New York Times*, 15 Jun. 1930; "London Screen Notes: The Curse of a Cultivated English Accent—Some New British Pictures," *The New York Times*, 28 Jun. 1931; Percy Hutchinson, "Chaucer's Tales 'Translated' for the Modern Reader: Mr. Hill Prepares a Fresh Draught From the 'Well of English Undefiled,'" *The New York Times*, 18 May 1930; no title, *The New York Times*, 16 Nov. 1901; and A. Walter Utting, "They Missed It," *Film Fun* 341 (Aug. 1917): n.p.

26. Examples: "The Answer Man," *Motion Picture Magazine* 14 (Oct. 1917): 132; The Answer Man, "The Movie Encyclopedia," *Motion Picture Classic* 10.1 (Mar. 1920): 84; "Answer Department," *Motion Picture Story Magazine* 7.5 (Jun. 1914): 143; and "Musings of 'The Photoplay Philosopher,'" *Motion Picture Story Magazine* 4.10 (Nov. 1912): 140.

with American subjects. This is not to say it was impossible to deploy Chaucerian tales to speak to American subjects and to generate simple stories about ordinary people, but doing so would entail considerable distortions of most Chaucerian stories, as *On Borrowed Time* attests.

A second reason for the dearth of Chaucerian films is the failure of his poetry to conform to another central convention of American film, a convention at least by the mid-1920s: Chaucer's tales of heterosexual couplings fail to offer the promise of futurity. As Lee Edelman argues, reproductive futurity structures contemporary American culture.[27] The cinematic celebration of futurity is evident in what Jacobs identifies as the rise to hegemonic prominence of heterosexual romantic coupling—especially as a motor of narration—in Hollywood film by the mid-1920s.[28] One could argue that reproductive futurity enjoyed a strong presence internationally from the earliest years of the moving image: for example, in Alice Guy Blaché's *La Fée aux Choux* (*The Cabbage Fairy*) (France, Solax, 1896) a shapely fairy of child-bearing age plucks naked babies from under large leaves in a cabbage patch. Chaucer's tales have little to offer a project of heteronormative generation, especially for early twentieth-century audiences surrounded by eugenics movements that insisted on the importance of breeding healthy stock to guarantee the success of future nations. Children are seldom present in Chaucerian stories, and when they are present, these children sometimes die, deaths rendered through dramatic means that are impossible to overlook, as in The Prioress's Tale, The Legend of Medea, and seemingly The Clerk's Tale. Many heterosexual unions in Chaucerian poetry end in failure, including all tales in the *Legend of Good Women,* the mating of Emily and the victor in The Knight's Tale, and Troilus and Criseyde's affair. Less disastrous heterosexual couplings are still largely failed matings and frequently sterile, such as Alison and her older husband in The Miller's Tale, the May-December romance in The Merchant's Tale, and the Wife of Bath's five marriages. The few marriages that do generate offspring are not structured by strong promises of futurity: witness the union between Griselda and Walter in The Clerk's Tale and Constance and Alla's married life in The Man of Law's Tale. The overall poor record on successful heterosexual mating, reproduction, and futurity in Chaucerian poetry decreased the likelihood of his tales inspiring American, especially Hollywood, films, increasingly so after the valorization of the heterosexual couple by the mid-1920s—and in Hollywood film thereafter.

---

27. Lee Edelman, *No Future: Queer Theory and the Death Drive* (Durham: Duke University Press, 2004).

28. See Jacobs, *Decline,* chap. 6.

A third reason that Chaucer was an unlikely choice for American filmmakers, at least between the wars, was his strong associations with the past and tradition and an accompanying sense that he, and the larger Middle Ages, belonged to the distant past, not to the future—nor even to the present. This view was grounded in part in strong associations between the medieval and the Victorian. Victorians had embraced medievalism at various sites, including in several artistic movements, such as the gothic revival in architecture, Pre-Raphaelitism, and the Arts and Crafts movement. Regarding Chaucer specifically, he was highly celebrated in the Arts and Crafts movement through William Morris's *Works of Geoffrey Chaucer*, also known as *The Kelmscott Chaucer*, which Morris considered the crowning achievement of the Kelmscott press,[29] and in Morris's creation of the "Chaucer type" font. More ubiquitously, Chaucer was associated with Victorians because his tales recurrently appeared in children's books in the Victorian and Edwardian eras.[30]

Before WW I, distant historical materials were frequent fodder for American film, as the sizable presence of folklore, fairy tales, and biographies of historical figures in moving images attest. However, between WW I and WW II, historical materials from dramatically earlier periods were not generally regarded with the same enthusiasm. Medieval subjects, given their historical distance, their associations with Victorians, and their foreignness, lost some cachet in the post–WW I American cinema. This waning of the Middle Ages is illustrated by an unrealized D. W. Griffith production. Seymour Stern explains that before WW I, Griffith planned to make *The Quest of the Holy Grail*: Griffith wrote the scenario and traveled to the Boston Public Library to film Edwin A. Abbey's frescoes. Forced by prior obligations to delay production, when Griffith wished to resume the medieval project after WW I, his financial backers rejected his proposal at a time when the American public clamored for modern themes.[31] If a director as central to Hollywood as Griffith could not secure funding for a movie about such a seemingly perennial favorite as Arthurian knights when his prestige was at its height, then surely the Middle Ages had declined in popularity. Nevertheless, some Arthurian movies were made between the wars, two of the most celebrated being *A Connecticut*

---

29. William Morris, *The Art and Craft of Printing* (New Rochelle, NY: Clarke Conwell at the Elston Press, 1902), 30.

30. On these children's books, see Richmond, *Chaucer*; Steve Ellis, *Chaucer at Large: The Poet in the Modern Imagination* (Minneapolis: University of Minnesota Press, 2000), chap. 4; and Siân Echard, "Bedtime Chaucer: Juvenile Adaptations and the Medieval Canon," *Printing the Middle Ages* (Philadelphia: University of Pennsylvania Press, 2008), 126–61.

31. "An Index to the Creative Work of David Wark Griffith," Part II, "The Art Triumphant (b) The Triangle Productions 1915–1916," compiled by Seymour Stern, Special Supplement to Sight and Sound, Index Series no. 7 (London: British Film Institute, 1946), 7–8.

Yankee in King Arthur's Court (U.S., Fox Film, 1920) and *A Connecticut Yankee* (U.S., Fox Film, 1931), both based on Mark Twain's novel. Reviewers frequently commented that an important key to the success of these films was the humor generated through dramatic updates to Twain's novel to appeal to modern moviegoers, such as the depictions of cars, motorcycles, airplanes, radios, telephones, and cigarette lighters.[32] Similarly, the two most important American interbellum Dante films, *Dante's Inferno* (U.S., Fox Film, 1924) and *Dante's Inferno* (U.S., Fox Film, 1935), deemphasized the poet's writings and focused on modern scenarios.

Likewise, MGM's promotion of *On Borrowed Time* insists that the film makes an old story modern. The film's trailer begins with vague visual allusions to the Middle Ages (namely, a nostalgic drawing of a cottage surrounded by fields that, through a wipe resembling a manuscript page, is replaced by a shot of buildings with medieval-style architecture) that are quickly superseded by an emphasis on the 1930s play and novel. The novel and play are depicted through rapidly dissolved images of the novel's mass production and icons of modernity: a typewriter, automobiles, a streetcar, shots of New York City at night, newspaper photographers, and urban crowds both inside and outside theaters—a montage that describes the transformation of the novel into a Broadway play and an impending cinematic success. Although the film proclaims its debt to Chaucer, the trailer does not mention him.[33] Because this film is a rare, if not the only, pre–WW II Hollywood film that explicitly claims to be based on Chaucer's poetry, it is striking that reviewers frequently remarked on the film's utter strangeness and its incongruity with other Hollywood productions, noting, for example, its centeredness on death and the personification of death as a man.[34] In the 1930s, Chaucer is intermittently positioned as the antithesis of the modern.[35] If Chaucer were situated in stark

---

32. Regarding *A Connecticut Yankee in King Arthur's Court*, see "Mark Twain's Satire Given Good Production and Has Many Laughs," *Wid's Daily* 15.35 (6 Feb. 1921): 3; "Connecticut Yankee in King Arthur's Court," *Motion Picture News* (12 Feb. 1921): 1383; "'A Connecticut Yankee in King Arthur's Court' One of the Screen's Greatest Comedies" and "The Screen," Richard Wallace Collection f 4, Margaret Herrick Library. Regarding *A Connecticut Yankee*, see "Rogers Goes Medieval in Twain Story," *Washington Post*, 19 Apr. 1931; "'A Connecticut Yankee'—with Will Rogers," *Harrison's Reports* 13.5 (11 Apr. 1931): 58; and "Two Laugh Films Open: Rogers Smart Cracks as Knight of the Olden Day, Mary Pickford Capers in Frenchified Role of 'Kiki,'" *LA Times*, 7 Apr. 1931.

33. Theatrical trailer, *On Borrowed Time* (U.S., MGM, 1939), available on youtube.com.

34. Examples: E. S., "'On Borrowed Time' Unique Venture into Supernatural," *LA Times*, 30 Jun. 1939; and Nelson B. Bell, "'On Borrowed Time' Is Picture of Unique Design . . . ," *The Washington Post*, 19 Jul. 1939.

35. Examples: "Beware of Shackles (editorial)," *Movie Makers* 10.7 (1935): 289; Campbell Nairne, "The Writer's Approach to Cinema," *Cinema Quarterly* 3.3 (1935): 137; and Angela Jane

contrast with the modern, then he would lose favor in a cinema of the 1920s and 1930s that congratulated itself for being thoroughly modern.

A fourth reason Chaucer was almost entirely overlooked in American cinema before WW II is that his writings were never massified. Despite the contested class basis of the beginnings of cinema as an institution, by the mid-1910s the cinema was a mass cultural institution that addressed a mass audience. As Uricchio and Pearson explain, Shakespearean films, typically featuring condensed versions of his plays or key scenes, enjoyed cross-class appeal by the nickelodeon period, since most Americans, middle- and working-class, native-born and immigrant, had exposure to the Bard. Americans routinely studied Shakespeare in school, and Shakespearean cultural ephemera circulated extensively. The working classes often attended Shakespearean performances, and some of their homes displayed inexpensive Shakespearean pictures.[36] Uricchio and Pearson argue that although Dante was much less well-known among the general population, at the turn of the century there was a Dante craze among certain sectors in the United States, especially middle- and upper-class women, and Dante courses flourished at universities. Italian immigrants appear to have been familiar with Dante, and the "lower orders" more generally did not necessarily lack familiarity with Dante's texts.[37] These combined forces were available as a means to position potential audiences for Dante films, although, as Uricchio and Pearson's work makes clear, Dante did not have a mass audience.

Chaucer lacked the cross-class appeal of Shakespeare, and even the more restricted appeal of Dante, and hence it was unlikely for Chaucer's writings to address a mass audience in the cinema. Nonetheless, Chaucer did enjoy some presence in mainstream American culture between the 1890s and WW II. American children studied Chaucer in elementary and secondary schools, as Richmond explains and as the Academy documents discussed earlier imply.[38] The 1914 Comus parade celebrating Mardi Gras in New Orleans featured as its theme the "Tales of Chaucer."[39] Most parade viewers, Barrington believes, would not have known Chaucerian tales but may have recognized Chaucer

---

Connor, "Highway Learning: Yellow Sign System Provides Stimulus for Motorists," *The New York Times*, 27 Oct. 1935. For an earlier mention of Chaucer being old-fashioned, see "Recent Fiction: Mr. Hewlett's 'New Canterbury Tales,'" *The New York Times*, 16 Nov. 1901.

36. Uricchio and Pearson, *Reframing*, 74–87; and "How Many Times Shall Caesar Bleed in Sport: Shakespeare and the Cultural Debate about Moving Pictures," *The Silent Cinema Reader*, ed. Lee Grieveson and Peter Krämer (London: Routledge, 2004), 155–68, at 158–63.

37. Uricchio and Pearson, *Reframing*, 95–99.

38. Richmond, *Chaucer*, chap 6. See also chap. 2.

39. Henri Schindler, *Mardi Gras Treasures: Costume Designs of the Golden Age* (Gretna: Pelican Publishing, 2002), 95–97, 112–15; and *Mardi Gras Treasures: Float Designs of the Golden Age*

as a name, reputed to be the Father of English Verse. Barrington ties this unfamiliarity to what she views as Chaucer's relative absence from popular culture.[40] However, Chaucer did enjoy some visibility in the first four decades of the twentieth century. Although Chaucerian ephemera did not circulate as extensively as Shakespeare's, typical Chaucerian ephemera of the era included postcards with Chaucer's portrait, prints of his tomb, magazine images reprinted from editions of his poetry, and his portrait on a cigarette card issued by a British tobacco company.[41] Chaucer's name frequently appeared in newspaper advertisements for editions of his writings, especially translations.[42] Steve Ellis demonstrates that there was a noticeable proliferation of books on Chaucer published in England in the first two decades of the twentieth century, books aimed at the general reader, reflecting the growth in the number of Chaucer's popularizers.[43] In the *New York Times,* references to editions of Chaucer's poetry and to books on Chaucer constitute the most typical citations of the poet, although his name consistently appears in various ways, most frequently in reports regarding manuscript sales but also intermittently in biographical pieces, such as in accounts of his newly discovered house or descendants, and occasionally in columns about miscellaneous topics, including the promotion of exercise and a discussion of automobile travel.[44]

(Gretna: Pelican Publishing, 2001), 84, 108–10. See the carnival collection in Tulane University's digital collection: http://louisdl.louislibraries.org.

40. Barrington, "'Forget,'" 810–11, 821, 824, 827.

41. The Metropolitan Museum of Art issued Chaucer's portrait on a 1937 postcard. A 1910 postcard from a different source features Chaucer's tomb. The magazine image reproduces a woodcut from *The Kelmscott Chaucer.* The 1923 cigarette card is from the set "Celebrities and Their Autographs," issued by Nicolas Sarony & Co., Cigarettes, London, England. These items were listed on eBay as "1937 Photogravure Geoffrey Chaucer Author Poet Canterbury Tales Portrait England," item 370919540540, auction ended 13 Nov. 2013; "1910 Print Chaucer Tomb Westminster Abbey London Wreath Chair Landmark Gothic," item 370922426358, auction ended 17 Nov. 2013; "1924 dd print printing kelmscott chaucer hammersmith," item 350915516449, auction ended 30 Nov. 2013; and "Geoffrey Chaucer Author Scarce 1923 Cigarette Card #95," item 350917730183, auction ended 3 Dec. 2013.

42. Examples: "Book Notes," *The New York Times,* 30 May 1934; "Books and Authors," *The New York Times,* 20 Oct. 1929; and Edward Larocque Tinker, "New Editions, Fine & Otherwise," *The New York Times,* 13 Nov. 1938.

43. Ellis, *Chaucer at Large,* 18–19.

44. Examples regarding manuscript sales include "Rare Literary Gems for H. E. Huntington: Ellesmere Chaucer Ranks with Milton Manuscript as Greatest Survival of Its Kind," *The New York Times,* 21 May 1917; and "George Smith Buys Bridgewater Mss.: Famous English Collection Sold," *The New York Times,* 18 May 1917. Reports of his alleged house or descendants appear in "Chaucer Line in America," *The New York Times,* 16 Mar. 1910; "Descendant of Chaucer: Search Results in Discovery of Kinsmen of Poet's Wife," *The New York Times,* 13 Mar. 1910; and "Chaucer Discovery Seen: London Workmen Find Part of His 13th-Century House, Believed His," *The New York Times,* 25 Feb. 1928. Regarding travel, see John H. Finley, "Long

Allusions to Chaucer were also part of ambient American film culture, appearing in fan and exhibitors' magazines. In addition to previously discussed deployments of Chaucer in these venues, the poet is intermittently associated with the personalities of stars, both generically and in specific instances. In *Photoplay*'s 1925 account of a typical day in the life of a leading man, the busy star spends a few minutes before bedtime "dipping into Chaucer."[45] Dale Summer, "the screen's most ardent and handsomest lover" in 1929, is a great thinker and revels in Chaucer, according to the Hollywood and Beverley Hills Society News in *Hollywood Filmograph*.[46] The refined Margaret Lindsay can discuss Chaucer but is not an intellectual, *Picture Play Magazine* proclaimed in 1935.[47] Chaucer is sometimes used as an example of those who have been martyred, exiled, or at least underappreciated as writers in their day.[48] A seeming contradiction, Chaucer is not infrequently employed to exemplify the maxim that good work and success often happens late in life.[49] Chaucer's name recurs in the pretentious regular column "Musings of the *Photoplay* Philosopher" in *Motion Picture Story Magazine*.[50] In these musings and elsewhere in film magazines, Chaucer is frequently lauded as a great poet or as the Father of English Poetry.[51] Contrasting Chaucer to modern authors, one writer in the British cinephile and craft publication *Cinema Quarterly* remarks, "Chaucer could write gaily that the grass was green, and leave it at that, sure of his effect," when he was writing what is "rightly regarded as the first English novel."[52] While repeating the frequent late nineteenth- and early twentieth-century alignments of Chaucer with nature,[53] claims such as these

---

Highroad Beckons to the Walker: Three Miles a Day . . . ," *The New York Times*, 12 Apr. 1925; and Connor, "Highway Learning."

45. Garrett E. Fort, "It's a Great Life, Etc.: Around the Clock with One of Our Most Popular Leading Men, According to Gossip," *Photoplay* 28.2 (Jul. 1925): 122.

46. Bert Levy, "Hollywood and Beverley Hills Society News," *Hollywood Filmograph* 9.31 (3 Aug. 1929): 11.

47. Leroy Keleher, "You'd Never Think It," *Picture Play Magazine* 43.2 (Oct. 1935): 34–35, 65, at 65.

48. Examples: "Musings of the *Photoplay* Philosopher," *Motion Picture Story Magazine* 5.5 (Jun. 1913): 108–11, at 110–11; and "The Martyrdom of the Pen," *Shadowland* 1.3 (Nov. 1919): 79.

49. Examples: "Come, Cheer Up, Old Folks!" *Shadowland* 1.3 (Nov. 1919): 80; and Dr. Max Thorek, "The Clipper's Health Department," *New York Clipper* 64.31 (9 Sept. 1916): 27.

50. Examples: "Musings of 'The Photoplay Philosopher,'" *Motion Picture Story Magazine* 3.4 (May 1912): 127–32, at 128; and 4.10 (Nov. 1912): 136–44, at 140.

51. Examples: "The World Above: An Essanay [sic] Gem with a Vital Sparkle," *Exhibitors' Times* 1.14 (23 Aug. 1913): 8; and "The Answer Man," *Motion Picture Magazine* 14 (Oct. 1917): 129–32, at 132.

52. Nairne, "Writer's Approach," 137.

53. Morris aligned Chaucer with nature. On Chaucer's associations with nature, see Ellis, *Chaucer at Large*, 1–2; Richmond, *Chaucer*, 66; Stephanie Trigg, *Congenial Souls: Reading*

betrayed that many, perhaps most, Chaucerian references in ambient American film culture were espoused with little knowledge of his writings. In film magazines, it is extraordinarily rare to find allusions to his specific characters, scenes, or verses, with the possible exception of the opening lines of the *Canterbury Tales*. The superficiality of typical references to Chaucer in these venues indicates that film culture heavily associated Chaucer with cultural capital but that the poet lacked a sizable public following, specifically a public sufficiently conversant with his tales to form large cinema audiences. In short, despite fairly frequent evocations of Chaucer's name in the world of entertainment and in the larger popular culture, Chaucer's actual writings were not massified or easily massifiable. Therefore, his tales were generally not deemed a suitable subject for the motion-picture screen.

Another reason for the dearth of Chaucerian films before WW II was that several key audiences conversant with Chaucerian poetry were not key audiences for the American film industry, such as academics. As Ellis explains, there appears to have been a gulf between academics and general readers of Chaucer by 1900; and by 1933, scholars and the general, educated reader are often said to have parted ways, while Chaucerian criticism by academics dominated.[54] Scholarly pursuit of Chaucer in the late nineteenth and early twentieth centuries, Stephanie Trigg notes, was frequently tied to philology, Latin, theology, history, rhetoric, and manuscript study.[55] Such a constellation of knowledge would not win favor for Chaucer in the American film industry, and, not surprisingly, newspapers and film magazines intermittently proclaimed Chaucer and the Middle Ages dull, a dullness in part associated with academe.[56] For example, in a review of G. K. Chesterton's *Chaucer*, Edward M. Kingsbury of the *New York Times* writes, "Chesterton is imperfectly medieval because he can never be dull."[57] Chaucer did not suffer such slings and arrows alone. In 1924 an article in *Exceptional Photoplays* remarks that it is fortunate that *Dante's Inferno* (U.S., Fox Film, 1924) adopted a modern example to tell an old story because it is extremely doubtful that a picture based on the Italian masterpiece could hold any audience outside Italy: "Dante's conception of

---

Chaucer from Medieval to Postmodern (Minneapolis: University of Minnesota Press, 2002), 170; and Barrington, "'Forget,'" 810.

54. Ellis, *Chaucer at Large*, 23–26.

55. Trigg, 179–80. See also David Matthews, *The Making of Middle English, 1765–1910* (Minneapolis: University of Minnesota Press, 1999), 190.

56. For example, Mitchell Leisen, "Timely Topics: No Motion Picture Is Perfect, Says Leisen," *Film Daily* 65.83 (10 Apr. 1934): 4.

57. Edward M. Kingsbury, "Speaking of Geoffrey Chaucer, Here is Mr. Chesterton: The Master of Paradox," *The New York Times*, 18 Sept. 1932.

Hell is so medieval . . . and in many ways so monotonous, that its appeal has narrowed down almost exclusively to scolastic [sic] circles."[58] An association with education in and of itself did not block an author's writings from cinemagraphic treatments. Educational films were valued at different moments in sundry ways: witness the existence of the long-running journal *Educational Screen*, the Academy's *In the Days of Chivalry*, and the American film education movements discussed by Eric Smooden and Dana Polan.[59] However, the *type* of educational associations mattered, and Chaucer's connections with university erudition, including philology, Latin, theology, rhetoric, and manuscript study, decreased the possibility that his work would receive a celluloid treatment, even as an educational short.

Young children constituted another large audience for Chaucer's works. Many Victorian and Edwardian children's books featured Chaucerian tales. Ellis explains that the first decade-and-a-half of the twentieth century comprised the golden age of Chaucer editions for children and that several of these collections were reprinted in the 1920s and 1930s, followed by a marked decline in frequency.[60] Richmond notes that Chaucer's tales for children in the Victorian and Edwardian eras were understood to epitomize morality and high sentiment,[61] the latter likely contributing to decreased interest in adaptations of Chaucer for children after the 1930s, when according to Siân Echard, the sentimental tales preferred by most adapters might no longer have suited contemporary tastes.[62] In part because of such texts, Chaucer himself was strongly associated with young children, an association reinforced by editorial remarks by some important adapters, who also frequently aligned the Middle Ages with childhood, reflecting a widespread understanding of Chaucer and the Middle Ages as childlike.[63] Despite our current recognition of Chaucer's bawdiness, Barrington maintains that in nineteenth-century America, Chaucer had been sanitized. In part because his entire corpus had not been translated into modern English until 1912, among the general population, Chaucer was only beginning to be separated from Victorian sensibilities by 1914, sensibilities

---

58. Review of "*Dante's Inferno*," *Exceptional Photoplays* 5 (Oct.–Nov. 1924): 4.
59. Eric Smoodin, "Film Education and Quality Entertainment for Children and Adolescents," *Regarding Frank Capra: Audience, Celebrity, and American Film Studies, 1930–1960* (Durham: Duke University Press, 2004), 76–118; and Dana Polan, *Scenes of Instruction: The Beginnings of the U.S. Study of Film* (Berkeley: University of California Press, 2007).
60. Ellis, *Chaucer at Large*, 46.
61. Richmond, *Chaucer*, 18.
62. Echard, "Bedtime Chaucer," 160.
63. Ellis, *Chaucer at Large*, 48–50, 56–57, 69–70; and Echard, "Bedtime Chaucer," 129. See also Richmond, *Chaucer*, 10–11.

associating him with exemplary morality and sententiousness.[64] Ellis explains that an acceptance of Chaucer's bawdiness appears in some scholarship in the 1930s and in Neville Coghill's translation in the 1940s.[65] Given Chaucer's associations with morality and the frequent obfuscation of his lewdness, it was not the latter that kept his work off the screen before WW II, especially since tales of adultery, rape, and murder were commonplace in film, despite industry self-regulation through the Hays Office.

Women formed a large audience for Chaucer not only because many of them read Chaucerian storybooks to children in either domestic settings or elementary schools but also because Chaucer was bound up with women's education movements beyond formal academic institutions. In late nineteenth- and early twentieth-century America, women both promoted education as a means of social reform and uplift for the masses and also consumed education and middle-brow refinement themselves. Enjoying a place in these movements (for example, as a standard figure in textbooks designed for Chautauqua literary courses),[66] Chaucer was associated with social uplift, gentility, and edification. As Barrington explains, Chaucer and other honored British poets were marketed to women by the adult education movement as a means of bettering themselves, their children, and their communities. Simultaneously, women were instrumental in disseminating Chaucer to non-academic audiences through public libraries, church parlors, and a loose coalition of women's clubs.[67]

Similarly, Chaucer was a figure in free lectures as part of education and social settlement movements in and around New York City. In 1900 the New York City Board of Education ran an extensive series of free lectures, including lectures on Chaucer. Such lectures were part of a project designed for those whom the *New York Times* identifies as "'the other half,' the common people, the workers." Begun in 1888, New York City lectures, "an antidote to the lurking snares and temptations of a great city," garnered over one-half million attendees by 1899. Speakers employed an important precursor to the moving image: lantern slides.[68] Lectures on Chaucer may have been accompanied by

---

64. Barrington, "'Forget,'" 808–12. See also Richmond, *Chaucer*, 15, 216; and Ellis, *Chaucer at Large*, 49–50.

65. Ellis, *Chaucer at Large*, 51. See also 21.

66. Examples: J. H. Gilmore, *English Literature*, Chautauqua text-books, no. 23 (New York: Hunt & Eaton, 1880); and Henry A. Beers, *From Chaucer to Tennyson: With Twenty-Nine Portraits and Selections from Thirty Authors* (Meadville, PA: Flood and Vincent, 1894).

67. Candace Barrington, *American Chaucers* (New York: Palgrave Macmillan, 2007), 123–26.

68. "Free Lectures: Courses in History, Literature, Art, and Science under the Board of Education," *The New York Times*, 20 Oct. 1900; and "This Week's Free Lectures," *The New York Times*, 5 Jan. 1908.

slides, since glass slides of the pilgrims and of themes related to Chaucer and the *Canterbury Tales* were available. Moreover, "electric film-slides," slides on a filmstrip manually turned from one image to the next (now often called an *educational filmstrip*), were also available to illuminate Chaucer lectures.[69] The social settlement movement in New York City was explicitly tied to Chaucer because in 1909, after part of the Rivington Street Settlement in Manhattan burned, the Barnard Chapter of the College Settlements Association arranged a performance of Percy MacKaye's *Canterbury Pilgrims* as a fundraiser to rebuild the settlement's country home.[70]

The audience of young children and the specific terms of reception of Chaucer by women and the working classes in educational movements produced a nexus of associations for Chaucer that made him an unlikely object for the American film industry, at least by the 1920s. As Jacobs explains in *The Decline of Sentiment: American Film in the 1920s*, discussions by American literary scholars about naturalism's place in the literary canon gave new energy to the rejection of sentiment, an energy that echoed throughout American culture and that eventually affected some assessments of popular culture. For some young literary intellectuals of the 1910s and 1920s, sentimentality was often aligned with a highly moralized view of literature and life. The taste for naturalism rejected morality as a key component of literary judgment and rejected literature that posited a morally comprehensible universe, with some scholars also scorning the idea of social uplift.[71] Across a wide spectrum of Hollywood filmmaking in the 1920s, Jacobs continues, there was a rejection of highly moralized narratives. The attack on sentimentality and genteel culture by literary intellectuals just before and after WW I contained "an unmistakably misogynist component. A similar misogynist strain can be observed in the antisentimental trends associated with the male adventure film." Naturalism in Hollywood provided a framework for filmmakers who sought to turn away from sentimental narrative prototypes. When criticizing films for being soppy, *Variety* sometimes claimed that such films appealed to women, lower-class viewers, or small-town audiences. Women were understood to epitomize gentility in literary discourses of the 1910s and 1920s and assumed

---

69. In a 1904 Chautauqua brochure, Mrs. Demarchus Brown advertised her Travel Talks, including one on Chaucer and Canterbury, illustrated by lantern slides (Barrington, *American*, 126; and http://digital.lib.uiowa.edu/cdm/compoundobject/collection/tc/id/32089/rec/1.). "The Film-Slide System: A Catalogue of Film-Reels," The Lantern Slide Gallery (London: Newton & Co. Ltd., 1904), 23, advertised a filmstrip of forty-eight slides titled the "Life and Times of Chaucer" (http://www.cineressources.net/consultationPdf/web/0000/227.pdf).

70. "An Open Air Play on Barnard Campus: 'Canterbury Pilgrims' to Be Given for Benefit of the Rivington Street Settlement," *The New York Times*, 16 May 1909.

71. Jacobs, *Decline*, 5, 7.

And, by various flying leaps to the saddle, he might have put pep in the day's ride of the Canterbury Pilgrims.

FIGURE 5.2. Employing Thomas Stothard's 1806 painting of the Canterbury pilgrims, one fan magazine imagined that Douglas Fairbanks, had he been born seven or eight hundred years earlier [sic], could have amused the Canterbury pilgrims as much as the tales did. The fantasy of Fairbanks salvaging the *Canterbury Tales* may have been a joke in this photomontage, but eleven years later the Academy of Motion Picture Arts and Sciences marketed Fairbanks in *In the Days of Chivalry* as doing exactly that. From "What Douglas Fairbanks Missed," *Film Fun* 352 (Aug. 1918: n. pag.).

to prefer sentimental, sad, and stirring tales.[72] Given the aesthetic changes in the American cinema in the 1920s, and because of the constellation of associations of Chaucer's tales with sentimentality, morality, edification, uplift, and women, Chaucer's poetry would have been a less-than-desirable source of material for the screen for most sectors of the American film industry in the 1920s and 1930s.

Douglas Fairbanks represented one alternative to sentiment in American cinema. Fairbanks starred in several adolescent boy adventure films, an increasingly popular genre in the 1920s, the decade when, Jacobs explains, sentimentality seems to have started being deemed inappropriate in male action stories.[73] Gaylyn Studlar argues that Fairbanks—personifying vigorous, idealized American manhood—was heavily associated with character building for adolescent boys, especially in the masculinist vein of Teddy Roosevelt. Fairbanks's film roles converged with white middle-class ideals of character building that sought a revitalization of American masculinity in a feminized era, a project insisting that "manhood not scholarship is the first aim of education." Perceived as a boyish man, Fairbanks assumed roles in the 1920s that reformers and educators considered among the most appropriate, manly ideals for boys.[74] By placing Chaucer alongside Robin Hood and King

---

72. Jacobs, *Decline*, 22–23, 27, 77, 273.

73. Jacobs, *Decline*, 128.

74. Gaylyn Studlar, "Building Mr. Pep: Boy Culture and the Construction of Douglas Fairbanks," *This Mad Masquerade: Stardom and Masculinity in the Jazz Age* (New York: Columbia University Press, 1996), 10–89. See also Scott Curtis, "Douglas Fairbanks: King of Hollywood,"

Arthur, the Academy's teaching guide for *In the Days of Chivalry* recruited Chaucer into a project of promoting manliness for American adolescents and young men. The use of Chaucer as a model of masculinity was not new, since, as Ellis notes, British writers, such as W. B. Yeats and Chesterton, often associated Chaucer with manliness and lusty boyhood.[75] The Academy's efforts to enlist Chaucer in this masculinization project, however, could not outweigh Chaucer's powerful alignments in the United States with effete academics who lacked Fairbanksian vigor; with women who promoted middle-brow interests, involving uplift and social reform; and with young children who learned at their mothers' knees. This third category bled into the problem of older boys subjected to maternal dominance, which, as Studlar explains, was of serious concern in the 1920s: maternal dominance, conceptualized as *petticoat rule* and *mollycoddlism* (the latter sometimes thought to involve too much European and insufficient American influence), was understood to imperil the developmental health of boys. Countering this threat, Fairbanks represented a version of masculinity posed as a salvation for feminized boys and young men.[76] Appropriately, as Scott Curtis demonstrates, Fairbanks was reputed to possess a penchant for rescuing people, both on-screen and off.[77] However, despite the Academy's promotion of Fairbanks's truncated *Robin Hood* to aid the study of Chaucer, and despite *Film Fun*'s fantasy of Fairbanks adding a boyish vigor to the Canterbury pilgrims (see figure 5.2), even the indefatigable Fairbanks was not man enough to rescue Chaucer for the American cinema.[78]

Idols of Modernity: Movie Stars of the 1920s, ed. Patrice Petro (New Brunswick: Rutgers University Press, 2010), 21–40, at 28.

75. Ellis, *Chaucer at Large*, 20–21, 33–34. See also 50.
76. Studlar, "Building Mr. Pep," 54–64.
77. Curtis, "Douglas Fairbanks," 26–27, 34.
78. I thank the Humanities Research Institute at Brock University for a grant to research at the Huntington Library and Margaret Herrick Library, Academy of Motion Picture Arts and Sciences. I am grateful to film historian Mark Lynn Anderson for invaluable guidance.

CHAPTER 6

LOST CHAUCER

Natalie Wood's "The Deadly Riddle" and the Golden Age of American Television

CANDACE BARRINGTON

Like Julian's experience of her revelation, our lives as scholars of archives or textual *corpora* tend to involve severe alternations of presence and absence: places at which our evidence and our work is "foul, black, and dede," and others at which it seems to stream as thick as the blood of Christ before Julian's visionary gaze. This is of the nature of our work with material that, whatever it is we research, has always, one way or another, suffered devastating loss, while also leaving us, once we can learn to see them, with glimpses of thoughts, experiences, and lives lived in the bodies that are no longer here.

—Nicholas Watson[1]

Some frames are so beautiful, they need
No painting. Some structures are glorious
In their ruin. Some maps show best
Where we have never gone nor ever will.
Some words mean more in their absence.

—Jeff Mock[2]

---

1. Nicholas Watson, "The Phantasmal Past: Time, History, and the Recombinative Imagination," *Studies in the Age of Chaucer* 32 (2010): 1–37, 36.
2. Jeff Mock, "Despite Our Not Seeing, No Void is Actually Empty" (unpublished).

MY SEARCH for Chaucerian American television began in a way familiar to medievalists.[3] Anticipated and outlined by R. W. Wilson's survey, *The Lost Literature of Medieval England*, this process starts by generating lists of productions that have "left some trace": rumors found (in the case of medieval literature) in catalogs of monastic libraries, collections of medieval wills, and reference in other literary works, and (in the case of early television) memoirs, biographies, and Internet fan sites.[4] I had my rumor—a "now-lost" 1955 television film, *The Wife of Bath*, starring Natalie Wood—and I thought I had time on my side.[5] I was wrong. Because I was searching for a cultural artifact just over fifty years old, I was surprised by the correspondences between Wilson's quest and my own. Like Wilson, I was attempting "to provide concrete evidence for the general statements often made on the subject."[6] And, like him, I was finding out how elusive that concrete evidence can be. It is easy to assume that, once we move out of manuscript culture, the problem facing a researcher is abundance, even superfluity, of textual evidence and paratextual documentation, not a paucity of material caused by fragile recording materials, careless disposal practices, frugal videotape recycling, or inadequate archival procedures.[7] Rather than scraps of vellum torn from manuscripts, I was looking for "film elements," a term used in commercial archives to denote parts or all of the continuous film used to shoot and then broadcast television episodes. I learned that film elements from early television broadcasts are often as ephemeral as fourteenth-century lyrics, both preserved only by happenstance. The fantasy of superabundance offered by current digital archives proved false. Moreover, what I was looking for was never concrete for its contemporaneous audience. A television broadcast is not the same as the "film elements"—a term

---

3. I have many colleagues to thank for help in this project. In particular, Gil Gigliotti instigated my search when he informed me of Natalie Wood's foray with The Wife of Bath's Tale; Anya Adair forwarded resources on Old English riddles; Katti Ritzenhoff and Burl Barr shared information on lost film footage; and Steve Larocco provided valuable feedback, pointing to places where my argument lost its way and suggesting new routes. Mike Shea, as always, supplied daily comforts, a provocative sounding board, and a wickedly sharp editor's pencil, all of which made this excursion possible.

4. R. W. Wilson, *The Lost Literature of Medieval England* (London: Methuen, 1952); R. W. Wilson, "The Lost Literature of Medieval England," *The Library* 5.4, 4 (Mar. 1925): 293–321; and Jennifer Summit, *Lost Property: The Woman Writer and English Literary History, 1380–1589* (Chicago: University of Chicago Press, 2000), 53–100.

5. Gavin Lambert, *Natalie Wood: A Life* (New York: Knopf, 2004), 116.

6. Wilson, *Lost Literature*, vii.

7. Magnetic videotape became a viable means for recording and distributing programs in 1956, with the added benefit of being able to be wiped clean and reused. Unlike medieval palimpsests, which sometimes preserve older texts in the process of destroying them, these used tapes have not been studied for possible traces of erased shows.

that nicely concretizes for what I searched—that were the immediate source of the broadcast. I was looking for surviving film elements and facts about the broadcast that would allow me to simulate imaginatively the conditions and contents of the broadcast. I was trying to recreate a moment comparable to Chaucer's reading his now-lost *Book of the Leoun* aloud at court (10.1086).[8] Yet the fact that it was not a stage production but a television broadcast (for which other televisions shows of similar vintage are available) makes it possible to think in terms of a rescued tin of film elements stashed and forgotten in a storeroom. So although I did not know the shape of the container housing the film elements, if I were lucky, they had been kept together, given an identity, and organized into cultural significance in an easily accessible reliquary (such as a DVD case or online link) indexed in a public archive.

For now, the film elements associated with American television productions of Chaucer's tales remain lost.[9] That ontological status, however, is more indeterminate than it might first appear, for *lost* does not mean *unrecoverable*; either the missing film elements could be sitting in an archive, undocumented yet eventually recoverable, or they could be destroyed and unrecoverable. Until they are found, or until incontrovertible evidence of their destruction (an unlikely outcome for the 1955 television film because of its peregrinations in the 1960s as an afternoon and late-night television feature) is uncovered, they will remain in this ontological limbo.[10] That is, unless these film elements are archived, not only sitting in a physical or electronic repository but listed in a published catalog, they have a potential but not an available existence.

This essay is about one set of lost film elements, those associated with that still-lost television movie starring Natalie Wood, "The Deadly Riddle." The episode's lost status can reveal much about its physical sources—the film elements—and the conditions of their production. Together with four extant paratexts, these contextualizing production conditions allow us to recreate imaginatively and, in a phantasmatic way, find the film's contents. Such a

---

8. Geoffrey Chaucer, *The Riverside Chaucer*, ed. Larry D. Benson, 3rd ed. (Boston: Houghton Mifflin, 1987); cited parenthetically.

9. I have found references to three televised Chaucerian tales originating in the United States: in addition to the *Warner Brothers Presents* version starring Natalie Wood, there is the Fireside Theater broadcast of "The Pardoner's Tale" (1949) and the Conrad Nagel Theater presentation of "The Three Searchers" (1956), each based on The Pardoner's Tale. See the corresponding entries at imdb.com. For subsequent British television productions, see Steve Ellis, *Chaucer at Large: The Poet in the Modern* Imagination (Minneapolis: University of Minnesota Press, 2000), 121–22; Kathleen Forni, *Chaucer's Afterlife: Adaptations in Recent Popular Culture* (Jefferson, NC: McFarland, 2013), 84–105; and the essay cluster in this volume.

10. Sharon Willis, "Lost Objects: The Museum of Cinema," *The Renewal of Cultural Studies*, ed. Paul Smith (Philadelphia: Temple University Press, 2011), 93–102, 94.

recreation, however, suggests that more than the film elements are lost; also lost are Chaucer, his tales, and their significance to the formation of American broadcasting. To find and fill in those missing medieval intertexts and Chaucerian tropes, we must again look outside the broadcast moment to the contextualizing form of early television in the United States.

LOST IN THE ARCHIVES

Our first riddle begins here: how does one view an obscure episode from a failed American television series? In contrast to today's ever-expanding number of television-watching practices, options for seeing footage from the 1940s and 1950s are limited, a confounding situation when the popular fervor for viewing historical broadcasts has caused the proliferation of easily accessible digital archives.[11] Despite these troves of archived television, significant gaps persist in the record because television was not initially viewed as a medium worth saving. Even the grand repository of all things American, the Library of Congress, did not consistently acquire television programs before the mid-1960s.[12] Some films disappeared through neglect; most disappeared through purposeful destruction: masters were often destroyed after broadcast and, with the commercial introduction of videotapes in 1956, many were erased and the tape reused. Sometimes these gaps are duly noted and, ironically, cataloged because the missing film is associated with broadcasts deemed essential to television's development: multiple episodes of *Texaco Star Theater* and the first evening of *The Tonight Show* with Johnny Carson hosting are frequently lamented as lost treasures.[13] In addition to these documented losses, some missing items are neither recorded as lost nor readily available for viewing. Although the "growth in the academic study of popular culture has led to the expansion of materials deemed appropriate for research library collections," cataloging efforts are dictated by academic, public, and (not surprisingly) commercial interest.[14] Whereas the post-broadcast past of television footage was once dictated by efficiencies of storage space and reuse, it is now determined by a heavily capitalized market. What was once cast aside as useless

---

11. Don Clark and Ian Sherr, "Next in Tech: Rethinking How We Watch TV," *The Wall Street Journal*, 30 Jul. 2013; and Marlene Manoff, "Theories of the Archive from across the Disciplines," *Portal: Libraries and the Academy* 4.1 (2004): 9–25.

12. See "Acquisition Practices," "Television in the Library of Congress," Library of Congress, www.loc.gov.

13. "Lost Programs," The Paley Center for Media, paleycenter.org/lost-programs.

14. Manoff, "Theories," 13.

ephemera has become a commodity used for advertising and other self-promotion. Consequently, the primary factor that determined what I was able to recover was the commercial interests in the episode, both the original business interests when the film was produced and the new profit potential when ardent fans purchase salvaged episodes from commercial archives.

My quest to find Chaucerian film elements began over a decade ago when I found a page photocopied from Gavin Lambert's *Natalie Wood: A Life* placed in my campus mailbox by a colleague. Circled in red was Lambert's offhand comment that seventeen-year-old Wood had starred in a now-lost Warner Brothers television movie, *The Wife of Bath,* which aired on 22 May 1955.[15] To see this television movie for myself, I began to look for it, using my four working facts: "made for television movie," "broadcast on 22 May 1955," "starred Natalie Wood," and "based on The Wife of Bath." When I initially turned to the Internet Movie Database (imdb.com), a generally reliable, nonacademic resource for all things cinematic, I found neither the film nor any film resembling it in Natalie Wood's filmography. As solid as my four facts might appear—a genre, a date, a star, and a title—they pointed toward nothing concrete and were no better than rumor. Over the years I periodically checked imdb.com, and information gradually began to appear (and disappear) as aficionados filled in gaps, the database resembling a magical crystal ball whose focus both sharpened and blurred, releasing details and taking them back. Eventually, I realized that two of my working facts were incorrect and a third one was a bit off-kilter. First, I had the wrong title. The film was titled "The Deadly Riddle," not "The Wife of Bath." Second, I had the wrong date. It seemed to have been broadcast not on 22 May 1955 but twice, initially on *Warner Brothers Presents* in 1956 and later on *Camera Three* in the 1960s.[16] Third, a "television movie" in the 1950s was not the same as the made-for-television movies popularized in the late 1960s. It seemed to fill a sixty-minute time slot, not the ninety- to -one-hundred-twenty-minute slots later associated with televised movies. My two amended facts—new title and new dates—did not immediately open up new resources. Although Natalie Wood's connection seemed solid, I found nothing following that led me in my search. I turned instead to an underexamined data point—the *Warner Brothers Presents* series—and its archive housed at the University of Southern California.[17]

---

15. Lambert, *Wood,* 116.

16. Occasionally, imdb.org also lists a 1955 broadcast of "The Deadly Riddle" on *Camera Three.* Such a broadcast was unlikely.

17. The Warner Bros. Archive "contains the paper records of Warner Bros. Pictures, Inc. [and] extensive production records for Warner Bros. Television Department from 1955 through

There I was able to detect the logic behind the creation and broadcast of "The Deadly Riddle." Although the online index to the Warner Bros. Archive indicates that no extant film elements are stored there, this index does reveal that *Warner Brothers Presents* was an early part of the studio's efforts to fend off television after ignoring its threat and its potential for a decade. Like other Hollywood studios that entered into television production, Warner Brothers did not take the new medium seriously and saw itself as stooping to a minor form of entertainment.[18] Producing television programming to lure audiences back into the cinema began as a business venture done cheaply and quickly. Working with "minuscule budgets [and] at a frenetic pace unseen at the studio since the B-grade movies of the 1930s," the *Warner Brothers Presents* episodes "were produced in five days" with actors, plots, costumes, sets, and even film footage imported from the silver screen.[19] To further confirm their secondary status, episodes in the show's omnibus format initially concluded with "Behind the Cameras," a ten-minute segment highlighting upcoming Warner Brothers films and stars.[20] Quickly, *Warner Brothers Presents* devolved into an advertising ploy "to increase public awareness of the Warner Brothers trademark."[21] Because all facets of the show sought to maximize attendance at movies shown in theaters and to minimize expenses, *Warner Brothers Presents* program titles and actors' names are not indexed in the archive; instead, the index focuses more on bureaucratic paperwork, with the name of the show's producer, Roy Huggins, providing the only successful search results, and these results are linked primarily to indexed lists of paperwork regarding contracts of preproduction personnel.[22] The "rationale (or lack thereof) of the filing system itself" in the Warner Brothers archive suggests the production was above all else a business, not artistic, investment, reflecting the prevailing attitude toward television's value.[23]

1968" (usc.edu/libraries/collections/warner_bros/). This archive is not to be confused with the Warner Archive, which is a publisher of DVD and online streams, or with Warner Bros. Corporate Archive Research Center, which is available only for in-house production research.

18. Christopher Anderson, "Warner Brothers Presents," *Museum of Broadcast Communication's Encyclopedia of Television*, 2nd ed., ed. Horace Newcomb (New York: Fitzroy Dearborn, 2004), 4.2485.

19. James Roman, *From Daytime to Primetime: The History of American Television Programs* (Westport, CT: Greenwood, 2005), 17; and Christopher Anderson, "Warner Brothers Presents," 4.2486.

20. Roman, *Daytime*, 17.

21. Anderson Warner Brothers Presents," 4.2485.

22. "Index by Film," 30 Dec. 1977, Index 1, pp. 261–62, Warner Bros. Archive of Historical Papers, cinema.usc.edu/about/wbarchives/index.cfm.

23. Lynn Spigel, "Our TV Heritage: Television, the Archive, and the Reasons for Preservation," *A Companion to Television*, ed. Janet Wasko (Malden, MA: Blackwell, 2005), 67–99, 90.

Because "The Deadly Riddle" was conceived merely as a toss-off for boosting attendance at movie theaters, its lost status becomes less a mystery. Although it featured two up-and-coming actors—Natalie Wood and Jacques Sernas, both featured in *Screen World*'s "Promising Personalities of 1955"—the television series seems not to have been considered serious work.[24] Moreover, the film's production staff was filled with men who had not yet left their marks on American television. The director, Don Weis, would later build his career producing family entertainment shows ranging from *Ironside* to *Fantasy Island*; the writer/producer, Roy Huggins, turned his penchant for writing hard-boiled detective fiction to creating or producing *Maverick, 77 Sunset Strip, Run for Your Life,* and *The Rockford Files*.[25] These well-known contributors were at the early stages of their careers; consequently, the episode is nearly forgotten and effectively lost (if not destroyed). In the "logic of [the television] archive," Warner Brothers did not retain copies of the film because neither television nor the episode's participants were yet significant enough to warrant the effort, and by the time they were significant, the film had been let loose on its odyssey around the country, appearing as an afternoon or late-night feature on "Hour of Stars," rebroadcast by local stations as late as 1963.[26] Because the film was not destroyed immediately after its initial broadcast or after *Warner Brothers Presents* folded at the end of the season, either it was tossed by a clerk clearing out a television station's storeroom or it remains there, lost to the moving-image archives scattered across libraries, museums, and commercial repositories. Despite my efforts, I have been unable to track down the film elements associated with "The Deadly Riddle."

The archive did provide, however, enough information to locate paratexts that allow us to recreate imaginatively some of the contents of "The Deadly Riddle." These paratexts confirm that "The Deadly Riddle" was originally broadcast on Tuesday evening, 22 May 1956, when ABC television aired its regular show, *Warner Brothers Presents*. They also outline the episode's basic plot—and cause us to wonder about the show's purported connection to Chaucer.[27] Advertised as an "adaptation of Chaucer's 'The Wife of Bath's Tale,'" "The Deadly Riddle" would seem to fit the series' mixture of criminal

---

24. Daniel Blum, *Screen World 1956* (New York: Biblio & Tannen, 1956), 191, 193.

25. Christopher Anderson, "Roy Huggins," *Museum of Broadcast Communication's Encyclopedia of Television*, 2.1147–48.

26. Spigel, "Heritage," 67; "Friday, November 7, 1958," *Chicago Daily Tribune* 1 Nov. 1958, sec. C, C20, ProQuest Historical Newspapers: *Chicago Tribune* (1849–1989); and "Wednesday, October 9, 1963," *Chicago Tribune*, 5 Oct. 1963, B14, ProQuest Historical Newspapers: *Chicago Tribune* (1849–1989).

27. As originally conceived, *Warner Brothers Presents* cycled episodes from three dramatic spinoffs of the parent studio's Hollywood films, *Kings Row, Casablanca,* and *Cheyenne*; see Alex

retribution, hidden identities, and exotic locale.[28] That manifestly dark side of the series (as well as The Wife of Bath's Tale) was undermined by four sets of paratexts: publicity shots plus three appearances in the daily papers (the daily television listing, a display advertisement, and a next-day review). The program listing announced the episode as an "adventure-romance set in the days of King Arthur," a sunny synopsis more akin to children's versions of The Wife of Bath's Tale than to Chaucer's original.[29] The display advertisement features a photo of a smirking, mannish crone, and it declares, "This is Marion [sic] . . . bride of Britain's handsomest man! The marriage shocked all England! Why had young Gawaine married this old hag? Only Gawaine himself knew the answer! Learn why he wed—and what he won" (see figure 6.1). The ad not only alerts us to the liberties taken with Chaucer's tale but also evokes more humor than mystery.[30] The next morning, a reviewer's breezy account in the *New York Times* further suggests that the episode was more lighthearted than *Warner Brothers Presents*' usual fare, with no mention of the life-and-death consequences the riddle has for the tale's characters:

> The program called *Warner Brothers Presents* turned back to Geoffrey Chaucer last night for inspiration for its filmed television presentation, "The Deadly Riddle," on Channel 7. The excursion into the classics was a sound idea.
>
> Muriel Roy Bolton's script, based on Chaucer's "The Wife of Bath's Tale," was a refreshing departure from the usual television dramatic pattern. The legend of King Arthur's search for the answer to the question—What one thing in the world does a woman most desire of a man?—provided a fascinating idea around which to build a play. And the production was done on a lavish scale, with impressive settings, costumes and effects.
>
> Some of the players were interesting, too. Geoffery Toone was a properly patrician Arthur and Torin Thatcher was appropriately diabolical as the

---

McNeil, *Total Television: The Comprehensive Guide to Programming from 1948 to the Present*, 4th ed. (New York: Penguin, 1996), 896.

28. "Television Programs," *The New York Times*, 20 May 1956, ProQuest Historical Newspapers: *The New York Times* (1851–2010) with Index (1851–1993).

29. "On Television," *The New York Times*, 22 May 1956, ProQuest Historical Newspapers: *The New York Times* (1851–2009); "Other 50," *Chicago Daily Tribune*, 19 May 1956, sec. D; and Candace Barrington, "Re-Telling Chaucer for Modern Children: Picture Books, the Marketplace, and Evolving Feminism," *Sex and Sexuality in a Feminist World*, ed. Katherine Hermes and Karen Ritzenhoff (Newcastle upon Tyne: Cambridge Scholars, 2009), 18–31.

30. "Display Ad 38," *Chicago Daily Tribune (1923–1963)*, 22 May 1956, D4, ProQuest Historical Newspapers: *Chicago Tribune* (1849–1989).

FIGURE 6.1. *Chicago Daily Tribune* display ad, 22 May 1956, for the first broadcast of "The Deadly Riddle." Reproduced with permission.

Red Knight of Cornwall. Marga Ann Deighton, as a bewhiskered hag, was triumphantly loathesome [sic].

Jacques Sernas and Natalie Wood, as the lovers of the legend, were at a serious disadvantage when called upon to act. But they photographed nicely.

About that riddle: King Arthur had trouble in finding the answer. And no wonder. It was "sovereignty." Even in the thirteenth century [sic], it seems, the girls really wanted to have their own way.[31]

Pertinent to this essay's interests, the reviewer's comments about the episode's characters and narrative cast doubt on the claim that Bolton's script was "based on Chaucer's 'The Wife of Bath's Tale.'" For instance, while the Wife sets her tale in "th'olde dayes of the Kyng Arthour," makes the offending knight "a lusty bacheler" in King Arthur's court, and establishes the king as the arbiter of justice in his kingdom, Arthur is not the one seeking the answer to the question (3.857, 3.882–83). Moreover, when the review identifies

---

31. J. P. S., "TV Review: 'The Deadly Riddle' Is Posed on Channel 7," *The New York Times (1923–Current File)*, 23 May 1956, 63, ProQuest Historical Newspapers: *The New York Times (1851–2010) with Index (1851–1993)*.

Sernas and Wood as playing young lovers, it suggests their relationship precedes the marital bed, a scene Chaucer's knight and former hag never have because their intimate relationship begins in their marriage bed. The publicity photo confirms the nicely photographed couple noted by the *Times* reviewer, while the blurb pasted on the reverse returns us to the noir-ish elements *Warner Brothers Presents* was known for: "Sir Gawaine (JACQUE SERNAS) gambles with the life of the one woman he loves, Lady Marian (NATALIE WOOD), in a desperate attempt to break the evil spell of the Red Knight of Cornwall and to solve 'The Deadly Riddle'" (see figures 6.2 and 6.3). The blurb adds more names to the Arthurian tale: Marian (incongruously borrowed from the Robin Hood legends) and the Red Knight of Cornwall (suitably Arthurian-sounding without bearing the burden of literary intertexts). And the blurb changes the Chaucerian narrative elements: the questing knight is risking Marian's life, not trying to save his own, and the evil spell is new. The only connection to Chaucer's Wife of Bath's Tale seems to be a knight's effort to solve a riddle with life-and-death consequences. Together, the display ad's copy, the review's commentary, and the publicity blurb point not to The Wife of Bath's Tale but to *Sir Gawain and Dame Ragnelle,* a Middle English Arthurian tale drawing on folklore motifs of the loathly lady and the life-threatening riddle.[32] Beyond a knight's quest to answer a question placed before him and a(nother) knight's marriage to a hag, little in these paratexts sustains purported ties to either Chaucer or his Wife of Bath's Tale.

These four sets of paratexts were as close to the film elements as I came. Ultimately, film elements or any recreatable broadcasts are lost in the archive. What is also lost in the archive is the fantasy that the version is worthy of the Wife of Bath and her tale.[33] All evidence points to the disappointing way these episodes were knockoff productions—quick, one-night stands not worth doing well or preserving. After a decade-long search, I'm forced to address the question that opens Laurie Finke and Martin B. Shichtman's *Cinematic Illuminations*:

> Why should serious medieval scholars take the time to comment on movies about the Middle Ages? They are, all too often, neither great art nor important historical documents; few are topics for serious scholarship. The vast

---

32. Robert M. Correale and Mary Hamel, eds., *Sources and Analogues of* the Canterbury Tales (Cambridge: Brewer, 2005), vol. 2. Another contemporaneous version of the tale is John Gower's "Tale of Florent," *Confessio Amantis*, ed. Russell A. Peck, 3 vols. (Kalamazoo: Medieval Institute, 2000), l.1407–861; it is not set in Arthur's court but in "daies olde" at the court of "th'emperour" (1.1407–10).

33. Slavoj Žižek, *The Plague of Fantasies* (London: Verso, 1997), 12–13.

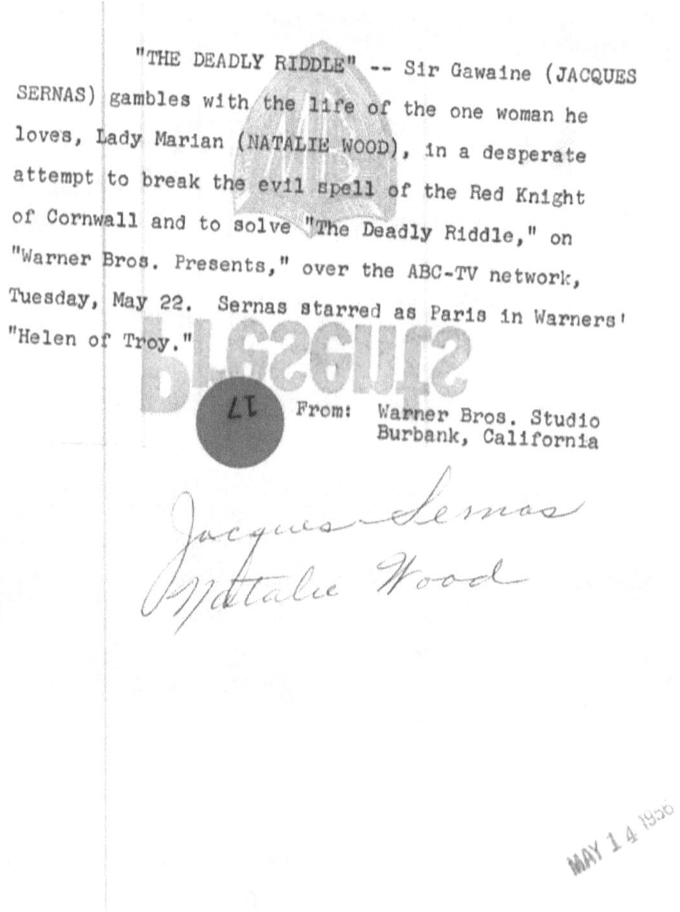

"THE DEADLY RIDDLE" -- Sir Gawaine (JACQUES SERNAS) gambles with the life of the one woman he loves, Lady Marian (NATALIE WOOD), in a desperate attempt to break the evil spell of the Red Knight of Cornwall and to solve "The Deadly Riddle," on "Warner Bros. Presents," over the ABC-TV network, Tuesday, May 22. Sernas starred as Paris in Warners' "Helen of Troy."

From: Warner Bros. Studio
Burbank, California

MAY 14 1956

FIGURE 6.2. Public relations blurb pasted to the back of a press photo for "The Deadly Riddle." Author's collection.

majority of movies about the Middle Ages may easily be dismissed as nothing more than mass-produced commercial fantasies. Do we not risk debasing our coinage, trivializing our scholarship by indulging such fantasies?[34]

They argue that we must come to grips with the pleasure that audiences receive from "these collective fantasies we call the Middle Ages" by unpacking

---

34. Laurie Finke and Martin B. Shichtman, *Cinematic Illuminations: The Middle Ages on Film* (Baltimore, MD: Johns Hopkins University Press, 2010), 6.

FIGURE 6.3. Warner Bros. press photo of actors
Jacques Sernas and Natalie Wood (1956). Author's collection.

"the social logic of the Middle Ages as it appears in contemporary film, the technology par excellence of modernity."[35] While I come to a different answer than they do, I do think this television episode has much to tell us about how the Middle Ages continues to shape our culture in ways we seldom recognize

---

35. Finke and Shichtman, *Cinematic Illuminations*, 7.

or acknowledge. Materially, Chaucer and his *Canterbury Tales* may be lost in America's earliest broadcast history; however, all is not lost. As Slavoj Žižek asserts, "When a certain historical moment is (mis)perceived as the moment of loss of some quality [here, the desired seriousness of Chaucerian medievalism on television], upon closer inspection it becomes clear that the lost quality emerged only at this very moment of its alleged loss."[36] To find that seriousness, as well as Chaucer's presence in American television, we need to shift our perspective and look anew at "The Deadly Riddle," the site of loss.

LOSS AND THE "RIDDLE"

Chaucer and The Wife of Bath's Tale seem to have lost their way in "The Deadly Riddle." Once it is clear that the episode's debt to Chaucer fades with each new piece of information, it might be tempting to dismiss "The Deadly Riddle" as an example of cinematic medievalism gone awry. If, however, we take seriously "The Deadly Riddle" and its insistence that its origins reach back to Chaucer's tale, then we see that it suggests three affinities between postwar United States and late-medieval Britain. First, "The Deadly Riddle" establishes detective fiction's genealogy as located in the Middle Ages and with the Father of English Literature, a lineage that might have intrigued the film's writer and producer, Roy Huggins. At the same time, the Chaucerian link helps "The Deadly Riddle" defuse Freud's "What-do-women-want?" question. Through these first two affinities, Chaucer's canonicity and "The Deadly Riddle" locate the present in the past by formulating the Middle Ages as a place and time that can accommodate both. This capacious understanding of the relationship between the medieval past and modern present downplays the radical alterity of the Middle Ages and provides soothing answers to the pressing questions that "The Deadly Riddle" presents. The third affinity looks to the framed storytelling structure shared by early television and Chaucer's *Canterbury Tales*. Here, I suggest, Chaucer's *Tales* provides hitherto untapped strategies for understanding the majority of early primetime television program in America. With the aid of "The Deadly Riddle," we might possibly perceive American television's phantasmatic filling in of the modern present with the medieval past.

Locating these affinities does not require finding the lost film elements. Even if these film elements—like saints' relics—were recovered, they would be only parts of a whole, incapable of providing more than a phenomenologically

---

36. Žižek, *Plague*, 13.

distorted viewing experience.³⁷ Whether attached or scattered, loose or reeled, the film elements recorded only parts of the pre-broadcast whole distilled into "The Deadly Riddle," a highly choreographed sixty minutes distilled from a longer creation period that included developing the idea, assessing the need, drawing up contracts, hiring personnel, writing the script, rehearsing lines, designing sets, creating costumes, filming the scenes (possibly with multiple takes), taking breaks, editing for continuity, scoring music, inserting titles, and developing publicity. Anyone on set or in the editing room would have perceived the fake sets, the retakes, the reused film stock, and the haste to get something on film on time and under budget. Moreover, the film elements represented only a part of the sixty-minute whole allocated to "The Deadly Riddle" broadcast. In addition to the movie, the hour comprised the Host's introduction and commercial breaks. So those film elements, whether or not they continue to exist in part or in whole, represent two forms of "The Deadly Riddle" hour: a distillation of the days or weeks needed to create those film elements, and the core around which the broadcast hour shaped itself. Although this short study cannot possibly delve into the work of writers, directors, set designers, costume designers, producers, and actors, it can begin to recreate the context that shaped "The Deadly Riddle."

The indexing structure of the Warner Bros. archives, in fact, helps explain what the film elements alone could not: the choice of The Wife of Bath's Tale and the changes made to it. Because "The Deadly Riddle" was part of *Warner Brothers Presents*' advertising ploy, it needed to tie into Warner Brothers' cinematic releases. Already, the three original revolving episodes were dramatic spinoffs of the parent studio's Hollywood films, *King's Row, Casablanca*, and *Cheyenne*—small-town drama, wartime noir, and Western adventure.³⁸ Adapting The Wife of Bath's Tale allowed *Warner Brothers Presents* to air an Arthurian romance, promote some up-and-coming stars, and reuse the costumes, settings, and film footage that so impressed the *Times* reviewer. Clearly, the Chaucerian tale suited corporate goals for *Warner Brothers Presents* programming. On the other hand, the changes to the tale—most evident in the breathless drama of the publicity blurb that plays fast and loose with Chaucer's tale—seem to be accounted for by Roy Huggins's interest in Chandleresque detective fiction because everything in the archive regarding "The Deadly Riddle" spins out from him. Behind him Huggins had several novels written in the style of Raymond Chandler, "the most typical author of novels whose books were made into classic noir film," and ahead he had years of

---

37. Willis, "Lost Objects," 95.
38. McNeil, *Total Television*, 896.

producing and directing many series that introduced noir to American television.[39] Turning to Chaucer as a source text for "The Deadly Riddle" allowed Huggins to medievalize detective fiction and provide the genre a more distinguished etiology than its supposed origins in the stories of Edgar Allan Poe. That is, hooking Chaucer to detective fiction via the riddle makes him a viable candidate for detective fiction's progenitor. His texts are rife with searchers looking for something lost, misplaced, hidden, or out of reach: the Knight in Black looking for White in *Book of the Duchess*; the *House of Fame* dreamer searching for the truth from a "man of gret auctorite" (2158); John and Aleyn hunting down their stolen flour in The Miller's Tale; Palamon and Arcite vying for Emily in The Knight's Tale; and the shamed knight in The Wife of Bath's Tale who seeks two answers, one that will save his life and another that will grant him marital bliss. With their pervasive questions to be answered, lost items to be found, and wrongs to be righted, Chaucer's tales provide a tempting genealogical basis for what John Ganim has identified as "medieval noir."[40] This association with detective fiction has been strong enough for Chaucer himself to be featured in numerous cases of medieval mystery fiction, a group of novels Kathleen Forni recognizes as paradoxically identifying "the obvious injustice and inequality that often [serve as catalysts] for crime" while failing "to bring the prominent malefactors to justice, often invoking the dubious defense of political inaction in the name of civic stability."[41] Both the poet and his *Canterbury Tales* provide a canonical British etiology for hard-boiled detective fiction, a distinctly American genre, recent examples being Bruce Holsinger's *A Burnable Book* (2014) and *The Invention of Fire* (2015), featuring Ricardian England's dynamic duo, Geoffrey Chaucer and John Gower.

Despite this convenient affinity between medieval Chaucer and Chandler's noir, the overlap is not perfect, and The Wife of Bath's Tale needs significant reorientation to reproduce mid-century American values and to accommodate the noir perspective. To help with that reorientation, "The Deadly Riddle" adds elements from the Arthurian tradition of honor and the Robin Hood tradition of injured rights, thereby uncovering what Ganim describes as "the disenchantment, rather than the idealism, of the chivalric quest as it faces the impossibility of its fulfillment" associated with noir.[42] American audiences

---

39. Anderson, *Encyclopedia*; John M. Ganim, "Medieval Noir: Anatomy of a Metaphor," *Medieval Film*, ed. Anke Birnau and Bettina Bildhauer (Manchester: Manchester University Press, 2009), 182–202, 187.

40. Ganim, "Medieval Noir," 182.

41. Forni, *Chaucer's Afterlife*, 82–83.

42. Ganim, "Medieval Noir," 191. See also Tison Pugh and Angela Jane Weisl, *Medievalisms: Making the Past in the Present* (London: Routledge, 2013), 64–65.

would have needed no introduction to these two legends; Warner Brothers and other Hollywood studios had turned to Arthurian and Robin Hood legends more often than to any other legend from the Middle Ages. And while juxtaposing Arthurian knights and Robin Hood outlaws might be comically anachronistic to scholars, audiences in the 1950s had been prepared for the unlikely combination by recent Arthurian films.[43]

In keeping with the Arthurian film tradition, "The Deadly Riddle" shifts its focus to male protagonists. With that new orientation, the rape is erased, and it is the male protagonist, not a woman under his protection, who is threatened by the antagonist, thereby establishing a manlier, less demeaning, situation for the heroic figures. Here, the knight is the righteous private eye determined to prevent an unjust murder, the hag becomes the beleaguered knight's unlikely source of clues, and his getting the dame at the end signifies his triumph. In The Wife of Bath's Tale, the riddle is offered as a gesture of mercy. In "The Deadly Riddle," on the other hand, Arthur and Gawaine face danger because honor requires them to accept the Red Knight's arbitrary challenge, suggesting similar situations that infect film noir with a "cynical attitude toward authority and due process."[44] By using a version of the narrative that separates the perpetrator of the crime from the solver of the mystery, "The Deadly Riddle" captures the hero's need to extricate himself from the pickle he gets himself into in the process of solving the crime. On the dark side of the detective noir, medievalization intensifies with its own Gothic darkness the figure of the Red Knight, who poses the riddle and reinforces the negative consequences of honor: unpredictability, horror, and danger. The episode's black-and-white film would have stood in contrast to the Technicolor brilliance associated with contemporaneous films set in the medieval past. If the review is to be believed, however, these noir sensibilities did not tame the sentimentality inherent in the romanticism of medieval films, and its injection of film noir cynicism and nihilism was eclipsed by the sight of the attractively photographed lovers.[45]

Transforming the Wife's tale into medieval noir produced a corollary transformation of the riddle at the tale's heart. The plot synopsis is built around a riddle—"What one thing in the world does a woman most desire of a man?" according to the *Times* review—similar (with significant differences) to the queen's question posed in The Wife of Bath's Tale. Unlike Chaucer's tale

---

43. *The Black Knight* (1954) culled characters "from widely separated time periods during the early Middle Ages," and *Prince Valiant* (1954) treated Arthurian legends with no respect for medieval sources (John Aberth, A *Knight at the Movies: Medieval History on Film* [New York: Routledge, 2003], 11–12; and Pugh and Weisl, *Medievalisms,* 83–90).

44. Ganim, "Medieval Noir," 182.

45. Ganim, "Medieval Noir," 183.

that leaves the species of question vague—it is called "this mateere" (3.910)—
"The Deadly Riddle" labels the centerpiece question into a riddle. By labeling
the question a riddle, the film draws attention to the dialectics between the
question and the answer, as well as to the dialectics between the questioner
and answerer; for not only does a riddle embed its answer in the question,
but (as in the Old English tradition) riddles are often posed by the answer to
the question. That is, the questioner holds the answer to the riddle: the book,
the onion, and the penis speak in the first person and provide clues about
themselves.[46] In retrospect, we see that Chaucer's queen follows this riddle formula when she asks the knight to determine what women want from men. By
asking *that* question and by establishing a situation in which she controls the
consequences of his failing to answer the question correctly, the queen enacts
the answer to the question she poses. To the wary observer, she demonstrates
what sovereignty looks like. To solve her riddle, the successful interlocutor
needs to overlook misleading information, focus on pertinent clues, fill in the
missing details, and look at the source.

This formula collapses in "The Deadly Riddle"; making the Red Knight
of Cornwall the source of the riddle redirects the answer away from women.
Plus, the film's riddle emphasizes the materiality of the riddle's solution with
"what one thing." By beginning not only with "what," a determiner that points
to a thing or to an abstraction represented by one or more metaphors, but also
"one thing," the answerer would be led into looking for an object. In this way,
the riddle in "The Deadly Riddle" points away from "sovereignty" as a dignity
naturally possessed by women and toward "sovereignty" as an object owned
by men and lent "to the girls [who] really wanted to have their own way."[47] The
film may identify the knight's quest with a riddle, but it more closely resembles
a detective mystery in search of material evidence.

In the same way that the publicity shot, one of the few physical remnants
of the film, exposes "the paraphernalia of our former existence" and makes
it easier for us to date the moment of production than to recognize the particular medieval moment being depicted, transferring the riddle from the
queen to the Red Knight of Cornwall tells us more about 1950s America than
it does late-medieval Britain.[48] For a 1950s audience not familiar with The
Wife of Bath's Tale, the riddle "What do women want?" would evoke a much
more modern context—Freud's famous question of exasperation: "What does

---

46. See Kevin Crossley-Holland, ed., *The Exeter Book Riddles* (London: Penguin, 1993), for riddles 26 (book), 65 (onion), and 44 (penis—or for the modest, key).

47. J. P. S., "Review."

48. Willis, "Lost Objects," 94, quoting Siegfried Kracauer, *Theory of Film: The Redemption of Physical Reality* (Princeton: Princeton University Press, 1997), 56.

a woman want?"⁴⁹ By making a man the source of this enigma, "The Deadly Riddle" mimics that famous chapter in the history of psychoanalysis. In this moment the film reflects a culture that turned the question into a medical question to be answered not by women but by a professional (and most likely a male one). Because the question does not belong to the woman, neither she nor the question provides the information necessary to answer it. Rather than pose a riddle, it poses a question and responds to it in a way conditioned by pop Freudian psychology in which a man asks it of other men. As Betty Freidan wrote less than a decade later, "The feminine mystique derived its power from Freudian thought; for it was an idea born of Freud, which led women, and those who studied them, to misinterpret their mothers' frustrations, and the fathers' and brothers' and husbands' resentments and inadequacies, and their own emotions and possible choices in life."⁵⁰ As she explains, the Freudian question and the inability to answer it become a dominant mode for approaching and marginalizing women in postwar America. Similarly, in the Red Knight's riddle, the answer is in an absence: one will never know the answer because the question has been wrongly framed. The Chaucerian question becomes lost when asked by the Red Knight of Cornwall. It is no longer the same riddle. And if it is not the same riddle, then an answer that appears to be the same is not the same because it is addressing a different question. And, based on the publicity photo, the answer that Gawaine finds is the answer embedded in the question: a young, beautiful woman who wants to please and be possessed by an older man. The deadliness of the riddle might seem to be the threat that looms over Gawaine (and Arthur) if he fails to answer it correctly. But in answering it, Gawaine demonstrates that it can prove equally deadly for Lady Marian.

In the landscape of American television, "The Deadly Riddle" stands out both for its singularity and for its self-deconstruction of what it purports to be: based on a Chaucerian tale. With only two other instances of a Chaucerian tale broadcast on American television, "The Deadly Riddle" seems to be the last Chaucerian tale filmed for American television audiences, a programming stain akin to the Lacanian "anamorphotic blot," which Žižek explains "opens up the abyss of the search for meaning" and in its superfluity "undermines our position as 'neutral,' 'objective' observers."⁵¹ By simultaneously drawing attention in its refusal to be incorporated into the landscape and incorporating

---

49. For Freud's question, see Ernest Jones, *The Life and Work of Sigmund Freud*, 3 vols. (New York: Basic Books, 1955), 2.421.

50. Betty Freidan, *The Feminine Mystique* (1963; New York: Norton, 2001), 103.

51. Slavoj Žižek, *Looking Awry: An Introduction to Jacques Lacan through Popular Culture* (Cambridge: MIT Press, 1991), 91.

us into that observation, "The Deadly Riddle" forces us to reconsider that broadcasting landscape anew in order to "take proper account of the intersections between [Chaucerian] medievalism and mass culture."[52] Because only a Chaucerian would notice this blot, it inscribes the knowledgeable observer into the observed scene and demands we interpret our presence therein. The blot requires us to expand our notion of how the Chaucerian tradition can help us read popular culture, urging us beyond a search for such intertextual engagements as appropriation and adaptation that medievalism studies has been accustomed to locating and explicating.

If, alerted by this blot, we look awry at the television archives, they then reveal that the whole notion of the "Chaucerian" needs to be reconsidered. The term *Chaucerian* has become a "double inscription," a semiotic function that Žižek, following the lead of Victor Shklovsky, marks as integral to detective fiction because it misdirects the wayward reader toward one referent purporting to solve the mystery, while the clear-eyed (but somewhat dawdling) detective eventually points to another that allows him to decipher the riddle and fulfill the reader's desire for completion.[53] Looking for Chaucer's narratological or thematic influence on American television is to be misdirected toward a dead end. The *Canterbury Tales* does not make for effective television: stripped of their language and their context, the tales are rather meager stories—which may explain why they eventually appear on British television in the form of animation or adaptations into modern contexts. Rather, the Chaucerian presence is to be found in the formal structure of the tale-telling sequence: an anthology of stories overseen by a genial, knowledgeable guide—a description applicable to Chaucer's *Canterbury Tales* as well as to *Warner Brothers Presents*, of which "The Deadly Riddle" was only one small bit. This structure does not describe what happens in one episode, but it does describe what happens in one evening or across the week, as well as what happens within a show over the course of a season. Repeatedly, we see the studios trying to recreate something like the *Canterbury Tales*—a Host who introduces a series of stories to his audience. The stories might seem to have little to do with one another. They are presented as a way to take one's mind off one's troubles. Not only did the framing work in the microcosm—a series with multiple embedded tales—but it worked in the macrocosm: each evening the audience was presented a series of stories—serial storytelling and entertainment. The new audience didn't have to ride on horseback but could sit in a comfortable chair before the newfangled box that brought the stories to life before the entire family.

---

52. Thomas Prendergast and Stephanie Trigg, "What Is Happening to the Middle Ages?" *New Medieval Literatures* 9 (2007): 215–29, 219.

53. Žižek, *Looking*, 50–57, esp. 54.

Of course, much of this format has its roots in radio programming, with music, talk, drama, news, religion, and special events alternating across time slots, which in turn can be traced to vaudeville shows and nineteenth-century literary anthologies. Ultimately, though, the format imitates the Canterbury pilgrimage, one tale following after the other. It is the framed storytelling that gets its start in English with a generation of writers in the late fourteenth century. They produced compendious works shaped by a framing device holding a series of tales introduced by a genial narrator or guide. This formula, so deeply associated with Chaucer, has infused modern mass culture to such an extent that it is no longer recognizable. This unrecognized correspondence—I'm reluctant to use "relationship"—between popular reconceptions of this framework and Chaucer's suggests that the work that scholars have done to read and understand the relationship in the *Canterbury Tales* between its framing device and its embedded tales can be fruitfully applied to understanding the early decades of American television. Although Chaucer may be lost within individual episodes, we find in his oeuvre a "recognition of an archive that lies below conscious memory," and we realize his *Tales* can provide a guide to the larger process of presenting the latest storytelling medium to the American masses.[54]

As these correspondences between The Wife of Bath's Tale and "The Deadly Riddle" suggest, my approach was not nearly as apophatic as it might have initially seemed. Not only can the contents of "The Deadly Riddle" be inferred through the extant paratexts, but also the episode reciprocates those efforts by filling its context phantasmatically. More than urging us to satisfy the fantasy of wholeness by imaginatively filling in the unrecovered elements, the lost "Deadly Riddle" invites us to consider the nature of the loss we experience when we note the absence of serious broadcasts deemed worthy of Chaucer's reputation and canonical status. By looking beyond narrative genealogies, we can locate a more substantial correspondence. In suggesting Chaucer as a more originary origin for television and radio broadcast than hitherto allowed, I acknowledge that this proposed reading of American television may have to retain its status as a suggestion, for to begin such a project would require diligent work in the archives guided by the fantasy—or rather *mal d'archive*—that frustrating aporias and repressions could be filled and brought to light.[55]

---

54. Ruth Evans, "Chaucer in Cyberspace: Medieval Technologies of Memory and the *House of Fame*," *Studies in the Age of Chaucer* 23 (2001): 43–69, 51.

55. Jacques Derrida, *Archive Fever: A Freudian Impression*, trans. Eric Prenowitz (Chicago: University of Chicago Press, 1995), 12, 19.

PART III
PRESENCE

CHAPTER 7

CHAUCERIAN HISTORY AND CINEMATIC PERVERSIONS IN MICHAEL POWELL AND EMERIC PRESSBURGER'S *A CANTERBURY TALE*

TISON PUGH

AT ITS HEART the past is now a narrative, stories we tell and are told about the way the world was, and so narratives of the past illuminate, even if they cannot answer, intrinsic questions of the human condition. Michael Powell and Emeric Pressburger's *A Canterbury Tale* (1944) posits the need for an experiential history, for the Chaucerian past to remain ever present so as to cure modern ills and to inspire Britain's citizens during their contemporary struggles against Nazi Germany and the Axis powers.[1] However, in their metanarrative excursus on film's role in engaging modern-day viewers with the Middle Ages, Powell and Pressburger castigate the cinema for numbing viewers to the meaning of history: the message that encourages their audience to celebrate Chaucer and his *Canterbury Tales* as emblems of a lost medieval paradise is thus devalued through its very medium. Constructing film as a simultaneously perverse yet redemptive art, the filmmakers reimagine the meaning of English character in a nation fighting for its survival during the horrors of World War II. Graham Fuller declares, "*A Canterbury Tale* beautifully celebrates the notion that England's mythic past is just a jumpcut back in time,"[2] yet the cinematic technologies necessary for reliving the

---

1. *A Canterbury Tale*, dir. Michael Powell and Emeric Pressburger, commentary by Ian Christie, DVD (1944; Criterion, 2006).
2. Graham Fuller, "A Canterbury Tale," *Film Comment* 31.2 (Mar. 1995): 33–36, 36.

Chaucerian past are ultimately implicated in the salvific perversity of the present, in its devolution from the ideals of yesteryear that nonetheless allows the opportunity for communal transcendence. Within Powell and Pressburger's imaginary, the trip to Chaucer's past, like the Canterbury pilgrimage, provides an opportunity to seek personal redemption, with a pernicious threat to salvation arising in the very condition of cinematic modernity. England needs inspiration from the past to save her present in *A Canterbury Tale*, but saving England also requires accepting the pleasures of contemporary cinematic perversities.

CHAUCERIAN HISTORY

A temporal irony defines *A Canterbury Tale*: it is a historical film set in the present. Its narrative action transpires contemporaneous to the time of the film's production, yet England's Chaucerian past resonates in this present and gives it meaning. Given its investment in advocating support for the war effort, the film's modern-day message resonates with a sense of urgency mostly lacking in its plot. Numerous scholars have addressed the genre of historical films, a category to which *A Canterbury Tale* both does and does not belong. David Eldridge defines history films as those whose narrative action "predates the year in which it was released by more than five years"; he also believes that "all films which utilize the past contact and reflect ideas about history."[3] According to this rubric, *A Canterbury Tale* does not adhere to the parameters of a history film in regard to its temporality and release date, yet by insistently reflecting on the meaning of history (despite being set in the present), it engages more directly with the significance of the past than many films set long ago. Leger Grindon suggests that historical films engage in historiographical questions, that historical-fiction films "interpret and comment on significant past events, as do historians; this interpretive role places historical films in a context of historiography and enables them to have an impact on the public that often exceeds that of scholarship in range and influence."[4] With its nostalgia for Britain's Chaucerian past while depicting its present, *A Canterbury Tale* modulates its historiographical impulse through an evocative paean to times long gone, and it does so with the explicit purpose of influencing public opinion about Britain's war-torn present and future.

---

3. David Eldridge, *Hollywood's Historical Films* (London: Tauris, 2006), 5.

4. Leger Grindon, *Shadows on the Past: Studies in Historical Fiction Film* (Philadelphia: Temple University Press, 1994), 2.

Charles Barr refers to *A Canterbury Tale* and other such wartime classics, including David MacDonald's *This England* (1941), Carol Reed's *The Young Mr. Pitt* (1942), and Laurence Olivier's *Henry V* (1944), as heritage films, those that encouraged an appreciation of longstanding British virtues during the wartime assault against the nation's sovereignty:

> Cinematically as in other ways, the war seemed to have validated precisely those qualities of restraint and stoicism which might previously . . . have appeared insipid. It had, in addition, opened up access to a rich historical and cultural *heritage*—in a sense, had only re-opened it, since the cinema has already tried from time to time to exploit this heritage in seeking out prestige material with import potential.[5]

Opening up the past cinematically creates the potential to relive that past, at least imaginatively, and these heritage films performed their cultural work in the present through their tacit interpellations of their audience into the mores of the nation's past. Furthermore, Chaucer's literary legacy—perhaps even more so than Shakespeare's, due to its greater age and foundational status—bespeaks the long history of British cultural achievement, which sets the stakes for the film both in the glories of the past and in the peril of the present.

If heritage films in some measure recognize the eternal co-presence of the past by positing history's living influence on the present, so too do recent trends in the scholarship of medievalism. The elusive touch of the Middle Ages has inspired innovative readings of history and its almost physical pull on the present, such as in the work of Carolyn Dinshaw, who declares that her "queer history [of the Middle Ages] has a relation to the tactile"; she sees in the work of theorists such as Roland Barthes, who "perform[s] his own caress, across time, of—and from—the dead," the model of an experiential relationship with history, one that coalesces and gravitationally alters readers in the present through their intimate encounters with the past.[6] In a similar vein, Catherine Brown illustrates the ways in which the medieval past colludes with the present in her reading practice: "In a mixture of hard scholarship and intense, almost hallucinatory imagination, I am *here* with this dead man's reading," she writes, capturing the tactile appeal of the co-presence of the

---

5. Charles Barr, "Introduction: Amnesia and Schizophrenia," *All Our Yesterdays: Ninety Years of British Cinema*, ed. Charles Barr (London: British Film Institute, 1986), 1–29, 11; italics in original.

6. Carolyn Dinshaw, *Getting Medieval: Sexualities and Communities, Pre- and Postmodern* (Durham: Duke University Press, 1999), 39–40.

past.⁷ With an unnecessarily cold eye, such critical stances may appear quirky, if not delusional, yet they strikingly capture the appeal of the past and the way readers can feel what is nonetheless irrevocably lost. That the past cannot literally touch us in no measure precludes its ability to touch us emotionally, spiritually, aesthetically.

From these perspectives, it is apparent that reaching across time, touching the past through the fantasy of touching the past, may enhance the artistic creation of historical films and the critical act of scholarship, and a similar vantage point of transhistorical temporality animates *A Canterbury Tale*. In his ruminations on history's allure and on filming *A Canterbury Tale*, Michael Powell ponders, "Why is it that legend is more potent than reality in stirring the emotions? Why do the songs and tales of our fathers and mothers and of their fathers and mothers touch our imagination more than our personal experience as children?"⁸ Legends, as distinguished from myths, are typically viewed as containing the potential of a lost truth, but it is a truth gilded over by communal illusions of social and cultural identity. For Powell, such a forgotten and distant legendary history resonates throughout contemporary society precisely because it has vanished through the haze of time. Yesterday's memories of childhood are too clear, too real, to reconstitute as a legendary history of one's culture. The distant past, to Powell's way of thinking, merits attention in the present so that by eternally reenacting the idealized mores of centuries ago, history can be recaptured (at least cinematically), and consequently, it can be experienced anew. So even though Powell dismissed the importance of Chaucer to the film—"It doesn't have that much to do with Chaucer," he stated in an interview—Chaucer iconically represents the legendary past of England in the film's themes, and he too must be reclaimed through a storyline only tangentially related to his literary masterpiece.⁹

A Canterbury Tale's experiential vision of the past unfolds as its protagonists happen upon a peculiar mystery in Chillingbourne, a small village on the Pilgrims' Road to Canterbury, in which the mysterious Glue Man frightens local women by pouring glue in their hair. American sergeant Bob Johnson (John Sweet), British sergeant Peter Gibbs (Dennis Price), and Women's Land Army girl Alison Smith (Sheila Sim) pursue the Glue Man, and, as they do so, the film's narrative structure loosely mirrors that of Chaucer's *Canterbury Tales*, in which these three "pilgrims" travel to Canterbury Cathedral. Toward

---

7. Catherine Brown, "In the Middle," *Journal of Medieval and Early Modern Studies* 30.3 (2000): 547–74, 551; italics in original.

8. Michael Powell, *Million-Dollar Movie* (New York: Random House, 1992), 67.

9. David Lazar, ed., *Michael Powell: Interviews* (Jackson: University Press of Mississippi, 2003), 40.

the film's conclusion, Thomas Colpeper (Eric Portman), Chillingbourne's magistrate, is revealed to be the culprit, but his motive in these bizarre and sexually suggestive attacks was to share England's history with the soldiers stationed at the village by ensuring that the local women did not distract them from his lectures. Johnson, Smith, Gibbs, and Colpeper complete their pilgrimage to Canterbury Cathedral, and the spiritual majesty of the closing shots establishes the salvific nature of their strange experiences. In regard to the film's temporal setting during World War II, Gordon Williams describes its reimagination of the past as a "new pilgrimage against Hitler," and, in considering the film's trans-temporality between medieval pilgrimages and modern wars as a propagandistic endorsement of English character, he concludes, "Powell and Pressburger achieved greatness by pervading their wartime vision with the fragrance of times past."[10] Merging past and present, *A Canterbury Tale* sutures over bloodily unpleasant aspects of medieval history—for example, no mention is made of the Hundred Years War, in which Chaucer participated, or of the Peasants Revolt of 1381—to posit the Middle Ages as an era of timeless virtues, rather than a time plagued (literally) by numerous political and social upheavals.[11]

The film's harmonious resolution and nostalgic reconstruction of Chaucer's Middle Ages should not lure viewers into overlooking the perverse underbelly of Colpeper's desires—he frightens women away so that he can enjoy homosocial pastimes with male soldiers—nor should the audience overlook the sexual subtext of pouring glue in women's hair, a striking metaphor for rape. Colpeper's apparent asexuality merely masks his transgressive desires for unadulterated homosociality, which he pursues by terrorizing the women of Chillingbourne. But while Powell and Pressburger condemn Colpeper for his transgressions, the character espouses the film's moral core in his lyrical proclamations of England's glorious history. Anthony Aldgate and Jeffrey Richards observe, "*A Canterbury Tale* rejoices in a sense of the living past, in country crafts, rural beauty, the intimacy of man and nature, and this joy is conveyed in passages of pure camera poetry, with much use of point-of-view shots to lead the audience into the countryside and the Cathedral."[12] Scenes such as Johnson's long discussion with the local wheelwright about planting and harvesting timber, his leisurely enjoyment of war games with the village

---

10. Gordon Williams, "Propaganda into Art: Wartime Films of Powell and Pressburger," *Trivium* 17 (1982): 39–65, 53, 59.

11. For Chaucer's activities in the Hundred Years War, see Donald Howard, *Chaucer: His Life, His Works, His World* (New York: Dutton, 1987), 69–73.

12. Anthony Aldgate and Jeffrey Richards, "Why We Fight: *A Canterbury Tale*," *Best of British: Cinema and Society from 1930 to the Present* (London: Tauris, 1999), 57–78, 67.

children, and Smith's energetic embrace of farm labor connect these modern defenders of British sovereignty to the nation's medieval forebears in terms of vocations and avocations.[13]

England's historical roots and Chaucerian charms, however, are not immediately evident to Johnson, Smith, and Gibbs, who must awaken to the living past that permeates the local atmosphere. Indeed, these protagonists do not travel to Chillingbourne with any sense of moral purpose other than fighting the war: Johnson arrives there accidentally and plans to leave for Canterbury as soon as possible; Smith has been assigned to the village as part of her duties in the Women's Land Army; and Gibbs takes a skeptical stance toward the virtues of English history, such as in the scene when Colpeper wonders whether Gibbs enjoyed his visit to the British Museum and Gibbs dismissively responds, "Yeah, I suppose it is pretty good." Gibbs also disparages Colpeper for his love of history: "You're a gentleman farmer with a fine house . . . Yet the first chance you get, you're off climbing mountains or digging up stuff which six hundred years ago was thrown out as junk." Roughly six hundred years before the film's narrative action coincides with Chaucer's birth; consequently, the comment suggests that it is likely for modern British citizens to cast aside their country's prized forefather. Johnson, Smith, and Gibbs must attune themselves to the ways in which the medieval past permeates life in Chillingbourne. Modeling the potential for an experiential coexistence with the past, Colpeper represents redemption while simultaneously, as the Glue Man, embodying perversion, and thus he undermines the spiritual value of history while endorsing it.

In their thematic consideration of experiential history, Powell and Pressburger open the film with the camera focusing on the text of Chaucer's General Prologue to the *Canterbury Tales,* then on a map of England (as the camera traces the route to Canterbury), and subsequently on a drawing of Chaucer's pilgrims that metamorphoses into their live incarnations riding on horseback. The sound effects accompanying the pilgrims—people laughing and horses' hoofs clopping—and the medievally inspired music score imbue the film with an aural ambience, one that recurs in key scenes to signify the continuance of the past into the present. The film concomitantly establishes the metacinematic pleasure of voyeurism by depicting a group of villagers watching the pilgrims. While modern cinematic viewers observe both Chaucer's pilgrims and these pilgrims' contemporaries (who treat the pilgrims'

---

13. The lyrical celebrations of nature throughout the film testify to its ecological investments, such that James Howard declares, "*A Canterbury Tale* has strong claims to be the first environmentally aware film" (*Michael Powell* [London: Batsford, 1996], 47).

journey as a spectacle, thus doubling the voyeurism of the shot), the parallels between past and present highlight the essential pleasure of scopophilia across the centuries. This cinematic prelude to the film's narrative action, which serves as Powell and Pressburger's condensed treatment of Chaucer's General Prologue, ends with a shot of the Squire setting his falcon to flight, which then transforms into a shot of a modern-day soldier watching a warplane, and this graceful segue between past and present reveals that the past is never past but continually present. Antonia Lant refers to this shot as a "most massive historical, six-hundred year jump cut,"[14] and Peter Conrad notes how Powell and Pressburger's play with time contributes to the film's sense of the timelessness of history: "The bird has been mechanized, but the man's face remains the same: despite mechanical evolution, the genetic stock of England is unaltered."[15] The roughly six hundred years between Chaucer's pilgrims and the modern soldier both establish and obliterate time's passage: the present is contemporaneous with the medieval past as measured on the actor's face, rendering time a meaningless barometer of human change in light of its eternal consistencies (see figures 7.1a and b). The opening sequence concludes as the screen fades to black, presaging the film's thematic treatment of the relationships among darkness, cinema, and wartime blackouts.

In contrast to Johnson, Smith, and Gibbs, who must learn to appreciate the eternally experiential nature of England's Chaucerian history, Colpeper enjoys a trans-temporal affinity with the past, one that imbues his present with meaning: in this regard, he sees his role in civic life as an advocate of medieval virtues. During his history lectures for locally stationed soldiers, he encourages them to see themselves as the latest incarnations of Chaucer's pilgrims, to live in and through the past:

> I don't know what you are in civil life. You might be cook, clerk, a doctor, a lawyer, a merchant. Let me remind you that as much as six hundred years ago, doctors and lawyers and clerks and merchants were passing through here on the old road which we call the Pilgrims' Way. . . . These ancient pilgrims came to Canterbury to ask for a blessing or to do penance. You, I hope, are on your way to secure blessings for the future.

The camera rests in turn on several of the soldiers, interpellating them into Colpeper's vision of timelessness and pulling them, at least momentarily, from

---

14. Antonia Lant, *Blackout: Reinventing Women for Wartime British Cinema* (Princeton: Princeton University Press, 1991), 207.

15. Peter Conrad, "Arrival at Canterbury," *To Be Continued: Four Stories and Their Survival* (Oxford: Clarendon, 1995), 7–45, 27.

FIGURES 7.1A AND B. These shots establish the timelessness of British character, in which fashions may change but core virtues remain the same. James Sadler, in an uncredited performance, plays both the Squire and the soldier.

the urgent pressures of the war. Colpeper does not explicitly mention Chaucer in this passage, but the temporal setting of six hundred years ago links his nostalgic fantasy to the period of the author's lifetime, as he also mentions the occupations of several of Chaucer's pilgrims, a certain allusion to the *Canterbury Tales*. Through this rhetorical move, Colpeper asks his audience to see themselves as pilgrims as much as soldiers, to enact their modern-day martial duties through the lens of medieval spirituality. Colpeper stands in for Chaucer in such scenes as this one, as he is the master storyteller of England in his lectures, one who forges fictions about various pilgrims traveling to Canterbury and experiencing spiritual revelations along the way.

Colpeper continues to exhort his audience to live in the present through communion with the eternal past, and his words grow increasingly hypnotic: "Follow the old road, and as you walk, think of [the Canterbury pilgrims] and of the old England," he urges. The salvific nature of his words becomes apparent as he is illuminated with the projector light as if with a halo, with the perverted Glue Man taking on the luminous symbolism of a saint. He then continues:

> They climbed Chillingbourne Hill, just as you did. They sweated and paused for breath, just as you did today. . . . When you lie flat on your back and rest and watch the clouds sailing as I often do, you're so close to those other people that you can hear the thrumming of the hoofs of their horses and the sounds of the wheels on the road and their laughter and talk and the music of the instruments they carried.

Embodying the medieval past, Colpeper's ahistorical character stands at odds against his contemporaries, and Eric Portman's performance as Colpeper accentuates the character's disjunction from his temporal setting and from the residents of Chillingbourne in numerous ways, such as his erect posture, crisp enunciation, and reserved nature. Powell said of Portman's performance of Colpeper that he "had the face of a medieval ascetic which could quite easily have been torn out of a monkish manuscript,"[16] and the blurring in this character as both embodying medievalism and ostensibly rejecting sexual desire bespeaks the film's interest in the torsions of consciousness necessary to desire a lost past while living in the present. For whereas medieval ascetics renounced sexuality as a means of achieving union with God, Colpeper's attempted renunciation of sexuality merely leads to his perverse acts as the Glue Man, spilling "sticky stuff," in Smith's words, into women's hair.

---

16. Michael Powell, *A Life in Movies: An Autobiography* (New York: Knopf, 1987), 441.

Of the three protagonists, Smith is the most readily sympathetic to Colpeper's vision of historical consciousness, and Powell and Pressburger accentuate this aspect of her character by focusing on her deeply felt sense of the medieval past. Smith's fascination with the Middle Ages is apparent when she notices a historical artifact in the innkeeper's lobby. The innkeeper attempts to educate her about Chillingbourne's local history—"That stone interest you, Miss? It comes from the old road . . . what some folks call the Pilgrims' Road"—but Smith reveals that she is already well versed on this subject: "Yes. From the bend. Up there on the hill." In a similar moment with Johnson, she informs him of the route of the Pilgrim's Road: "That's where the Pilgrims' Road runs. . . . From the bend at the eastern edge of the hill, pilgrims saw Canterbury for the first time." As viewers learn, Smith's knowledge of the Pilgrims' Road derives from her time spent caravanning with her former lover Geoffrey, who, she believes, has died in enemy action. For both Colpeper and Smith, England's history—his desire to share it with other men, her memories of the man she loved as she learned of its landmarks—is implicated with sexuality, such that the experience of reliving history is invested with erotic desire. Furthermore, her lover's name of Geoffrey clearly alludes to Geoffrey Chaucer, thus suggesting the possibility of a libidinal investment in the literary pleasures of the past.

Smith, the victim of the Glue Man/Colpeper's attacks, is most rapturously affected by his evangelical plea to embrace England and to relive its past, beyond all other members of his audience. During his lecture, her countenance is brightly lit amid the darkness around her, and these shots link her to Colpeper as their faces shine through the blackness. In a later scene in the film, she proves Colpeper's words about the experiential nature of history true when she hears sounds—again, people laughing and horses' hoofs clopping—from the medieval past. Colpeper informs her, "It's a real voice you heard. You're not dreaming," and Smith confirms that she understands his lesson concerning how history resonates in the present: "You have to dig to find out about people, as well as roads," she avows, and the two apologize for their initial dislike of each other. It is then apparent that Smith understands that all of life—past, present, and future—is an excavation into the past so that one can understand the ways in which the past constructs the people of the present.

As much as *A Canterbury Tale* alludes to England's past as a lost Eden through Colpeper's and Smith's medieval reveries and their attempts to experience history anew, it is very much a film of its times in terms of its thematic registers: it directly addresses the threat that Nazi Germany poses to Britain, and as such it belongs to the genre of "why we fight" films designed both to enhance civilian morale and to unite British and American forces into a coherent whole. Recalling her participation in the film and its contribution to the war effort, Sheila Sim called it a "propaganda film" to show "it was a war worth fighting,"[17] and Nanette Aldred proclaims, "*A Canterbury Tale* was made towards the end of the war when American troops were arriving in Britain and it was explicitly a way to introduce the Americans to a 'British' way of life and to show an 'ordinary' American soldier to a domestic audience, and it was an implicit valorization of Britain as film subject for an American market."[18] Given the characters' musings over the Chaucerian past, their meditations on England's pastoral charms, and the urgent matter of identifying the Glue Man, Johnson, Smith, and Gibbs have surprisingly little time to discuss the war that has brought them to Chillingbourne, except for such scenes as when Johnson talks with some young boys about their war games and makes a joke about his need for them to "lease-lend . . . two generals" for his investigations into the Glue Man. His military humor confuses the children, who question the meaning of the phrase "lease-lend," to which Johnson replies, "If the isolationists were to hear you back home, they'd be mighty sore." He also extols the virtues of engagement in contrast to isolationism, whose advocates he refers to as "short-sighted folks." Couching its pro-war message in England's Chaucerian history, *A Canterbury Tale* proselytizes to its viewers through the idyllic cast of English character, but as the film also makes clear, it ironically achieves this thematic objective through the corrupt and alienating force of cinema. As the perverse Glue Man/Colpeper espouses these salvific themes in the film's narrative, so too does the perverse medium of film become implicated with an ultimately moral message about Chaucerian history.

CINEMATIC PERVERSIONS

For Colpeper, cinema is an inherently distracting, juvenile, and perverse form of recreation, one that alienates viewers from the eternal, experiential, and redemptive virtues of English history. It is, of course, ironic that the perverse Glue Man decries the perversions of others, but given his joint status as the film's moral core and its minatory prophet, his denunciations of film highlight the potential for cinematic entertainments to distract England's citizenry from their nation's history. In regard to the aberrant potential of cinema, theorists have long noted the ways in which its focus on the gaze and spectatorship

---

17. "Sheila Sim Interview," from "Disc 2: The Supplements" of *A Canterbury Tale* DVD.
18. Nanette Aldred, "*A Canterbury Tale*: Powell and Pressburger's Film Fantasies of Britain," *A Paradise Lost: The Neo-Romantic Imagination in Britain, 1935–1955*, ed. David Mellor (London: Lund Humphries, 1987), 117–24, 122.

ferments potential perversities. Gaylyn Studlar acknowledges "[t]he close resemblance of the cinematic apparatus to the structures of perversion, and specifically, to masochism" in the ways in which films invite viewers to embrace the disciplinary force of its technologies.[19] Janet Staiger tempers a definition of cinematic perversity as inherently wayward, asserting that "each act of deviant (*and normative*) viewing requires historical and political analysis to locate its effects and 'judge' its politics"; while modulating the semantic range of perversions, she further highlights the potential for the cinematic experiences to (d)evolve into perversity.[20] When one sits in the darkness, viewing narratives shot on the silver screen, no end of desires, whether pure, impure, or merely chaotic, can be aroused.

In *A Canterbury Tale,* cinema's potential perversion enters the narrative when Colpeper condemns films as a distraction from England's beauty. In a conversation with Johnson concerning the films that the American soldier enjoyed in Salisbury, Colpeper's contempt for cinema is expressed in measured terms, but his disdain is nonetheless clear:

> JOHNSON: Yeah. [Salisbury has] got some swell movies.
> COLPEPER: Really? You're a great moviegoer, Sergeant Johnson?
> JOHNSON: You bet. It's a great thing to sit back in an armchair and watch the world go by in front of you.
> COLPEPER: The drawback is, Sergeant Johnson, that people may get used to looking at the world from a sitting position.
> JOHNSON: I don't quite get you.
> COLPEPER: Then when they really do pass through it, they don't see anything. Shall you being going to a movie in Canterbury?
> JOHNSON: Is there anything good on?
> . . . .
> COLPEPER: Pity . . . when you get home, and people ask you what you've seen in England, and you say: "Well, I saw a movie in Salisbury, and I made a pilgrimage to Canterbury and saw another one."
> Johnson: You've got me all wrong. I know that in Canterbury I have to look out for a cathedral.
> COLPEPER: Do look out for it. It's just behind the movie theater. You can't miss it.

---

19. Gaylyn Studlar, "Masochism and the Perverse Pleasures of the Cinema," *Feminism and Film,* ed. E. Ann Kaplan (Oxford: Oxford University Press, 2000), 203–25, 220.

20. Janet Staiger, *Perverse Spectators: The Practices of Film Reception* (New York: New York University Press, 2000), 32.

Johnson appreciates the passivity inherent in the cinematic experience, the idle luxury of "sit[ting] back in an armchair and watch[ing] the world go by in front of you." Colpeper, on the other hand, views cinema as corrupting the human potential to experience history and nature, and in regard to his appreciation of England's natural beauty, Colpeper is an impressively active man: during a conversation with Gibbs, viewers learn of his passion for mountain climbing, and he tells Johnson that he once walked the fifty miles from Chillingbourne to London. Johnson's tour of the British Isles, regrettable due to the military circumstances that necessitated it but fortuitous in its illuminative potential, faces the divergent opportunities for a spiritually uplifting transformation by visiting Canterbury Cathedral and reliving the Chaucerian past or for an aesthetically vacuous experience by visiting the local theater. Colpeper's ironic description of the cathedral as located behind the theater, when their respective sizes should give precedence to the cathedral, evinces his recognition that in some aspects of British culture, relatively new cinematic technologies have eclipsed England's longstanding spiritual traditions.

As part of his rebirth into England's eternal Middle Ages, Johnson quickly learns that Chillingbourne allows him to experience life rather than merely watching it in a movie, and he soon dismisses invitations to film showings. When he shares a leisurely ride along a country road with Smith and enjoys England's pastoral greenery, she suggests to Johnson that he visit the local movie theater: "There's a movie. It's Saturday. They have a matinee" Johnson replies, "What? Go to a single feature? Not me."[21] When Gibbs and Johnson attend Colpeper's lecture, Gibbs attempts to encourage Johnson's enthusiasm by comparing the event to the cinema—"Hey, Bob. Movies"—but Johnson again disparages the viewing experience: "I don't like free shows. Something always goes wrong." In contrast, Johnson, soon after arriving in Chillingbourne, proclaims to the crowd of men at the wheelwright's shop, "Yes, sir. I'm crazy about that old road and . . . those old Canterbury pilgrims," and the wheelwright affirms the allure of the medieval past in regard to time-tested vocations: "Ah, them was the days for a wheelwright." This quick reversal in Johnson's stance on cinema—from eager cinephile to leisurely aficionado of England's beauty—appears to endorse Colpeper's anticinematic stance, but it cannot be overlooked that *A Canterbury Tale* (as well as the "why we fight" genre as a whole) was intended to galvanize support for the war from its audience of British and American soldiers and civilians. If, as Colpeper argues and

---

21. It could be argued that Johnson is implying that he would attend a double feature, if not a single show. Such an interpretation is feasible, yet it would overlook the character's growing investment in experiencing England's history as part of his pilgrimage to Canterbury.

Johnson soon comes to agree, cinema is an inherently corrupting medium, it is certainly ironic for a film to argue thematically for the danger inherent in people enjoying cinematic pastimes rather than England's eternal history, when the preservation of England's present and future stands at the heart of this cinematic endeavor.

In condemning film on the level of metanarrative, Powell and Pressburger cast Gibbs as an employee of the cinematic world, and, as such, his stance regarding the cinema echoes that of Johnson's initial enthusiasm. Gibbs works as a theatrical organist and presents himself as proud of his vocation; Colpeper, however, deflates his sense of professional fulfillment:

> GIBBS: I'm a cinema organist. A good one.
> COLPEPER: I'm sure you are. Have you always wanted to be a cinema organist?
> GIBBS: Not when I was a kid. I wanted to be a church organist. I studied for nine years. Then, luckily for me, I met a chap who told me about a job—a new theater, brand-new organ. . . .
> COLPEPER: You never played a church organ?
> GIBBS: Not a big one.

Through Colpeper's implied comparison of church and cinema, Gibbs must confront the hollowness of his employment, which merely gilds with financial recompense the ways in which it has deprived him of spiritual nurturing. In a subsequent conversation concerning organists' pay between Gibbs and Dr. Kelsey, the organist at Canterbury Cathedral, Powell and Pressburger expand on their implicit contrast of Gibbs's spiritual and financial motivations. Kelsey fails to understand that Gibbs receives the princely sum of thirty pounds (rather than thirty shillings) per week, but his mistake is forgotten—indeed, it is inconsequential—in light of the spiritual majesty of the cathedral. At the film's conclusion, Gibbs realizes his ambition to play Canterbury Cathedral's organ, and so he too, like Johnson, ultimately reassesses his relationship to cinema and rejects it in favor of the eternal and medieval truths espoused by Colpeper.

While Colpeper's primary motivation for his bizarre acts as the Glue Man is to deprive soldiers of amatory pursuits so that they will attend his history presentations, he also sees an intimate connection between cinema and sexuality that likewise threatens his endeavors. In recalling his difficulties in staging his lectures, he conflates his male audience's pursuit of women with their enjoyment of women via the silver screen and thus offers another reason to condemn cinematic pastimes:

I planned a series of lectures—no one came. I tried again and again—nobody turned up. I went to see their C.O. He sympathized. Said when the men had finished their work, they had dates with the girls in the village, or they went to the movies to see glamour girls on the screen, or they got up dances. They were always with girls or after girls.

If the men were not pursuing sexual activity with local women, they were voyeuristically pursuing sublimated sexual satisfaction with the "glamour girls on the screen." Viewers are given ample reason to distrust Colpeper's dismissal of cinema, as it is so clearly linked to his perverse desire to build a homosocial community of history buffs with himself as their leader, and with no women allowed. For Colpeper, cinematic sexuality obscures the possibility of living in history, and he apparently sacrifices his sexuality to live in and through history, yet only to see his sexual desires surface in his furtive attempts to prohibit the local soldiers from acting on their sexual desires, as well as in the gluey discharges he pours in women's hair.

Those who police perversions are often hypocrites, and Colpeper embodies such hypocrisy when staging his lectures for the local soldiers: his slide shows approximate the film-going experience, and so he condemns the cinema while relying on its technologies to stage his lectures and thus to direct the gaze of numerous soldiers toward him. Furthermore, as he feared that the local soldiers would become smitten with "glamour girls on the screen," it is certainly ironic (and again somewhat hypocritical) that he finds Smith in his audience and realizes their ultimate kinship. Upon Smith's entrance in the lecture hall, she is greeted with the soldiers' wolf whistles, and this unleashed expression of male desire establishes her as the film's "glamour girl"; however, her interest is piqued not sexually in regard to these men but historically in regard to Colpeper. Smith comes to appreciate Colpeper in this scene, although she initially feared him, sensing his perversity: "There's something about him [Colpeper] I don't like," she declared to Johnson when they lodged at the Hand of Glory, the local inn. Later, when spying Colpeper scything in his yard, she reappraises him, declaring to Johnson as they ride in a horse-drawn cart: "But this morning, if ever a man looked—looked right, he did." At Colpeper's lecture, when Smith tells him that she will donate her antique Belgian coins excavated from the Pilgrims' Road to his institute, the two share a moment of union that is immediately disrupted by a burst of applause, but as Gibbs explains, the applause is "not for you," but for the soldier who fixed the broken projector.

Colpeper succeeds in luring men to his lectures, yet he fails to engage many of them beyond the most superficial levels, which highlights both the unfulfilled nature of his homosocial desires and the irony of his nascent (albeit asexual) relationship with Smith. As Colpeper begins his slide show again, a soldier uses the projector's light to read, and an earlier shot showed that he was entertaining himself with a racy book—one featuring a woman's legs in stockings on the cover—suggesting that he ignores Colpeper's lecture in pursuit of sexual satisfaction via the "glamour girls" available through the printed word. Another shot features a portly man dozing in a corner. Having lured the men to his historical presentation, Colpeper fails to entice them to pay attention to him while he simultaneously reassesses his relationship with Smith, the woman who was never welcome to attend. In the cinematic darkness, Colpeper and Smith see each other anew, realizing a clarity of vision they could not achieve under other circumstances and thus realigning the perceived degradations of cinematic technologies. This potential for communion, predicated upon their mutual appreciation for England's ever-present history, emerges out of the darkness.

Cinema relies on the dark, as does Colpeper for his nighttime attacks as the Glue Man, and through the interplay of the darkness of cinema and the darkness of night, as well as, metaphorically, the darkness of desire, cinematic and sexual perversions bleed together. To survive enemy attacks during the war, Britain must rely on her citizens to act for the common good by enforcing blackouts to protect one another and their land. In this overlap between cinematic darkness and blackouts, Powell and Pressburger merge the perverse possibilities of the theater with the beneficial communalism of the wartime blackouts. Given *A Canterbury Tale*'s temporal setting during WW II, the townspeople of Chillingbourne must maintain the region's blackouts to preserve them from bombings, and these blackouts serve as metaphors both for the characters' spiritual journeys and for the cinematic experience. Along these lines, Scott Salwolke suggests that the "blackness will be a striking metaphor for the emotional darkness in which each of the characters will find themselves."[22] The divergent temporalities of medieval past and war-torn present, as well as the divergent technologies of medieval artisans and modern filmmakers, appear to operate according to a binary logic of beneficent and baleful, but *A Canterbury Tale* is, of course, a film, and so the modern technologies of cinema are perversely necessary to share this paean to England's Chaucerian roots. With respect to the blackout theme, the film's audience is reminded both of the threat of war and of the necessity to defend themselves through the communal experience of darkness. The trip to the cinema, in this

---

22. Scott Salwolke, *The Films of Michael Powell and the Archers* (Lanham, MD: Scarecrow, 1997), 112.

metaphor, is a trip into perversity and darkness that is ultimately, yet ironically, illuminating.

Infractions of the blackout enlighten (in a literal sense) the mystery of the Glue Man, incriminating Colpeper as the perpetrator. After the Glue Man attacks Smith and she and Johnson investigate in the town hall, Officer Brooks informs Colpeper that he has breached the blackout codes—"You're showing your light, sir"—and Colpeper admits the severity of his transgression to Johnson: "Very careless of me. We take our blackout seriously in East Kent." When Johnson, Smith, and Gibbs determine the identity of the Glue Man, it is in part because they remember that Colpeper's light was turned off when they approached the town hall but was turned on later in the evening, indicating that he had surreptitiously entered the building. Johnson solves the mystery by interpreting the meaning of this light in Colpeper's office: "We hadn't seen a light, so it follows . . . ," he reasons, and the three protagonists thus solve the mystery (with the additional evidence that the Glue Man's attacks occurred on nights when Colpeper was assigned to fire-watch duty). Here is the film's strongest condemnation of Colpeper: in perversely terrorizing women in his effort to lure male soldiers to his lectures glorifying England's history, he potentially sacrifices England's future by undermining the blackout. When Colpeper requires a blackout prior to his slideshow, requesting to the soldiers, "Would some of you mind doing the blackout, please?" the merging of wartime blackouts and cinematic darkness makes possible the disintegration of the binary between historic wholesomeness and cinematic perversity. Calling the soldiers to stage a blackout for his lecture yet failing to adhere to the blackout upon which the nation depends, Colpeper privileges cinematic darkness as a means of advancing his homosocial desires over his historical ones. The film's final treatment of its blackout theme, when Johnson, Smith, Gibbs, and Colpeper ride together on the train to Canterbury and are cast into darkness as the train enters a tunnel, prepares viewers for Johnson's proclamation of sanctification: "Pilgrims for Canterbury, all out and get your blessings."

As much as *A Canterbury Tale* condemns film as a distraction from medieval values, it concludes with an homage to the cinematic experience. When Johnson reunites with his army buddy Mickey Roczinsky (Harvey Golden) in Canterbury, they retire to a tea shop to talk. Viewers know that Roczinsky has been pursuing women in London during his three-day leave—he mentions the "million[s]" of women's telephone numbers he's taken down—and so they might expect him to voice themes counter to the film's dominant ethos of spiritual communion with the past. In many ways, the sexually active Roczinsky stands in direct contrast to the ascetic Colpeper, and along these lines, he encourages Johnson to view the world cinematically, to gaze out the tea shop's front window and enjoy the "show": "There you are, you Canterbury pilgrim. You can sit right there and watch the world go by, like in the movies." Despite all Johnson has learned about the experiential nature of the past, the two men then observe the parading soldiers from the tea-shop window. Johnson appears at this moment to have regressed to his earlier passivity, "watch[ing] the world go by," but he then completes his pilgrimage to Canterbury Cathedral. By enacting both the passivity of the cinematic experience and the activity of pilgrimage, Johnson exposes the false binary at the heart of Colpeper's anticinematism, proving the potential of any given individual to embody perversion and sanctity. He earlier proclaimed to Alison while they shared their cart ride through the countryside, "Yeah, it don't add up. . . . But you know, Alison, things don't add up in life," and this simple endorsement of life's complexity purges the film of its surface exploration into perversions and resignifies them as instruments through which one may receive a blessing at Canterbury Cathedral, thus achieving the narrative end denied Chaucer's pilgrims due to his masterwork's incompletion.

As *A Canterbury Tale* concludes, it is apparent that the film need not be experienced cinematically (as paradoxical as this might be) but can be experienced religiously. Its opening shots feature the bells of Canterbury Cathedral ringing, calling viewers to the cinematic "service," and its closing shots bookend the narrative, as the bells now toll the service's end. As this film likens its medium to a religious event, it rewrites its message, in much the same manner as Chaucer rewrites the profane pleasures of his many bawdy tales through his retraction at the end of the *Canterbury Tales*, claiming "For oure [Bible] seith, 'Al that is writen is writen for oure doctrine,' and that is myn entente" (10.1083). As Chaucer's masterpiece begins with a paean to pilgrimage, journeys through numerous sinful and vulgar stories yet ends with the prayer of his apology, so too does *A Canterbury Tale* begin and end with spirituality yet detour through numerous perversities during Powell and Pressburger's loose adaptation of Chaucer's narrative. Powell criticized his schoolteachers for their censorious renditions of Chaucer's masterpieces—"It is my recollection that the courtly and witty poet was not presented to us as such by our English masters: rather he was forced into our consciousness in a bowdlerized and anglicized version which we automatically resisted"[23]—and his film purifies cinematic perversities while nonetheless preserving them, establishing a narrative affinity with the *Canterbury Tales* beyond the surface structural similarity of pilgrimage. With Colpeper as its preacher/prophet and with Chaucer

---

23. Powell, *Life*, 74.

as its spectral inspiration, *A Canterbury Tale* sanctifies perversion—on both the narrative and the metanarrative levels—as a necessary antidote to modern ills. The film celebrating Chaucerian history that you have just watched, Powell and Pressburger imply, was a perversion of life as you should live it, but if you embrace the perversion at the heart of the experience, the Glue Man might save your soul—and England's as well—under the protective and perverse cover of cinematic darkness.

CHAPTER 8

IDOLS OF THE MARKETPLACE
Chaucer/Pasolini

KATHRYN L. LYNCH

I am beginning to forget how things were *before*. The loved faces of yesterday are beginning to turn yellow.
—Pier Paolo Pasolini[1]

In me thou see'st the glowing of such fire,
That on the ashes of his youth doth lie.
—William Shakespeare[2]

IN 1971, 1972, AND 1974, Pier Paolo Pasolini released three magisterial films set in the Middle Ages, a time in which he located treasured aspects of humanity fast disappearing from his contemporary, increasingly commercialized world. These were his cinematic interpretations of the beloved and canonical storytelling collections, Boccaccio's *Decameron*, Chaucer's *Canterbury Tales,* and the anonymous Middle Eastern *Thousand and One Nights,* a grouping he presented optimistically as the *Trilogia della vita.* It can be fairly said that this trilogy marked a kind of apex, while also a crisis, in Pasolini's remarkable career. They were an astonishing box-office success and made him secure financially for the first time. Official objections to the nudity and obscenity of the films mobilized critics in their defense and elevated Pasolini's already significant reputation as a central figure of the Italian arts. Over the

---

1. Pier Paolo Pasolini, "Trilogy of Life Rejected," *Lutheran Letters,* trans. Stuart Hood (Manchester: Carcanet New Press, 1983), 52.

2. William Shakespeare, Sonnet 73, *The Riverside Shakespeare,* ed. G. Blakemore Evans, 2nd ed. (Boston: Houghton Mifflin, 1997), lines 9–10.

years, though, critical responses to *I racconti di Canterbury*, Pasolini's *Canterbury Tales*, have been very mixed. In 1972, when the movie appeared, it won the Golden Bear Award at the 22nd Berlin International Film Festival. Pasolini was still alive and held a revered if controversial place in the contemporary film world. But *I racconti*, the most internally conflicted of the *Trilogia della vita*, never enjoyed the critical acclaim of the other two films, and when Pasolini himself renounced (or "abjured") the trilogy and soon thereafter died in violent and scandalous circumstances, the critical reputation of Pasolini's Chaucer sank further and faster than that of its two companion films.

By 1980, on the occasion of *I racconti*'s American debut, *New York Times* critic Victor Canby, who had lauded Pasolini's *Decameron* as "one of the most beautiful, turbulent and uproarious panoramas of early Renaissance life ever put on film,"[3] dismissed *I racconti* as "aggressively infantile" and "slapdash." Perhaps even more insulting to Pasolini's version of Chaucer's masterwork was Canby's insinuation, often repeated by others in different registers, that the filmmaker was indifferent to the Chaucerian text—that other cultural preoccupations of his present moment "were clearly of more immediate interest to Mr. Pasolini than Chaucer's tales."[4] As Maurizio Viano writes about "Pasolini's most uninteresting film," he was "clearly less at ease with the English author [than he had been with Boccaccio]."[5] The notion that Pasolini did not deeply care about Chaucer's original text, that he was callous in respect to the medieval English past and was prone to subordinate it to his late twentieth-century political agenda, is an aspersion that this essay will attempt to refute. When *I racconti* was banned by the censors and denounced by the Church, Pasolini defended his presentation of Chaucer, whom he identified as Dante "for

---

3. Vincent Canby, "Pasolini's Decameron at the Film Festival," *New York Times*, 5 Oct. 1971.

4. Vincent Canby, "Film: *Canterbury Tales*," *New York Times*, 30 May 1980. By 2009, when the Criterion Collection reissued the films, Phelim O'Neill (in *The Guardian* [1 May 2009]) refers to the group as a "refreshingly honest and gritty take on human nature, via some of the world's most enduring literary endeavors." At the same time, *I racconti* is regarded as "the weakest," about which the best that can be said is that its "farcical" take on the original "holds the interest." The notion that *I racconti di Canterbury* is the weak link in the trilogy is repeated so often as to have become a truism; see also Robin Wood, *New York Times Educational Supplement*, 16 May 1975, quoted in Richard Dyer, "Pasolini and Homosexuality," *Pier Paolo Pasolini*, ed. Paul Willemen (London: British Film Institute, 1976), 57–63, 57. For the sense that Pasolini "has little interest in a faithful or earnest representation of Chaucer's poetic text," see Kathleen Forni, "A 'cinema of poetry': What Pasolini Did to Chaucer's *Canterbury Tales*," *Literature/Film Quarterly* 30 (2002): 256–63.

5. Maurizio Viano, *A Certain Realism: Making Use of Pasolini's Film Theory and Practice* (Berkeley: University of California Press, 1993), 280.

the Anglo-Saxon world," on the basis of its substantial fidelity to its original.[6] He elaborates, "When making a film of the text which marks the beginning of English literature . . . I didn't want to make a simple illustration of the work. . . . But it would be also wrong to consider the umbilical cord linking my text to its matrix as irrevocably cut."[7] As Pasolini presents it, his is a rigorous, if sometimes flawed, "critical reading" of an "inspiring" Chaucerian original.

Indeed, Pasolini had built his career as a man of letters, a career that was at once distinguished and flamboyant, on the signifying links between literature and film. He was, before all else, a poet and a student of language. He was also a serious disciple of art history and of the classic texts that repeatedly informed his cinematic work. In his *Decameron,* he was persuaded to play the part of the "best pupil" of the painter Giotto, a role in which he clearly took pleasure.[8] His choice then to cast himself in the role of the poet Chaucer in his version of the *Canterbury Tales* has a kind of inevitability about it. But this choice was not trivial. Nowhere else on film does Pasolini play the role of "literary author," and his move here suggests the close connection he felt with Chaucer as well as his ambition to use film to craft a visual language that could be transnational. There is poetic justice in the modern Italian writer filming in the English countryside, turning to the English poet who had at least twice traveled to Italy and who had built his own national literature on the backs of such Italian masters as Dante, Petrarch, and Boccaccio. If there are incoherencies in this film (and there are), they are not only Pasolini's fundamental incoherencies but also Chaucer's, which Pasolini percipiently recognized. Indeed, rather than the weak partner in the *Trilogia della vita,* as it is often viewed, *I racconti* can be seen as the dark key to the trilogy's mythology. It is the film at the center of the triptych, the one that has perhaps the *most* suggestive power to reveal the contradictions that animate Pasolini's larger moral and artistic project of recuperating the medieval past.

It is an irony of the *Trilogia*'s critical and production history that only now may we be fully able to appreciate its complex achievement. When the films first appeared, their effect was overwhelmed by the sheer force of Pasolini's controversial personality and reputation. "Everything that had to do with

---

6. Pasolini, *Paese sera* (newspaper), n. p.; quoted in Barth David Schwartz, *Pasolini Requiem* (New York: Vintage, 1992), 592.

7. Pasolini, "Libertà es sesso secondo Pasolini," *Corriere della Sera* 2.4 (1973), quoted in *Pier Paolo Pasolini: A Future Life,* ed. Laura Betti (Associazione Fonde Pier Paolo Pasolini, 1989), 163 (hereafter cited as *A Future Life*).

8. One will, in criticism, sometimes see him referred to as Giotto, as the screenplay suggests was the plan. The film, however, is clear that he is a disciple of the great painter, though Stephen Snyder suggests that "the pupilage [is] a part of his disguise," and we should actually regard him as Giotto (see Snyder, *Pier Paolo Pasolini* [Boston: Twayne, 1980], 180, note 4).

him caused an uproar," observes Elena Ferrante.[9] That uproar led to severe early restrictions on the circulation of *I racconti*.[10] The quality of a 1990 VHS version was poor and could not add to the reputation of a film that gains substantial power from its cinematography. Not until 2012 have audiences had access to a high-quality reproduction in the superb Criterion Collection *Trilogy of Life*, which truly replaces famine with feast.[11] Now viewers can watch all three films together in first-rate digital restorations as well as gain access to a cornucopia of critical materials, including interviews, documentaries, and video essays. The DVD format further allows for the kind of close and iterative "reading" of the films that is well rewarded by Pasolini's intricate and sophisticated, even scholarly, reinvention of Chaucer. In this sense technology and "reading practices" lagged behind Pasolini and can now be said to have caught up with him.

Many more examples than I have space for here could be adduced to demonstrate the depth and complexity of Pasolini's understanding of Chaucer. These extend throughout the film and range from local details of costuming and color to citations of text and scripture to larger structural echoes and variations like the creative reassignment of entire speeches to alternate characters. I will concentrate on four of Pasolini's Chaucerian adaptations to create a suggestive rather than exhaustive range of contexts and reference, including an icon in The Reeve's Tale, a gesture in The Summoner's Tale, the elaboration of Chaucer's self-reflexive structural frame, and the use of voice in The Merchant's Tale. While these will ultimately be seen as connected examples, they can also usefully be treated separately, as instances that demonstrate Pasolini's lively and close reading of Chaucer.

To begin, when the two Cambridge students in The Reeve's Tale arrive at the conniving Miller's domain in Pasolini's film, one of their first sights is of two fleshy bottoms protruding from a window, presumably suspended over a device used as a privy. As several critics have noted, this is a detail taken from Brueghel's sixteenth-century painting *Netherlandish Proverbs*. The proverb here illustrated is "They both shit from the same hole," providing the lesson that, as Patrick Rumble explains, "These two are forced to make a virtue

---

9. Elena Ferrante, *The Story of a New Name*, trans. Ann Goldstein (New York: Europa, 2012).

10. Such that, for example, Stephen Snyder in his Twayne series *Pier Paolo Pasolini* concedes in his preface that his discussion of the film was inadequate "due to absurd distribution problems which restricted me to a single viewing" (xii).

11. The 1990 VHS version was produced by Walter Bearer films. The 2012 Criterion Collection *Trilogy of Life* is licensed by Twentieth Century Fox and Metro-Goldwyn-Mayer Studios.

of necessity."[12] But as the usually sympathetic Rumble goes on to say dismissively, "Within the context of Pasolini's episode, this original lesson seems quite irrelevant."[13] Viewing Pasolini more intently through the lens of Chaucer, however, suggests that this aphorism in fact represents Pasolini's astute reading of Chaucer.

Chaucer's Reeve's Tale is all about recycling, double uses, and making the best of what one can find. The Cambridge students John and Aleyn are tricked out of the full measure of flour to which they are entitled by the Miller's cheating, so Aleyn determines that he will find an alternate means of payment, using the very language of proverb: "al sal be for the beste. / . . . For . . . gif a man in a point be agreved, / . . . in another he sal be releved" (1.4176, 4181–82).[14] His recompense will be found in the arms of the Miller's daughter. In *his* turn, the young clerk John resents the repayment in pleasure anticipated by his friend Aleyn, so he crafts a plan that will let him have at the Miller's wife as a substitute for both the flour and the daughter who he expects is at that very moment servicing his companion. In the logic of the tale, one kind of milling, a conventional medieval image for sexual intercourse, takes the place of another. And all of these shenanigans depend upon a confusion of beds, a "bed-trick," that makes the various men and women interchangeable in the dark. It is hard to imagine a more perfect visual icon for this application of fungibility to practical use than the two Brueghelesque bottoms that introduce Pasolini's interlude.

Further, Pasolini continues to stress these Chaucerian elements in his version of the story. He emphasizes the similarity of the two students both visually in their bright red academic gowns and in their speech, where one frequently echoes the song, the rhythms, and even the exact wording of the other (as in Chaucer, both speak in a Northern dialect). Pasolini's phallic milling apparatus, the hopper of which extends through the center of the mill structure, underlines the sexual metaphor at the heart of the tale, and his Alan repeats word for word the justification of his Chaucerian counterpart ("All shall be for the best. . . . If a man be aggrieved in one way, he shall be relieved in another"). As in Chaucer, the second student, John, is motivated by a spirit of emulation, wanting to avoid looking like "a sissy or a fool" when the story is told back in Cambridge (Chaucer's John had dreaded the reputation back at school of "a daf, a cokenay" [1.4208]). In Pasolini this male homosocial/

---

12. Patrick Rumble, *Allegories of Contamination: Pier Paolo Pasolini's* Trilogy of Life (Toronto: University of Toronto Press, 1996), 58.

13. Rumble, *Allegories*, 58.

14. Geoffrey Chaucer, *The Riverside Chaucer*, ed. Larry D. Benson, 3rd ed. (Boston: Houghton Mifflin, 1987); cited parenthetically.

homoerotic rivalry is further underscored when the two clerks feel each other's erections under the blankets as a way of affirming and admiring their male equivalency; while this specific detail is not taken from Chaucer, it is consistent with the motivation of Chaucer's students. At the tale's end, in both Chaucer and in Pasolini, the clerks' original stolen portion of flour has been recycled and returned to them in the form of a cake, and their interchangeable appetites emerge one final time as they ride away from the mill back to school, each taking a parallel pleasure in consuming the same cake. Indeed, by eliminating the introductory Chaucerian material that reveals the Miller's social pretensions and marriage plans for his daughter, Pasolini, in his own recycling of Chaucer, focuses the story even more tightly than did Chaucer on the theme of recompense and substitution. The visual epigraph from Brueghel is entirely appropriate.

An equally telling visual moment, a gesture, occurs near the beginning of Pasolini's wondrously irreverent, boisterously iconoclastic rendition of The Summoner's Tale. Chaucer's tale opens with sixty lines describing the friar whose gluttony prompts his licensed begging of all manner of food from the folk around the countryside. This introduction aptly contracts in Pasolini to that friar's brief but lip-smackingly appreciative taste of "delicious" cake. Quickly and expertly transitioning from the secular to the divine while echoing his Chaucerian original, Pasolini's friar then intones "Hic Deus" (God be here), just before he disdainfully lifts a cat up from a chair by the scruff of the neck and drops it on the floor with a distasteful waggle of his fingers, as if trying to rid them of germs. This sequence constitutes an expressive enactment of an identical gesture in Chaucer ("And fro the bench he droof awey the cat" [3.1775]), a moment that close readers of the medieval poet have found to be highly evocative. In Derek Pearsall's words, "That action tells us more of the friar than a quantity of exposition: the cat is sitting, as is the wont of cats, in the most comfortable seat in the place, and the one therefore that the friar has his eye on and naturally appropriates as his own; his actions, further, have the easy and insinuating assumption of privilege, the unhurried deliberateness, the gentleness, of a cat's and withal the ruthlessness, and obliviousness of all but physical advantage."[15] Pasolini has captured Chaucer's friar's actions and their banal consequences perfectly, down to the cat's little screech as it drops to the floor. Such a moment reminds us of the friar's trivial but remorseless brutalism and significantly contrasts with his unctuous and patronizing demeanor as he pressures the bedridden Thomas for more gifts.

---

15. Derek A. Pearsall, *The Canterbury Tales* (London: Allen & Unwin, 1985), 224.

On a larger scale, one of the most important ways that Pasolini models himself on Chaucer is through casting himself in the role of the medieval author, a choice frequently remarked upon by critics. These critics, however, are less likely to acknowledge fully the way that Pasolini adopts this self-reflexive move from Chaucer. It is clear from the opening lines of Chaucer's *Canterbury Tales* that "the pilgrim Chaucer" is meant to be seen throughout as the observer and reporter of the action (see, for example, 1.19–34) and that he is recognized by the other travelers and tale-tellers as the medieval poet Chaucer. His own narrative perspective is alternately one of embarrassment at the coarseness of the stories he will be forced to repeat (1.725–42) and unease in the face of his own poetic incompetence (1.745–46). At the end of the whole work (but before the "explicit" that moves us outside of its formal boundary), this modesty takes a more serious form in the poet's "retraction" not only of those Canterbury tales that "sownen into sinne" (10.1086) but of most of his other poetic works, including some we no longer possess if they indeed ever existed. This is not the only place where Chaucer's *Canterbury Tales* looks outside itself at other parts of the poet's literary oeuvre. The Introduction to The Man of Law's Tale, for example, has long fascinated Chaucerians with its tantalizing self-references; here the Man of Law protests that it will be difficult for him to find a tale to tell due to the fact that Chaucer (though poorly schooled in his knowledge of prosody [2.47–48]) has already exhausted the store, "and if he have noght seyd hem, leve brother, / In o book, he hath seyd hem in another" (2.51–52). The list again includes many works we know plus a couple that seem to have been made up for the occasion.

Clearly this kind of bravura performance of authorial elusiveness appealed to Pasolini, and he took pains to incorporate and even to extend it in *I racconti*. Since the storytelling framework requires each pilgrim to contribute, Chaucer had assigned *himself* a romantic tale, The Tale of Sir Thopas, to be composed in verse like those of the other tellers, until it is interrupted by the master of ceremonies, the Innkeeper, because of its poor quality ("Thy drasty rymyng is nat worth a toord!" [7.930]). To compensate, "Chaucer" tells a second story, this time more serious and in prose, since clearly he cannot be expected to produce acceptable light verse. The joke, of course, is on the famous poet and romancer Chaucer, who is exposed as less capable at his craft than any other random traveler. In the screenplay, Pasolini's intention originally was to imitate Chaucer here by including a "Racconto di Chaucer"—The Tale of Sir Thopas—between The Cook's and The Wife of Bath's tales, but as in the original tales Chaucer/Pasolini would be cut off by the impatient Innkeeper: "Per Dio! Perchè, per dirtelo chiaro e tondo, questa tua leggenda poetica non vale una merda!" (By God, it's loud and clear that your reputation as a poet isn't worth a shit!"). But the "Racconto di Chaucer" was the one tale from the screenplay that did not make it onto the screen—perhaps Pasolini felt that the film itself had come to substitute for The Poet's Tale, perhaps the tale did not fit the evolving work generically, perhaps he simply was looking for places to cut: we will never know. Nonetheless, the inclusion of Chaucer's tale in the original plan does suggest the poet's central interest in Chaucer's range of self-reference and his poetic *legerdemain*. We will see that, in other ways, this interest found its way into the final version of the film.

All three of the films that compose the *Trilogia della vita* are framed storytelling collections, but Pasolini treats the frame in *I racconti di Canterbury* in a way that is quite distinctive from the other two films. In the *Decameron* and especially in *Il fiore delle mille e una notte*, Pasolini eliminates the traditional frame entirely—there is no brigade of Florentine nobles escaping the city to narrate stories on their country estate as in Boccaccio, nor is there the compelling fiction of Scheherazade inventing nightly tales to stave off her execution. The reduction of the poetic armature enables a fluid and recursive counterpoint of tales with no point of view accessible outside of them, allowing the tales to bleed into one another and inviting the audience to participate in the construction of the narrative's meaning. In Patrick Rumble's formulation, these story collections are "contaminated": an initiating tale may become the frame for another tale or tales, which may in turn frame or contain their originating stories, making the text "like a glove pulled inside out" or "an allegory of a text without an author."[16] Pasolini's *I racconti*, however, is tightly framed, if not by the tales' individual tellers then by its medieval author. Far from being absent, the author becomes all important.

In consequence, the general view is that this film, while still highly provocative in its subject matter, lacks "the structural complexity" of the other films in the trilogy.[17] But the difference lies in the *kind* of structure we encounter in *I racconti*, not in the complexity of that structure. Just as he had in the first and third films of the *Trilogia della vita*, Pasolini also experiments with the frame of the *Canterbury Tales*, precisely by taking the tales out of the mouths of the individual pilgrims and returning them to the control of their "author." While his method in the other films puts pressure on the audience to supply

---

16. Patrick Rumble, "Stylistic Contamination in the *Trilogia della vita*: The Case of *Il fiore delle mille e una notte*," *Pier Paolo Pasolini: Contemporary Perspectives*, ed. Patrick Rumble and Bart Testa (Toronto: University of Toronto Press, 1994), 210–31, 215. While Rumble sees *Il fiore* as Pasolini's *pièce de résistance* of this kind of narrative abyss, he clearly believes that it also informs Pasolini's *Decameron*; see his chapter "Framing Boccaccio: Pasolini's Adaptation of the *Decameron*," in Rumble, *Allegories of Contamination*, 100–134.

17. Rumble, *Allegories*, 52.

a framework of meaning for the tales, his approach in *I racconti* explores and challenges the role of the author, the human creator, that is the character of "Chaucer," who Pasolini claimed "bears the meta-linguistic meaning of the film."[18] Far from being simplified, these tales are aggressively "framed" by their autobiographical author, ultimately Pasolini, just as Chaucer asserted and repeatedly exploited his own role as biographical author.

Within the film, this author is the hybrid Chaucer/Pasolini, the twentieth-century Italian rebel-poet self-cast as the mischievous but urbane fourteenth-century Father of English Literature. We first meet Chaucer/Pasolini just shy of five minutes into the film, at his entrance to the public square, where his horse nudges him into unceremoniously bumping faces with an intimidating-looking man dressed in burlap and covered in tattoos. Chaucer/Pasolini instantly becomes angry but in a quintessentially Chaucerian gesture quickly writes off his hard words as a joke, to which the tattooed man replies pacifically, "Between a jest and a joke many a truth can be told." In the first of many inversions, this formulation echoes Chaucer's own "men shal nat maken ernest of game" (1.3186). The authorial "eye" of this "narrator" continues to exert its control over the scene, if intermittently. Chaucer/Pasolini is next seen briefly surveying his fellow pilgrims inside the inn as the Innkeeper/Host establishes the storytelling framework. In his third appearance Pasolini confronts the problem of naturalism by showing us when Chaucer may have commenced composing the tales, revealing him in the middle of the night observing his fellows mostly sleeping around the hall as he (literally and figuratively) sharpens his pens; at this point he writes the incipit for The Cook's Tale, which here follows. Directly after that tale, Chaucer/Pasolini is shown at work on his opus in his study at home, creating it presumably from his memory—but also by consulting a pile of other books for inspiration, chiefly the *Decameron,* over which he chuckles before burying that tome discreetly at the bottom of the teetering stack. This reference to the intertextuality of Chaucer's poems and Pasolini's films is both interrupted and underscored by the appearance of Chaucer's wife, surveying him from an interior balcony and screeching "Geoffrey Chaucer," which awakens him from a catnap to his task. I have not, however, seen mentioned anywhere that the appearance of Chaucer's wife in *I racconti* is itself an extratextual reference (outside the frame of the *Canterbury Tales*) to a moment in Chaucer's dream vision the *House of Fame* when the poet Geffrey is similarly awakened

---

18. Pasolini, Press Conference at the Berlin Festival (1972), quoted in "Pasolini on Film," *Pier Paolo Pasolini,* ed. Willemen, 67–77, 73.

abruptly by "oon I koude nevene," commonly assumed by modern critics to be his wife (562).

We see Chaucer/Pasolini three more times in the movie, reinforcing his continuous presence as author—in his study taking up his quill to pen The Pardoner's Tale, then hard at work again at his text following the friar's vision of hell in The Summoner's Tale, and finally after the pilgrims have made their arrival at Canterbury, completing the script of his tales with the words "Here end the Canterbury tales told only for the pleasure of telling them." His expression of amusement in all these instances suggests that an impish joy in tale-telling has indeed been his chief or even exclusive motivation. But should we take Pasolini at his word here? Chaucer stated the opposite at the conclusion of his work: that "'Al that is writen is writen for oure doctrine,' and that is myn entente" (10.1083). And remember that earlier, while Chaucer cautioned against making game into earnest, Pasolini indicated the reverse, that behind the screen of jest, "many a truth can be told." And yet though the two lose their narrative faith for complementary reasons, ultimately, when the director recants his films, he does so with a peculiar Chaucerian irony and "rhetoric of concession" that blames the viewer for the abuse of his art.[19] Don't blame me, implies each artist, if you cannot comprehend my work. The complexity of literary relationships here suggests that Pasolini is inviting us inside an authorial *mise en abyme* parallel to the structural *mise en abyme* of his other two medieval films. The creator's imprimatur, certified by a playful artist like Chaucer/Pasolini, alerts the audience to a different kind of failure of the "frame" from that of his other "allegories of contamination." Yet the contamination, understood as the removal of a stable ground of understanding, remains constant.

Visually, Pasolini employs the "frame" in such a way as to remind his audience that a filmmaker stands behind all this magic and that any "perspective" achieved by a camera is perhaps even less to be trusted than that supplied by a viewer or reader. While the figure of Chaucer/Pasolini is explicitly inserted into several transitions between tales to remind us of his presence, it might be said that he is just as present when two tales bump up against each other abruptly with no transition. Far from being a sign of clumsiness, as some have thought, such visible quilting in the film is meant to startle the viewer and focus attention on implicit linkages between stories and scenes. The images on the screen themselves compose the "frame," their visual presentation and

---

19. The phrase is Patrick Rumble's; see his excellent chapter on the parallels between Pasolini's "ironic recantation" and the retractions of Chaucer and Boccaccio, in Rumble, *Allegories*, 82–99.

arrangement providing all the scaffolding that is needed to understand them. We might think back in this regard to a famous scene in the *Decameron,* when after having arrived in Naples, Pasolini as the disciple of Giotto sets up his scaffolding in the church where he will be painting. He and his apprentices are visually enclosed within the wooden frames of this device; the model of the fresco he is planning sits before him. But for Pasolini, the real as well as the artifact have signifying importance, as we realize when the next scene takes us "outside" where Pasolini "frames" his vision of the actual public square by twice placing over his eye the director's square of two fingers laid across another. Pasolini was noted for the disciplined, painterly composition of his films, whether he was taking his subject matter from art or from life, as is in evidence both here in the *Decameron* and throughout *I racconti.* Even in a film as respectful of the "real" Naples as was the *Decameron,* the "natural" provides a language that must be selected and arranged, and Pasolini's theatrical practice continually calls attention to this fact. The absence of a fully articulated narrative transition suggests that the viewer should look elsewhere for the link, in images, repeated themes, the blocking of a scene; it does not suggest an abrogation of directorial oversight.

To take an example from *I racconti,* the previously described The Summoner's Tale follows directly upon The Pardoner's Tale, with no transition. The dead and dying bodies of the three revelers beneath a tree are instantly replaced with a friar performing the sign of the cross "in nomine Patris, et filii, et Spiritus Sancti." He stands behind a large wooden chair that dominates the center of the scene. As viewers of the film, we are looking through it from the point of view of the sick man in the bed. First, the hollowed-out square of the chair back literally frames the friar as he utters his empty blessing and then crosses obliquely to taste the cake, returning to the center of the "frame" of the chair, closer in, for his Deus Hic. It is surely no accident that the shallow, materialist friar appears as if he were a talking head broadcast from a television set, a medium whose "petit-bourgeois . . . instrumentality" Pasolini loathed, as one sees in the image in figure 8.1.[20]

The frame takes center stage as we move back and forth across it, next glimpsing the ailing Thomas through the chair back from the friar's point of view. The friar is zeroing in on Thomas's most private matters as he approaches his bedside more closely, and our perspective shifts again to that of the ailing Thomas, who now views the friar in the chair with the "frame" positioned

---

20. Pier Paolo Pasolini, "New Linguistic Questions," *Heretical Empiricism,* ed. Louise Barnett, trans. Ben Lawton and Louise Barnett (Bloomington: Indiana University Press, 1988), 3–22, 13.

FIGURE 8.1. Pasolini's vision of Chaucer's acquisitive friar in The Summoner's Tale.

just above his head.[21] The entire brief scene evolves in a perfect visual balance, as such framing links it not only to the empty literalism of the preceding tale but also to the scene that directly follows, which locates the friar in *his* bed, observed by a visionary guide situated above him and enclosed by an arched window. Pasolini has reversed the order of events from the original *Canterbury Tales,* where a friar's vision of hell had preceded the encounter with the dying Thomas. But this artistic liberty is meticulously controlled by the filmmaker's eye within a visual composition that discloses the radically mediated nature of his artistic practice. The vision of hell itself, coming right up, provides further evidence of artistic self-consciousness. Pasolini bases this final landscape, filmed at Mount Etna, closely on Hieronymus Bosch's vision from his representations of *The Last Judgment,* though the friars who pop out of Satan's ass are pure Chaucer. In the series of visual and literary references, the real and the literary form a seamless signifying web from which authorial presence is never allowed to disappear and in which multiple contexts are put into productive dialogue with each other.

A particular concern with the shaping power exerted by the authorial role is in evidence in *I racconti* not only in the presentation and interleaving

---

21. Such changes of perspective are classic examples of Pasolini's directorial use of free indirect discourse to articulate varying perspectives and as in contrast with the use of this technique in The Merchant's Tale described below; see note 25. (My thanks to my colleague Maurizio Viano for pointing this out, as well as for the observation about the friar on television, above.)

of tales but also in their selection and ordering. For one thing, Pasolini has exercised a significant pruning authority over Chaucer by eliminating all the tales not covered by Chaucer's retraction—and including only eight of the most scurrilous. He has also departed widely from the order of Chaucer's tales, though it is clear from the screenplay that Pasolini's initial thought was to follow that order more closely than he did. The first of the tales in the screenplay is The Miller's Tale, followed by The Reeve's Tale and The Cook's Tale (just as Chaucer ordered these three as the second, third, and fourth of his *Canterbury Tales*). In Pasolini's text, The Merchant's Tale comes fifth, after The Wife of Bath's Tale and before the Friar's and the Summoner's tales; this is a slight alteration from the original, as in Chaucer's *Canterbury Tale,* The Friar's Tale interrupts the Wife of Bath, but the variation is minor. The final tale in the screenplay is The Pardoner's Tale, directly preceding the pilgrims' arrival at Canterbury. The Pardoner's Tale, the last of Pasolini's selected tales from Chaucer, forms a logical choice, as the Pardoner is often seen as a sinful preacher whose hypocrisy contrasts with the virtue of the Parson, and the Parson concludes the tale-telling in Chaucer.

Editing for the final film version, however, turned this order upside down, moving the Merchant from fifth to first and reshuffling other stories as well. Pasolini viewed this editing process as an important last stage of his creation: "Herein lies the exciting mystery of the film. I would like to devote a study to this question because editing *I racconti di Canterbury* has been a mad experience. It had gone through countless combinations before I found that which satisfied me as far as the rhythm was concerned."[22] Just as Chaucer's placement of The Knight's Tale as the lead narrative in the original *Canterbury Tales* was clearly deliberate, so Pasolini understood that what came first would establish the philosophical parameters of his filmic accomplishment. The positioning of The Merchant's Tale as the first of Pasolini's Chaucerian tales is far from a random act, as is sometimes claimed;[23] rather, this tale forcefully raises

---

22. Pasolini, in *Had* 11 (1972), quoted in Agnès Blandeau, *Pasolini, Chaucer, and Boccaccio: Two Medieval Texts and Their Translation to Film* (Jefferson, NC: McFarland, 2006), 12. On pp. 265–66, Blandeau provides a helpful table showing the changes in the order of the tales from Chaucer to the script to the final edited version of Pasolini's film.

23. See, for example, Steve Ellis, *Chaucer at Large: The Poet in the Modern Imagination* (Minneapolis: University of Minnesota Press, 2000), 125. While Pasolini conceded that he could not tell "why the first tale is first rather than seventh, or why the seventh isn't first or third or whatever," in context it is clear that he is not here denying the centrality of these choices but is simply reluctant to articulate his reasons for choosing: "The material did have its own exigencies which I had to learn to understand and adhere to in the editing stage. The choice of tales depended on structural and rhythmic requirements I had to discover for myself" (interview from *Seven Days*, 17 Nov. 1971, in "Pasolini on Film," *Pier Paolo Pasolini*, ed. Willemen, 67–77, 73).

the questions of sexual and epistemological corruption that deeply motivate and inevitably haunt *I racconti*. It is also itself a kind of allegory of authorial tyranny.

The Merchant's Tale launches abruptly with no transition, but its connection to what has just come before should be clear. The dramatist is establishing the setting(s). From our prior location inside the Tabard we find ourselves suddenly within the house of the lecherous old burgher January.[24] The audience may be expected to be confused about where or even whether the scene has changed, until the door opens (stage right) and January descends, speaking lines directly out of his Chaucerian source. The spatial ambiguity opens questions about narrative authority and the relation of tale to frame that this episode is designed to exploit. Played by the very loud and unctuously hirsute Hugh Griffith, January swaggers, or given that his elderly condition requires some propping up, staggers into the hall with the booming announcement that "I have convinced myself that marriage is a Paradise" (cf. Chaucer, *Canterbury Tales* 4.1265).[25] He is a kind of viewpoint totalitarian as we soon realize, for his wealth has afforded him the power to command both the flesh and the imaginations of all who reside within his sway. It will be a full fifteen minutes before any other character's voice is permitted to speak (except for the brother's five-word directive, discussed below, and a priest mumbling Latin blessings over the marriage bed, whom January quickly shuts up)—and then only the pagan god Pluto has the power to break into January's monologue.[26] The film has been utterly swamped by a single speaking voice. This is a startling and dramatic move, especially within the context of the whole. The stark silence of the supporting cast represents a significant intervention into the characteristically noisy arena of voices in Chaucer.

As Pasolini explains, the "gift" and structure of Chaucer's masterpiece was "chatter." While the filmmaker recognized that "chatter can hardly be visualized" and that he would have to "replace it with something else," in the first

---

24. In Chaucer he is identified as a knight (4.1246), but his crassness and the focus on his wealth identify his values, if not his social class, as mercantile.

25. In this locution January surprisingly appropriates free, indirect discourse—a trope valued by Pasolini for its power to conjure up the perspectives of others (see above, note 21)—to the first person. This poetic technique should permit an author to maintain his own perspective while also imaginatively entering into the world of his character, acting as both director and protagonist. January curiously collapses or flattens this double vision, as he seemingly eliminates the need for a distinct narrator (not "he had convinced himself" but "I have convinced myself"). See Pasolini's "Comments on Free Indirect Discourse," in *Heretical Empiricism*, 79–101; and Paolo Fabbri, "Free/Indirect/Discourse," *Pier Paolo Pasolini*, 78–87.

26. The Merchant's Tale begins at 7:58 into the film, and Pluto does not speak until 22:58; in the interim January's is the only voice heard, with the small exceptions noted.

seven minutes of *I racconti* chatter dominates. Even before the first character appears, we hear the pilgrims' voices over the primitive title and introductory credits. We meet them first through their sounds. For nearly the first three minutes, over the credits we hear a buzz of random chatter, dominated by a woman selling roses and culminating in the song of an unknown man. Then we are introduced to a market square of various pilgrims. The camera moves restlessly from one to another, and their voices whisper, gossip, thunder, boast, and overlap with one another in a cacophonous multilogue, which begins to assume shape only when the Host provides an order to the storytelling by setting up its rules. Indeed within these first minutes of *I racconti di Canterbury,* Pasolini makes it very difficult to pick out a dominant speaker; here we have a carnival of truly Bakhtinian voices.

It is all the more shocking, then, to experience the first of Pasolini's tales as a heard event. His will be a "rigid pared-down style," as he explained, compared to his source.[27] Rather than being dialogic at all, this Merchant's Tale, as I've suggested, is entirely dominated by January's voice. Further, January's dictatorial relationship to the narrative that he is essentially writing is not only spoken; it is also highly visual (like a film director's). Indeed, when he steps into the public square to select his bride, his role is somewhat resonant of Pasolini's. Just as Pasolini had done earlier in *I racconti,* or as the pupil of Giotto had done in the *Decameron,* January emerges through a doorway into the market street of the town to select the perfect actress for his domestic drama: "What pretty figures, what pretty faces, my God, my God, what pretty neighbors I have around me. It's only a matter of choosing!" He might as well raise the director's square to his eye when he selects May ("lovely, lovely") as his bride, the visual attractions of her derrière overcoming his initial hesitation at her youth. The decision to cast Geraldine Chaplin, daughter of the famous star of silent film Charlie Chaplin, in the role of May deepens the irony, since as we will see she is variously dominated and silenced—and yet also given voice. (The significance of this choice is confirmed in Pasolini's Cook's Tale, which he described as "a[n] homage to Chaplin."[28])

Throughout Pasolini's tale, January continues to direct, even to subjugate, the scene, presiding over the wedding feast from a dais on high and controlling the pace and timing of the celebration. His "wish to God these guests were long since gone!" is immediately translated into action with his brother's command to the wedding guests, "Stop eating and start dancing!" But the

---

27. Pasolini, "Libertà e sesso secondo Pasolini," *Corriere della Sera* 2.4 (1973), quoted in *A Future Life,* 163 (all quotations in this paragraph and in the one preceding).

28. Pasolini (interview), *Jeune Cinéma,* n.d., n.p. provided in "Pasolini on Film," *Pier Paolo Pasolini,* ed. Willemen, 67–77, 70.

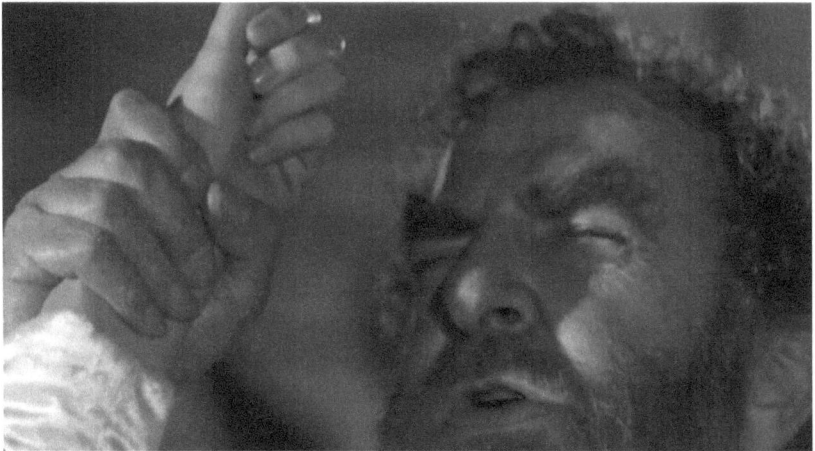

FIGURE 8.2. January clutches May in the "Merchant's Tale," yet his grasp eventually falters in light of her duplicity.

bleakest and most disturbing emblem of this husband's iron grip lies in his literal grasp upon his young wife. Even in sleep his fingers tightly encircle his wife's wrist—as a close-up in the film emphasizes—though none of his efforts prevent May from unwinding his hand, leaving their bed as he snores, and secretly writing her reply to the squire/suitor Damian's love note. All of these oppressions and answering acts of resistance are suggested by Chaucer, where May escapes the marital bed to a privy that affords her the freedom to write. Likewise, Chaucer's January ("That hadde an hand upon hire everemo" [4.2103]) believes that the way to secure his woman when he can no longer monitor her visually is to clasp her to him like a prisoner. So once blinded, Pasolini's January leaves no doubt that he will never allow May out of his physical control: "From now on I hold onto you and never let you go! I can't see you, but I can hold onto you!" His carceral grip is clear in the image in figure 8.2. Even at meals, he keeps her wrist in his fierce grasp. But clearly the more one strives for absolute power like this, the more impossible the quest becomes. Wanting to be left in solitude with "his May," the blind January shrieks, "Get out of my sight!" to the assembled diners in his hall. Although most leave in disgust, Damian stays behind, his disobedient eyes and her wayward lips sending unambiguous messages.

Indeed, well before January loses his sight, there is much in his world that he cannot see and does not control; as in Chaucer, his literal blindness simply confirms a preexisting moral condition. Although still sighted, Pasolini's

January does not observe May and Damian making eyes at each other as early as the wedding feast (Damian's eyes clearly have a greater power than January's).[29] He does not see May's aversion to their lovemaking, as she sticks her tongue out at him comically behind his back (Chaucer similarly draws attention to May's missing subjectivity, "God woot what that May thoughte in hir herte" [4.1851]). A man's eyes cannot be everywhere. Perhaps most significantly, January does not know that Damian and May are communicating through secret notes, for the power of the written word is an alternative to the visual language of the film. In the garden he has created, to which he holds the sole key, he is already the laughable object of the gaze of the gods well before he is deprived of his eyesight. In fact, the instruments of May's confinement—the key to the garden, her spouse's grip on her arm—become devices to enable her liberation, as she resolutely leads January by the hand to the tree where Damian awaits her and as she manipulates his illusion that she is pregnant (also in Chaucer) to persuade him to make his back her stepladder to her lover. This story of a man's attempt to harness the entire world to his own fantasy and desire becomes instead a fable of the impossibility of such control and the disruptive inevitability of the lusts of others. Such a man might be confused with a film director. As Pasolini "repeated many times, . . . it is a film about film, a film conscious of itself."[30]

Yet why would Pasolini kick off *I racconti* with a parable so self-undermining? Some of the reasons may have been personal. During the filming of *I racconti*, Pasolini's biographer tells us, he was a miserable man. In public interviews he described his "spirit [as] anguished": "I was very unhappy when I made the film." In a private letter, he confessed to being "insane with grief." And in poetry written at this time, he pondered suicide and described himself as "a rag of a man."[31] The ostensible reason for his pain was the news that his beloved Ninetto Davoli (featured in many films and as the Cook in *I racconti*) had just given him that he was engaged to be married, an engagement that Pasolini regarded as an unforgivable betrayal. At the same time, Pasolini was enjoying material and financial success beyond anything he had previously experienced in a life that had often been haunted by economic insecurity, and that success itself must have been something of a double-edged

---

29. Can it be a coincidence that he so closely resembles the young Pasolini? See the photo on p. 56 in *Pier Paolo Pasolini*, ed. Willemen.

30. Pasolini, Interview from *Seven Days*, 17 Nov. 1971, in "Pasolini on Film," *Pier Paolo Pasolini*, ed. Willemen, 67–77, 73.

31. Quoted in Schwartz, *Pasolini Requiem*, 587. The newsweekly that published his remarks was *Panorama*, n.d. and n.p.; the letter was to Paolo Volponi; and the poem sequence cited is *L'hobby del eonetto*.

sword. As Maurizio Viano rightly points out, the filmmaker who denounced the "commercialization of sexuality" himself was making quite a pretty profit on it.[32] This bad faith is unlikely to have been lost on Pasolini. But though Pasolini's personal despondency and his sense of his own contamination may have been the bitter wells from which he drank during the creation of *I racconti*, they do not provide a sufficient explanation for the darkness of a film that feels (always) already uncomfortably located inside a series titled the *Trilogia della vita*. Even in the *Decameron*, Pasolini had begun to foreshadow the artistic crisis that would find its fullest expression in *I racconti*, for the *Decameron* already includes a visual citation of Brueghel's famous painting *The Triumph of Death*, possibly a more appropriate title for the film's sequel, in which Pasolini's quest for a utopian origin is most at risk.

In the trilogy Pasolini attempted to find, in a lost preindustrial past, a sense of enchantment associated both with an earlier time and with the common people, the subproletariat—or at least any social class other than the bourgeoisie. He characterized these films as "a fascinating and marvelous experience" in which ideology, while avoiding "escapism," took a back seat to "a pure act of narration."[33] This description returns us to Chaucer/Pasolini's claim that he has told these tales "only for the pleasure of telling them." But in Pasolini's restless and resistant artistic practice, these three films were not only an "experience" but also an "*experiment* [my emphasis] with the ontology of narration, an attempt to engage with the process of rendering a film filmic."[34] And especially in *I racconti*, the film where he most fully identified with the author, Pasolini engaged in a fully self-conscious exploration of metanarrative. Pasolini understood Chaucer as a man who was already transitioning to a modern world with a modern bourgeois mentality. In Chaucer's England, as in Pasolini's Italy, "there was already a contradiction: on the one hand the epic aspects of the work (coarse heroes full of the vitality of the Middle Ages), and on the other hand the irony and self-mockery which are specifically bourgeois phenomena and signs of a bad conscience."[35] Where better to start than with a tale told by that most bourgeois of characters, a merchant, and one that represents a ridiculous old lover run amok, whose gross narrative appetite and hypocritical appropriation of others are condemned by a narrative that reveals the full limitations of his ambition?[36] Just as Chaucer's January consults

---

32. Viano, *A Certain Realism*, 269; see the section titled "A Realism That Failed," 267–73.
33. Interview from *Seven Days*, 17 Nov. 1971, in "Pasolini on Film," 77.
34. Interview from *Seven Days*, 77.
35. Interview from *Seven Days*, 71.
36. Of course, at the same time, that irony redeems the very art that it condemns. Interestingly, Chaucer's Merchant's Tale has been also a locus of narratorial problematics, as the voice

his dreaming imagination in the search for a wife, "As whoso tooke a mirour, polisshed bryght, / And sette it in a commune market-place" (4.1582–83), so Pasolini holds a mirror up to Chaucer and finds that same marketplace with the reflection of himself at its center. That act of vision is at once redemptive and culpable.

In the final analysis, it is impossible to determine where exactly Pasolini comes out in his exploration of the problematics of authorship in *I racconti di Canterbury*. As he described it, the making of this film was "*consciously* a game alternating irony and pity, superimposing one upon the other."[37] There is joy and beauty in his rendition of Chaucer's playful tales. Yet these bawdy jokes are also cruel, and as we have seen in the presentation of the old, foolish January, who can be seen as a dark surrogate to the filmmaker himself, they do not reflect well on either the man or his art. But Pasolini's engagement with Chaucer was profound. In the act of remaking himself in the fourteenth-century poet's image, he conveyed something of himself and of his source that students of both poets should learn to appreciate better than they have. He may also, in the process of making it, have rid himself of some of his demons—those "alibis of conscience" that plague the bourgeois sensibility as he defined it[38]—for the *Il fiore delle mille e una notte,* the film that would follow, conveys a candid, innocent sweetness that is very un-Chaucerian. Still, perhaps, to borrow another metaphor from the marketplace, Chaucer was the price of admission.

---

of the Merchant who tells the tale is often, perhaps deliberately, to be confused with the voice of its merchant protagonist. The tale is told by a man who claims to be disappointed in marriage about a marriage that is itself disappointing, leading critics around the time that Pasolini was making his film to interpret the subject matter as a reflection on the teller. C. David Benson summarizes and argues against this kind of "dramatic reading" in *Chaucer's Drama of Style: Poetic Variety and Contrast in the* Canterbury Tales (Chapel Hill: University of North Carolina Press, 1986), 14–17. Although more recent readers have avoided the most naive conflations of narrator with character (with author), a more common approach in recent criticism has been to see the tale as reflecting mercantile values rather than the narrator's marital misery, an alternative conflation of narrative concerns that equally complicates the role of the narrator and the characters he "creates." See, for example, Christian Sheridan, "May in the Marketplace: Commodification and Textuality in The Merchant's Tale," *Studies in Philology* 102 (2005): 27–44.

    37. Pasolini, "Pasolini sur son film," *Jeune Cinéma* 68 (1973), quoted in *A Future Life*, 163.

    38. Pasolini, "C'est le Décameron qui m'a choisi," *La Galérie* 3 (1971): 88, quoted in *A Future Life*, 153.

CHAPTER 9

"SORRY, CHAUCER"

Mixed Feelings and Hyapatia Lee's Ribald Tales of Canterbury

GEORGE SHUFFELTON

THE PORNOGRAPHIC FILM *The Ribald Tales of Canterbury* (1985) necessarily occupies an especially strange place in any discussion of Chaucer's absence and/or presence in modern film. Its existence has only rarely been acknowledged by scholarship.[1] The film has largely disappeared from view, though its recent rerelease as a DVD ensures that it will continue to live on, if not quite in public consciousness, then on Internet discussion boards. But the film's unusual contribution to any consideration of Chaucer's absence or presence in modern film does not ultimately derive from its status as pornography. As I will argue in the second half of this essay, its most distinctive trait is its deliberate and thorough feminine displacement of Chaucer's male authority. The film celebrates a nostalgic and entirely conventional version of medieval bawdy while simultaneously rejecting the imprint of Chaucerian masculinity: thus the "mixed feelings" of my title and the two-sided nature of the argument that follows.

•

---

1. Prior to my brief discussion of the film in "Chaucer's Obscenity in the Court of Public Opinion," *Chaucer Review* 47 (2012): 1–24, the only other mention of it known to me is a brief note by Steve Ellis, *Chaucer at Large: The Poet in the Modern Imagination* (Minneapolis: University of Minnesota Press, 2000), 190, note 2.

FIGURE 9.1. Cover image of *The Ribald Tales of Canterbury*. Film originally distributed by Caballero Home Video. Photo by author.

The Ribald Tales of Canterbury runs approximately ninety minutes and was directed by Bud Lee (see figure 9.1). His wife at the time, Hyapatia Lee (née Victoria Lynch), serves as both star and screenwriter. Few other precise details about the film's production history are available, beyond the brief comments about it made by Hyapatia Lee in her 2000 autobiography.[2] The pornographic film industry is notoriously secretive and unreliable in reporting its budgets, revenues, or other details of production history, but based on Hyapatia Lee's claim that the film cost $300,000 to produce, it is often cited as one of the most expensive pornographic films ever made.[3]

The film's connection to Chaucer's *Canterbury Tales* is both direct and oblique in equal measures. The frame narrative remains largely intact. The film opens with a crane shot of a boisterous meal at an inn, and the first scene ends with six pilgrims (the Hostess, the Knight, the Lady of Bath, the Miller, the Carpenter, and the Monk) pledging to engage in a storytelling contest on their way to Canterbury. After an interlude at the inn featuring a sex scene between the Carpenter and a "tavern girl," the next scene begins the following morning as the pilgrims set out. The Knight tells the first tale, after the Hostess prevents the Monk from beginning the journey with a sermon. The drunken Miller then attempts to tell the next tale but is disallowed by the other pilgrims, and instead the next storyteller is the Carpenter, who tells what is clearly an adaptation of Chaucer's Reeve's Tale. The pilgrims rest for the night (and for more sex), and the next day features The Lady of Bath's Tale followed by The Hostess's Tale. The pilgrims then arrive in Canterbury, where two pairs have sex with each other and where the Monk—in the film's closing scene—receives oral sex from another "tavern girl" in a setting identical to that of the first scene.

With the exception of the aforementioned Reeve's Tale, none of the inset episodes of *The Ribald Tales* appear directly connected to the *Canterbury Tales*, but the Chaucerian text has clearly shaped the film in a variety of other ways that go beyond the narrative outlines of the pilgrimage and the storytelling game. Indeed, in certain respects, *The Ribald Tales* is one of the most steadfastly conventional adaptations ever made of the *Canterbury Tales*. The film adheres in almost every way to the conventions of mainstream pornographic film, a genre that is itself rigorously conservative. The camera work, the acting, the restricted use of dialogue, and the tone (oscillating between smirking sexual innuendo and earnest sexual directives) will all be familiar to anyone who has seen any pornographic film from the 1970s or 1980s. *The Ribald Tales* also adheres to fundamental aspects of Chaucer's tales: the episodic structure of the *Canterbury Tales* lends itself well to the episodic format of mainstream pornographic film, just as Chaucer's tale-telling game and the confessional

---

2. Hyapatia Lee, *The Secret Lives of Hyapatia Lee* (1st Book Library, 2000), 102–3.
3. Daniel Comiskey, "The Naked Truth," *Indianapolis Monthly* (Mar. 2008): 120–38. Even adjusting for inflation, the claim would seem to have little basis in fact, and various subsequent films have reportedly involved much larger budgets.

tendency of his pilgrims to reveal aspects of themselves in their tales fit well with pornography's fondness for "true confessions" of the Penthouse Forum variety. *The Ribald Tales* takes advantage of this in multiple ways. For example, the story told by the Knight is presented as straightforwardly autobiographical, and the actor (listed in the credits as Mike Horner) who plays the pilgrim Knight plays himself in his tale.

Beyond its format as a collection of short narratives, the diversity of the *Canterbury Tales* also translates easily into the (carefully limited) diversity of sexual permutations expected in pornography. Where Chaucer gives us romance, fabliau, saint's life, and tragedy, *The Ribald Tales* gives us boy-girl, girl-girl, orgy, two-on-one, and all the other standard geometries of the mainstream (i.e., heteronormative) pornographic lexicon. Readers may not recall any moment in the *Canterbury Tales* in which a black serving man has sex with an upper-class white woman, but when *The Ribald Tales* gives us exactly that, it is an entirely logical concession to the typical expectations of porn. Chaucer's plenitude of plots suits the porn film's need for variation.

To push the comparison further, one could argue that in 1985 nothing more closely resembled the insistent vernacularity of Chaucer's popularizing medium more than the feature-length pornographic film, with its correspondingly wide distribution across boundaries of class and its resulting influence on both "high" and "low" cultural forms in its wake. While the cultural position of Chaucer's Middle English verse may not have been the same as "pornography's position at the very bottom of the very lowest rungs of the cultural hierarchy," both media occupy a broadly similar, dubious place in their respective worlds.[4] From this angle, *The Ribald Tales* sits much closer to the *Canterbury Tales* in its fundamental similarities than many more ostensibly faithful and/or high-minded adaptations before or since. If one considers that a BBC miniseries or children's picture book must make significant formal compromises to present Chaucerian narratives as legible to modern audiences, then the adaptations involved in turning Chaucer's work into porn seem straightforward by comparison.

The Ribald Tales cannot be called a spoof, but the film nonetheless marches alongside similar pornographic parodies that take famous literary works as their starting point. Naturally, Shakespeare can claim the greatest number of pornographic spinoffs, and the titles of his plays have provided ample opportunity for puns and innuendo.[5] But Chaucer's work generated its own

---

4. Laura Kipnis, "Pornography," *Film Studies: Critical Approaches*, ed. John Hill and Pamela Church Gibson (Oxford: Oxford University Press, 2000), 151–55, 153.

5. Among Shakespeareans, Richard Burt has written most extensively about these films; see his *Unspeakable ShaXXXpeares: Queer Theory and American Kiddie Culture* (New York: St. Martin's, 1998), 77–126.

series of soft-core 1970s films, which traded on the reputation of the tales for "bawdy." The attention garnered by Pasolini's *I racconti di Canterbury* provided a winning formula for pornographers: ample sex accompanied by literary pretensions, historical costumes, and art-film touches. The results were numerous cheap, soft-core pornographic knockoffs made across Europe and the United States, such as *I racconti di Canterbury numero 2* (released in the United States as "The Lusty Wives of Canterbury"), *Gli altri racconti di Canterbury*, and *Canterbury proibito*.⁶ In these and other film titles, "Decameron" and "Canterbury" took on the role of code words hinting at pornographic spectacle, rather like the function of words *sexy* or *lusty* in pornographic films today. In some cases, the word *Canterbury* was even used in international releases of Italian films that had not originally contained the word. So *Sollazzevoli storie di mogli gaudenti e mariti penitenti* became *More Sexy Canterbury Tales*, and the French release of *Le mille e una notte all'italiana* was titled *Canterbury interdit*. The latter film's title not only follows this tradition of using *Canterbury* as a code word for light-hearted sex, but it also apparently imitates an earlier medieval-themed sex comedy, *The Ribald Tales of Robin Hood* (1969).⁷

Released in 1985, *The Ribald Tales of Canterbury* comes at the end of this era of quasi-medieval erotica. The *translatio imperii* from European soft core to American hard core was virtually complete. Also nearly over was the prominence of the feature-length, 35mm pornographic film. Within a few years the pornographic film industry shifted almost entirely to video. Adult movie houses closed, and the direct-to-consumer model (achieved through the VHS rental market), with its emphasis on cheap, quickly made videos released in rapid succession, made elaborate productions like *The Ribald Tales* increasingly rare.⁸ Caballero Control Corporation, the company that produced the film, was also one of the pioneers in this rapidly expanding VHS market and seems to have shifted resources away from feature films like Lee's.

For these reasons the film looks like it might have been produced in 1980, or 1975, but could never be attributed to the 1990s. Given the trends in pornography that emerged after 1985, the film seems especially obsolete.⁹ The

---

6. See Kathleen Forni's essay in this volume, "Profit, Politics, and Prurience," for additional perspective on the pornographic "franchise" generated by Pasolini's film.

7. This film, apparently made in both the United States and West Germany, appeared under several other titles (e.g., *The Erotic Adventures of Robin Hood*) as well; consult its entry at imdb.com.

8. For an account of this shift in the market, see Chuck Kleinhans, "The Change from Film to Video Pornography: Implications for Analysis," *Pornography: Film and Culture*, ed. Peter Lehman (New Brunswick, NJ: Rutgers University Press, 2006), 154–67. See also the essays by Penley and Schaefer, cited below, notes 9 and 15.

9. Constance Penley has argued that "as porn films 'progressed' as film, technically and narratively, and began to focus on the woman and her subjectivity, they became more socially

"amateur" and "gonzo" porn of the last two decades, with their emphasis on gritty production values and ferocious sexual aggression, make Bud and Hyapatia Lee's film seem gentle and innocent by comparison. The profuse body hair and unenhanced physiognomy of the actors and actresses in *The Ribald Tales* markedly contrasts with the plasticized bodies of contemporary porn. While the film makes regular use of "meat shots"—that is, the close-ups of genital penetration customary to pornography—the body parts on display here look natural.[10] The bodies in twenty-first-century pornography have often been altered by silicone implants, cosmetic surgery, peroxide hair treatments, and (according to accounts of male performers' habits) anabolic steroids. In contrast, this film's many orifices, breasts, and genitalia are unmistakably human, neither sanitized nor grotesque. In contemporary porn, such homely bodies might be featured in "amateur" porn and subject to grainy pseudo-realism. But the mode of *The Ribald Tales* is conventional fantasy, from the costumes (tunics, robes, etc.) to the camerawork (professional and clinical). What the film offers is a decidedly premodern sexual reverie, when everyone had pubic hair and no one visited tanning booths.

In most outward respects the film also obeys the usual dictates of Hollywood medievalism, without the kind of ironic "neomedievalism" of later films such as *A Knight's Tale* (2001) or *Black Knight* (2001). Characters speak in a mongrel approximation of Middle English that critics have labeled "eth-ness," a mix of old-fashioned vocabulary (*drunken sot, harlot*), inverted syntax, and frequent use of the old forms of second-person pronouns ("What say ye?").[11] Even those tunics and robes are quite literally borrowings from an earlier era of Hollywood medievalism: Hyapatia Lee reports that they were taken from the wardrobe for *Camelot* (Joshua Logan, 1967), an adaptation of the famous Broadway production.[12]

It is not simply the costumes, the language, or the scenes on horseback that render the film antiquated; it also makes ample use of outdoor settings in a vaguely Mediterranean-looking landscape, bathed in soft natural light.

---

conservative as they lost the bawdy populist humor whose subject matter was so often the follies and foibles of masculinity" ("Crackers and Whackers: The White Trashing of Porn," *Pornography: Film and Culture*, 99–117, 108).

10. Linda Williams, *Hard Core: Power, Pleasure, and the "Frenzy of the Visible"* (Berkeley: University of California Press, 1989), 72–73.

11. Carol O'Sullivan, "A Time of Translation: Linguistic Difference and Cinematic Medievalism," *Medieval Film*, ed. Anke Bernau and Bettina Bildhauer (Manchester: Manchester University Press, 2009), 63. See also Richard Osberg and Michael Crow, "Language Then and Language Now in Arthurian Film," *King Arthur in Film: New Essays in Arthurian Cinema*, ed. Kevin J. Harty (Jefferson, NC: McFarland, 1999), 39–66.

12. Lee, *Secret Lives*, 102.

Unlike many post-Bergman film versions of the Middle Ages, there is no fog, mud, or other gloomy weather.¹³ Although some of the film was shot in Scotland, the Californian climate prevails.¹⁴ The sun shines, and the pilgrims traverse grassy downs with nary a hovel or a muddy track in sight. When the Knight and the Carpenter have told their tales, night falls with a lovely orange sunset and birds flocking to roost. The pilgrims sit around a campfire outside their tents, in a scene that gently evokes the genre of the Western, before the Hostess and the Lady of Bath retire for some well-lit sex inside their tent. The Dark Ages this is not.

All of this contributes to a sense that *The Ribald Tales* comes from some pastoral golden age, neither medieval nor fully modern. Indeed, many histories of the porn industry refer to the 1970s and early 1980s as the "golden age" of pornography, when porn stars became well known and porn seemed cloaked in the romance of counterculture adventure. *Boogie Nights* (dir. Paul Thomas Anderson, 1997) and many other popular representations of this era tell a similar story: before AIDS, drugs, and the radical economic upheavals created by VHS rentals ruined the production model and many of the lives of its producers, the porn industry had artistic ambitions (or at least pretensions) and a sense of an artistic community. Subsequent scholarship has not significantly changed this history of the genre, except to point out that this "golden age" now seems like a brief aberration in the longer history of pornography, as Eric Schaefer argues:

> What has become increasingly evident is that the feature-length hard-core narrative constituted merely an entr'acte between reels of essentially plotless underground stag movies in the years 1908 to 1967 and the similarly plotless ruttings of porn in the video age (emerging in the mid-1980s and continuing in the present).¹⁵

Like all golden ages, this one now seems improbably distant, a subject for nostalgia and thoughts of what might have been. The film thus embodies a now

---

13. On the use of filth and fog to signify the Middle Ages in film, see Laurie Finke and Martin B. Shichtman, *Cinematic Illuminations: The Middle Ages on Film* (Baltimore, MD: Johns Hopkins University Press, 2010), 48–49.

14. Hyapatia Lee's autobiography notes that the film was shot over nine days in the United States and two in Scotland, but "Because of the legal ramifications, only non-sex scenes could be shot abroad" (Lee, *Secret Lives*, 102). Lee's account of the filming is the only one I have found, but the Internet Movie Database lists Petaluma, California, as the location.

15. Eric Schaefer, "Gauging a Revolution: 16mm Film and the Rise of the Pornographic Feature," *Porn Studies*, ed. Linda Williams (Durham: Duke University Press, 2004), 370–400, 371.

well-recognized form of atemporality or asynchrony.¹⁶ But this is not simply because its Middle Ages are an ahistorical fantasy but also because the film itself is the product of a lost moment outside the historical arc of pornography and modern film.

In the age of the Internet, when pornography takes the form of thousands of short clips and grainy webcam spectacles, the grand aspirations and traditional narrative of *The Ribald Tales* seem like narrative relics from a distant past. The era of *The Ribald Tales* may not seem exactly closer to Chaucer's than our own, but the film nonetheless appears as quaint as taverns, jousting, or minstrels. The commitment of films like *The Ribald Tales* to storytelling, dialogue, and the conventions of plot now looks like a short-lived concession to the expectations of "serious" film. After the golden age ended, the porn industry found it no longer needed to make these concessions, and their fragmentary, disposable products of the later 1980s and 1990s took "porn back into a format that is more closely aligned with many of its heterogeneous and fleeting moments of pleasure," that is, non-narrative or loosely narrative fragments that do not strenuously attempt to resemble traditional forms of storytelling.¹⁷

Each of the scenes in *The Ribald Tales* features an entirely conventional plot, albeit one that aims to include as many opportunities for sex as possible. This is most evident in the tales that do not take Chaucer's tales as their starting point. For example, the Knight begins his tale by recalling a time when he had been poor and deprived of his inheritance by his older brothers. Riding in the countryside, he comes across a young abbot escorted by an older monk on a journey to see the Pope. The three join company, and when they share lodgings in the evening, the abbot reveals herself to be a woman in disguise and joins the Knight in his bed. In a voice-over at the conclusion of the sex scene, the Knight declares that the young woman turned out to be the daughter of the King of England, pledged to "the Heir of Flanders." Although the time allotted to the plot of this tale (two minutes) may be insignificant in comparison to the sex scene at its center (ten minutes), it is clearly a familiar model of romance, featuring a lowly knight earning the love of a wealthy heiress, as well as common elements of medieval romance such as the idea of disguised identity and the hero's quest to restore his displaced family.

---

16. Bettina Bildhauer and Anke Bernau, "Introduction: The A-chronology of Medieval Film," *Medieval Film*, ed. Bernau and Bildhauer, 1–19. For a wider-ranging consideration of atemporality and medievalism, see Carolyn Dinshaw, *How Soon Is Now? Medieval Texts, Amateur Readers, and the Queerness of Time* (Durham: Duke University Press, 2012).

17. Peter Lehman, "Revelations about Pornography," *Pornography*, 87–98, 91.

The conventions of romance also govern the sense of closure offered by the film. Like so many adaptations of the *Canterbury Tales*, the film obliges viewers with an arrival in Canterbury. But it takes this satisfaction one step further by uniting the two most likeable pilgrims—the Knight and the Hostess—in a final sex scene that culminates the meaningful, flirtatious glances they exchange at various stages along the way. If this is not exactly the Right Boy ending up with the Right Girl in the usual way (there is absolutely no suggestion of marriage), it nonetheless offers modern viewers a conventional romance structure for what might otherwise be merely unconnected episodes.

In every outward respect, *The Ribald Tales* thus seems not only conventional but also conservative. Richard Burt suggests that pornographic adaptations of Shakespeare have worked "to undo the romantic couple and the institution of marriage" and "give reign to a sexual pornotopia, including gay and lesbian sex and even incest, rather than uphold heteronormative sexuality."[18] No such radicalism would appear to be at work in this Chaucerian world. Although the film satirizes Christian piety and its fear of the flesh, and does not promote marriage, it never strays from fantasies familiar to Burt's sense of heteronormative sexuality. In its nostalgia and thoroughgoing adherence to traditional forms of narrative, as well as in its indebtedness to both Hollywood medievalism and conventional pornographic aesthetics, *The Ribald Tales* is neither a subversive nor surprising exercise in adaptation.

However, *The Ribald Tales of Canterbury* constitutes a radical departure in a few essential respects, and in its own way the film documents not only a Chaucerian absence but also a brave negation of Chaucerian authority. To begin with, Chaucer appears only once in the film, as a name in the opening credits that tell us the film is "Based on an Adaptation of the Novel by Geoffrey Chaucer." The redundant double displacement ("Based on an Adaptation") emphasizes Chaucer's removal from the project. At no other point is Chaucer invoked, and his name seems to be largely absent from the promotional material for the film. He appears neither as a voice-over narrator (as in the BBC animated *Canterbury Tales*) nor as a prologue. Unlike other forms of Chaucerania, such as Powell and Pressburger's 1944 film *A Canterbury Tale*, this film makes no attempt to refer to the textuality of its source.[19] Only the Monk has a book, and his learning seems to be a hypocritical veneer of piety rather than any proof that he has hundreds of "olde textes" in his cell. Nor is there any moment of writing in the film. The obvious contrast is with

---

18. Burt, *ShaXXXpeares*, 82.
19. See the description of *A Canterbury Tale*'s opening sequence in Tison Pugh's essay in this volume.

Pasolini's *I racconti di Canterbury* in which brief scenes of a Chaucer (Pasolini) writing his work are interspersed with the film's episodes, reminding us of a very different connection between author, auteur, and *auctoritas*.

The film's real author is never in doubt: from the opening title to the closing credits, this is "Hyapatia Lee's *Ribald Tales of Canterbury*." Hyapatia Lee is credited as the screenwriter, and as the Hostess she governs the film's action in all important respects. The film opens with a crane shot of the feast at the tavern, as a large group of guests enjoys a raucous meal of iconic medieval food (cue the boar's head) and drink as they grope and leer at each other. Although the characters we will soon recognize as the Carpenter, the Miller, and the Lady of Bath are given the first speaking lines, the scene is one of joyous anarchy until the Hostess silences the crowd. She proposes the storytelling game, and the narrative is set in motion. Lee's Hostess also tells a tale of her own later in the film, and at every step of the way she directs the pilgrims without any contestation of her authority. Chaucer's Host is an unsteady would-be despot: subject to various indignities from rebellious pilgrims, carefully deferring to the *gentils*, and (as he eventually reveals) under the yoke of his wife. Harry Bailly's authority is compromised in every respect, not least by the shadowy presence of his own author. No such limits appear to constrain Hyapatia Lee's Hostess, who reigns benevolently over her *compagnye* with the confidence that she is the star of the show she has written.

Hyapatia Lee's autobiography provides an illuminating, if brief and elliptical, version of the film's origins. Having only recently moved from a career in strip clubs to pornographic film beginning in 1983, Lee describes meeting a film producer in Lansing, Michigan, who can be identified as strip-club impresario Harry Mohney with reasonable confidence.[20] After several successful porn films—*Body Girls* and *Let's Get Physical*—Lee and her husband Bud had fully entered the California-based porn business, and this in turn elevated her status on the nationwide circuit of strip clubs. According to Lee, "I was in my own little heaven," and she clearly felt newly empowered to make her own career decisions within the porn industry.[21] Lee then approached Harry Mohney about making a film based on her script about a radio DJ. He agreed

---

20. Lee never mentions "Harry's" last name, and given that she acknowledges changing names for various people mentioned in her autobiography, it is possible that this is a pseudonym for an otherwise unmentioned pornographic impresario. But *The Secret Lives of Hyapatia Lee* first describes him as "Gail Palmer's boyfriend," and Bud and Hyapatia meet "Harry" at a strip club in Lansing, Michigan (64). These two details strongly suggest that this is Harry Mohney, a porn distributor now primarily known for his large network of Déjà Vu strip clubs; see Tom Horgan and Jennifer Bjorhus, "The King of Clubs," *Minneapolis Star Tribune*, 19 Jul. 2011; web.

21. Lee, *Secret Lives*, 101–2.

to make the film, "if [Lee] would write the movie he had always wanted to do, *The Ribald Tales of Canterbury*." In Lee's account, this follows naturally from Mohney's ambition:

> When we first met him, [Mohney] did not consider making X-rated movies an art.... [But] doing these two movies [i.e., *Body Girls* and *Let's Get Physical*] had helped him to have pride in his work. They were socially responsible movies, with a real plot and character development, not your average "pizza delivery boy gets laid instead of paid" scenes.[22]

The origins of *The Ribald Tales* thus begin with male fantasy and as a concession to the conventional authority of male producers within the world of pornography. Also fundamental to this aim is a kind of conventional envy of "high" art on the part of pornographers. "Real plot and character development" assume greater importance than the pragmatic concerns of erotic pleasure. As a female porn star whose acts on film must balance these two competing demands for both pleasure and respectability, Lee would seem an unlikely figure for artistic independence.

But once Harry Mohney set the film in motion, Hyapatia Lee's desires apparently took some control of the project, and the respect for conventional authority was slowly displaced by other motives:

> I started to research the book. If you have ever read "The Canterbury Tales," you know that it does not treat women with respect and they are not in positions of power. Wives and daughters are considered property and there is even a rape scene in it. I refused to reflect this in my version, so I had to do a major rewrite. Sorry, Chaucer.[23]

As literary criticism, Lee's conclusions are certainly subject to argument: depending on how one counts, there are either several "rape scenes" in the *Canterbury Tales* or none at all, and one might also contest the claim that women *never* occupy positions of power. But the larger implications of her reading are entirely in keeping with an important strain of 1980s Chaucer criticism, a feminist critique that may be said to culminate in Elaine Tuttle Hansen's 1992 *Chaucer and the Fictions of Gender*.[24] While some feminist

---

22. Lee, *Secret Lives*, 101.
23. Lee, *Secret Lives*, 102.
24. Elaine Tuttle Hansen, *Chaucer and the Fictions of Gender* (Berkeley: University of California Press, 1992).

scholarship of the late 1970s and 1980s argued that Chaucer's female characters represent his powerful response to conventional patriarchal sexism, others insisted on Chaucer's complicity with this sexism.[25] If Hyapatia Lee's response seems a little naïve ("there is even a rape scene in it"), it is nonetheless justifiable. Hansen's *Chaucer and the Fictions of Gender* reaches a broadly similar conclusion and so have many subsequent reappraisals of feminist theory and Chaucer's tales.[26] If this particular kind of feminist reading has ceded ground to queer readings and broader considerations of gender in Chaucer's work, it is primarily because these later modes have subsumed the practices of earlier feminisms.[27] And subsequent scholarly analysis of Chaucer's depiction of sex has found it to be just as dark and disturbing—filled with "cutting, stabbing, bleeding, and dying"—as Hyapatia Lee apparently did.[28]

Lee's rejection of Chaucer also resembles a nearly contemporary moment when the worlds of Chaucer, pornography, and 1980s feminism intersected. In the early 1980s, feminist activist/scholars Andrea Dworkin and Catherine MacKinnon launched a series of attempts to restrict pornography on the grounds of civil rights (rather than the more traditional grounds of moral turpitude). One of the most famous of these attempts was the Minneapolis Civil Rights Ordinance proposed in 1983. This ordinance was debated in public hearings before the city council and featured testimony from rape survivors, social scientists, and activists. In the midst of the hearings, Rick Osborne, a member of the Minnesota Commission on Civil Rights, raised several objections to the proposed ordinance, specifically to its prohibition of "graphically depicted" and "sexually explicit" material that "subordinates women" and portrays them as enjoying sexual submission. Osborne suggested that Chaucer's Wife of Bath's Tale could easily fall under such a prohibition:

> It is possible that somebody can try and bring an action against the Commission [on Civil Rights] for the following materials: from Geoffrey Chaucer,

---

25. The different tracks of feminist readings of Chaucer may be familiar to Chaucerians but less so to others. For important early feminist readings that view Chaucer as criticizing the gender politics of his world, see Mary Carruthers, "The Wife of Bath and the Painting of Lions," *PMLA* 94 (1979): 209–22; and the later versions of a series of influential articles by H. Marshall Leicester, *The Disenchanted Self: Representing the Subject in the* Canterbury Tales (Berkeley: University of California Press, 1990).

26. Ethan Knapp, "Chaucer Criticism and Its Legacies," *The Yale Companion to Chaucer*, ed. Seth Lerer (New Haven: Yale University Press, 2006), 324–58, 349–50.

27. Glenn Burger, "Gender and Sexuality," *Chaucer: Contemporary Approaches*, ed. Susanna Fein and David Raybin (University Park: Pennsylvania State University Press, 2010), 179–98.

28. W. W. Allman and D. Thomas Hanks, "Rough Love: Towards an Erotics of the *Canterbury Tales*," *Chaucer Review* 38 (2003): 36–65.

The Wife of Bath's Tale, "He took her in his arms and kissed her, overcome with joy. Thereafter she obeyed him in everything that might add to his bliss, and thus they lived for the rest of their lives in perfect happiness." It is sexual.... She is definitely subordinate.... By someone's definition that she is being treated as an object, a thing, or a commodity, it might mean that she is being presented in a posture of sexual submission, because we don't know what Geoffrey Chaucer means, when she is overcome with joy.[29]

This hypothetical reading seems closely aligned with Hyapatia Lee's interpretation: Chaucer's women are objectified by their subordination to men's sexual desires. Osborne goes on to suggest that by this same legal definition, a particularly abhorrent cover of the pornographic magazine *Hustler* would *not* be subject to the same restrictions that might prohibit The Wife of Bath's Tale. Osborne's larger point is effectively the opposite of Hyapatia Lee's—he rejects the Civil Rights Ordinance because its vagaries would censor Chaucer—but both take a similar counterperspective on Chaucer's sexual politics. Viewed from a certain angle, Chaucer's work looks more regressive and misogynist than some widely reviled twentieth-century pornography.

Lee's reaction to the *Canterbury Tales* upends a long-standing tradition of celebrating Chaucer's premodern "bawdy" as a counter to the degradations of modern pornography. This tradition has typically used Chaucer's work as a standard to define the limits of obscenity and to demarcate unacceptable forms of pornographic representation.[30] Osborne's comments are recognizably part of this legal and scholarly tradition, whose proponents have mostly been men. And it seems reasonable to assume that the original premise for *The Ribald Tales*, as voiced by "Harry," the producer who gave Hyapatia Lee the idea for the film, was a broadly similar desire to legitimize pornography on the basis of Chaucer's authority. But Lee's reaction heads off in an altogether different direction, *preferring* her own pornographic enterprise to Chaucer's, and refusing to use his authority to justify her own.

Viewing *The Ribald Tales of Canterbury* as a rejection of Chaucer's authority and as a celebration of female authority ends up making sense of Lee's otherwise puzzling choices. Foremost among these is the rejection of all the fabliaux other than The Reeve's Tale as source material for the film. The Merchant's Tale might seem a surprising omission from any pornographic adaptation, since it features multiple sex scenes and scopic precision worthy

---

29. Catharine A. MacKinnon and Andrea Dworkin, eds., *In Harm's Way: The Pornography Civil Rights Hearings* (Cambridge: Harvard University Press, 1997), 85–86.
30. For the outlines of this tradition, see my "Chaucer's Obscenity," 1–24.

of any pornographic film. January's vision of May's tryst in the pear tree ("Ye, algate in it went!" [4.2376]) accords well with Linda Williams's suggestion that the "frenzy of the visible" characterizes pornography's obsession with genital penetration, performed female orgasm, and ejaculation.[31] But Hyapatia Lee has not used it as a source for the film, perhaps because The Merchant's Tale features both an unsympathetic heroine and an underlying tone of male cynicism.

Even more remarkable is Lee's decision not to use The Miller's Tale, surely most readers' choice as a particularly memorable example of Chaucer's bawdy. And in this case, it is not a silent omission but a deliberate rejection. As in the *Canterbury Tales*, the Miller of *The Ribald Tales* boorishly inserts himself into the order of storytelling after the Knight has told the first story. But in *The Ribald Tales* he is successfully silenced—not by the *gentils*, but by the Hostess herself. Dennis Dugan, the actor playing the Miller, bears a much closer resemblance to a fat, middle-aged, and bearded Chaucer (i.e., the Chaucer of late-medieval portraiture) than he does to the "thikke knarre" of The General Prologue (1.549). If Lee is conflating Chaucer with one of his most famous surrogate narrators, it is a conflation that many readers might agree with. But if so, she makes the association to punctuate her rejection of Chaucer's authority. Her Miller is systematically punished at every turn.

The audience is invited to dislike the Miller in the film's opening scene before we know who he is. Watching one of the tavern revelers grope and kiss a serving woman, he protests, "How disgusting!" But the Lady of Bath sitting next to him retorts, "Well, it certainly seems to have gotten a rise out of you," at which point the camera pans down to reveal a bulging erection as proof of his hypocrisy. A few minutes later, after the Hostess proposes the storytelling game, the Miller boasts that he will certainly win, with condescending arrogance rather than the (arguably) lovable bravado of Chaucer's "janglere and a goliardeys" (1.560). Once again, the Lady of Bath warns of comeuppance, and the Miller is decisively cast as the one character in this film whom we are expected to root against. Plenty of Chaucer's readers have rejected the Miller and his tale without rejecting Chaucer himself, but for Lee that seems to be precisely what we are meant to do.

After the Knight completes his tale, the Miller—drinking heavily—boasts that he has a better one to follow. The Hostess rejects him in terms that directly adapt Chaucer's text: "You're too drunk to tell your tale now. Leave a better man to tell his tale now. Pipe down until you've recovered your wits" (cf. 1.3129–31). But in this exchange the Hostess prevails, and her suggestion

---

31. Williams, *Hard Core*, 93–94, and *passim*.

that he cede to a "better man" goes unchallenged by the Miller. The roles of the exchange between the Carpenter and Miller are then swapped, so that when the Carpenter is given the privilege of telling the next tale and announces that his story involves a miller of "Oxenford," it is the Miller who takes offense, with a sense of defamation that clearly resembles Oswald the Reeve's protest (1.3144–48). This Miller is both boorish *and* touchy, a combination of the worst traits of Chaucer's Miller and Reeve. And he is also powerless: the pilgrims quickly shout down his interruptions, and the Carpenter is given free rein.

The Miller's humiliation is then fully confirmed by The Carpenter's Tale, a reworking of The Reeve's Tale, with the actor playing the Miller also playing Simkin. And in keeping with Hyapatia Lee's refusal to portray women as "property" or as the victims of rape, both Simkin's daughter and his wife initiate sex with the visiting students, Alan and John. They take pity on the students during Simkin's theft of the grain while the young men chase down their horse, and the resulting dinner is a wonderfully ludicrous feast of flirtatious eating. Simkin's wife luridly pantomimes fellatio with a loaf of bread, and the students respond with what must be the first filmed evocation of cunnilingus with chicken wings. Only Simkin seems unaware of the erotic bacchanal around him, and when his daughter and then his wife end up in a four-way orgy later that night, no bed trick is needed. Instead, Simkin's wife sneaks out of her husband's bed when she hears the fun in the next room. The episode does not end with violence (as it does in Chaucer's Reeve's Tale) but with Simkin tripping and falling flat on his face, allowing the students to escape; the inept husband is not even granted the mock heroism of a violent struggle for his family's honor. As John and Alan flee, and as Simkin lies prostrate and groaning on the floor, the women laugh. The conclusion thus effects a double humiliation: of Simkin, as the patriarchal ogre who would seek to control his women; and of the Miller, who would subvert the *jouissance* of storytelling for his own egotistical ends. Later in the film the Miller makes a final bid to tell a story, but the Hostess silences him once again: the pilgrims have arrived at Canterbury and it is now too late.

Pornography before and after *The Ribald Tales of Canterbury* hardly shies away from fantasies of rape and reluctant women, but as the revision of The Reeve's Tale demonstrates, this film insistently puts women in charge of their own bodies. Good men, such as the Knight, are saved by women (such as the "princess" disguised as an abbot who rescues him from poverty), and the bad husbands are humiliated. When the Lady of Bath tells her tale, it only obliquely portrays the "wo that is in mariage" (3.3), and (as her changed epithet suggests) she does not seem to be a wife herself. Instead, she describes a story of her revenge upon a rich lord who reduced her parents to poverty. She enables a tryst between the evil lord and the queen of England, while simultaneously arranging sex between the lord's wife and one of his grooms. The Lady of Bath (played by Colleen Brennan) reveals the lord and lady's infidelity to each other at the moment when the king has arrived for a visit, and she regains her family's lost lands by blackmailing the evil lord in the resulting moment of vulnerability.

Viewed from a proper distance, The Lady of Bath's Tale contains many of the crucial elements of The Wife of Bath's Prologue: women's struggle for property rights, the exploitation of jealous husbands through cunning, and the willingness of wives to take lovers outside marriage when their husbands do the same. But these elements have been entirely rearranged to remove any hint of misogyny, violence, old age, or ambivalence. Once again, Lee has not merely rewritten Chaucer's text to make room for pornographic spectacle but has also replaced male authority with an untroubled vision of female *soveraynetee* over pleasure.

Lee's ultimate assertion of her authority emerges in her Hostess's Tale, a strange episode that is the last of the tales before the pilgrims reach Canterbury. The Hostess recalls a time when she was a young gypsy girl—the unlikely ethnic transposition is never explained—in love with two men between whom she could not choose. The devil appears to her one night and offers her a magic fiddle that will charm any man, and she soon enjoys both lovers in her tent. Although the image of Lee being penetrated from behind by one man while fellating another may seem like a traditional form of male fantasy, the narrative clearly presents this as the triumph of her seductive art rather than some triangular, mimetic desire.

Lee's otherwise curious choice to imagine herself as a gypsy fiddler also makes sense in the context of her autobiography, *The Secret Lives of Hyapatia Lee*. There, she nostalgically recalls her childhood success as an actress and dancer in community theater. She mentions with particular fondness a production of *The Twelve Dancing Princesses*, a musical based on the Grimms' fairy tale, and this scene in *The Ribald Tales* is broadly patterned on familiar folktales of a gift from the devil.[32] That Lee would insert a narrative built around her happy childhood days as a child actor in the midst of her pornographic movie seems poignant given that her childhood was not particularly happy. Interspersed with her memories of acting, dancing, and violin lessons is her account of the repeated sexual assaults she endured from her stepfather, trauma that (in Lee's account) triggered the onset of her multiple-personality

---

32. Lee, *Secret Lives*, 6–16.

disorder. Although Lee never attributes her involvement with the porn industry to this trauma and the resulting mental problems she suffered, this is a familiar enough narrative from the grim pantheon of troubled porn stars.[33] Lee managed to escape her stepfather's household in her early teens, and her autobiography recalls one particular memory from her escape: on the airplane back to her grandmother in Indiana, a flight attendant noticed that this obviously distraught girl traveling by herself carried a violin case, and she asked her to perform for the passengers. Lee obliged, and the result is a rare bright spot in the darker memories of her unhappy adolescence.[34] The moment seems to herald the later ways in which she invented a sexually confident performer (Hyapatia Lee) to overcome the powerless sexual victim (Vicki Lynch). This in turn resembles the film's odd spectacle of a gypsy fiddler bargaining with the devil for the ability to hold men in her sway. And it seems entirely consistent with an urge to remake a man's text so that it demonstrates women's sexual control.

Naturally, one need not have been a rape victim to find Chaucer's depiction of sexual struggle repugnant, and a reading that connects Hyapatia Lee's displacement of Chaucer's patriarchal authority to the trauma of her stepfather's abuse is admittedly unsophisticated. But such a reading seems nonetheless unavoidable, given Lee's assertions about her lifelong dilemma between her pride in performing and her vulnerability as a woman. This reading also suggests a terrible irony: a sufferer from multiple-personality disorder assumes the place of one of English literature's most polyvocal ventriloquists. But in Lee's opinion, the encounter was clearly a victory for her artistic independence. In giving herself a space for her triumphant self-articulation as a gifted performer within the frame of her *Canterbury Tales,* Lee has avoided Chaucer's influence and asserted her own.

However, as much as we might try to view the film in Hyapatia Lee's terms, Bud Lee (the director) and Harry Mohney (the producer) created a work of entirely conventional pornography, and it is difficult to view it as anything else. Hyapatia Lee's revisions ensured that the film does not genuflect in any meaningful way to Chaucer's cultural authority, as Mohney may have intended it to. But Mohney and Bud Lee ensured that straight male viewers would receive all the predictable pleasures that pornography delivers. The visual language

---

33. The fallout of Hyapatia Lee's career in pornography has been no happier than its origins. According to a 2008 profile of her, she now lives (as Vicki Lynch) a modest, largely isolated life in rural Indiana and continues to struggle with the difficulties of her mental disorders (Daniel Comiskey, "The Naked Truth"). Lynch reports that she receives little or no royalties from her pornography.

34. Lee, *Secret Lives,* 15–16.

of "meat shots" and "money shots" remains the essential *lingua franca* of this film, not its faux Middle English. Focusing on its subtle feminist subtext requires a viewer to fast-forward past the lengthy sex scenes aimed squarely at male arousal. This essay naturally cannot take up the vexed, larger question of whether mass-market pornography made by women has ever been or can ever be successful in creating a space for genuinely "pro-woman" pornography. But Hyapatia Lee's involvement in *The Ribald Tales* is at best an incomplete gesture in this direction, and not an unqualified success.

In retrospect, the film embodies some of the usual ambivalence about adapting Chaucer's work for modern audiences, albeit in a unique form. As has often been the case in America, Chaucer is a figure for both veneration and disgust. His work has a prestige that can legitimize "low" forms like pornography and let the producers and cast of *The Ribald Tales* feel as though they are finally engaged in "real" art. And at the same time he is too revolting, too premodern, and too obscene even for pornography. Sorry, Chaucer.

CHAPTER 10

THE NAKED TRUTH

Chaucerian Spectacle in Brian Helgeland's
A Knight's Tale

SIÂN ECHARD

> Also I prey yow to foryeve it me,
> Al have I nat set folk in hir degree
> Heere in this tale, as that they sholde stonde.
> –Geoffrey Chaucer, The General Prologue 1.743-45[1]

> And everybody else here *not* sitting on a cushion!
> –*A Knight's Tale*[2]

TWO CHAUCERS speak in my epigraphs. The first is the Chaucer-pilgrim of The General Prologue of the *Canterbury Tales,* apparently apologizing (though we would do well not to take him at face value) for any perceived failure to maintain social order in his presentation of the pilgrims and their tales. The second is Geoff Chaucer, acting as herald to William Thatcher, the peasant turned tournament contender in Brian Helgeland's *A Knight's Tale.* Geoff is stirring up excitement in the waiting crowd before William displays the skills that will eventually win him a knighthood, the friendship of the Black Prince, and a high-born ladylove, thus proving his father right that a man can "change his stars." Geoff's cheerfully subversive appeal to the groundlings at

---

1. Geoffrey Chaucer, *The Riverside Chaucer,* ed. Larry D. Benson, 3rd edition (Boston: Houghton Mifflin, 1987); cited parenthetically.
2. *A Knight's Tale,* dir. Brian Helgeland, perf. Heath Ledger and Paul Bettany (Columbia Pictures, 2001).

this early point in the film becomes, at its finale, an explicit narrative about Will's change of stars—or degree, to use that other Chaucer's term. As Geoff proclaims, "Days like these are far too rare to cheat with heavy-handed words. And so, I'm afraid without any ado whatsoever, here he is, one of your own, born a stone's throw from this very stadium and here before you now, the son of John Thatcher, Sir William Thatcher." The tournament ends with the aristocratic and nefarious Count Adhemar lying in the muck of the lists as Will and his friends gaze down at him. "Welcome to the new world," says Will, underlining the film's emphasis on change and social mobility. Geoff, for his part, muses, "I'm going to have to write some of this story down."

Clearly the social arc of Will's story is at odds with the Chaucer-pilgrim's anxious framing of "degree"; equally clearly, *A Knight's Tale* is not Chaucer's Knight's Tale, despite Geoff's final words. Yet both tale and film have at their heart a focus on spectacle. Chaucer's Theseus constructs an elaborate stadium in a futile attempt to contain the violent conflict between Palamon and Arcite, and Chaucer's Knight similarly constructs a spectacular poetic edifice, replete with classical imitation and rhetorical decoration, in the service of asserting that, in the end, some principle of control reigns over the universe. But the careful architectonics of The Knight's Tale are disrupted both within the tale and, afterwards, by the Miller's drunken disruption of social and literary order as he offers a tale to "quite" the Knight's (1.3127). In the film, the lists, presented in terms of social hierarchy and exclusion, become the arena (literally) in which William Thatcher creates his own social inversions, ultimately becoming the Knight of the title. And in the middle of both poem and film is the figure of Geoffrey Chaucer. Chaucer-as-poet is characteristically disguised in the Russian doll structure of the *Canterbury Tales*: a reader views every move the Knight makes through multiple filters, including the Chaucer-pilgrim and the far more shadowy Chaucer-poet. There is a pleasing fantasy, then, in the amount of time that the film's Chaucer spends literally naked—here the poet is completely revealed and talks cheerfully to us, too, about his work. This Chaucer's greatest moment, however, comes when he inhabits the lists, and—in an example of the modesty topos that would make any medieval poet proud—claims to set aside ornate speech in favor of plain speaking.

This chapter explores unexpected points of contact between the spectacle of tale and film, suggesting that despite the obvious gaps between Chaucer's and Helgeland's narratives, resonances and affinities establish profitable crosscurrents between them. My approach in what follows is not a straightforward, linear comparison of Chaucer with not-Chaucer. Instead, it involves what might be thought of as a sequence of sidelong approaches to the pairing of tale and film to allow the unpacking of clusters of meaning that result from putting one next to the other.³ Each of these clusters ("Edifices and Order," "The Adapter's Gaze," "Naked Words," and "Complicity") offers a way to excavate formal, thematic, and readerly interplay between Chaucer and his many audiences. Chaucer—despite Geoff's frequent nudity in the film—is not exactly on display in *A Knight's Tale,* and yet reading one Chaucer while watching the other proves to be an unexpectedly rewarding experience.

EDIFICES AND ORDER

V. A. Kolve pointed out long ago that Chaucer's poem swirls around two architectural images: the prison/garden dyad where we first encounter Palamon and Arcite and the amphitheater where they settle their conflict over Emily. The literal prison, he argues, "expands into a metaphoric prison that includes all human life," while the amphitheater "allows Chaucer to assess . . . the possibilities of creating human order within a world apparently governed by chance."⁴ Kolve's study is richly illustrated with medieval manuscript illuminations from works such as Boethius's *Consolatio,* Boccaccio's *Teseida,* and other texts that amply present the mental furniture from which a medieval reader could have constructed a setting for The Knight's Tale. In these works, images of gardens, towers, prisons, amphitheaters abound (though, as Kolve points out, Chaucer's amphitheater is very much his own). Architectural and poetic edifices are consonant and meaningful in Kolve's reading of Chaucer's tale, and I would argue that the same can be said of *A Knight's Tale.*

Helgeland's film, despite its departure from the tale's narrative, contains visual cues that similarly organize the narrative arc around two key structures: the prison (understood broadly) and the lists. First, carceral imagery brackets Will's experience. At the start of the film, opportunity presents itself to Will when his master, the washed-up tournament knight Sir Ector, dies before his final bout. Will takes his place and wins the tournament. His companions, Wat and Roland, fixate on the financial value of the trophy, but Will wants to invest the funds to "change his stars." The conversation starts at a crossroads, where the trio have exchanged the trophy for coin. A crane shot presents the scene to the audience, making clear that this is a moment of decision and

---

3. I am inspired in this approach in part by James J. Paxson's suggestion that rather than explore film adaptation through the lenses of accuracy and anachronism, we think instead about possible homologies; see "The Anachronism of Imagining Film in the Middle Ages: Wegener's *Der Golem* and Chaucer's *Knight's Tale,*" *Exemplaria* 19.2 (2007): 290–309.

4. V. A. Kolve, *Chaucer and the Imagery of Narrative: The First Five* Canterbury Tales (Stanford: Stanford University Press, 1984), 98, 105.

change—a metaphorical as well as a literal crossroads. The action soon moves up the dusty road as Will tries to persuade his companions to invest their winnings in the equipment and training necessary to turn the peasant Will into a tournament knight. Looming behind Will as he makes his case is a gallows and a gibbet; Roland gestures angrily toward the dead bodies to counter Will's subversive suggestion, and when Roland and Wat wrestle with Will to reclaim the coins, they do so on the patch of roadway etched by the gallows' shadow.

While Roland and Wat are persuaded to join Will in his venture, the film never lets us forget the potential risks of Will's social imposture. Will's first encounter in the lists with his nemesis, Count Adhemar, ends in Adhemar's stunning him, and in the resulting flashback we see a young Will watching a tournament parade with his father. John Thatcher props his son up on the stocks so that the boy can see better, and we learn that Will's reference to changing his stars originates in what his father told him that day. The man imprisoned in the stocks jeers at the idea that a peasant could ever become a knight. He is apparently proved wrong by the next appearance of the stocks, as Will rides past a young boy perched on the stocks (empty this time) to watch the parade of knights coming to London for the World Championships. (The point is underlined by the boy's morphing into the young Will under the adult Will's gaze.) But the next time we see stocks in the film, Will is the prisoner, having been exposed by Adhemar, and the boy who watched him ride into the city is the first to run up and strike him. Before he is placed in the stocks, Will is imprisoned, and we view him in his cell from overhead, just as we saw the crossroads at the beginning of the film: here, the juxtaposition seems to say, is where attempting to change his stars will lead a man. Indeed, that is the point Roland makes by gesturing toward the gibbet at the film's start. The final shot of Will in prison melts into Will in the stocks, but then this apparent low point is transformed when the Black Prince arrives, orders Will freed, and knights him. Will triumphs over Adhemar in the lists, and the closing music plays as he kisses his lady, the high-born Jocelyn, against the backdrop of a starry night. Despite the film's emphasis on prison and punishment, this last shot says that Will has indeed changed his stars. In Chaucer's poem, Theseus asserts the order of the universe—"Thanne may men by this ordre wel discerne / That thilke Moevere stable is and eterne" (1.3003–4)—and while his words are intended to reassure the witnesses about the troubling results of the final tournament, they can speak, too, to a social fixity that is cheerfully upended, in a decidedly modern rags-to-riches narrative, in Helgeland's film. The stars here are aspirational rather than an image of eternal order; nevertheless, it is the same activity (the tournament) that prompts the reflection, and here I come to the second physical feature that structures the film both literally and in narrative terms—the tournament lists.

The night sky at the film's close appears gradually, in a morph from the backdrop of the lists. The film, like Chaucer's tale, features an amphitheater; indeed, it features many. The most important is clearly the stadium in London, where the World Championships are held and where Will faces his final encounter with Adhemar. Helgeland lavishes considerable detail on the (re)creation of the lists and their surroundings in medieval London, an emphasis underlined by frequent overhead and panning shots of the structure, the city, and the crowds, as Will and his band prepare for the climactic battle. In this respect, Helgeland's film accords with the emphasis, if not the narrative details, of The Knight's Tale.[5] The "noble theatre" (1.1885) built by Theseus is described in minute detail in Chaucer's poem and is revisited in another extensive segment when the protagonists visit the temples to pray. In these latter lines the pleas of the speakers are front and center, but the physicality of the temples is underlined in each case by the response of some aspect of the architecture to the prayers: the statue of Venus shakes for Palamon, the fires die on the altar for Emily, and the doors and Mars's hauberk ring for Arcite. Finally, the battle between the forces of Palamon and Arcite occurs in the newly built amphitheater, and the arrival of the opposing forces is decorously described in a scene that is reminiscent of the parade of the knights into London for the World Championships in Helgeland's film. The details of banners and heralds, too, are consonant with the staging of the tournament scenes in the film:

> Up goon the trompes and the melodye,
> And to the lystes rit the compaignye,
> By ordinance, thurghout the citee large,
> Hanged with clooth of gold, and nat with sarge.
>   Ful lik a lord this noble duc gan ryde,
> Thise two Thebans upon either syde,
> And after rood the queene and Emelye,
> And after that another compaignye
> Of oon and oother, after hir degree.
> And thus they passen thurghout the citee,
> And to the lystes come they by tyme.

---

5. Indeed, Paxson finds a cinematic quality in the ekphrasis's "semiosis of perspectival movement, mobility"; he argues that "the sensory phenomenologies of the *Knight's Tale* bespeak a proto-cinematic consciousness" ("Anachronism," 303, 305).

> . . . .
> And westward, thurgh the gates under Marte,
> Arcite, and eek the hondred of his parte,
> With baner reed is entred right anon;
> And in that selve moment Palamon
> Is under Venus, estward in the place,
> With baner whyt and hardy chiere and face.
> . . . .
> Whan that hir names rad were everichon,
> That in hir nombre gyle were ther noon,
> Tho were the gates shet, and cried was loude:
> "Do now youre devoir, yonge knyghtes proude!" (1.2565–75, 2581–86, 2595–98)

In The Knight's Tale, the amphitheater is the physical, psychic, and emotional point to which the whole of Chaucer's narrative is tending, a "theatre" both literal and metatheatrical, as the site of the poem's climax and the spur for its reflection on the meaning of that climax. I have already suggested a similar movement in Helgeland's film; what is surprising is the frequency with which this central structure (physical and narrative) is reduced in prominence in many more self-consciously faithful adaptations. A brief glance at some of these should help to clarify the importance of assessing the spirit, rather than merely the letter, of any Chaucerian retelling/remediation.

THE ADAPTER'S GAZE

Brian Helgeland is hardly the first to take on Chaucer's Knight's Tale. It was one of the most frequently adapted of the *Canterbury Tales* in the postmedieval period and is a particular favorite in illustrated adaptations aimed at children.[6] These narratives are recognizably Chaucer's in a way that Helgeland's is not, but the effect of the retelling is quite different, underlining that even adaptations that make claims to faithfulness (in a way that the film rarely does) can produce radically divergent readings of their medieval original. In the case of the juvenile adaptations of The Knight's Tale, the visual presentation redirects and reframes Chaucer's text. That is, the images that accompany

---

6. For example, in more than a dozen instances of excerpted adaptations between 1833 and 1947, of the adaptations aimed at children, The Knight's Tale is the most frequently featured tale; see my *Printing the Middle Ages* (Philadelphia: University of Pennsylvania Press, 2008), 130. See also Velma Bourgeois Richmond, *Chaucer as Children's Literature* (Jefferson, NC: McFarland, 2004).

FIGURE 10.1. Illustration of The Knight's Tale. From Mary Eliza Joy Haweis, *Chaucer for Children: A Golden Key*. London: Chatto and Windus, 1877.

FIGURE 10.2. Drawing of The Knight's Tale final battle. From Anne Anderson in Emily Underdown, *The Gateway to Chaucer*. London: Thomas Nelson and Sons, 1912.

these adaptations (as well as a few aimed at adults) overwhelmingly emphasize, not the spectacle and violence of the tournament, but rather Emily (and Emily as the object of the prisoners' gaze). Figure 10.1 is an example of this type of illustration: drawn by Mary Eliza Joy Haweis to accompany her version of The Knight's Tale in *Chaucer for Children: A Golden Key* (1877), it places Emily at the center of the picture with the prison tower in the background.[7] One would not in fact know from the image, or from the snippet of Chaucer's text below, that the tower at left is a prison: the light, flowers, and birds surrounding Emily defang the implications of the carceral tower. In a similar way, even when these illustrations feature the combat between Palamon and Arcite, the potential for violence and tragedy is overwritten by the standard

---

7. Mary Eliza Joy Haweis, *Chaucer for Children: A Golden Key* (London: Chatto and Windus, 1877), plate 4, 37. I discuss Haweis's adaptation in *Printing*. See also Mary Flowers Braswell, "The Chaucer Scholarship of Mary Eliza Haweis (1852–1898)," *Chaucer Review* 39.4 (2005): 402–19; and David Matthews, "Infantilizing the Father: Chaucer Translations and Moral Regulation," *Studies in the Age of Chaucer* 22 (2000): 93–114.

decorative vocabulary of late-Victorian and Edwardian illustrations of knights and, again, by the emphasis on Emily, as seen in figure 10.2, in which Anne Anderson's drawing of the final battle is photo-bombed by Emily and her attendants, so that while the caption refers to the "fight," in fact we see a decorative and ceremonial scene.[8]

Prison and amphitheater feature in these illustrations, but it is Emily who is repeatedly at the center of the image, and indeed many of the nineteenth- and early twentieth-century adaptations seem fixated on the female characters—not only Emily in The Knight's Tale but also Constance and Griselda, for example. In one collection aimed at children, Janet Harvey Kelman's *Stories from Chaucer,* the four tales told—Knight, Man of Law, Clerk, and Franklin—are titled with the women's names, and the illustrations emphasize the women (though in the case of The Knight's Tale, Heath Robinson includes an image of a ragged Palamon in addition to the usual wistful image of Emily in the garden, as shown in figure 10.3).[9] Robinson's famous illustrations of wacky machines are quite different in mood from these fairy-tale drawings, and indeed it is common to find illustrators who specialized in fairy tales and mythology working with these Chaucerian adaptations and illustrated editions, whether for children or adults. Both Warwick Goble (1862–1943) and Sir William Russell Flint (1880–1969), for example, illustrated Chaucer collections aimed at adults, and both emphasized the female figures in their (quite lovely) illustrations. But for all her importance to the plot of The Knight's Tale, Chaucer's Emily is hardly pictured at all. The Knight's laconic description of her seems awkwardly unspecific:

> Yclothed was she fressh, for to devyse:
> Hir yelow heer was broyded in a tresse
> Bihynde hir bak, a yerde long, I gesse.
> And in the gardyn, at the sonne upriste,
> She walketh up and doun, and as hire liste
> She gadereth floures, party white and rede,
> To make a subtil gerland for hire hede;
> And as an aungel hevenysshly she soong. (1.1048–55)

To be sure, we know that Palamon and Arcite are instantly struck with Emily's beauty, but the point is that Chaucer's poem does not show her in the same

---

8. Illustration by Anne Anderson in Emily Underdown, *The Gateway to Chaucer* (London: Thomas Nelson and Sons, 1912), 80.

9. Janet Harvey Kelman, *Stories from Chaucer* (New York, n.d.). This is one of the "Told to the Children" series and likely dates to the early years of the twentieth century.

FIGURE 10.3. Illustration of Emily in the garden. From Janet Harvey Kelman, *Stories from Chaucer*. Illustrator Heath Robinson. New York, n.d. Photo by author.

way that the illustrated editions and adaptations do: she is not central, if by that we mean that her experience is not the point of main interest. And yet the illustrators seem to be moved by impulses similar to those that informed the rather odd iTunes description of *A Knight's Tale* discussed later in this essay: they present us with a fairy story and a princess.

The visual is obviously central to the film's intersection with the tale, and several visual elements suggest affinities with these juvenile adaptations. Take, for example, the film's Jocelyn (once called "the princess"; though her actual status is unclear, she is obviously aristocratic). She is often displayed for the audience, and as in these illustrations just discussed, she is often framed and centered—by the stained-glass windows of a church; by crowds, canopies, and admirers in the stands; and even by Geoff's gaze as he watches, and narrates as he watches, her slip into Will's tent after the latter has proven his love by losing and then winning at tourneying. But decorative as Jocelyn and her preposterous costumes might be, the film's gaze remains most lovingly fixed on the lists and on the controlled mayhem exhibited within them. Slow-motion close-ups abound of splintering lances (actually balsa wood filled with pasta, according to the "making of" material on the DVD). We see knights knocked from their horses, somersaulting over the barriers, dragged with their feet caught in stirrups, all to the accompaniment of Helgeland's cheekily modern soundtrack. Here again we can draw a parallel to Chaucer's treatment of tourneying. The Knight's description of the final battle emphasizes the action and the gore, and the poetic decoration of the passage—the repetition, the alliteration, the directional words that shift the reader's perspective from point to point—offer a poetic counterpart to the filmmaker's tricks:

In goon the speres ful sadly in arrest;
In gooth the sharpe spore into the syde.
Ther seen men who kan juste and who kan ryde;
Ther shyveren shaftes upon sheeldes thikke;
He feeleth thurgh the herte-spoon the prikke.
Up spryngen speres twenty foot on highte;
Out goon the swerdes as the silver brighte;
The helmes they tohewen and toshrede;
Out brest the blood with stierne stremes rede;
With myghty maces the bones they tobreste.
He thurgh the thikkeste of the throng gan threste;
Ther stomblen steedes stronge, and doun gooth al. (1.2602–13)

Chaucer's Knight describes a melee rather than a single combat, and for all the crashing around in Helgeland's version, very little blood is on display, apart from the wound Will receives in the climactic battle when Adhemar treacherously uses a tipped lance. The potential menace and actual tragedy of the lists in Chaucer's tale is absent: there is no "furie infernal" (1.2684) to turn Will's victory into defeat, as happens to Arcite, and no one dies a grisly, protracted death like his. The film's end is upbeat and triumphant. But to the extent that both poem and film rivet the audience's attention on the violent action in the amphitheater—action that is the door through which resolution must be reached—the visual, narrative, and affective structures of both works are strikingly similar.

NAKED WORDS

Kathleen Forni argues that Helgeland's Chaucer is a "pastiche" of many historical constructions of Chaucer, also noting that the film "fails to engage Chaucer's tale on any thematic or aesthetic level."[10] Nickolas Haydock, while acknowledging that the film's pastiche may in fact suggest affinities with Chaucer's own poetics, clearly finds the "medieval imaginary" of the film exasperating and lacking in the appropriate postmodern "suspicion of meta-narratives."[11] While these observations are, on one level, incontestable, I have suggested thus far ways in which we can see negotiations between

---

10. Kathleen Forni, "Reinventing Chaucer: Helgeland's *A Knight's Tale*," *Chaucer Review* 37.3 (2003): 253–64, 254, 255.

11. Nickolas Haydock, *Movie Medievalism: The Imaginary Middle Ages* (Jefferson, NC: McFarland, 2008), 81 and 82.

text and film. I would further nuance Forni's and Haydock's remarks by suggesting that in a sense, the pastiche *is* a thematic and aesthetic engagement, not, perhaps, with the emphasis on fate and social structure suggested by the architectural emphasis discussed above but rather with an idea of the Middle Ages and, especially, of Chaucer. This engagement is embedded not only in the postmedieval scholarly and popular consciousness to which they refer but also in the poet's own works and, indeed, as exemplified in the architectonics of the amphitheater of The Knight's Tale. In part, both Forni and Louise D'Arcens approach the film in terms of what it has to say about scholarly desire (both acknowledge debts to scholars like Stephanie Trigg and Steve Ellis). And in arguing that there is something meaningful in Helgeland's naked Chaucer and his veering between plain and adorned speech, I could doubtless be accused of showing the "residual desire for medieval presence" which, D'Arcens argues, is frequently displayed in scholars of medievalism.[12] If I draw attention to medieval tropes of speech and silence, of display and withdrawal, then I risk displaying what she has called a wishful Platonism with respect to the Chaucerian text. And yet in exploring Geoff's words next to the words of Chaucer's Knight's Tale, I have no desire either to expose or to rescue the film's anachronisms. I have no argument with the critiques of the film's ideology launched by Forni, or by Candace Barrington in *American Chaucers*;[13] enough has, I think, been said about Brian Helgeland's oft-quoted suggestion that "people back then were probably a whole lot like we are today."[14]

I hope instead to suggest ways that parallel readings of the medieval and modern Chaucer-figures might explain the film's undeniable appeal. Reviewing for *The Guardian*, Peter Bradshaw wrote, "This is a deeply silly film. It deserves a special Silly Oscar of its own. It has the silliest lines, the silliest set-pieces, the silliest performances of anything I can ever remember seeing. And yet I came out of the cinema with a great big grin on my face."[15] Most scholarly analyses of the film have refused that grin *tout court,* but I am with Bradshaw: I cannot stop smiling when I watch this movie. That pleasure, I argue, leads

---

12. Louise D'Arcens, "Deconstruction and the Medieval Indefinite Article: The Undecidable Medievalism of Brian Helgeland's *A Knight's Tale*," *Parergon* 25.2 (2008): 80–98, 81. D'Arcens suggests that scholars of medievalism often invoke the Chaucerian text as Derrida's "transcendental signified" (87). Both Forni and D'Arcens cite Stephanie Trigg, *Congenial Souls: Reading Chaucer from Medieval to Postmodern* (Minneapolis: University of Minnesota Press, 2000); and Steve Ellis, *Chaucer at Large: The Poet in the Modern Imagination* (Minneapolis: University of Minnesota Press, 2000).

13. Candace Barrington, *American Chaucers* (New York: Palgrave Macmillan, 2007).

14. Brian Helgeland, "A Write Knight Takes on Hollywood—and Lives to Tell the Tale," *Los Angeles Times,* 14 May 2001; both Forni and D'Arcens quote this remark.

15. Peter Bradshaw, "*A Knight's Tale,*" *The Guardian* (31 Aug. 2001); web.

me back to Geoffrey (rather than Geoff) Chaucer, and as was the case with the treatment of the prison/amphitheater dyad, the result has been to see ways in which this most improbable film at times marches in surprising tandem with its inspiration.

The Chaucer-pilgrim, according to Harry Bailley, is short and chubby:

> "Now war yow, sires, and lat this man have place!
> He in the waast is shape as wel as I;
> This were a popet in an arm t'enbrace
> For any womman, smal and fair of face.
> He semeth elvyssh by his contenaunce." (Prologue of Sir Thopas, 7.699–703)

Helgeland's Chaucer is played by Paul Bettany, who is 6 feet, 3 inches tall; more to the point, Bettany is a remarkably charismatic actor, nothing at all like the meek avatar Chaucer constructs for himself in The Prologue to The Tale of Sir Thopas. *The Daily Mail Online* review of the film makes Bettany's presence the central fact of its appeal:

> And then a character called Geoffrey Chaucer turns up, played by Paul Bettany in a performance of such individual maverick intelligence that it's like the film has been struck firmly in the chest while travelling at speed. Oof! Crikey! What happened? . . . When he first meets Hedge and the guys he is walking barefoot and naked down a French hill, having just lost all his clothes. But can he live by his wits and wiry charisma, this man? Verily, he can and does. He can also act everybody else off the screen.[16]

It would be easy to see Bettany's performance as lifting the script beyond its quality, but the film's punctuation of Will's story with Geoff's appearances is remarkably canny.

We first see Geoff from the back. Will, having persuaded Wat and Roland to invest in his plan to change their stars, rides an ambling horse over the crest of a hill. Gone are his dreadlocks, tangled beard, and clothing apparently made of medieval pillowcases; he is now the picture, if not yet the reality, of a knight (in civilian clothes). He has donned the costume of knighthood, and then the naked figure of Geoff walks past him—and us—and continues down the road. Geoff responds to Roland's perplexed question as to his identity by calling himself *Lilium inter spinas*, obligingly translating the Latin tag from the Song

---

16. Lynne Truss, "*A Knight's Tale* (Cert PG)," *The Daily Mail Online*, n.d.

of Songs and continuing in a far more modern register with "Geoffrey Chaucer's the name, writing's the game." The whole first conversation veers giddily back and forth between visual and linguistic punning, specifically medieval and/or Chaucerian references, and modern idiom. Geoff produces the Latin tag after spitting out a thorn he removes from his (staggeringly pale) bare foot with his teeth. His colloquial self-introduction is, appropriately enough, followed by his entrepreneurial presentation of writing as the production of writs and patents of nobility, but he then adds, "You've probably heard of my book, the *Book of the Duchess*?" At this point a Chaucerian might remember that names and games occur in that book, in the lamenting knight's account of the game of chess: "Ful craftier to pley she was / Than Athalus, that made the game / First of the ches, so was hys name" (*Book of the Duchess*, 662–64). The internal audience of the film, however, greets the announcement with blank stares; Geoff concedes, "Well, it was allegorical," and then offers his own incredulous look when Roland responds, "That's for each man to decide for himself."

This last exchange draws cheerful attention to a disjunction between authorial awareness and what an audience does and does not understand. Throughout the rest of the film, Geoff both downplays and revels in his writerly abilities. When challenged by Will about his failure to own up to his gambling problem, Geoff responds, "I lied. I'm a writer. I give the truth scope." He has been naked, for the second time in the film, when he says this, apparently revealing some essential truth both about himself and about the craft of writing. Similarly, there are moments in the *Canterbury Tales* when the Chaucer-pilgrim's voice addresses the audience and appears to confess to the mechanics of writing. So, for example, he introduces the Miller's "quiting" of the Knight with these imploring words:

> And therfore every gentil wight I preye,
> For Goddes love, demeth nat that I seye
> Of yvel entente, but for I moot rehercè
> Hir tales alle, be they bettre or werse,
> Or elles falsen som of my mateere. (The Miller's Prologue, 1.3171–75)

Far from giving the truth scope, this Chaucer-figure claims that his job is to present the absolute truth, and yet the persona making the claim is a fictional mask. Even as Geoff is naked and abject, his words are sufficiently powerful to persuade Will (after a long pause) to pity him and pay his debt. From this point, Geoff's words are at Will's service, but the film continues to play with alternative visions of efficacious language.

In the scene when Will tries to write a love letter to Jocelyn, Chaucer is the scribe. He acts too as a gentle critic, hesitating over Will's halting efforts, but it is the non-poets who band together with Will to craft the letter, with even the inarticulate Wat providing language that Geoff simply transcribes. Here the writer is the recorder the Chaucer-pilgrim claims to be, but Geoff also commands the attention of stadium audiences with his verbal performances, whether they be outrageous fictions like the one he spins in which Will lives for two years in silence in the Holy Land and then rescues an Italian virgin from her villainous uncle, or the speech by which he halts the final encounter with Adhemar long enough for the wounded Will to prepare his lance; here, Geoff says, he "would lay rest the grace in [his] tongue and speak plain." This is not quite the ubiquitous medieval modesty topos, as the speech that follows *is* plain compared to Geoff's usual productions. And yet the film underlines both Geoff's performance—as the lanky, magnetic Bettany leaps into the royal box and strides over the Black Prince, drawing all eyes to him (and, crucially, away from the work being done to deal with Will's injury)—and the performative nature of his plain speech, as he names Sir William Thatcher, whose subsequent victory confirms that name and title.

Geoff's persuasive powers fail temporarily when he tries unsuccessfully to calm the angry crowd jeering at Will in the stocks—the intervention of the Black Prince seems to suggest that there is a limit to the power of the poet's language, whether adorned or plain. And yet the film's most knowing reference to the medieval Chaucer paints a different picture. Rejecting the enticements to another game from Peter the Pardoner and Simon the Summoner, Geoff promises he will not have anything to do with them again, "Except to exact my revenge. . . . I will eviscerate you in fiction. Every pimple, every last character flaw. I was naked for a day. You will be naked for eternity." A viewer recalling The General Prologue will remember gleefully that the Summoner "hadde a fyr-reed cherubynnes face, / For saucefleem he was, with eyen narwe" (1.624–25). The threat has been realized, and our realization is part of the fun. At this point, then, I turn to my final theme, our involvement in the film's game.

COMPLICITY

After serving a number of years as a squire, an earnest young commoner poses as a knight and establishes himself in the jousting tournaments of Europe. He and a princess fall in love, but she is unaware of his deceit and common roots. The false knight is estranged from the princess once his true roots are revealed. He struggles to amend their relationship.

The perplexing plot summary above greets a would-be buyer of *A Knight's Tale* on iTunes. It gets just about everything about the film wrong, and so in a way, considering the violence some critics feel Helgeland does to Chaucer's story, there is a kind of poetic justice here. The difference between Helgeland's departures and this ham-fisted summary, however, lies in the former's cheerful enlisting of his audience's complicity. There is a kind of layered collusion between filmmaker and audience, and this is, I argue, a very Chaucerian move.

Some viewers of the film will not have read Chaucer, but they will have some sense of what "medieval" might mean, and those viewers are brought into the film's aura of knowingness by the pastiche of medieval and modern. The Nike swooshes that Kate the blacksmith etches on the experimental armor she makes for Will have attracted considerable negative scholarly commentary,[17] but in addition to offering an example of the kind of blatant product placement ubiquitous in Hollywood films, they also give the audience the sense of being in the know, as a viewer recognizes both the swooshes and the fundamentally ridiculous fact of their appearance in medieval Europe. The reconstruction of medieval London includes the London Eye (in appropriate medieval dress), and again the effect depends upon audience recognition as well as on the indignation or amusement that the recognition incites. The film's soundtrack, featuring David Bowie, Thin Lizzy, Queen, AC/DC, and so on, provokes a similar response: recognition, disbelief, and then delight, this last prompted by a sense of both the absolute incongruity and the absolute rightness of the choice. The oft-remarked-on elements of stadium sports function in a similar way: audiences do the wave, Will's companions sing football songs in a bar, Wat yells, "Give us a shout out, London," at the parade for the world championships, and so on. For the modern equivalents of those "not sitting on a cushion" in the film—those whose knowledge of the medieval past and poet is hazy and nonspecific—there is nevertheless ample room for the kind of recognition of anachronism that in this film paradoxically produces identification rather than critical distance.

Other moments depend on a quick ear and fondness for puns, as, for example, when Wat's accent renders Rouen as "ruin," in his sneering question to Geoff: "This is the road to Rouen, isn't it?" Some audience members might hear a reference to The Ramones or The Foo Fighters; film aficionados have several films of the same title to refer to, including the campy 1934 exploitation film that recounts the ruining of its young female protagonist's life by

---

17. See Barrington, *American Chaucers*; Kathleen Forni, "Reinventing"; and Carl James Grindley, "Arms and the Man: The Curious Inaccuracy of Medieval Arms in Contemporary Film," *Film and History* 36.1 (2006): 14–19. D'Arcens discusses this critical preoccupation at some length in "Deconstruction and the Medieval Indefinite Article."

promiscuity and drug abuse; and there is a resonance with the narrow and broad paths of Matthew 7.13—"Enter through the narrow gate; for the gate is wide and the road is easy that leads to destruction, and there are many who take it." (Or maybe this is simply a lovely accident.) Some of the puns are visual. After Will is described as "the lance that thrilled France," the tournament flag markers flip up erect to record the losses he incurs to please Jocelyn; as the *Mail* review slyly notes, "There is, quite simply, more locomotive lance action than you would care to shake a stick at."[18] And the film also trades on the fact that at least some members of its audience know their Chaucer. I have already suggested ways in which viewers might channel familiarity with the *Canterbury Tales* and the *Book of the Duchess* into their interactions with the film. It is fascinating to see the extent to which critics happily did the same. Peter Bradshaw's review begins with a tour de force imagining of the pitch meeting for the film. He has Helgeland say, "'and the hero is really just a squire, and he needs to be a very perfect gentle knight to compete in tournaments.' . . . There is a pause before one exec removes a cigar and says: 'I think you'll find that is a common misreading of "verray, parfit gentil Knight."'" Later, Bradshaw suggests that Heath Ledger, "With his tousled, beach-blond hair . . . is actually a pretty good approximation of Chaucer's Squire: 'A lovyere and a lusty bachelor.'"[19] Displaying his familiarity with the "real" Chaucer, Bradshaw seeks to assure us that his pleasure in the film is not the result of ignorance.

The Chaucer-pilgrim reminds us that "men shal nat maken ernest of game" (The Miller's Prologue, 1.3186), yet the display that many of the film's more informed viewers make of their knowledge of Chaucer and of the fourteenth century suggests an anxious earnestness that risks missing the "game" of this film entirely. We know that in the context of the *Canterbury Tales,* the words are not simple and plain—the game of the tales is complex and often bewildering, but play (and delight in play) lies at the heart of the text. By reading Brian Helgeland's "deeply silly" film against and through Geoffrey Chaucer's work, I have suggested how allowing ourselves to revel in the playground that is the film is not a problematic exercise, at least not with regard to any sense of responsibility we might feel to the Middle Ages or to Chaucer. In an interview with Nitrate Online, Paul Bettany reports that the film was fueled by "a truly mesmerizing amount of alcohol"; that filming was "a real joy for four and a half months"; that his own preparation involved reading the *Canterbury Tales*; "and there's just one fart gag after another after another after another" before

---

18. Lynne Truss, "*A Knight's Tale* (Cert PG)."
19. Peter Bradshaw, "*A Knight's Tale*."

concluding that the film is "not pretending to be anything else other than what it is (or what you see)."[20] The naked truth of *A Knight's Tale* is that it is fun, and funny, and sometimes improbably and surprisingly in tune with the output of that other Geoff.

---

20. Elias Savada, "*A Knight's Tale*: Interview with Paul Bettany," NitrateOnline.com, 11 May 2011.

PART IV
THE BBC *CANTERBURY TALES* (2003)

CHAPTER 11

PUTTING THE SECOND FIRST

The BBC "Miller's Tale"

STEVE ELLIS

THE "MILLER'S TALE," as the first in the 2003 BBC series of Chaucer's *Canterbury Tales*, gave a clear indication of how much the series approximated Chaucer's original and how much the series provided an independent narrative with various Chaucerian borrowings or allusions. At the outset it was thus established that we had no roadside framework, no General Prologue, no Chaucer persona, and no pilgrim-narrators; rather, the tales were self-contained, hour-long dramas of a type that might be equated with the erstwhile BBC *Play for Today* format.[1] Because of the absence of narrators, there was also no sense of the pilgrims' aiming their tales at one another, and thus no sense of the Miller's desire to "quite" The Knight's Tale (1.3127) and of course of the Miller's being answered in turn by the Reeve, so that the original thematic and structural correspondences between Chaucer's tales were also in abeyance.[2] Given this, the series was free to elect its own ordering, with the "Knight's Tale" following not only the Miller's but also the Wife of Bath's. In short, it is not simply that the tales' tellers were omitted, and thus the relation between tale and teller, but with this the whole Chaucerian context

---

1. See the remarks of Tony Marchant (writer of the "Knight's Tale"), quoted in Stephen Pile, "Asylum Seekers, Karaoke—It's Chaucer for the 21st Century," *Daily Telegraph*, Arts Section, 30 Aug. 2003, 8.

2. Quotations from the *Canterbury Tales* are taken from Geoffrey Chaucer, *The Riverside Chaucer*, ed. Larry D. Benson, 3rd ed. (Boston: Houghton Mifflin, 1987).

of narratorial interactivity, which may be the first point to make in response to the surprising judgment (albeit rather loosely phrased) that the series was "true to the spirit" of the Chaucerian original.[3]

Of course, the six tales make thematic linkages of their own, in that the (Chaucerian) imperatives of human nature, as often portrayed in the fabliaux—greed, lust, treachery, gullibility, and so forth—are frequently on display, again as several reviewers remarked. The absence of the various layers of narrative artistry that we have in Chaucer is but one element in the somewhat reductive version of the original in the series as a whole, a version moreover already familiar from modern television, film, and stage retellings, involving the highlighting of Chaucer's bawdy—even supplementing this with its own extra sex scenes, as with Jankyn's behavior (as an actor off-set) in the "Wife of Bath's Tale." Kathleen Forni's claim that the 2003 series is therefore progressive in giving us something more than the commonly received Chaucer—what she calls "a more complex engagement" with the *Canterbury Tales*—is problematic, certainly in relation to the first two tales, the Miller's and the Wife of Bath's, which not unexpectedly received the highest viewing figures.[4] The BBC press release for the "Miller's Tale" had at its head the words of its director John McKay: "the appeal of taking on the 'Miller's Tale' is that it is the 'Carry On' of Chaucer's Tales. Big characters. Brassy humour. Lots of nudge nudge. And of course a red-hot poker up the bum."[5] In this sense the opening publicity for the series shows little development from that of the earliest BBC television version of the *Tales*, broadcast in 1969, which was marketed in the *Radio Times* under the heading "Chaucer's bawdy pantomime."[6]

This is not, of course, to contest the dramatic or entertainment value of the adaptations or to decry the interest of the issues that were added to the original. The major change to Chaucer's Miller's Tale is the enhancement of the role of Nicholas, who becomes the central figure in the modern version.

---

3. See Robert Shrimsley, "Clearing the Chaucerian Haze," *Financial Times*, 12 Sept. 2003, 20. Similar phrasing can be found in accounts that investigate this relationship in much greater detail—for example, "the general concerns of the tales as told here may be virtually the same as those of the originals," and "in curious ways, [the BBC series] captures the original even as it distorts it." See Margaret Rogerson, "Prime-time Drama: *Canterbury Tales* for the Small Screen," *Sydney Studies in English* 32 (2006): 45–63, 55, 58.

4. Kathleen Forni, "Popular Chaucer: The BBC *Canterbury Tales*," *Parergon* 25 (2008): 171–89, 171–72. According to the Wikipedia entry on the series, the viewing figures progressively declined from 8.18 million for the "Miller's Tale" to 4.3 million for the final transmission, the "Man of Law's Tale."

5. "The Miller's Tale," Press Release, 6 Aug. 2003; bbc.co.uk.

6. On the 1969 series, see my *Chaucer at Large: The Poet in the Modern Imagination* (Minneapolis: University of Minnesota Press, 2000), 121–24.

In addition, "Nick" (as he is addressed throughout, and as played by James Nesbitt) clearly embodies the devil, and the opening shot of him driving his bright red sports car establishes an appropriate color symbolism.[7] His clothing never varies during the several days' action of the tale from the red suit, tie, and shirt he always wears, even when he affects friendship for one of the village inhabitants by gardening for her. As Alison (Billie Piper) says to him at one point, in relation to his manipulation of his rival Danny Absolon, "You're evil you are." Even though Nick's voice recites the opening lines that serve as an epigraph, so to speak, for the episode—"That Nicholas must hatch some stratagem / To fool the silly jealous husband; / When, if everything went well and turned out right, / She'd sleep in the arms of Nicholas all night"[8]—his quest in this tale goes beyond this specific sexual conquest. By the conclusion, his indiscriminate and generalized immorality leads not only to his seducing Alison but also to his defrauding John and other villagers out of large amounts of money and cleaning out the stock of the village shop. Of course, a one-hour episode would need more material to sustain it than we have in the original Miller's Tale; at least one critic, Peter Brown, regards these "invented subplots" as impairing the coherence and focus that Chaucer maintains, so that in particular "the exhilarating pace of Chaucer's finale is lost."[9]

The other major addition to Chaucer, and, one might feel, an entirely appropriate modernization for a television version, is Nick's exploitation of the wannabe dreams of stardom and celebrity that drive the small-town inhabitants he encounters. He first espies Alison during her karaoke performance in the village pub that her husband owns. Karaoke night is advertised with a banner outside: "Your chance to be somebody." Nick pretends to be a metropolitan record producer to worm his way into Alison's confidence and that of John, who sees a lucrative future in the prospect of Alison's stardom as vividly painted by Nick. It hardly needs stressing how the cult of celebrity and the opportunity for unknown talent to achieve it has become such a feature of British (and American) television over the last twenty years or so. The updating of the following episode in the series, Chaucer's Wife of Bath's Prologue and Tale, depicts the Alison of this story no longer as a wool manufacturer but as the leading star of a television soap. The entire Prologue and Tale are set in the world of television production, viewing figures, and celebrity fandom. It is an appropriate irony then, returning to the "Miller's Tale,"

---

7. Forni finds "the color red (suggesting perhaps vitality) acting as a linking device across the series as a whole" ("Popular Chaucer," 175), although in the "Miller's Tale" the color clearly has a specific resonance, as noted above.

8. These lines are inspired by Chaucer's Miller's Tale 1.3403–6.

9. Peter Brown, *Geoffrey Chaucer* (Oxford: Oxford University Press, 2011), 210.

that the foregrounding of the role of Nicholas becomes a star-vehicle for the actor James Nesbitt who plays him and whose hypnotically expressive features dominate much of the visuals. He is slick, cool, confident, plausible, and effortlessly articulate—everything that the villagers, whose dreams of the big time come to nothing, are not.

And at the end of the tale he is victorious. The last few lines of Chaucer's tale rehearse the punishments meted out to John, Absolon, and Nicholas, thus emphasizing the overthrowing of the male triad that they compose—and which is effected at the "exhilarating pace" Brown approves of through the key ingredient of water (or rather its absence). At the end of the modern version, not only John, Danny Absolon, and other villagers have been tricked and let down, but so has Alison herself, deserted by Nick after his promise to flee with her to London. Again, that the action continues beyond the adultery and its immediate consequences into the resolution of the other subplots emphasizes the wider scope of Nick's operations. The tale closes with Nick, having abandoned his car, on a coach traveling to London, already inveigling another young and impressionable couple into a new scam as he poses as a television recruitment agent. He represents an irrepressible resourcefulness that finds no shortage of human folly to feed it, with the ending of the tale raising interesting questions about the moral stance of this story (if there is one) and how the viewer is to receive it. Chaucer's Miller's Tale ends in the emphatic context of laughter—laughter common to three audiences: John's neighbors in the tale, who when they hear of the trick played on him "gan laughen at his fantasye" (1.3840); the pilgrim-listeners who "for the moore part . . . loughe and pleyde" in response (1.3858); and the tale's readers (with some notable exceptions).[10] How far viewers are laughing at the end of the television version, and, if so, what precisely they are laughing at, will be discussed below. Again, the absence of the pilgrimage framework to these tales removes not only any interpretative guidance their tellers may offer but also any provided by their listeners' reactions.

If so much is different from Chaucer's original, what then remains? We have the adultery theme; the jealous old man guarding his young wife; and two younger men, Nick and Danny Absolon, competing for her. Danny is a hairdresser, keen on fashion, male cosmetics, and looking at himself in

---

10. See Elaine Tuttle Hansen's reading of the tale: "I find it . . . difficult to praise or enjoy, as so many critics do . . . a tale in which the more polite of the two male rivals intends and attempts to assault the 'pryvetee' of the woman he claims to adore with a red-hot iron blade" (*Chaucer and the Fictions of Gender* [Berkeley: University of California Press, 1992], 225–26). The television version makes this assault more graphic by having Danny heat up the weapon with a blowtorch underneath Alison's window.

the mirror, all of which accords well with Chaucer's original, but, given Nick's "demonic" powers, Danny is no match for Nick in the rivalry over Alison. Viewers who know Chaucer would doubtless have felt shortchanged if the posterior-kissing episode were not retained, even if the television version handles it, in the eyes of some, with a disappointing discretion.[11] Here, even though Nick is indeed, like Nicholas, "scalded in the towte" (1.3853), the recovery seems pretty immediate, indicating how the mechanics of male triangulation are constructed differently. As Karma Lochrie emphasizes, Chaucer's Miller's Tale is not so much a tale of adultery as of a more complicated cuckoldry: it is driven not so much by Nicholas's desire to seduce Alison as by the gratifications in this seduction of outwitting another man, her husband.[12] In fact Nicholas could have "had" Alison at any time, given John is often away—as at Osenay, on the bishop's business (1.3274, 3400)—but part of the game for Nicholas is sleeping with the wife while simultaneously duping the husband by means of the second flood story. The fact that Alison and Nicholas's lovemaking takes place in the marital bed emphasizes the themes of inter-male rivalry and usurpation, with the woman as the site of masculine competition. The situation is rather different in the television version: John's jealousy is violent and obsessive, with the result that he won't let Alison out of his sight (in this he is more like the January of The Merchant's Tale). During his brief foray into the cash-and-carry to buy stock for the pub—an amusing gesture toward the Osenay theme—he even appoints Nick to look after Alison and keep her from the clutches of Danny, who he believes is the real threat. Nick and Alison are ready to exploit this brief window of opportunity until Danny turns up to keep them company. We can thus say that Nick, for all his devilish cleverness, manages nothing as clever as Nicholas's deceptive stratagem, but there again the modern version is not a gown-versus-town story pitting a sophisticated clerk against a "sely" carpenter. And we might note that Nicholas's cleverness is a condition of Chaucer's own in the brilliant denouement it enables at the plot's finale.

With the impossibility of Nick's bedding Alison on John's home ground, the modern version offers a more varied setting to match its more diffuse plot. Nick breaks into a recording studio, rather implausibly situated just down the road, and it is there he takes Alison, with John in accompaniment of course, to make the demo disc that will lead her to stardom, and it is also there that Danny comes serenading under the window and receives his "kiss." Getting

---

11. See Katrin Rupp, "Getting Modern on Alisoun's Ass: The BBC and Chaucer's Miller's Tale," *Neophilologus* 98 (2014): 343–52.

12. Karma Lochrie, "Women's 'Pryvetees' and Fabliau Politics in The Miller's Tale," *Exemplaria* 6 (1994): 287–304.

John out of the way, so elaborately and brilliantly effected in Chaucer, is done rather crudely: it transpires that Nick has a sideline in making marijuana-laced biscuits, and after John eats a quantity of them and falls into a stupor, Nick and Alison are free to turn from making music to making love, all of which John is still able to hear (but is too drugged to respond to) through the headphones he is wearing. After the fracas occasioned by the "scalded . . . towte," John wakes up and sees Alison ministering to Nick's wounds, but they persuade him (in his woozy state) that this is a dream—again there may be some infiltration of the climax of Chaucer's Merchant's Tale here—and in wandering off falls down a flight of stairs and breaks his arm as the tale enters the territory of knockabout farce.

It is true that the seduction of Alison goes hand in hand, as in Chaucer, with some humiliation of John; indeed, when the latter recounts these events in his pub, Alison complains to Nick that he has gone too far: "Why do you want to humiliate [John] like this? I'm leaving him for you, isn't that enough?" But such reservations represent a different situation from that of Chaucer's tale. Not only does the fourteenth-century context of The Miller's Tale involve parallels with a range of biblical and religious narratives, but also, returning to Chaucer's design of having the tale "quite" that of the Knight, we can perceive a cultural context of carnivalesque humor at play in the tale. The gloomy stoicism of The Knight's Tale, emphasized by its key image, as V. A. Kolve demonstrates, of the "foule prisoun of this lyf" (1.3061), is "answered" by the Miller's drunken reveling in a world ("so attractively and exuberantly alive") of beauty, energy, and pleasure-seeking which his youthful lovers represent.[13] John is not simply the husband to be cuckolded; he also has a more extensive symbolic import as the embodiment of the world of Christian piety, fearfulness, work (rather than holiday), routine, and elderly caution, which Nicholas, as a "free spirit," subverts. In John's fall these aspects of Christian respectability and seriousness are overturned by carnivalesque forces, with moreover, as Bakhtin puts it, the sexuality and promiscuity of the young wife dealing death to the old year and the winter represented by the husband in the further symbolism of organic renewal.[14] Moreover, the escalation of the punishment to all the men in the tale can be read as a more general "de-crowning" of patriarchal authority by the female agent, while the widespread laughter at its end

---

13. V. A. Kolve, *Chaucer and the Imagery of Narrative: The First Five* Canterbury Tales (Stanford: Stanford University Press, 1984), 98, 162.

14. Mikhail Bakhtin, *Rabelais and His World,* trans. Hélène Iswolsky (Bloomington: Indiana University Press, 1984), 241.

indicates the status of the carnivalesque, as, in Bakhtin's emphasis, belonging to, and being shared among, "all the people," the entire culture of the "folk."[15]

It is generally accepted that carnivalesque "subversion" is an authority-licensed interval of suspension of official power rather than any permanent challenge to it, and this can be substantiated in Chaucer's own work. But whatever the debates about the efficacy of the carnivalesque, its presence in Chaucer as an informing context points up the different relations of power and gender in the modern television series. The facts that both Alison and John are finally betrayed by Nick, and that Alison protests, as noted above, about how far Nick is taking things, ultimately unites husband and wife as victims rather than maintaining a symbolic opposition between them.[16] Indeed, that such an opposition is workable in any case founders on the implausibility of such a marriage in modern circumstances. As Paul Hoggart notes in his review,

> it was impossible to work out why [John's] pert young wife Alison had ever married him. In medieval England such mismatches were commonplace. Young women married horrible old men because they had no choice, and their infidelities became the stuff of folklore. Here the psychology was unfathomable.[17]

Elsewhere in a somewhat contradictory way the series acknowledges a post-feminist context that is markedly un-Chaucerian: in the BBC "The Wife of Bath," for instance, we have no female battling against the authority of the Church and its clerkly personnel, but women at the top of their professions, whether as actresses or production managers, and where Jankyn, the man, is much more professionally vulnerable. In the BBC "Knight's Tale," Emily holds the authoritative position of visiting tutor to the "knight" prisoners, and so on. Without carnivalesque opposition and its consequences there can be no carnivalesque laughter and applause, joined in by all; what we have rather, at the end of the BBC "Miller's Tale," is something more uncertain and uneasy: admiration indeed for the trickery and survivability of its devilish "star," but alongside this a sense of how little such things as deceit and the survival

---

15. Bakhtin, *Rabelais*, 240, 82.

16. Alison's moral "turn" in the tale is mirrored by the rather strange development in the BBC "Pardoner's Tale" in which the two villains gang up on the third not through greed for the gold but in moral outrage at the latter's other crimes.

17. Hoggart's review appeared under the indicative heading "'The Miller's Tale' Lost Much of Chaucer's Coarse Humour and, like Most Television Drama, Proved to Be Amiably Pointless," *Times* 2, 12 Sept. 2003, 22.

instinct really need to exert themselves, given the amount of human gullibility generated by our fame-obsessed culture.

According to Hoggart, the "amiably pointless" "Miller's Tale" was also "one of the least interesting" adaptations of the series.[18] This criticism focuses on the tale as adaptation rather than as a drama in its own right (though Hoggart was lukewarm about this also). The various responses of reviewers to the opening tale in the series rehearse, once more, a number of customary debates about the validity and value of modernized Chaucer, from the "Chaucer needs such things to survive" camp to the outcry against misrepresentations of the original. Robert Shrimsley, in his "Clearing the Chaucerian Haze" review, welcomes the effect the modernizations would have in clearing "the haze of uncertainty" attached to the tales that is the legacy of the difficulties of studying Chaucer at school.[19] In a similar if more extreme vein Gill Hudson, the editor of the *Radio Times,* enthused about a "fabulous" series that would redress the fact that Chaucer "bored the brains out of me" at school and even "succeeded in making me want to dust down ye olde copy of the original."[20] Why approval of the spin-off has to go hand in hand with this patronizing response to the "original" is a mystery; or rather the mystery is that the "boredom" Chaucer provokes is ascribed to him rather than the way he is educationally received and transmitted.[21] While there is no call to be po-faced about the interest and value of modernized Chaucer, the response to it should be, as with modern translations of Chaucer, an inclusive both/and, rather than an either/or, attitude, one that embraces the opportunity for, as Susan Hitch puts it, a "conversation" between the medieval and the modern.[22]

But part of that "conversation" will be to reflect on what remains in some ways the oddity of the BBC enterprise and on its being marketed at all under the "Chaucer" brand. To return to Hoggart's skepticism, he notes that the requirement that the modern tales "do something interesting with Chaucer . . . may sound like a stuffy, pedantic quibble, but the plays are called the *Canterbury Tales* after all. . . . Presumably they must relate to Chaucer in some way, at least a little bit."[23] Hoggart doesn't make the obvious point that the title of the televised "Miller's Tale" becomes meaningless outside of the original pilgrim-context, given that any notion of a miller or millers is totally absent

18. Hoggart, "Miller's Tale," 22.
19. Shrimsley, "Chaucerian Haze," 20.
20. Gill Hudson, "Trick of the Tales," *Radio Times,* 6–12 Sept. 2003, 7.
21. I have discussed Hudson's (symptomatic) response further in "Introduction: Chaucer Today," *Chaucer: An Oxford Guide,* ed. Steve Ellis (Oxford: Oxford University Press, 2005), 1.
22. Susan Hitch, quoted in Pile, "Asylum Seekers," 8.
23. Hoggart, "Miller's Tale," 22.

from it. In other words, the retention of the link with Chaucer is an inevitable invitation to comparison, or "dialogue," with the original for those who know that original; and the danger is that the comparison will work out much to the detriment of the retelling. But for those who do not "know" Chaucer and are content to follow in the footsteps of a reductive received knowledge, this series arguably does little to promote a writer who was a sophisticated, advanced, and intellectual figure of European culture and whose greatest act of sophistication was his persona-construction as none of these things in the *Canterbury Tales*.

CHAPTER 12

MIDLIFE SEX AND THE BBC "WIFE OF BATH"

SARAH STANBURY

IN AN EARLY scene in the BBC "Wife of Bath," Beth (played by Julie Walters) tells a story to Jerome (Paul Nicholls), her much younger co-star on a television series, while giving him a ride home after a day at the studio. At a party at the vicarage, Beth says, the vicar's daughter has a breast-related clothing failure, to which the vicar's wife quickly responds by hustling guests to the window to admire the garden—where two dogs, unexpectedly, just happen to be "shagging" on the lawn. Big laughs from both Beth and Jerome, from the backseat of Beth's limo. Later, in one of the program's final scenes—and after Jerome is out of the picture—we see Beth with a new, unnamed, young man, telling exactly the same story, and with exactly the same relish. Wherever you look, Beth's anecdote seems to be saying, you might find sexual surprises—female clothing failures, canine couplings—and of course you might find Beth herself, an enthusiastic sexual partner. In both scenes Beth is easily recognizable as a twenty-first-century version of Chaucer's Alisoun. She loves a good story and embraces power, money, and the bawdy with gusto. She has no qualms in coming on to a much younger man.

Beth's story, a parable of the program's larger theatrics, plays with the lines not just between the fourteenth and the twenty-first century, but also between film and real life: turn away from something happening in real time and you may well find a similar event, in this case the scene out the vicar's window, unspooling in "reel" time. The anecdote also points to the program's central identity problem: how does the public respond to an off-color story told by an older woman to a much younger man? In the BBC "Wife of Bath," multiple lines of sight—of its characters, of viewers of the miniseries in which Beth and Jerome co-star, and of the viewers of the BBC—are appraising and judging Beth. Everyone is looking at Beth; and to look at Beth is to gaze on a diva who is neither young (she is fifty-three), slender, nor beautiful, but who nevertheless is an international superstar with immense talents and appetites. Jerome (who is twenty-two) explains her potent attraction for him: when you are in a room with her, she makes you feel like you are the most important person there.

The BBC "Wife of Bath," written and directed in 2003 by Sally Wainwright, reprises Chaucerian questions of female power and subjectivity by weaving Chaucer's Prologue and Tale into a single fable about age, female desire, and public spectacle. At the opening of the episode Beth, a film company executive and star of a popular miniseries in its fifth season, has been happily married to James (Bill Nighy), an age-appropriate dentist, for sixteen years. Early in the program, however, James tells her he is leaving her for another woman. Enter Jerome, a combination of Jankyn from The Wife of Bath's Prologue and the rapist knight from The Wife of Bath's Tale. The central plot-problem for the TV series, Beth's show-within-a-show, is that "Gary," played by Jerome, has been accused by a young woman of date rape. Beth proposes to the writers that her character ("Roz") offer to get the young and handsome Gary off the hook, on the condition that he sleeps with her. This central plot-point, an echo of Chaucer's Wife of Bath's Tale, serves as catalyst for the show's subsequent primal scene. In bed in front of the cameras and studio audience, Beth ("Roz") whispers to Jerome ("Gary") offering him not just a staged shag, but the real thing. This event—whose comedy lies in the fact that we, unlike the studio audience watching as cameras roll, are in the know—ignites the relationship that becomes the central story of the adaptation.

Wainwright's episode, an award-winning comedy with a more or less happy ending, appears to offer in Beth a refreshing alternative to the cult of youthfulness. She is a media superstar and film executive who is both self-confident and happily appetitive. Perhaps tapping into the desires of the BBC's midlife viewers, the adaptation presents a midlife diva. In *Autographies,* A. C. Spearing calls Chaucer's Wife of Bath a "conspicuous body" that, like Falstaff, has a potent afterlife.[1] In the BBC "Wife of Bath" episode, her afterlife is as an "It" girl—though "It-woman" might be a more precise term. Beth, a remade

---

1. A. C. Spearing, *Medieval Autographies: The "I" of the Text* (Notre Dame: University of Notre Dame Press, 2012), 69.

Alisoun, is a charismatic public personality with the same qualities that Elinor Glyn articulated in 1927: "To have 'It,' the fortunate possessor must have that strange magnetism which attracts both sexes. He or she must be entirely unselfconscious, indifferent to the effect he or she is producing. There must be physical attraction, but beauty is unnecessary. Conceit or self-consciousness destroys 'It' immediately."[2] Magnetic, flamboyant, attractive but not beautiful, Julie Walter's Beth embodies unselfconsciousness and what Joseph Roach calls the "effortless look of public intimacy" that is a defining quality of "It."[3] At the beginning of the program Beth is sitting in a chair, comfortably addressing the camera, and talking, like the Wife of Bath, about her life and marriages. At the end, she sits in a beach chair, again addressing us, as she breezily recounts her post-Jerome life.

In projecting Chaucer's Alisoun into a role as star of a contemporary miniseries, the BBC "Wife of Bath" has, as in the other episodes of its *Canterbury Tales* series, created a kind of intertextual puzzle for well-read viewers: where in this story, which is set in today's world of celebrity glamour—at a film studio, at an elegant London home, and in the seats of various expensive twenty-first-century sports cars and limousines—can we find traces of Chaucer? Plot threads and tics from The Wife of Bath's Prologue and Tale weave their way through the adaptation:[4] the Wife's unfaithful fourth husband becomes the dentist-husband; Jankyn becomes Jerome (with an echo of Jerome's *Against Jovinianus*); the tale's quest for "what women most desire" is reprised as TV ratings; Alisoun's admiration of Jankyn's legs, when he is helping carry her husband's bier, resurfaces in a shot of Beth and Jerome side by side at the dentist's funeral; and the wish, by Chaucer's crone, for youthful beauty gets an update in Botox and plastic surgery. As one study quips, she becomes the "Wife of Botox" (see figure 12.1).[5] In a discussion of her program, writer Sally Wainwright describes the Wife as "a feminist ahead of her time" who nevertheless is constrained by her "Achilles heel," which is her need for a man.[6] In her dependence on male admiration, Beth is easily recognizable as a modernized version of Chaucer's Alisoun—a rich, successful older woman whose actions are driven by a mixture of lust, need, and longing for true love.

---

2. Joseph Roach, *It* (Ann Arbor: University of Michigan Press, 2007), 4.

3. Roach, *It*, 3.

4. For textual interpellations see Kathleen Forni, "Popular Chaucer: The BBC's Canterbury Tales," *Parergon* 25.1 (2008): 171–89; and Mikee Chisholm Delony, *From Textual Interpretation to Film Adaptation: The Narratorial, Readerly, and Directorial Gaze at the "Joly Body" of Geoffrey Chaucer's Wife of Bath* (University of Houston, PhD dissertation, 2007), 323–49.

5. Alan Baragona and Gloria Betcher, "The Wife of Botox," paper presented at the Southeastern Medieval Conference, Daytona Beach, FL, October, 2005.

6. Forni, "Popular Chaucer," 184.

FIGURE 12.1. Beth recuperates after surgery in the BBC "Wife of Bath."

The real Achilles heel is not a woman's need for a man, though, but rather an older woman's desire for a young one, and in this the adaptation departs notably from Chaucer. Age differences are present in Chaucer's Prologue and Tale, of course. At over forty the Wife is already into old age, according to medieval writers on the life cycle.[7] In The Prologue, Alisoun takes a partner twenty years younger when she marries Jankyn, and in the tale, an old woman transforms magically into a young beauty. The knight's horror of the crone's aged body is no doubt meant to evoke a corresponding frisson in Chaucer's readers. Yet the more important issues in Chaucer's Prologue and Tale are textual and experiential authority, not sexual cougardom. Alisoun and the crone both gain some of their power and authority, or *sovereynetee* and *maistrie*, by being older than their husbands. In The Prologue, Chaucer endows the Wife with the authority to lecture and gloss biblical texts, in part, through her literary genealogy in a line of textual older women and go-betweens that reaches from Ovid's Dipsas through the *Romance of the Rose*'s La Vieille. In both Prologue and Tale, the older woman's age also gives her the "experience" to sound off on issues of marriage, virginity, power, and money. Age and experience put The Prologue's Alisoun and the Tale's crone in positions to both speak and act.

In the BBC "Wife of Bath," the aging diva is, in essence, the story itself. Commentary on the program has noted its pointed address of the tolls of celebrity culture but has not fully addressed the particular transformation of

---

7. William Matthews, "The Wife of Bath and All Her Sect," *Viator* 5 (1974): 413–43, 418.

its Chaucerian source into a fable about female midlife sexuality and desirability.[8] In Wainwright's "Wife of Bath," the issues of marriage and *maistrie* that organize Chaucer's Prologue and Tale are largely subsumed under "cougardom," with power, money, and multiple marriages all by-products of Beth's older-woman status rather than, as in Chaucer, material for sermonizing as topics of interest in themselves. As a midlife It girl, desiring a younger man, Wainwright's Beth defies her public's critique of her life choices. Nevertheless, the program focuses obsessively on Beth and Jerome's age difference. The twenty-year age difference in Chaucer stretches, in Wainwright's remake, to thirty-one years, with Beth fifty-three and Jerome twenty-two. Age difference enters even before the breakup of Beth's marriage, when Beth tells the off-color story to Jerome about the Vicar's daughter. After Jerome gets out of the car, with sex palpably in the air, Beth leans forward and says to her driver, "He is *such* a pretty boy." Later, when she gets involved with Jerome, people she tells are not just shocked but appalled: her assistant Jessica, her producer Jane, and—in a scene filmed with particular theatrical relish—Jerome's parents, when Beth and Jerome come for lunch and announce they are to be married. After Beth and Jerome share their news—to the parents' stunned silence—we find Beth upstairs in the bathroom with Jerome, lamenting the disastrous lunch: "They hate me! She's thinking, by the time he's forty, she'll be a geriatric." Then her recapitulation of what the parents must be thinking quickly turns on herself: "I'll be seventy, and you'll be forty! You'll have nubile seventeen-year-old girly wirlies swirling around trying to get into your knickers, and I'll be incontinent."

Beth's twenty-year imagined leap forward lands at old age, a territory that has been remarkably absent from feminist theory and only occasionally visible in the cinema. Beth's midlife sexuality repeatedly looks forward to this dark continent of the incontinent elderly. In a 2006 study of aging, Toni Calasanti and Kathleen Slevin argue that ageism permeates feminism and that unlike race, class, and gender, old age and aging have rarely been topics in feminist discourse.[9] Betty Friedan's 1993 *Fountain of Age* did little to dispel this

---

8. Forni briefly notes the film's picture of the tyranny of age ("Popular Chaucer," 185); and Delony argues that the film is an indictment of the cultural construction of femininity, but without direct attention to the issue of age (*Textual*, 384).

9. Toni M. Calasanti and Kathleen F. Slevin, eds., *Age Matters: Realigning Feminist Thinking* (New York: Routledge, 2006), 1–17. See also Lois Banner, *In Full Flower: Aging Women, Power, and Sexuality* (New York: Knopf, 1992). Banner, writing in 1992, assumed that feminist analyses were on the cusp of remediating the neglect of the category of age (331–34). As Calasanti and Slevin note, fourteen years later, the neglect persists.

lacuna, with its title even suggesting the book's own ageist agenda.[10] Feminist film theory, for all its attention to the body, has also rarely included analyses of age—and perhaps with good reason, since older women have made such infrequent appearances in film.[11] There has not been a great deal to write about. Whenever older women do appear on screen, their sexuality is usually cast in a dubious or downright negative light. The older, sexualized film diva was noirishly encoded in *Sunset Boulevard*'s Norma Desmond (Gloria Swanson), a figure who herself recollects Dickens's Miss Haversham—rich, destructive, lost in the past, grasping at youth.[12] In Hollywood's cult of youth, when older women appear to be embracing sexuality, as with *Sex and the City*'s Samantha (Kim Cattrall), that exuberance is belabored or at risk. Samantha, particularly as represented in the film *Sex and the City 2*, wages constant war against her aging body and is a figure of lurid fascination: what act of excess and indecorousness is she going to do now? In a recent study of the "older bird" chick flick, Margaret Tally notes that while Hollywood seems to be producing some films that allow older women a measure of sexual rediscovery (*Something's Gotta Give, Under the Tuscan Sun*), rediscovery has to be, as she says, "contained in the family."[13] It also has to have an age-appropriate object. As Mary Russo, best-known for her book *Female Grotesques,* puts it, "Not acting one's age . . . is not only inappropriate but dangerous, exposing the female subject, especially, to ridicule, contempt, pity, and scorn—to the scandal of anachronism."[14] The sexualized older woman, that is, violates sequential life-span chronicity. She risks making herself grotesque. If she endangers herself (through ridicule), she also endangers others by challenging, in her own polychronic body, temporal boundaries that keep old age safely in its own preserve. In that, she perhaps commits what Lucien Febvre in 1942 condemned as not just a scandal but as a sin: anachronism—"the worst of all sins, the sin that

---

10. Ruth E. Ray, "The Personal as Political: The Legacy of Betty Friedan," *Age Matters,* 36–42.

11. In many classic studies of feminist film theory the category of aging does not appear; see, for example, *Issues in Feminist Film Criticism,* ed. Patricia Erens (Bloomington: Indiana University Press, 1990); and *Multiple Voices in Feminist Film Criticism,* ed. Diane Carson, Linda Dittmar, and Janice R. Welsch (Minneapolis: University of Minnesota Press, 1994).

12. For *Sunset Boulevard,* see Banner, *Flower,* 27–55; and Sally Chivers, "Baby Jane Grew Up: The Dramatic Intersection of Age with Disability," *Canadian Review of American Studies* 36 (2006): 211–27.

13. Margaret Tally, "Hollywood and the 'Older Bird' Chick Flick," *Chick Flicks: Contemporary Women at the Movies,* ed. Susanne Ferris and Mallory Young (New York: Routledge, 2008), 119–31, 120.

14. Mary Russo, "The Scandal of Anachronism," *Figuring Age: Women, Bodies, Generations,* ed. Kathleen Woodward (Bloomington: Indiana University Press, 1999), 20–33, 21.

cannot be forgiven."[15] While Febvre was writing about historical anachronism, the remark may apply as well to perceived violations of the life course. The real sin of the sexualized older woman is to bring aging into plain sight.[16]

In the BBC "Wife of Bath," Beth risks the scandal of anachronism through her position at the center of multiple sight lines. Even while she appears insouciantly self-confident, the program repeatedly annotates her conspicuous body through the gazes and comments of others. Choices and desire are as much in the hands of the public, a voracious celebrity market, as they are under her own control. As the shagging joke illustrates, desire of all kinds is mediated by stories, angles of view, and screens. When Beth is having sex in her trailer, her driver is listening outside. When anyone in the program is having sex anywhere, someone else seems to be paying attention—listening to thumpings through the wall, watching the chandelier shake overhead, or gathering around Beth and Jerome's "staged" consummation scene, ironically the real thing. Studio sex and sex lives of studio personnel are public acts.

More insidiously, the public also judges. There seems little distinction between private and public life—between choices independently made and the public will. When James, Beth's dentist husband, confesses to Beth that he is having an affair, his motive for confession is not marital scruples but the fact that the press has finally gotten wind of it. "It's going to be all over the papers tomorrow," he tells her. And public judgment is particularly harsh when it comes to age difference. The narrative poses Chaucer's question—later Freud's question—"What do women want?" as a question answerable by networks and ratings. While the viewers of the TV series celebrate Beth's chutzpah in marrying a much younger man, they disapprove of Jerome. Ratings cost Jerome his job, not because of his screen performance but because of his off-screen relationship with his co-star. As Jane, the show's director, says about the viewers that have given Jerome a thumbs down, "Maybe they don't know what to do with a twenty-two-year-old boy who wants to sleep with someone old

---

15. Cited in Margreta De Grazia, "Anachronism," *Cultural Reformations: Medieval and Renaissance in Literary History*, ed. Brian Cummings and James Simpson (Oxford: Oxford University Press, 2010), 13–32, 13.

16. Midlife female sexuality and marital age differences have also been underexamined in Chaucer scholarship, which has had little to say about the Wife in the context of real-time practices of marriages between older women and younger men or of female aging in the late Middle Ages. For a survey of the topos of old age, see George R. Coffman, "Old Age from Horace to Chaucer: Some Literary Affinities and Adventures of an Idea," *Speculum* 9 (1935): 249–77. Coffman is chiefly concerned with male old age and mentions sexuality only in passing. Though readers have noted the Wife's fear of getting old, it has been to situate that fear within Chaucerian constructions of age and youth and to note that for Chaucer, age is primarily associated with negativity and decline. See especially Alfred David, "Old, New, and Yong in Chaucer," *Studies in the Age of Chaucer* 15 (1993): 5–21.

enough to be his mother. Maybe they don't trust his motives. Maybe they think he's just a bit . . . sad."

"They," the invisible audience for the show-within-a-show, have significant, perhaps even godlike, powers. Beth responds to Jane's decision to fire Jerome with various desperate strategies: Defy the ratings. Quit the show. As Jane calmly points out, neither one would be a good idea. Both Beth and the public are celebrities of sorts, and both are crucial for the show's success. In his study of celebrity culture, Joseph Roach speaks of the "secular magic" of celebrity appeal, a religiosity that endows the celebrity with quasi-divine status.[17] Both the audience and the It-person participate in this devotional set of projections, though, with invisible forces governing visibility's remarkable allure. Wainwright plays with these visual paradoxes, among them the complex, even inverse, relationship between female visibility and power, in which Beth's older body becomes a disquieting marker of the fault lines between ingénue and crone and between object of desire and sign of anachronism. Peggy Phelan, in her study of the structures of power and "to-be-seenness," notes that film visibility, at least for women, often constitutes not power but vulnerability. As she wryly puts it in *Unmarked*, "If representational visibility equaled power, then almost-naked young white women should be running Western culture."[18] Phelan's comment can be applied as well to Hollywood lines of sight that historically have projected the female film star as fetishized object of largely male desire, on screen before an invisible audience. Film studies of the 1980s and 1990s built a monumental body of work examining the ways that cinematic lines of sight and the "gaze" collude to objectify, disempower, and even dismember the starlet on the screen.

Beth, of course, is not a young woman. Neither is she a Hollywood production. She is the vision of the BBC, which has been much more willing than has Hollywood to create starring roles for older women: Judy Dench, Maggie Smith, and Helen Mirren. And not just older women but also older women on the make. In BBC comedy the sexualized older woman is something of a stock character. In the BBC hit sitcom *Birds of a Feather*, which aired from 1989 to 1998, Dorien Green (played by Lesley Joseph) is a middle-aged, married woman who has repeated affairs with younger men. Indeed, the TV series format may offer a particularly apt platform for socially risqué topics, particularly when those topics are presented as comedy. Laughter and an episodic format both guard against seriousness. In *Birds of a Feather* and "The Wife of Bath," which is also part of a series, we get the cougar in a genial, one-hour dose.

---

17. Roach, *It*, 3.
18. Peggy Phelan, *Unmarked: The Politics of Performance* (New York: Routledge, 1993), 10.

In the BBC "Wife of Bath," the look at the aging diva is not, in fact, entirely genial. Filmic gazes circulate around Beth's midlife sexuality with an inquisitorial prurience. One of the program's most relentless inquisitions targets her age, even with a quiet unease about her aging body. In Chaucer's Prologue, Alisoun speaks of female sexual desire with an authority that derives from her own experience; she has had occasion to know. Wainwright distills desire to the perverse emanations of an older body. The narrative's concern is not with the scandal of female desire, as in Chaucer's Prologue, but with anachronistic desire. There is always something potentially indecorous about Beth; indecorousness, the possibility of outrage, is part of her It-effect. Yet her appeal is also tainted with something darker. To be old is to be, in the world of celebrity culture, as good as dead and gone, or perhaps even worse. The indecorousness might be generated in part by casting Julie Walters as a stand-in for the Wife. If the character of Beth bears traces of Elizabeth Taylor, as Andrew Higl suggests, the actor performing her character comes with the shadow of a grandmother.[19] Julie Walters is a well-known figure to film and TV viewers, particularly in the United Kingdom, for portrayals such as the fairy godmother in *Jack and the Beanstalk* (1998) and the grandmother in *Little Red Riding Hood* (1995), with her most familiar persona perhaps as Molly Weasley in the *Harry Potter* series (2001–11). Walters brings to the role, that is, a mature film identity associated with motherhood, not sexuality. When Jane points out that viewers might be uneasy with Jerome for wanting to sleep with someone "old enough to be his mother," that observation is also brought home by another level of film masquerade and recognition: Walters, well-known for her maternal roles, playing non-maternal Beth who falls in love with a "boy" young enough to be her son.

Beth's flamboyantly "conspicuous body," investigated by a mix of prurience and desire to alter, is also marked by a kind of unease, even to the point of near erasure in some scenes. As Roach notes, there's a "fearsome religiosity" to the It-effect,[20] and in Beth, that religiosity is generated by the oscillation or interplay between the godlike, invisible viewers who love her and rate her performance, and Beth's own aging body, a thing that is only partly seen. Shots of Beth, throughout the program, skirt her body. One of the opening scenes pictures Jerome in his trailer in a "shag" with a young woman, with their nubile bodies both getting ample airtime. Beth's body, in contrast, is

19. Andrew Higl, "Wife of Bath Retold: From the Medieval to the Postmodern," *Inhabited by Stories: Critical Essays on Tales Retold*, ed. Nancy A. Barta-Smith and Dannette DiMarco (Newcastle upon Tyne: Cambridge Scholars, 2012), 294–315, 306.

20. Roach, *It*, 17.

always decorously covered. In the consummation scene, she and Jerome are tucked in by sheets. Youthful fashion is aspirational; when Jerome moves in, she is on a treadmill—working, as she tells him, to be able to fit into her red wedding dress. "Do you think it's easy getting into a dress that size?" Always comic, potential crone-horror is also palpable in Beth's own recognition—and fears—of aging. In a reprisal of the classic medicine cabinet tell-all scene, made famous by an episode of *Seinfeld,* while she is on the treadmill Jerome investigates her medicine closet, pulling out items like royal jelly. To his question, "What's this for?" Beth, with a look of consternation on her face, says evasively, "Oh, it keeps you supple." The subject of investigation, of course, is her body, with the medicine cabinet a stand-in for her own interior, but in the scene her body is only partly visible. What we see: Jerome pulling pillboxes out of the cabinet, Beth's anxious face, and Beth's arms pumping back and forth on the machine.

If the Wife of Bath seems like one of Chaucer's most fully realized characters, the main reason is the dimensionality of her life in time.[21] She is his only character to recount her own life story as a history with temporal markers. Wainwright, in contrast, constructs Beth's character on the dimensionality of her life not in, but against, time. That, perhaps, contributes most directly to the narrative's temporal illusionism. The actual time line of the plot is vague. It is unclear how much time has passed between James's announcement of his affair and his death, or between his death and Beth's marriage to Jerome. The program's main temporal markers are the thirty-one years separating Beth and Jerome. Beth attempts to live outside the scandal of anachronism; others expose it. The chronicity of the BBC "Wife of Bath" is not structured as much by events proceeding in time as it is by the romantic relationship's potential collapse of life-cycle conventions. When Beth faces the interviewer's camera in the program's penultimate scene, the desire to stop time is literally etched on Beth's skin. In one of the program's cleverest twists on both Chaucer's Prologue and Tale, Jerome's physical off-screen violence (assaulting Beth when she refuses to let him leave her) has miraculously generated youthful beauty. When Jerome penitently comes to visit her, her face is a purple mask of stitches. He assumes, as do we, that the bruises are the results of his assault. But no. The bruising is the aftermath of surgery, not his fists. Beth has had the plastic surgery that her doctor was recommending at the opening of the episode (see again figure 12.1). The reader may ask which of these actions on her body, Jerome's fists or the surgeon's knife, is the more violent. Jerome protests that he loved her the way she was. "You were perfect!" he says. "Will you

---

21. Spearing, *Autographies,* 77.

FIGURE 12.2. Beth rejuvenated after Jerome and after surgery, in the BBC "Wife of Bath."

still look like you when you're done?" The answer is equivocal. Interviewed in the lawn chair in the next shot, Beth appears markedly younger, thinner, and lovelier. The cosmetic surgery, its effects perhaps bolstered by a diet, has been notably successful (see figure 12.2). In this interview, which takes place at some unspecified time in the future, she tells us that Jerome is long gone: "In the end it was an age thing." Even in this acknowledgment of the remorseless disciplines of age—and of the sin of anachronism—Beth's own body turns back the clock.

Where the clock turns back to is one of the show's most unsettling questions. For Beth, temporal reversal is bodily: having departed her chronological age of fifty-three, she has now remade herself to a svelte fortyish. This final interview almost overrides the temporal unease that continues to circulate in the episode's narratorial seductions. When Beth tells the joke about the vicar's daughter to her new young co-star in the very next scene, we are reminded that the antitype to the daughter's luscious breasts, and to Beth's own surgical transformation, is canine coupling. The beauty/hag dichotomy remains a trace. And someone is always watching. In the next scene, the show's last, Ernie, Beth's paunchy, middle-aged chauffeur, smokes outside her trailer while Beth and her new leading man (presumably) laugh and close the blinds.

The episode's own unease with time—the future, time passing, even the past—comes through most tellingly in a scene that also contains its nearest Chaucerian echo. Indeed, the echo suggests not only that middle age is indecorous but also that the Middle Ages, the temporal source for the program's storyline, is equally unseemly. In a stunning act of impropriety—expressly embarrassing many of the wedding guests but also unsettling the episode's viewers—at her wedding Beth, dressed in red, stands on a table and gives a drunken speech full of bawdy puns celebrating her "chamber of Venus." Repeatedly the camera pans to the faces of the guests, who respond with laughter as well as dismay. In this surprise resurfacing of the episode's medieval origins and language, the Wife of Bath herself seems to step into Beth's body and give the wedding toast. A bride's toast to the joys of the marriage bed might be seen to offend wedding decorum; from a bride who is more than thirty years older than the groom, that speech is likely to verge on burlesque or grotesque. Old is inappropriate, this scene suggests; and old includes as well the Middle Ages, in an echo of popular associations of the medieval with "getting medieval": obscenity, dirt, instruments of torture, eating with your hands, and wenches at the annual Renaissance Fair.[22] Resurrected is not the Wife of Bath as much as a twenty-first-century image of soft-core Chaucer and of the Middle Ages as uncouth.

In this scene, as throughout the show, the arbiters of age are the audience—both the wedding guests in the program and its viewing audience—who join together in discomfort at Beth's toast to her sexual self. As one guest remarks to another on leaving the wedding, "What the hell was all that about, her . . . Venus flytrap?" Clearly the guest has not been reading her Chaucer. Viewers of the adaptation, though, may have caught the Chaucerian echoes, along with their reminder of the ways that signs and language of the past, and of time passing, can indecorously shout out at unexpected moments. For much of the program, it requires active thinking to recognize the connections with Chaucer's Prologue and Tale; Wainwright's adaptation, in keeping with other episodes in the BBC *Canterbury Tales* series, is seamlessly situated in the present—with the exception, that is, of the wedding toast. The Chaucer echo suggests that to be fifty-three, female, and sexually active is also to be queerly medieval. Middle age, along with the premodern Middle Ages, is a stain, or perhaps a dark continent, that even the most charismatic It-ness can't quite Botox away.

---

22. Carolyn Dinshaw, *Getting Medieval: Sexualities and Communities, Pre- and Post-Modern* (Durham, NC: Duke University Press, 1999), 185; and Laurie Finke and Martin B. Shichtman, *Cinematic Illuminations: The Middle Ages on Film* (Baltimore, MD: Johns Hopkins University Press, 2010), 18, 48.

CHAPTER 13

SERVING TIME

The BBC "Knight's Tale" in the Prison-House of Free Adaptation

LOUISE D'ARCENS

THE BBC'S adaptation of The Knight's Tale is about "serving time" in two different but intertwined ways. At the first, more conspicuous, level of narrative, acclaimed screenwriter Tony Marchant intensifies Chaucer's tale of imprisonment by setting most of the story within the walls of a prison—in this case, although it is not named, London's Wandsworth Prison, a grim Victorian institution based on the panoptic models of Jeremy Bentham and his peers. In Marchant's version, Chaucer's chivalric heroes Arcite and Palamon are turned into the petty criminals Ace (John Simms) and Paul (Chiwetel Ejiofor), friends since boyhood who find themselves sharing a cell as they serve time together. The beloved Emily (Keeley Hawes), no longer the distantly glimpsed paragon of Chaucer's tale, enters this carceral scene in the form of a young, idealistic literacy teacher with whom the two friends fall in love, leading to a breach in their steadfast friendship. In a parallel to the banishment suffered by his medieval counterpart Arcite, Ace is released early on a home curfew arrangement that restricts his nighttime movements; and just as Arcite flouts his exile, returning to Athens—and Emily—disguised as the page Philostrate, Ace tries to get close to Emily by enrolling at the community college where she works her second job. The mutual jealousy between the now-separated friends escalates, culminating in a standoff in which Ace douses Emily and Paul, who has escaped prison, in petrol and threatens to torch them, only to be accidentally incinerated moments after reconciling with them. By preserving the core elements of Chaucer's love narrative, Marchant renders into drama the Knight's question—"You lovers axe I now this questioun: / Who hath the worse, Arcite or Palamoun?" (1.1347–48)—retaining the medieval *demande d'amour* trope in which imprisonment goes beyond the domain of the physical and becomes a metaphor for the torments of impossible loves.¹

This program also "serves time" at a second, reflexive, level in that its narrative offers a recognizable allegory of the BBC *Canterbury Tales* series' cultural mission to render a service of a distinctly trans-temporal nature, bringing Chaucer's magnum opus into the present where it can enjoy renewed appreciation in the twenty-first century. This service is formulated as a consciously pedagogical intervention that enables British audiences to gain access to an early stage of their cultural heritage. Despite opening with the voice-over "'All's fair in love and war'? / Love is a mightier law, upon my soul, / Than any made by any mortal rule,"² and despite its dramatization of the friends' descent into romantic rivalry, this "Knight's Tale" is equally a story about what Marchant calls "the transforming nature of education,"³ which simultaneously takes the Chaucerian tale as its frame to tell a pedagogic love story *and* to educate its modern audience about their Chaucerian heritage. The narrative and reflexive levels of the episode mutually reinforce each other, which marks this tale's distinctive place in the series as it both dramatizes and meditates on the BBC's educative intent. Tracing this parallel offers, I suggest, a way into understanding an adaptation that might otherwise seem only tenuously connected to its Chaucerian source, and it allows us to evaluate its particular contribution to the history of Chaucer on screen.

The reflexive dimension has so far received no sustained critical attention, despite the fact that a pedagogic encounter is at the heart of this adaptation. Virtually all commentary on this episode lauds Emily's feminist-inflected rehabilitation from Chaucer's hieratic idol to a fully realized female character with agency, psychological complexity, and a backstory, yet little is said about the meaning of this character's specific transformation into a prison literacy teacher.⁴ From a narrative perspective, this transformation provides plausible grounds for bringing the tale's female love-interest into the exclusively male

---

1. Chaucer is cited from *The Riverside Chaucer*, ed. Larry D. Benson, 3rd ed. (Boston: Houghton Mifflin, 1987).

2. These lines quote David Wright's rendering of "'who shal yeve a lovere any lawe?' / Love is a gretter lawe, by my pan, / Than may be yeve to any erthely man" (1.1164–66) in his *The* Canterbury Tales (Oxford: Oxford University Press, 1985), 30.

3. "The Knight's Tale," BBC Press Kit," 6, http://www.bbc.co.uk/pressoffice/pressreleases/stories/2003/08_august/06/canterbury_tales.shtml.

4. See, for instance, Kathleen Forni, "Popular Chaucer: The BBC's *Canterbury Tales*," *Parergon* 25.1 (2008): 171–89; and Kevin J. Harty, "Chaucer for a New Millennium: The BBC

domain of the prison, where she interacts with Paul and Ace while remaining inaccessible to them. But this narrative contrivance is complemented by a deeper performative significance: reimagining Emily as a teacher who wants to "make a difference" to the lives of illiterate inmates offers the opportunity for the BBC to tell a tale, scaffolded by Chaucer, about its own well-known forays into bringing literature to the masses and about the value and the pleasures of gaining cultural literacy.

Despite their many differences, one important feature that Marchant's adaptation retains from Chaucer's romance is a preoccupation with the question of freedom. Chaucer's Knight explores freedom not only through his portrayal of different forms of physical and emotional imprisonment, but also famously through his extensive account in *pars tercia* of the roles of the classical deities in determining the lovers' fates. The social realism of Marchant's version means, as Forni also notes,[5] that rather than focusing on questions of divine intervention and determinism, it focuses on the entrapping nature of social disadvantage and the vital role of education in liberating people from ignorance and diminished prospects. Early in the story, viewers learn that Paul, although clearly intelligent and sensitive, is trapped in a state of semiliteracy, a tacit explanation of his resort to petty crime. Although he is initially unwilling to take the literacy class because he "hated school," he is allowed to enroll after surprising the prison superintendent with his appreciation of the song lyrics of the hip-hop band Arrested Development. In an apposite (if somewhat heavy-handed) allusion, he quotes the lyrics to their track "Give a Man a Fish," about the confining nature of ignorance ("Lately I've been in a life like limbo / Looking out of a smudged up window") and the sustained liberation to be had from education ("Give a man a fish, and he'll eat for a day / Teach him how to fish and he'll live forever"). The song's message is reinforced in Emily's first lesson with the inmates during which she enumerates the practical autonomies afforded by literacy, including being able to determine "what food you might like to order, what the Benefits Agency are doing about your claim, or whether that might be a job you'd like to apply for." In an interview Marchant reinforces this vision of socioeconomic freedom, expressing the hope that prison education classes can "equip [the prisoners] to overcome some of the economic circumstances or the drug habits that put them there in the first place."[6] This is supplemented by the

---

Canterbury Tales," *Mass Market Medieval: Essays on the Middle Ages in Popular Culture,* ed. David Marshall (Jefferson, NC: McFarland, 2007), 13–27.

5. Forni, "Popular Chaucer," 175.
6. BBC Kit, 6.

more Boethian interpretation of Chiwetel Ejiofor (Paul), who argues that the classes also perform the stoic function of "free[ing] you from the mental constraints of prison life."[7] The comprehensive personal freedom promised by the pedagogic exchange is reinforced in a later scene when Emily and Paul play a "snap"-style word game using flashcards on which they have each written "personal key words." The game ends when they both turn over cards with the word "free" written on them. This is the moment when the two yet-to-be-lovers disclose a shared yearning for freedom: Paul from ignorance, poverty, and hopelessness, and Emily from the dissatisfaction of teaching apathetic students in a community college and from a controlling relationship with her sinister and seemingly unfaithful boyfriend Gareth.

Given that this program, and indeed the whole series, was conceived as an adaptation of a canonical literary text, it is striking that the model of everyday literacy outlined by Emily is expressly distinguished from book learning, which she characterizes as frustrating and disengaging. Stressing to the inmates that "reading isn't just about trying to get through a book you can't be bothered with," she encourages them to formulate an expanded and non-hierarchical notion of "social texts" that includes television guides, takeaway menus, and, importantly, the song lyrics Paul favors. Once reading becomes detached from literature, it becomes both accessible and meaningful for Paul, who then makes such quick progress that he soon writes the love letter to Emily that ruptures his friendship with Ace. The first lesson scene is not the only one canvassing the idea that literacy needs to be uncoupled from its burdensome cognate, literature, to attract the learner. Returning to the scene featuring Paul and Emily's "key word" game, a significant sequence leads up to the moment when they mutually turn over the word *free*. As the game moves toward its culmination, Emily turns over the word *learn*, after which Paul turns over the word *wank*. Within the frame of the love narrative, this could be understood, to use the well-known term from Michèle Le Doeuff's *The Philosophical Imaginary*, as a moment of "erotico-pedagogical transference" in which Emily reveals her desire that Paul will learn while Paul discloses that his desire is directed as much toward his teacher as it is toward the knowledge she imparts.[8] Read allegorically, however, this scene reinforces the superior value

---

7. BBC Kit, 11.

8. In *The Philosophical Imaginary*, trans. Colin Gordon (Stanford: Stanford University Press, 1989), 100–128, Michèle Le Doeuff describes the idea of the "erotico-theoretical transference," a dynamic in which the female student's relationship to knowledge is mediated via an eroticized relation with a male teacher; later, in *Hipparchia's Choice: An Essay Concerning Women, Philosophy, Etc.*, trans. Trista Selous (Oxford: Blackwell, 1991), 59–60, 162–65, Le Doeuff renames this "the Heloise complex," after medieval scholar-lovers Peter Abelard and

of the "social text" approach taken by Emily over education that treats book reading as the pinnacle of literacy. In British slang, *wank* does not refer solely to masturbation but also disparages behavior and pursuits deemed pretentious or self-indulgent. It is clear from the inmates' flippancy in the first lesson that they regard the literacy classes as a *wank*; it is just this perception Emily sets out to disabuse by differentiating what they are doing from the study of literature. Later, the sequence that moves from *learn* to *wank* to *free* marks the fact that Emily's nonliterary curriculum has fostered Paul's shift from suspicion and fear of education to an embrace of the real freedoms it promises.

But what has all this to do with BBC's "Knight's Tale" as a specifically Chaucerian adaptation? The pedagogic love story at the heart of Marchant's version, despite having drifted from Chaucer's chivalric tale, in fact is central to the program's searching meta-analysis of the cultural meaning of Chaucer in the modern world, for just as the school-hating Paul is enlivened by Emily's real-world approach to reading, so too does this "Marchant's Tale," precisely by being a "free" adaptation, aim to free the British viewing public from the "foule prisoun" (1.3061) of their previous institutionalized contact with Chaucer—a contact that has made it, to cite Emily again, into "a book [they] can't be bothered with" but feel they "have to get through." This escape from the constraints of "curricular" Chaucer began with the cast, with Ejoifor claiming that even though he "actually studied [The Knight's Tale] at school," it was Marchant's script rather than his studies that showed him "how it could lend itself to being adapted to a modern time."[9] The apparent success of Marchant's strategy is borne out in his tale's positive critical reception in which praise for its nonliterary and, especially, nonacademic nature becomes a leitmotif. An especially well-expressed instance of this is Graeme Blundell's review in *The Weekend Australian*. Recalling his university studies, Blundell says:

> Geoffrey Chaucer . . . was incomprehensible. . . . Chaucerian English was a thicket from which I could never emerge (even though its mastery was seen as a badge of scholarly supremacy). It took years before I was able to see that buried in those elongated vowels and strangled consonants were grave insights into the actuality of life, its confusion and sadness and the truth of its laughter.

Heloise. While Le Doeuff's thesis describes a historically unequal gender dynamic, I apply it to the unequal dynamic in which the illiterate prisoner-student accesses knowledge through the teacher who has both knowledge and freedom. Emily openly acknowledges this power differential in her dealings with Paul.

9. BBC Kit, 10.

The BBC series, by contrast, is successful for Blundell because both viewers and performers are freed: "there is none of that difficult-to-read Middle English for mumbling modern actors to learn."[10] This determination to leave behind the schoolroom is not limited to this series but is a common trope among Chaucer's recent adapters. Jonathan Myerson, whose celebrated 1998 animated version of the *Canterbury Tales* won numerous awards, also argues that Chaucer's modern audiences have been poisoned by drinking at the educational well, saying "that memory of yomping through it at school, with your teacher reading out the Middle English like the Muppets' Swedish Chef, probably destroys half the potential readership."[11] Critics of the series' modernization strategy, on the other hand, have argued that far from freeing audiences from Chaucer, it confines and patronizes them under the populist imperative of "contemporary relevance," which, in the words of *The Guardian*'s Tania Shakinovsky and Tara Conlan "simply pander[s] to the lowest common denominator."[12] This counterargument relies, interestingly, on positing an audience that, in direct opposition to the former bored schoolkids depicted by the show's defenders and embodied in Paul, has been "gripped" by the *Canterbury Tales* "for centuries."[13] Such critical voices have been far outnumbered, however, by those who argue for adaptation as liberation.

As Blundell's and Myerson's comments reveal, the notion of freeing readers from academic Chaucer is closely aligned to another, inverse, trope that reappears regularly throughout the production and reception of this series, in which Chaucer is also busted out from the prison-house of Middle English. This trope is exemplified by the opening of Stephanie Merritt's review in *The Observer*: "If you've ever wondered why Chaucer's magnificent *Canterbury Tales*, the first substantial work of fiction in English, has not yet enjoyed a television airing like so many of its classic successors, that'll be because it involves lines such as 'Fayn wolde I do yow myrthe, wist [sic] I howe.'"[14] Aside from Merritt's elision of earlier medieval English fiction, immediately striking is her assumption that quoting, more or less at random, a line of Chaucer's Middle English (in this case, 1.7616 from *The General Prologue*) self-evidently proves the unfriendliness of his text to televisual adaptation. Nevertheless, in quoting Chaucer, she employs a trope that has persisted in Chaucer reception from the

---

10. Graeme Blundell, "Tales Quite Unexpected," *The Weekend Australian*, 13 Aug. 2005, 24.
11. Jonathan Myerson, "The Adaptor's Tale: Jonathan Myerson on Bringing the *Canterbury Tales* to Our Televisions," *The Guardian*, 19 Dec. 1998, 8.
12. Tania Shakinovsky and Tara Conlan, "Karaoke and Soap Stars as BBC Butchers Chaucer," *The Guardian*, 26 Apr. 2003, 16.
13. Shakinovsky and Conlan, "Karaoke," 16.
14. Stephanie Merritt, "OTV: Box-Fresh: *Canterbury Tales*," *The Observer*, 7 Sept. 2003: 5.

late seventeenth century onward, in which Chaucer's language is deemed to be an awkward medieval carapace for his ageless wit and wisdom. Since the time of Dryden, the promoters of Chaucerian modernization subscribed to what John Sitter has perceptively described as an eighteenth-century "mentalist" approach founded on a Platonic "dualism of thought and language," which argues that thought resides in the mind of the author in a way that can be detached from the products of that mind. This detachment was central to Dryden's famous distinction in *Annus Mirabilis* (1667) between "wit writing" and "wit written,"[15] a distinction that also underpins the definition of "paraphrase" in his *Preface Concerning Ovid's Epistles* as "translation with Latitude, where the Author is kept in view by the Translator, so as never to be lost, but his words are not so strictly follow'd as his sense."[16] Following Sitter's account, throughout the late seventeenth and eighteenth centuries, numerous translations and modernizations of earlier texts relied on the assumption that the writer's "imagination or genius . . . in its loftier identity has no visible connection with writing."[17] This belief in Chaucer's ineffable yet durable wit was reiterated across the eighteenth century by his modernizers before it was challenged by the emergence of the philological approaches of the nineteenth century. A remarkably similar set of assumptions and motifs returns in both Marchant's and reviewers' postphilological recourse to a platonic notion of "Chaucer" as a timeless cultural entity that can be unshackled, courtesy of free adaptation, from the constraining language that alienates modern readers.

For the BBC adapters and the program's reviewers, the essence of "Chaucer" seems to inhere in the tales' narratives. Again as a representative example, Merritt follows her lampooning of Chaucerian language with the statement "the poetry may have dated but the tales themselves survive admirably into the present."[18] Although a minority opinion argues that Marchant's rendering "couldn't quite shake off the restraint of having to follow another writer's plotline,"[19] most commentators' opinions reflect uncritically Jonathan Myerson's sentiment that for the British public Chaucer's narratives "transcend literature, [becoming] a bedrock myth at the heart of English consciousness."[20] Arguably

---

15. John Sitter, *Arguments of Augustan Wit* (Cambridge: Cambridge University Press, 1991), 81.

16. John Dryden, "Preface Concerning Ovid's Epistles," *The Poems of John Dryden*, ed. John Sargeaunt (London: Oxford University Press, 1913), 509.

17. Sitter, *Arguments*, 81.

18. Merritt, "OTV: Box-Fresh," 5.

19. Thomas Sutcliff, "Last Night's Viewing: Dismembered for TV Consumption," *The Independent*, 26 Sept. 2003, 29.

20. Myerson, "Adaptor's Tale," 8.

the limit case of this view can be found in a comment by the actor John Simms (Ace): "I tried to re-read [the *Canterbury Tales*]. It was like ploughing through treacle.... But I kind of knew the story.... I didn't really think about Chaucer. I felt there's no point in me doing that because I'm playing a kind of white black guy, in prison. So Chaucer's not going to help me at all."[21] The corollary to this comment is that "the story" of The Knight's Tale has been freed from Chaucer to the extent that resorting to his medieval text is not only unnecessary but obstructive. "The story" in this case, as mentioned earlier, is almost exclusively a compressed version of the friends' love rivalry. Gone are the parts of Chaucer's narrative that digress from this, including the entirety of *pars tercia*, which details Theseus's construction of the lavish amphitheater; the arrival of Arcite's and Palamon's forces; the three central characters' prayers to Venus, Mars, and Diana, respectively; and Saturn's intervention into the conflict. In addition to these excisions, Marchant's resolution of the pedagogic love triangle marks the adaptation's most striking divergence from Chaucer's narrative: he follows Chaucer in ultimately bringing Emily and Paul together, yet his Emily, unlike her medieval counterpart, freely chooses Paul over Ace, leading the jealous Ace to threaten the pair with immolation before his own tragic death. But this resolution also points back to Chaucer's text in an unexpected way, for although Marchant's social realist version seemingly avoids the cosmic determinism of Chaucer's (Forni says, "God appears to be no longer operative, having been replaced by ubiquitous security cameras"[22]), there is nevertheless a suggestion that Fate has caught up with Ace. Earlier, in the main confrontation scene when Ace and Paul realize they are love rivals, Paul suggests that he and Emily might be fated to be together because they both arrived in the prison on the same day. Ace dismisses this idea, calling it "synchronicity bullshit," and mocks the idea of fate. But the camera appears to collude with Paul's perspective, opening the story with a series of establishing shots (through the panoptic view of the CC TVs) that cut between Emily's and Paul's simultaneous arrivals in the prison in a way that suggests the providential nature of their meeting. When the episode closes with Emily visiting the now-recaptured Paul in prison, the prophecy of these opening shots is fulfilled.

This adaptation's somewhat incongruous retention of Chaucerian practice does not end there. Despite the insistence from the series' executive producers Laura Mackie and Franc Roddam that the "timelessness" of Chaucer's narratives makes them congenial to adaptation (Mackie says, "Chaucer held up a

---

21. In Eleanor Sprawson, "An Old Wife's Tale," *The Daily Telegraph*, 17 Aug. 2005, 5.
22. Forni, "Popular Chaucer," 176.

mirror to the 14th century and we intend to do the same to the 21st. The characters in the tales are timeless"[23]), there is equally an insistence on the strong historical pedigree of adaptation as a textual practice. Roddam alludes to the Elizabethan practice of "turning," saying, "They were given stories by Plutarch and Homer and told to rewrite them in their own style. We are turning Chaucer."[24] For others, however, adaptation is a specifically Chaucerian practice, with Myerson singling out Chaucer's use of Boccaccio's *Teseida* in The Knight's Tale as a key example.[25] As I have argued elsewhere, it is common for medievalist adapters to employ a circular logic in which shedding the cumbersome premodernity of medieval texts is validated on the basis that modernization is a "medieval" thing to do;[26] here this same logic is invoked to underwrite the program's aim to combine, in Myerson's words, "gravitas, credibility and, let's face it, sexiness."[27]

The idea that Chaucer needs to be "sexily" packaged would appear, as I discussed earlier, to be played out both through modernization and in the program's dramatization of knowledge being transmitted through an eroticized pedagogic exchange. But as the narrative unfolds, it becomes clear that the underlying premise that education must be based on pleasure and diversion is treated highly ambivalently. Just as Chaucer is only partially freed by modernization, so too the heady educational encounter between Emily and the two friends does not universally guarantee autonomy. Although Ace appears to be making progress, impressing the class with his research into the history of gardening, when he later enrolls at community college it becomes clear that this is only to be near Emily: he is trapped in the erotico-pedagogic economy where his desire for learning is secondary, mediated by his desire for Emily. Paul, on the other hand, transcends this economy to genuine learning, despite forming a couple with Emily, as is made clear in the program's final scene, when Emily visits Paul in jail. His advance in literacy, and by extension in social consciousness, is evident in the impressive reading course on which he has embarked, which includes no less than George Orwell, social theorists Frantz Fanon and C. L. R. James, and cultural theorist Richard Hoggart, as well as popular poet Lynn Peters, whose feminist poem "Why Dorothy

---

23. Tom Leonard, "BBC Puts Modern Pilgrims on the Road to Canterbury," *The Daily Telegraph*, 16 Dec. 2002, 3.

24. Stephen Pile, "Asylum Seekers, Karaoke—It's Chaucer for the 21st Century," *The Daily Telegraph*, 30 Aug. 2003, 8.

25. Jonathan Myerson, "Tales of the Unexpected," *The Observer*, 31 Aug. 2003, 9.

26. Louise D'Arcens, "Deconstruction and the Medieval Indefinite Article: The Undecidable Medievalism of Brian Helgeland's *A Knight's Tale*," *Parergon* 25.2 (2008): 80–98.

27. Myerson, "Tales of the Unexpected," 9.

Wordsworth Is Not as Famous as Her Brother" has appeared on the syllabus of British prison education classes.

What this conclusion reveals, and reinforces, is the deep tension in the episode's conception of the relationship of popular (in this case televisual) and literary texts, for although this "Marchant's Tale" in one respect queries institutionalized literary canons and poses an expanded concept of "text" that implicitly includes television, ultimately it reaffirms not just book reading, but demanding book reading, as the definitive intellectual and cultural accomplishment. In this respect it echoes the sentiments expressed by Kate Bartlett, the producer of the entire series, who claims that far from replacing Chaucer, the series is "also making people want to read his books again."[28] By placing reading at the center of its adapted storyline, the "Knight's Tale" is thus the most telling episode in the BBC *Canterbury Tales* for exposing the confusion at the heart of the series' conception, highlighting the conflict between the producers' modernizing agenda and a crypto-conservative impulse that aspires, via Chaucerian adaptation, to bring the Middle English text back into circulation. Ultimately, then, in Marchant's "Knight's Tale" it is not just "timeless" Chaucer who is purportedly being set free but also medieval Chaucer, whom the series means to give a new lease on life. Like many a released prisoner, though, medieval Chaucer is so changed as to be almost unrecognizable, and if reviewers' comments are any guide, it is by no means certain that he can return to how he was, being consumed *en masse* as literature rather than on screen. And perhaps that is the paradox of the BBC Tale experiment: while the medieval text is released into the fresh air of renewed relevance, the imperative to be accessible inevitably risks confining it anew.

---

28. "Beeb's Bartlett Is Telling Tales," *Variety* (13–19 Oct. 2003): 24.

CHAPTER 14

THE COLOR OF MONEY
The BBC "Sea Captain's Tale"

KATHLEEN COYNE KELLY

> The existing order is complete before the new work arrives; for order to persist after the supervention of novelty, the *whole* existing order must be, if ever so slightly, altered; and so the relations, proportions, values of each work of art toward the whole are readjusted; and this is conformity between the old and the new.
>
> —T. S. Eliot[1]

Chaucer's Shipman's Tale is about commerce, avarice, and sex; about a woman, like May in The Merchant's Tale, who speaks under the protection of Persephone; about puns; and about the exchange and circulation of money, bodies, and language. In fact, the eighty-three manuscripts in which the *Canterbury Tales* are collected, in whole and in part, are themselves studies in exchange and circulation: modern scholars continue to take pleasure and some pains in stitching up the tales in logical order and to pin the tale on the appropriate teller. In the space that I have, I can only nod at the numerous scholarly interventions into determining whose body is meant in the line, "My joly body schal a tale telle" (2.1185) in The Epilogue to The Man of Law's Tale—the Shipman's, the Wife of Bath's, or the Man of Law's?

To further complicate matters, in the beginning of his tale, the Shipman observes that

The sely housbonde, algate he moot paye,

---

1. T. S. Eliot, "Tradition and the Individual Talent," *The Sacred Wood: Essays on Poetry and Criticism* (London: Methuen, 1920), 47–59, 50.

> He moot us clothe, and he moot us arraye,
> Al for his owene worshipe richely,
> In which array we daunce jolily. (7.11–14)

It is doubtful that the Shipman slips into the royal "we" to emphasize his fervent identification with a beautiful "wyf" invested in conspicuous consumption. Did Chaucer intend for Alisoun, the Wife of Bath, to tell the Shipman's fabliau? Suffice it to say that the *Canterbury Tales* reminds us quite particularly that all tales are capable of circulation, often in unpredictable and untraceable ways. Moreover, the *Canterbury Tales* also teaches us that all tales are susceptible to adaptation, rewriting, repurposing—and updating, as when Chaucer "modernizes" classical stories for the tales.

The BBC production of Chaucer's Shipman's fabliau, the "Sea Captain's Tale" (dir. John McKay, 2003), is more than just an adaptation: it exemplifies what Jay David Bolter and Richard Grusin call *remediation*. They use this term (following Marshall McLuhan) to mean "the representation of one medium in another"—the process by which new visual media refashion old media, often quoting the conventions and imitating the aesthetics of prior media.[2] Bolter and Grusin argue that any new medium achieves its cultural significance through "defin[ing] itself in relationship to earlier technologies of representation."[3] By repeatedly asserting their commitment to remain "true" to Chaucer's tales, the BBC makes explicit its relationship to earlier media; that is, to privileged manuscript and standard printed edition and even to a pony (David Wright's Oxford translation was the go-to text for the BBC, as the renaming of The Shipman's Tale indicates). However, remediation is only half the story, for we are dealing with two mutually dependent, inseparable processes: one a shift from one medium to another (whether poem to novel or painting, book to screen or television, or screen to video game) and the other a shift from the past to the present. I call this practice *updaptation*.

For the specialized segment of the viewing audience—medievalists—the BBC *Canterbury Tales* offers an opportunity for revisiting Chaucer's works, perhaps if only to confirm a commitment to a historicized reading of the *Canterbury Tales*. However, one might also discover surprising à la mode readings in the context of a newfangled medium. Chaucer's Shipman's Tale, scholars tend to agree, is a tale of two economies, financial and sexual, and how they intersect or, better, mobilize each other. What scholars do not agree on is the

---

2. Jay David Bolter and Richard Grusin, *Remediation: Understanding New Media* (MIT Press, 2000), 45.

3. Bolter and Grusin, *Remediation*, 8.

degree to which any character in the tale profits from the exchange of money and sex—a particularly charged issue when taking gender difference into account. The "Sea Captain's Tale" remains "true" to such a reading of Chaucer's tale, foregrounding gender by examining who has power and who does not, as well as by examining what *counts* as power. Moreover, by unsettling whiteness as the assumed locus of power and status, this updatation also interrogates not only what constitutes "Englishness" but also English literary history, as I will suggest.

Screenwriter Avie Luthra sets the tale in a South Asian enclave of Gravesend, Kent—his version of Chaucer's "queynte world" (7.236). Meena (Indira Varma) is married to a wealthy importer, Jetender Kapoor (Om Puri). Addicted to shopping, Meena is in debt to a jeweler who threatens to go to her husband. Meena seduces Pushpinder (Nitin Ganatra), who has just arrived from India to open a health bar, financed, apparently, by drug money. Pushpinder borrows £11,000 for Meena from Jetender. Pushpinder learns from Jetender of Meena's past adulteries and how she exploits men for gifts. Disillusioned and angry, Pushpinder tells Jetender that he paid back the loan to Meena. Jetender, furious, strikes Meena, who then goes to Pushpinder's shop and wreaks havoc with a croquet mallet as Pushpinder stands helplessly by. Romi (Surendra Kochar) tells Jetender, who goes to the shop, attacks Pushpinder, and tells him to go back to India. The Kapoors reconcile.

Perhaps taking a cue from Chaucer's description of the Shipman in The General Prologue ("Of nyce conscience took he no keep" [1.398]), Luthra makes Jetender a mafia-style godfather and moneylender. Meena is beautiful, spoiled, conniving, and shallow; Pushpinder combines drug-dealer bravado with naïveté. Jetender and Meena occupy all-too-familiar polarized gender positions, whereas Pushpinder veers between the two. In The Shipman's Tale, debts are finally balanced or canceled; in "The Sea Captain's Tale," debts beget debts, both private and public, never to be erased. In Luthra's hands, Chaucer's fabliau becomes a much darker tale—characteristic, it has been argued, of all of the BBC *Canterbury Tales*.[4]

Professing unfamiliarity with Chaucer's works, Luthra says, "The specific cultural context isn't that important in itself; it doesn't really matter that these people are Asian, it just matters that they're rich and separate from the rest

---

4. See my "The BBC *Canterbury Tales* (2003)" in *Medieval Afterlives in Contemporary Culture*, ed. Gail Ashton (London: Bloomsbury Academic, 2015), 134–43; Kathleen Forni, *Chaucer's Afterlife: Adaptations in Recent Popular Culture* (Jefferson, NC: McFarland, 2013), 84ff.; Kevin J. Harty, "Chaucer for a New Millennium: The BBC *Canterbury Tales*," *Mass Market Medieval: Essays on the Middle Ages in Popular Culture*, ed. David Marshall (Jefferson, NC: McFarland, 2007), 13–27.

of the world. . . . The influence is film noir; the ethnicity of the characters is really incidental."⁵ Luthra's remarks are provocatively disingenuous. As his other BBC projects suggest (*Indian Dream* [2003], *Cross My Heart* [2003]), Luthra is very interested in interrogating stereotypes of South Asians on British television and in film. Moreover, by creating a community that chooses its isolation, Luthra challenges any tendency to define South Asian subjectivity in relation to white norms. Naming classic film noir as one of his influences permits Luthra to foreground genre and to ask that we judge his adaptation of Chaucer's tale against a set of received aesthetic values rather than against such clichés as "relevance" and "authenticity." Since the BBC uses as one of its classifications of programming the descriptive term *colour*, we might understand why Luthra would want to short-circuit critical discussions that would make ethnicity and race the sole focus. However, race *does* matter, in theory and in practice in postcolonial Britain; I would argue that suppressing or ignoring difference and the politics of difference simply makes race all the more present.

It may be useful to consider briefly the BBC's tale, from the BBC's inception in 1922 as a conservative, government-sponsored, and therefore government-controlled, radio monopoly to its current splintering into regional radio stations and into an array of channels dedicated to a mix of high culture, news reporting, and popular entertainment. In the late twentieth century, the BBC, committed to socially responsible broadcasting, went up against more popular programming made possible by deregulation and available through digital TV, resulting in a fiercely competitive ratings race—pun intended. For example, Independent TV's popular soap opera *Coronation Street*, broadcast since 1960, developed story lines for South Asians and other ethnic minorities; the BBC's *EastEnders* now features minority characters. And both ITV and the BBC face competition from "niche channels" (a euphemism for "ethnic") on satellite and cable television, such as *Dish Asia Network*. But competition has also created clichéd crime and hospital drama series on the BBC, amid general cries about declining standards. The controversy over the BBC, ongoing, bitter, and discussed endlessly in the British media, is one of the more visible sites of class and culture wars in Great Britain.

Since most of the directors and writers involved in the *Canterbury Tales* project were BBC veterans, one might well ask if the BBC tales are any different from other television drama series. The glossy promotion of the tales on

---

5. "Interview: Avie Luthra Is the Writer of *The Sea Captain's Tale*," bbc.co.uk. http://www.bbc.co.uk/pressoffice/pressreleases/stories/2003/08_august/06/seacaptains_al.pdf

the BBC website suggests not. The BBC *Canterbury Tales* and its promotion serve as a case study in the commodification of culture. Producer Kate Bartlett says:

> Chaucer held up a mirror to the 14th century and we intend to do the same for the 21st, exploring themes such as the cult of celebrity, bigotry and the obsession with youth. . . . We wanted writers who saw something in Chaucer's tale[s] and had a fantastic idea for modernising [them]. We spoke to a lot of writers, but we wanted the ones who would grab the material.[6]

And Laura Mackie, head of drama serials, states that "the BBC wanted a prestige series for the new millennium that reflected the identity of Britain today."[7] (Mackie had previously updated Othello as a police captain for ITV.) Race, class, and gender have been turned into fungible products in the BBC retellings.

In the "Sea Captain's Tale," director John McKay deploys an aesthetics of commodification, so to speak, by restricting his palette to shades of blue—specifically, he creates a *mis-en-scène* of indigo blue. While we often think of adaptation in terms of plot and character alone, the processes of remediation and updaptation offer myriad ways to riff on an original text. In the BBC tale, visual allusion remediates not only Chaucer but another precursor "text"—India itself, sold as moody blue, and with a history: in antiquity and the Middle Ages, natural blue dyes were extremely rare, and indigo, the powdered dye derived from *Indigofera tinctoria*, was considered a luxury in both the East and the West, thought to be far superior to other blue dyes such as English woad. The word *indigo* came into English through the Romance languages, through Latin *indicum* from the Greek: Dioscorides used the word ἰνδικόν—literally, "the Indian (substance)" (*OED*). Instead of a film noir per se, McKay has made a *film bleu*: in the opening scene at Meena and Jetender's anniversary party, she wears a royal blue sari, he a cobalt blue suit. Pushpinder hovers in the margins in a light blue sharkskin suit. Most of the characters wear variations on indigo, violet-blue, cobalt, navy, and gray-blue throughout, as, for example, at the opening of Pushpinder's "Hindu Health" shop. We see customers in shades of muted blue waiting in the street, in high contrast with the cheerily lit shop and its neon sign. Indigo *is* India.

The saturated blue of the film, like the flickerings of a television in an otherwise darkened room, approximates the effects of early black-and-white

---

6. Stephen Pile, "The Scriptwriters' Tales," *The Telegraph*, 30 Aug. 2003, telegraph.co.uk.
7. Pile, "Scriptwriters' Tales."

films noir. It is the (occasional) blue of English weather and of the sea over which goods are transported; it is the color of melancholy, sadness, and heartbreak; it is the color of Krishna, god of love in the Hindu pantheon. Within these themes of color and culture, blue links crucial scenes throughout. Meena and Jetender's bedroom is bathed in sapphire light, as is Jetender's warehouse office. Thus the blue of the bedroom is juxtaposed with the blue of commerce. Jetender strikes Meena in the face as they sit in their blue car in their blue garage, and in the following scene, Meena trashes Pushpinder's shop in a glowing blue dark. Blue is also the color of sex in this program's quintessential film noir moment: when Pushpinder goes out to his van at his shop's grand opening, he hears a low whistle, and the camera cuts to a sultry Meena leaning against a brick wall in the indigo darkness. She kisses him passionately. When they return to the shop and rendezvous in the dimly lit, blued supply closet, we hear a swell of clichéd film noir music (think of the *Perry Mason* theme) as Meena, now in blue lace bra and panties, triumphantly wraps her blue scarf around Pushpinder's neck.

And finally, blue is the color of skin reflected in the camera lights. The history of color words and what they denote, not only in a single language but across languages and cultures, is notoriously difficult to untangle. For example, the complex etymological and historical relationship between the modern English words for *black* and *blue*, together with a number of other color words, is best illustrated by the fact that one Indo-European root, *bhel*, gives us, in various centum Indo-European languages, words for *white, fire, shine, blaze, brightness, blonde, golden* or *reddish-yellow, blush, blue, bleakness, burnt, black,* and *blind*. The words *blue-black-brown* as descriptors for skin color have roots in the ancient and medieval science of physiognomy. In fact, we find references to "blue" Indians, Ethiopians, and Saracens in a variety of Middle English texts. In the *Brut* (c. 1205), Laȝamon says that the king of Africa came to Rome, and "mid him com moni Aufrican / of Ethiope he brohte þa bleomen." In *Kyng Alisaunder* (c. 1300), we meet men whose "visages ben blew so ynde."[8] I am not claiming that McKay or Luthra knew any of this history; rather, I am suggesting that the indigo blue of this remediated, updapted Shipman's Tale exemplifies how an adaptation can invite (even impel) viewers to pursue meanings beyond, and sometimes against, a precursor text.

---

8. Laȝamon, *Brut*, ed. G. L. Brook and R. F. Leslie (London, 1963, E. E. T. S. O. S. 250, 277; 1978), line 12666; and *Kyng Alisuander*, ed. G. V. Smithers (London, 1952; E. E. T. S. O. S. 227, 237; rpt. with cor. 1969), line 63. See my "'Blue' Indians, Ethiopians, and Saracens in Middle English Narrative Texts," *Parergon* n.s. 11.1 (June 1993): 35–52, from which I borrow this material.

And what of other skin colors? The only characters in the "Sea Captain's Tale" who are not South Asian are service workers, such as the white clerk in Jetender's warehouse and the East Asian waiter in a restaurant. Most spectacularly white is the trio of pale-faced patricians who work in Pushpinder's shop. Difference is foregrounded through an arch reversal of roles: "Let me see your hands," commands Pushpinder as he inspects the waitstaff, who are elegantly garbed in white. When one of them tells Pushpinder that they are out of mangoes, obsequiously calling him "sir," Pushpinder hands over his keys to his van only to snatch them back, saying that he will fetch the mangoes himself. He says to Jetender with a smirk, "You can't trust them, can you?"

As the mango scene suggests, Luthra's "Sea Captain's Tale" is a study in cultural mimicry. In postcolonial theory, the terms *mimicry* and *hybridity* are much contested, imbued with both positive and negative valences depending upon the degree to which assimilation is understood as occurring at the cost of one's "own" "original" identity. I use scare quotes to emphasize that, as many argue, in a globalized world, identity is no longer neatly binarized between that of the colonizer and the colonized. In the "Sea Captain's Tale," most of the signs of hybridity are nicely ambiguous. For example, Jetender and Meena are conspicuous consumers of privileged Englishness. Meena wears both Western clothes and saris; she indulges in French manicures, but with a mehndi pattern. Jetender and Meena's house is a showcase of traditional English design. Their bedroom is dominated by an imposing entertainment center—but instead of a television hidden behind the doors, the Kapoors keep a Hindu shrine dedicated to Krishna. Meena and Jetender's bespoke kitchen with its expanse of indigo tile is only a bourgeois prop, for Meena imports Indian takeaway food and passes it off as homemade.

While these superficial signs of hybridity do not necessarily imply cultural conflict or anxiety in the "Sea Captain's Tale," the same cannot be said of the function of a Rajput sword and a croquet mallet. Jetender appears to have made his fortune in the trafficking of cheap third-world goods, but his true wealth, aside from money lending, comes from smuggling Indian antiquities into England. These are stockpiled in a secret storeroom at his warehouse behind a facade, just as that Hindu shrine in his bedroom is locked behind cabinet doors. Jetender, it seems, is in the business of selling his own heritage. Perhaps he no longer sees the precious artifacts as having any connection with himself. Or does selling these goods represent some form of displacement, or even self-loathing?

One night, drunk, Jetender waves a sixteenth-century Rajput sword at Pushpinder: "When maharajahs discovered their ranis were sleeping around . . . then . . . Yah! Shhk! Like a fish," he says, and takes a mock stab at

Pushpinder, who already acutely feels the prick of conscience. On one level, the sword is a prop introduced to foreshadow the conclusion. On another level, and like the color blue, the sword, a precolonial artifact, points us to that other text, "India," and functions as a metonymy for a lost, romanticized past. It also signifies loss of honor and masculine retribution, which is not a feature of The Shipman's Tale. Chaucer's Merchant displays not jealousy or anger but husbandly exasperation when he says to his wife, "ne be namoore so large. / Keep bet thy good" (7.431–32). These words resonate with a double meaning for readers, for we know more than the Merchant. In Luthra's adaptation, however, the sword encourages readers-in-the-know to think *against* and *beyond* Chaucer's text.

If the "Sea Captain's Tale" were a true film noir, the sword would be the murder weapon—and the croquet mallet stored in the Kapoors' garage would be another. Meena first uses the mallet, a quintessential sign of genteel Englishness, as a defense against her husband. After he has slapped her, she fears that he may do worse. Fleeing the garage, bent on revenge, Meena takes the mallet to Pushpinder's and smashes everything in the shop, finally handing it to Pushpinder, kissing him goodbye, and walking out. The next day, an enraged Jetender, who now knows the truth about Pushpinder and Meena, goes to see Pushpinder. Sword in hand, Jetender chases Pushpinder around the shop. Jetender sees the croquet mallet, proof of his wife's involvement, and takes it home. When he enters the kitchen where Meena sits, he casually but deliberately slides the mallet onto the kitchen table (see figure 14.1). The mallet is thus transformed into proof of *his* complicity. Both sword and mallet, overdetermined cultural artifacts, are transformed into misappropriated signifiers: Jetender uses the sword not against his wife, as the Rajput rulers supposedly did, but against her lover, and only to threaten; Meena plays not a harmless lawn game but another, more dangerous, one, paying Pushpinder back for telling Jetender the truth and thus inciting even more violence. Both objects operate as analogues in a tale of commercial and marital negotiations; both objects circulate as *stories*.

The story that Chaucer's Shipman tells is a variation on an ancient motif known as "The Lover's Gift Regained," found in the Sanskrit *Śukasaptati* (*Seventy Tales of the Parrot*)—not unknown to Chaucerians, as J. W. Spargo's work on sources and analogues for The Shipman's Tale demonstrates.[9] Compiled perhaps as early as the sixth century, the *Śukasaptati* contains tales of various vintages; it most likely circulated close to its current form in the

---

9. J. W. Spargo, "Chaucer's Shipman's Tale: The Lover's Gift Regained," FF [*Folklore Fellows*] *Communications* 91 (1930): 5–70.

FIGURE 14.1. Screen shot of Meena's mallet: a sign reciprocated in the BBC "Shipman's Tale."

twelfth century and is extant in a fifteenth-century manuscript. The frame tale has particular resonance for the adultery theme in both Chaucer's tale and the BBC's updatation: Madon Vinod, reformed through the words of a wise parrot, takes a journey, leaving his wife Prabhávati behind with the parrot and a mynah bird. Persuaded by "women friends of questionable character" to take a lover in her husband's absence, she prepares to go out one evening for a rendezvous.[10] She tells the mynah, who advises her not to go; she attempts to wring its neck. (In some versions, she succeeds.) The parrot asks her where she is going, and when she tells him, he says, "That is fine, and merits doing. . . . Go if you have the wits to handle any problems which may arise."[11] He proceeds to tell her a story that keeps her home, and does so for sixty-nine nights. When Madon Vinod returns, his wife confesses and the parrot urges forgiveness, tells a seventieth story, and the husband and wife are restored to harmony. (In some versions, she is stoned to death.) The Thirty-Fifth Tale, "How Sambak Got Back His Ring," relates the story of Sambak, a buyer of sesame seeds who desires the wife of a merchant and gives her his ring in exchange for sex. He regrets the trade, and attempts to get his ring back from the husband by claiming that he has paid for the sesame in advance. The merchant returns the ring.[12]

Thus Chaucer may have riffed on a tale that most likely traveled from East to West long before the anonymous French author wrote his version of "The Lover's Gift Regained" known as *Le bouchier d'Abevile*, or before Boccaccio

---

10. *Sukla Saptati: Seventy Tales of the Parrot*, trans. A. N. D. Haksar (HarperCollins India, 2000), 4–5.

11. Sukla, *Seventy Tales*, 5.

12. Sukla, *Seventy Tales*, 116–17.

added his version to the *Decameron*. Scholars disagree on whether Chaucer knew these continental tales. Sources, or analogues? Spontaneous generation? Over the past four decades, the debate over whether Chaucer knew (remembered, or had to hand?) the *Decameron* has shifted from a flat denial that he did to a tempered acceptance that he must have. In some of its forms, this debate seems to have nothing to do with what Peter Beidler calls the "evidence of influence."[13] Leonard Koff suggests that the *Decameron*'s "moral uncertainty, not merely the 'immorality' (though perhaps that, too) . . . its open-endedness within its formal perfection" causes "varying degrees of distress" for Chaucerians who prefer to see the *Canterbury Tales* as "reaching . . . for . . . comprehensiveness, a stability of vision."[14] In his analysis of the debate, Beidler says that some scholars, out of a feeling of patriotism or nationalism, argue that Chaucer did not know, let alone borrow, anything from the *Decameron*, because to do so would be to "admit that Chaucer was merely an imitator or footnote to Boccaccio, rather than a native-born English genius"; that in fact, such scholars seem to believe that if Chaucer "learned even part of his amazing artistry from another artist . . . [that] somehow diminishes his greatness."[15]

Keeping the terms of this debate in mind, let us return to Luthra's adaptation of the fable that Chaucer's Shipman tells. The five-hundred-year-old story of how Chaucer came to be known as the "Father of English Literature" is too complex and fraught to be rehearsed here,[16] but I would like to note that the privileging of "Englishness" makes up the bulk of the narrative—an Englishness that Luthra calls into question, as his adaptation demonstrates. Thus Luthra earns a place in the great sources and analogues debate; I would argue furthermore that he also challenges the premises of an English literary history that depends upon linearity and chronology.

When I emailed Luthra to ask if he knew the *Śukasaptati* and its possible connection to Chaucer's tale, he said no.[17] While Luthra seemed merely amused by my question, I take his answer as a rebuke. "Critical inquiries, unlike bets, are not settled" by asking an author what she or he meant, W. K.

---

13. Peter Beidler, "Just Say Yes, Chaucer Knew the *Decameron*: Or, Bringing The Shipman's Tale Out of Limbo," *The* Decameron *and the* Canterbury Tales: *New Essays on an Old Question*, ed. Leonard Koff and Brenda Deen Schildgen (Madison, NJ: Fairleigh Dickinson University Press, 2000), 25–46, 27, 29.

14. Leonard Koff, "Introduction," 11–18, 14.

15. Beidler, "Just Say Yes," 27, 28.

16. See Stephanie Trigg, "Chaucer's Influence and Reception," *The Yale Companion to Chaucer*, ed. Seth Lerer (New Haven, CT: Yale University Press, 2006), 297–323.

17. Personal email, March 2006.

Wimsatt and Monroe Beardsley say tartly. "There is," they argue, "a gross body of life, of sensory and mental experience, which lies behind and in some sense causes every poem, but can never be and need not be known in the verbal and hence intellectual composition which is the poem."[18] Luthra's answer opens up other possibilities. After all, readers read according to their own "sensory and mental experience"—and now mine includes the *Śukasaptati*. Luthra named his female protagonist *Meena,* which for me recalls the mynah bird of the Indian tale. Moreover, in the *Śukasaptati,* the parrot reveals to Madon Vinod how his wife Prabhávati spent sixty-nine nights poised on the edge of adultery. In the "Sea Captain's Tale," we find a similar figure: Romi, who sees all and tells all, is a tattletale. (The Manciple's Tale also comes to mind.)

It is to story itself as something that circulates, as a signifier in itself, perhaps even as agential, that I now turn. The BBC "Sea Captain's Tale" is a lover's gift, regained by Avie Luthra. Such a circuit complicates what we mean by sources and analogues and the notion of "host" text and "symbiont" text, as David Cowart describes precursor and derivative texts.[19] Like Jetender's Rajput sword, "The Lover's Gift Regained" is preserved in the West in storerooms of Eastern antiquities—in this case, the *Decameron* and the *Canterbury Tales*—its provenance indeterminable, yet attestable even in Kansas, in a version involving George, Janet, their "Jew buddy" Bill, and a slipcover for a couch.[20]

In the BBC analogue, as we may now describe it, Jetender loses money but gains a story suppressed in this *mise en abîme* of narratives. Meena also "pays" for a story suppressed, and twice over, first to the jeweler and then to Pushpinder. But neither Jetender nor Meena succeeds in controlling the market. Their exchanges and bargains are indeed as much about *telling* as they are about *tallying* (a pun beloved by Chaucerians: "I am youre wyf; score it upon my taille," says the merchant's wife [7.416]).

Pushpinder, unlike Chaucer's monk—but like Romi—also cannot keep a tale to himself. Consider his exchange with Jetender about the loan:

PUSHPINDER: You don't have to worry about me, Jet. . . . I paid it back. I gave it to your wife. The full £11,000.

JETENDER: Why the hell did you do that?

---

18. W. K. Wimsatt and Monroe Beardsley, "The Intentional Fallacy," *The Verbal Icon: Studies in the Meaning of Poetry* (Lexington: University of Kentucky Press, 1954), 3–18, 17, 12.

19. David Cowart, *Literary Symbiosis: The Reconfigured Text in Twentieth-Century Writing* (Athens: University of Georgia Press, 1993).

20. Joan O'Bryant, "Two Versions of The Shipman's Tale from Urban Oral Tradition," *Western Folklore* 24 (1965): 101–3.

PUSHPINDER: She asked me to. She owed money to some jeweler's and she wanted me to help her out.

Pushpinder thus betrays Meena to Jetender. Later, Jetender says to Meena, "Why did you take the money from Pushpinder? Why didn't you tell me?" When he questions his wife, Chaucer's Merchant seems most anxious about keeping his ledgers in balance; however, Jetender also seems to be demanding a different tale altogether—and one, to generalize to the BBC *Canterbury Tales* as a whole, Chaucer's modern adapters are eager to supply.

On the diachronicity of literature, Mikhail Bakhtin argues: "Works break through the boundaries of their own time, they live in centuries, that is in great time and frequently . . . their lives there are more intense and fuller than are their lives within their own time."[21] Perhaps what lifts a symbiont text out of mere parasitism is the degree to which it asks us to re-see the host text while also generating new meanings. A symbiont text both confirms the authority of its host text (in a conservative reading) as it subverts its cultural capital (in a radical reading). After Luthra, Chaucer's Shipman's Tale is simply not the text it was *before* Luthra. In a Bahktinian economy, unfettered by chronology, we can look from Luthra's apparent unknowing retrieval of a Sanskrit tale to Chaucer's text, or from Chaucer's text to Luthra's film—and take pleasure in wondering which is host and which is symbiont.

---

21. Mikhail Bakhtin, "Response to a Question from the *Novy Mir* Editorial Staff," *Speech Genres and Other Late Essays,* trans. Vern McGee, ed. Caryl Emerson and Michael Holquist (Austin: University of Texas Press, 1986), 1–9, 4.

CHAPTER 15

SEX, PLAGUE, AND RESONANCE
Reflections on the BBC "Pardoner's Tale"

ARTHUR BAHR

I'VE ALWAYS loved The Pardoner's Tale—the grim pleasure I take in its *riotoures*' elegantly realized downfall, the tautness of its narrative core as contrasted with its teller's expansive self-presentation, and the unsettling strangeness of the Pardoner's final exchange with the Host. I was excited to take up the 2003 BBC adaptation of Chaucer's text for other reasons, too, chief among them the fact that the "story" of The Pardoner's Tale, properly speaking, comprises only about 235 of the nearly 700 lines that the Pardoner speaks in Fragment VI. I was therefore curious as to how, with so much of the interest of The Pardoner's Tale bound up in the Pardoner himself, the BBC adaptation would translate Chaucer's text into a televisual medium that—as Steve Ellis points out in his contribution to this collection—has dispensed with pilgrim-narrators altogether. The adaptation's omission of Chaucer's frame-tale radically minimizes both the sexual queerness that the Pardoner embodies and the contextual queerness of his story's relation to the Canterbury pilgrimage as a whole.[1] Partly as a result, the nature of its moralizing

---

1. Here and throughout this essay, I adopt a capacious understanding of queerness as designating both non-normative, transgressive expressions of sex and gender and, more metaphorically, what is strange, uncanny, or inassimilable to established explanatory paradigms. On the overlap between these two dimensions, see Paulina Palmer, *The Queer Uncanny: New Perspectives on the Gothic* (Aberystwyth: University of Wales Press, 2012). The Pardoner's Tale is of course a key site for queer readings of medieval literature, as in Carolyn Dinshaw, *Chaucer's*

is also fundamentally different, concentrating on sexual violence rather than greed and using individuated characters rather than archetypes. These changes make the episode less complex than its source-text when approached on its own, but they also highlight fissures between medieval and modern, then and now, out of which new forms of literary, historical, and social resonance can emerge from Chaucer's still-evolving project.²

The opening shot of the BBC "Pardoner's Tale" is of stained, yellow teeth. We zoom out and discover that the teeth are those of an old man singing Louis Armstrong's "What a Wonderful World," and the vocals continue as the camera shifts to an attractive young woman, eighteen or so, riding her bicycle through an idyllic English townscape. As the music fades out, we hear a voice that many will recognize as Jonny Lee Miller's (more recently of *Elementary* fame) declaiming the famous "This sceptered isle, this England" speech from Shakespeare's *Richard II*.³ He performs in front of a cathedral for a crowd of camera-toting American and Japanese tourists. As the girl stops her bicycle to watch, two seedy youths pickpocket one of the tourists who is hanging, rapt, on Miller's celebration of England.

This scene establishes the program's main characters and also some of the ways in which the production will play with Chaucer's text. The three petty criminals are clearly the three *riotoures* of The Pardoner's Tale, but here they are differentiated from one another, unlike in Chaucer's treatment: one recites Shakespeare in a posh accent, while the other two are made obviously lower-class. (This distinction is treated more explicitly later in the narrative.) More significantly, Jonny Lee Miller's character, Arty, emerges as an amalgamation of one of the *riotoures* from within The Pardoner's Tale and of the Pardoner himself: here, bilking the gullible and naive in an ecclesiastical setting, just as the Pardoner does. (Subsequent flashbacks reveal Arty to have been a choir-boy in his youth, so he, like the Pardoner, is a singer.) I will return to the girl on the bicycle and the old man with the yellow teeth in a moment, but we should remember that although an old man is central to The Pardoner's Tale—he tells the *riotoures* how to find death—there are no individuated women in Chaucer's narrative.

Sexual Poetics (Madison: University of Wisconsin Press, 1990); Steven Kruger, "Claiming the Pardoner: Toward a Gay Reading of Chaucer's Pardoner's Tale," *Exemplaria* 6 (1994): 115–39; and Glenn Burger, *Chaucer's Queer Nation* (Minneapolis: University of Minnesota Press, 2002).

    2. On the concept of resonance as a literary phenomenon created by a text's evolution across time, see Wai Chee Dimock, "A Theory of Resonance," *PMLA* 112 (1997): 1060–71. I discuss this concept more fully later.

    3. Quotations of Shakespeare are taken from G. Blakemore Evans, ed., *The Riverside Shakespeare*, 2nd ed. (Boston: Houghton Mifflin, 1997), at 2.1.40.

This scene also works at a subtler level by testing its audience's knowledge of the culture-object that they are consuming. Many viewers will recognize Miller's speech in general terms, but only those who know Shakespeare well will recall that it is spoken by John of Gaunt, to whom Chaucer dedicated his *Book of the Duchess,* his first long poem and a memorialization of Gaunt's first wife, Blanche of Lancaster. She apparently died during an outbreak of the Black Plague, a potentially significant tangent point with The Pardoner's Tale, which opens with a description of pestilence stalking the land.[4] Likewise, only Shakespeare aficionados will remember that Gaunt's apparently triumphant nationalism—"This earth of majesty, this seat of Mars / This other Eden . . . This blessed plot, this earth, this realm, this England" (2.1.722–32)—is only the preface that makes even more bitter his ultimate condemnation, "that England, that was wont to conquer others, / Hath made a shameful conquest of itself" (2.1.747–48). These levels of resonance, which reside beneath the obvious structural correspondence between adaptation and poem (three ne'er-do-wells in each), propose the adaptation as a complex object that rewards critical reading. This sense is confirmed as it progresses and we realize that Arty quotes many famous authors, not just Shakespeare but also Dickens, Blake, and even Douglas Adams, who wrote *The Hitchhiker's Guide to the Galaxy.* This is a clever move on the part of the screenwriter, Tony Grounds, for it reinforces that such fixtures of the literary canon, not passages from the Bible, are "scriptural authorities" for the kind of audience likely to be watching a televised adaptation of the *Canterbury Tales.*

Before going any further, I should outline the basic plot of this adaptation. The three young men are indeed the counterparts of Chaucer's *riotoures,* but it emerges only gradually, and somewhat confusingly, that the girl with the bicycle, Kitty, is the ghost of a girl who was killed the previous year. She is visible to and interacts with some characters (like the *riotoures*) but is invisible to others (like her parents). Her parents learn that a second girl, Amy, has gone missing, and Kitty leaves to help in the search. Elsewhere, Arty pretends to join the search party and secures "donations" from the patrons of a local pub (more shades of the Pardoner there), but refuses to share the proceeds with his companions, Baz and Colin. At this point Arty notices and flirts with Kitty; she is curiously unresponsive but goes home with him anyway. After they have sex, Arty goes to wash up and returns to find Baz and Colin leering at Kitty threateningly. He indignantly shoos them away, and she abruptly announces that she knows who killed Amy. Arty is eager to find and kill the

---

4. References to Chaucer's *Canterbury Tales* are taken from *The Riverside Chaucer,* ed. Larry D. Benson, 3rd ed. (Boston: Houghton Mifflin, 1987), with these lines at 6.678–79.

malefactor so that he can become famous and admired. She leads the three *riotoures* to her parents' house, which has been abandoned since her death, and tells them to go inside; she watches from without. Frustrated and confused at finding the house empty, they start smashing up the place and then notice a glint of gold under the floorboards. They discover a cache of gold bullion, one bar of which Arty takes to have appraised, promising to bring back Indian takeout for dinner. Baz and Colin watch the news as they wait, and they see that Amy has just been found, dead. They recognize her, and we flash back to a scene of all three *riotoures* first hassling her on a lonely playground and then preparing to rape her in the woods nearby. Arty was the last to take his turn at her, so Baz and Colin now assume that he killed her after he was done. They are horrified at their friend's behavior; they were just having a bit of fun, but to kill her! They decide that someone like that doesn't deserve the money they have found, so they ready their cricket bats for his return. Arty, however, has put rat poison in the Indian food, and the denouement proceeds as in Chaucer's tale. After shots of the three bloody and foam-flecked corpses inside the house, Kitty gives a kiss to her sleeping parents and then leads Amy up a set of stone stairs into the sunlight.

In a way, this moral trajectory is quite similar to that of The Pardoner's Tale: Chaucer's gamblers and drinkers are revealed to be murderers, and these petty criminals are revealed to be rapists. The decision to make sexual predation the core of the episode is especially significant, however, for The Pardoner's Tale initially seems like it might be going in that direction as well, but then conspicuously declines to do so. At the beginning of the tale proper, for example, the Pardoner says that taverns such as those frequented by his *riotoures* are also home to dancing girls and singers, officers of the devil who kindle the fire of lechery (6.191–96)—but quickly changes the topic to that of drunkenness. Lust never comes up again, so we could take a quasi-psychoanalytic approach and regard the Pardoner's quick turn away from what would seem to be a naturally contiguous vice to those he describes (and I use that word *natural* advisedly) as evidence of his own unresolved relation to sex and gender.[5] The rhetorical bombast of the Pardoner's apostrophes on the sins that he *does* condemn lends some credence to that argument.

Either way, this anxiety on the part of the Pardoner (if that is how we choose to interpret it) finds an analogue in some of the changes that the BBC adaptation makes to its source-text. In the first place, by making heterosexual

---

5. For an analysis of the appeal and limitations of psychoanalytic theory as it pertains to medieval literature generally, and The Pardoner's Tale especially, see Lee Patterson, "Chaucer's Pardoner on the Couch: Psyche and Clio in Medieval Literary Studies," *Speculum* 76 (2001): 638–80.

rape central both to the plot and to our gradually deepening loathing of its *riotoures,* the adaptation suppresses the queerness of the Pardoner and his tale. Partly by removing the sexually ambiguous Pardoner, the program takes his rather eerie tale and makes it simply, and all too comprehensibly, ghastly. In Chaucer's tale, it is the hubris of the *riotoures'* belief that they can kill Death (capital D) that starts them on the path to death (lowercase d). This is hardly admirable, not least because it makes clear their ignorance of the fundamental law of mortality, but there is nevertheless something rather grand about the scale of their ambition, however doomed it proves to be (one thinks, if only glancingly, of Don Giovanni or Doctor Faustus). The adaptation's *riotoures,* by contrast, are never more than petty thugs, even and perhaps especially in their most heinous actions. The old man of Chaucer's poem is queer in the sense of uncanny and liminal; he seems to invite allegorical interpretation but never provides enough cues for us to feel confident of exactly who or what he is. The episode, by contrast, gives his function in the story to a character, Kitty, who is personally invested in the proceedings: her vigil outside her parents' house at the episode's end, as she waits and watches as the *riotoures* destroy themselves, clearly implies that she seeks revenge. It thereby imposes normative comprehensibility upon the proceedings.

It is in the conclusions of the adaptation and tale, however, that this contrast emerges most pointedly. Famously, Chaucer's Pardoner concludes his tale by encouraging the pilgrims to buy his pardons and relics, and he singles out the Host, Harry Bailly, as especially sinful: "Com forth, sire Hoost, and offre first anon, / And thou shalt kisse the relikes everychon, / Ye, for a grote! Unbokele anon thy purs" (6.943–45). The Wife of Bath has already established a man's "purse" as slang for his genitals, so it is hard not to perceive the sexual innuendo of these lines. The Host certainly seems to, for he reacts furiously, accusing the Pardoner of asking him to kiss his old underwear even though it is stained with excrement. He wishes that he had the Pardoner's balls in his hand; let them be cut off, he says, I'll help you carry them, and I'll put them in a reliquary of hog shit. The Pardoner is so enraged that he cannot speak—a striking moment for someone whose identity is defined by always having a smooth-talking word at hand. The Knight intervenes and effects a reconciliation so the tale-telling contest can continue, and he urges the Host to kiss the Pardoner; they do, and that's how the tale and Fragment VI end.

There is queerness aplenty here, and it is not just sexual, for while the Pardoner undoubtedly has an ambiguous relationship to biological sex, socially constructed gender, and sexual orientation, his social gambits on the pilgrimage itself, and his relation to his tale, are also deeply strange. What con man reveals his tricks to his audience and then attempts to con the very audience whom he's disabused? By stripping the narrative core of the tale of its complex framing devices—the pilgrim-Pardoner, his Prologue, and the tale's almost-violent grace note—the makers of the adaptation remove not just the sexual but also the contextual queerness of The Pardoner's Tale as a literary enterprise. The decision to tie up the loose ends in its closing frames, by using a voice-over from the news to make explicit that Arty is responsible for the deaths of both Kitty and Amy, is antithetical to Chaucer's closing gambit, which raises unsettling questions instead of answering them.

This (for me) unsatisfying aspect of the adaptation reinforces how intimately sexual and literary forms of queerness are related here, which leads to another of the screenwriter's most significant changes to Chaucer's text: the decision to make what is stalking the town a predator rather than a plague. This change enables its ironic twist by which the monster that the *riotoures* seek is, quite literally, themselves. But it fundamentally alters the nature of the drama in ways uncannily congruent with the de-queering of the Pardoner by means of the violent heterosexuality of his quasidouble, Arty. He and his fellows prey upon young women: horrible, but hardly indiscriminate. The plague of Chaucer's Pardoner's Tale, by contrast, slays "man and wommam, child, and hyne, and page" (6.688). This makes the BBC production about villainy rather than death—unsurprising, perhaps, given contemporary Western culture's pervasive refusal to acknowledge the reality of death (recall the hysteria over "death panels" that attended the quite modest attempts to include end-of-life counseling in the recent U.S. health care reform law). But this change aligns the program's makers with the *riotoures* of Chaucer's story in the sense that both attempt to transform death, the one universal human reality, into a concrete adversary who can be vanquished: Arty, Baz, and Colin, who are righteously slain by their own iniquities and the retributive force of their victim's ghost.

Furthermore, the nature of the fears engendered by these two phenomena—plague as opposed to predator—is fundamentally different. What is scary about a plague is not just that it targets its victims indiscriminately but also the sense of helplessness that it imposes, the fact that we cannot fight back against it in anything like the visceral, clawing-and-biting way that we can against a physical aggressor. (It is presumably to compensate for this helplessness that we so often use a martial lexicon—"I'm going to fight/beat this"—to talk about our relationship to many diseases.) In that sense, then, cancer would have been the better modern analogue for Chaucer's Black Death. But three young men who want to go out and kill cancer? That sounds like some of the MIT students whom I teach and write recommendations for, not the vile thugs of the adaptation—which in turn suggests one way in which the adaptation might have made its antagonists more complex and thus more deeply troubling.

But precisely because of how thoroughly the episode sidelines its source-text's queerness, the plague that kept recurring for me was AIDS, for it was initially regarded *not* as an indiscriminate killer, like so many other frightening diseases, but rather, as Pat Robertson put it, as "God's way of weeding his garden." Eve Sedgwick quotes that line as part of a queer reading of *Billy Budd*,[6] which is enabled in part by the *double entendres* that a whole group of words (such as *mysterious, peculiar, obscure,* and *secretive*) that, as Wai Chee Dimock brilliantly explains, "boosted by the noise of homophobia, now rise above the threshold of detectability to be heard as if for the first time."[7] Dimock uses Sedgwick's reading as an example of what she calls *resonance,* by which she means how the historically evolving semantic range of particular words creates evolving interpretive potentialities in and around the texts in which those words appear. Adaptations that are distant in time or medium from their source-text can have a similar effect,[8] and that is what this episode did for me: its suppressions enabled me to find in Chaucer's text forms of contemporary resonance—and relevance, as I will argue in the last paragraphs of this essay—that were obscure to me before. That resonance centers on two phenomena: insouciance and forgetfulness.

I am too young to remember the early 1980s, but I vividly remember the late '80s, which is when, as a boy, I learned what homosexuality was: it was bad, and it would kill you (me). Those realities substantially preceded my discovery both of what the word actually meant and of the fact that I myself was an initially reluctant, now proud, member of the tribe. My behaviors are still shaped by that early recognition that a pestilential predator is out there, stalking the unwary. But I have met many a gay (in both senses of the word) young *riotour* with no memory of AIDS as a ruthlessly killing rather than a chronic disease and who, as a result, regularly engages in behavior not just risky but death-seeking. There's a kind of perverse forgetfulness here that evokes not just that of Chaucer's *riotoures*, who forget both their initial quest

---

6. Eve Kosofsky Sedgwick, *Epistemology of the Closet* (Berkeley: University of California Press, 1990), 129.

7. Dimock, "Resonance," 1068.

8. For an argument along similar lines, see Kathleen Coyne Kelly's contribution to this volume, specifically her contention that "after Luthra [its director for the BBC], Chaucer's Shipman's Tale is simply not the text it was *before* Luthra."

and their vows of comradeship as soon as they find the gold, but also what the Pardoner himself assumes of his audience at the end of his tale—since his final rhetorical gambit would seem to suppose that they have forgotten what he has just told them of his duplicitous modus operandi.

Bringing the focus back to Chaucer, it is worth thinking a bit about timelines. The Black Plague first hit England in 1348 and decimated the country, receding by 1350. During a subsequent outbreak, in 1368, John of Gaunt's wife Blanche died, a bereavement that Chaucer dramatizes in his first long poem, the *Book of the Duchess*. While writing the majority of the *Canterbury Tales* in the 1390s, Chaucer would have had vivid memories of the outbreak that killed Blanche and hazier but still formative ones of the first outbreak of 1348–50 (he was born around 1340). And because of his extensive European travels, he would also know of the apparent randomness, itself deeply frightening, with which various recurrences of the disease struck different parts of the continent. This, then, is another form of historical resonance that helps Chaucer's text to emerge as a warning against forgetfulness.

It is also a warning against what I call, provisionally at least, insouciance. By that word I mean to evoke the carefree, even hedonistic, elements of the gay male subset of queer culture. This aspect of queer culture evolved at least partly as a response to oppression, which produced a need to release pent-up and otherwise inexpressible energies. Doing so can be immensely liberating, not just for queers like me but also for all of us in a profession, like academia, that valorizes and incentivizes a work-centered understanding of life. But care*free*-ness, in the sense of the Castle of Sans Souci from Oscar Wilde's fairy story "The Happy Prince," can readily become care*less*-ness, insouciance in its negative sense, a kind of self-destructive heedlessness—to which, as we all know, Wilde himself succumbed with the ill-judged libel case that he brought against the Marquess of Queensbury. Chaucer was more circumspect. Biographies of the poet regularly marvel at how adroitly he navigated the treacherous political shoals of late Ricardian England, managing to keep both his head (whereas friend Thomas Usk lost his) and, for the most part, his annuities.

Doing so requires knowing where one is situated and what the lay of the land is. But the queerness of the conclusion of Chaucer's Pardoner's Tale, even as it cautions against forgetful insouciance of the realities of evil and death, also unmoors us from the interpretive security that would constitute a literary analogue to Chaucer's biographical circumspection. And that may be the poem's most challenging paradox: its narrative core demands from us a rigorously trained self-awareness that its contextual queerness makes difficult or impossible to feel fully secure in.[9] By smoothing over those difficulties, the BBC adaptation makes the even more unsettling nature of its source-text emerge with new resonance. In that sense it helps to keep Chaucer's poem lively and vital: a final, salutary rebuke to death, both lowercase and capital D.

---

9. On the contextual difficulties posed by Fragment VI, see Donald Howard's influential characterization of it as "floating," in *The Idea of the* Canterbury Tales (Berkeley: University of California Press, 1976), 333–39. This notion has been further developed by a range of scholars working within a host of different theoretical frameworks.

CHAPTER 16

TIME, MEMORY, AND DESIRE IN THE BBC "MAN OF LAW'S TALE"

KATHLEEN DAVIS

OPENING SCENES: expanse of still, blue water, gentle sound of wind chime, bird call; *Quick cut* to parched gold-brown dirt, blurred fast-paced movement, panicked breathing, panicked woman's face, bloodied gold cross on open dead hand, buzzing flies.

When is this? It could be the eighth century, or the fourteenth, or it could be now. As it turns out, it is now, if by that we mean the early twenty-first century. But it is also "now" in the sense of what Carolyn Dinshaw calls "a temporal simultaneity in which past and present appear in the *now* simultaneously."[1] In these opening scenes of the BBC version of Chaucer's Man of Law's Tale, the panicked woman is Constance (Nikki Amuka-Bird), a Nigerian woman caught in the midst of Christian-Muslim violence. The dead hand belongs to her Christian mother; her dead Muslim father is just inside. Soon, Constance will drift into those still, blue English waters in a small lifeboat, a lone refugee from religious strife, just as Chaucer's Custance drifted onto the Northumbrian shore. "That is an image whose time has come again," says Olivia Hetreed, author of the BBC version of the The Man of Law's Tale, who

---

1. Carolyn Dinshaw, *How Soon Is Now? Medieval Texts, Amateur Readers, and the Queerness of Time* (Durham: Duke University Press, 2012), 70.

adds, "The more I looked into it, the more it became about immigrants and faith." The tension between Christianity and Islam, too, Hetreed muses, "seems to be sadly relevant to our times."[2]

Unlike the other BBC versions of the *Canterbury Tales*, which focus on aspects of human relationships long enduring in literature—love triangles, jealousy and greed, sex and aging, lust and sexual predators—the BBC "Man of Law's Tale" attends to such themes but also focuses on specific historical events that correlate with those Chaucer contemplated: bloodletting between Christians and Muslims, interconnected with economic motivation and European intervention in points south and east. For viewers of this BBC production who are familiar with Chaucer's fourteenth-century tale, the irony that *his* Custance finds herself a religious refugee/boat person/immigrant to England becomes palpable, if not downright eerie, and it invokes the question of the entire complex of economic and political forces connecting then and now. The tale's attention to the possibility of temporal heterogeneity by which "past and present appear in the *now* simultaneously" operates both on the level of the viewer and of the characters and underscores the degree to which Chaucer's tale engages questions of historical time and memory. At the same time, by naming the heroine Constance "Musa" (Muslim for "Moses"), the BBC version explicitly invokes one of Chaucer's textual models (in this case the biblical story of bloodletting between Egyptians and Israelites) and thereby extends its reference to endless cycles of ethnic and religious violence. *This* Constance, set adrift like the baby Moses, also reminds viewers familiar with Chaucer of his frequent musings on historical repetition and its interconnections with textuality.

The relationship between historical time and the time of memory is emphasized throughout the BBC production, which pares Chaucer's geopolitical triangle—Rome, Syria, England—down to two: England and Nigeria. The marriage proposed for Chaucer's Roman princess Custance with the Sultan of Syria, who agrees to convert from Islam to Christianity, is reflected in the interfaith marriage of the BBC Constance's parents. Likewise, the massacre ordered by the Sultan's outraged mother in Chaucer's tale parallels the Muslim/Christian violence in which Constance's parents are murdered before her eyes. Fearing for the young woman's safety, an aunt secures Constance passage (presumably illegal) on a freighter, but when customs officials intercept the freighter, the fearful crew sets her adrift in a lifeboat. Thus Constance—traumatized, clutching her mother's cross, and with no memory of the recent

---

2. Quoted from Stephen Pile, "The Scriptwriters' Tales," *The Telegraph*, 30 Aug. 2003, www.telegraph.co.uk.

violence—drifts into the Thames estuary, where she is found by Mark Constable and carried to his home and to his African wife, Nicky. Mark and Nicky correspond to Chaucer's constable and his wife, Hermengyld, and within their household, interfaith and interracial relations begin to interchange within the larger issue of immigration. Just as Chaucer's Custance swears that she has lost her memory and could not (or would not) explain who she is, Constance has no memory of the events that brought her there. "I had to leave Nigeria," she recalls, "but . . . I do not remember." This inability to account for herself raises Mark's suspicions and fear of immigration authorities, particularly when Constance awakes screaming from nightmares (that provide piecemeal glimpses into the past she forgets). But Nicky, empathetic, insists that they claim her as her niece who has come for a visit, thus substituting herself for the aunt who sent Constance across the sea.

The strong bond between the women, like that between Custance and Hermengyld, forms in spite of—even depends upon—its disconnect with historical time. Indeed, Constance's oblivion of her past, like the amnesia of Chaucer's Custance, allows for the temporary stasis of this domestic arrangement, a suspension of history in which political difference plays no part. Mark wants answers in the form of historical explanations, but Nicky insists upon a simple, empathetic embrace. The violent details of historical events, unremembered, are irrelevant to the women's relationship, which, to the degree that it is "out of sync" with ordinary measurements of temporality, subsists in what Dinshaw calls an asynchronous, or "queer," *now*. For Dinshaw, such a time can be "wondrous, marvelous, full of queer potential," and such potential is evident in the BBC's and Chaucer's portrayal of this temporality.[3] However, for Nicky and Constance, as for Chaucer's Hermegyld and Custance, this comforting time also bears a conflicted relation to patriarchal historical time. As the BBC version emphasizes, this asynchronous *now* does have political dimensions in that it results from the trauma of political-ethnic-religious-economic violence, which is also to say state authority. For this reason it is fated not to survive. The BBC "Man of Law's Tale" makes the implications of this paradoxical relation apparent by connecting Constance's amnesia to the role of oblivion in British domestic policy. When Nicky suggests that Constance pose as her niece, Constance objects, "I am Fulani." Nicky replies, "And I'm Yoruba. Frankly, as long as we're both black, no English person will question it." Whereas in Nigeria Fulani herders and settled Yoruba are among the peoples struggling against each other for scarce resources, in England immigrants are simply "black," a generic racial

---

3. Dinshaw, *How Soon*, 4.

designation that need not attend to—or remember—the specificities of this economic struggle, its connections to a global economy, or the history it shares with Europe.⁴

In *History, Memory, and State-Sponsored Violence*, Berber Bevernage studies the implications of such oblivion with respect to the relations of historical time, memory, and justice. Like others before him, he observes that dominant conceptions of time are generally aligned with the perpetrators of injustice. He argues that the authoritative "time of history" conceives of time as always moving forward, positioning the past as irretrievably gone and insisting upon "a break between past and present that is threatened by a memory that refuses to let the past go."⁵ For Dinshaw, this "time of history" is the linear time of patriarchal reproduction, and in Bevernage's analysis it usually supports state power at the expense of victims of injustice. The forgetting of past injustice is precisely what state authority often demands: for the sake of unity and peace, victims must consign their past to oblivion despite their insistence that it is *not* past, that the "disappeared" are not "dead." For these victims this past (if *past* is even the appropriate term) is irrevocable and persists, haunting the present and defying the very operation of dividing present from past. Ironically, then, Constance's amnesia in part accords with the needs of state authority. The past that haunts her present must not be allowed to exist—be *present* in British domestic space—as the tale's references to immigration authorities and threats of deportation constantly remind us. "Constance" will never recall her past while she is in Britain, but as her name implies, she bears memory's struggle for "eternal contemporaneity," always under assault by forces determining the historicity of the past.⁶

As in Chaucer's tale, the destruction of the women's relationship comes in the form of erotic violence, which is here also associated with religion and spiritual desire. Terry, a member of the local evangelist Christian congregation to which Constance (likely a Pentecostal Christian) has gravitated, is the

---

4. Most commentators note that the violence in Nigeria is at root economic and is more ethnic than religious, with religion often providing either a conveniently visible target or a means to gain outside support. See, for example, Murray Last, "Muslims and Christians in Nigeria: An Economy of Political Panic," *The Round Table* 96.392 (Oct. 2007): 605–16.

5. Berber Bevernage, *History, Memory, and State-Sponsored Violence* (New York: Routledge, 2012), 4. Bevernage contrasts the "time of history" with the "time of jurisdiction," which allows for the persistence of the past and thus the availability of justice for victims. He focuses particularly on "truth commissions" set up after extreme ethnic violence and studies the implications of their compromise between recognizing past injustice and at the same time consigning it irrevocably to the past, thus eliminating its continued existence in the present. See especially his introduction.

6. Bevernage, *History*, 14, citing Yosef Yerushalmi, *Zakhor: Jewish History and Jewish Memory* (Seattle: University of Washington Press, 2002), 96.

counterpart to Chaucer's lustful knight. Incapable of parsing or controlling his desires, Terry becomes the mechanism for the tale's correlation of spiritual and sexual desire—thus foregrounding another latent current in Chaucer's tale. Indeed, the BBC episode explicitly connects Terry and his desire to the violent religious strife in which Constance's parents died: when the congregation welcomes her and the minister leads the responsum "Lord have mercy," Terry hovers near, his gaze already a leer. Constance is transported to her own murmur of "Lord have mercy" just before her mother is shot, and she faints. The camera cuts directly from Terry's gaze to the flashback of Constance's panicked desperation at the moment of her mother's death, a scene that is later replayed when Terry murders Nicky. That later scene is foreshadowed here when Constance comes to, with both Nicky and Terry leaning over her, already in competition, with Terry unable to stop touching, touching . . .

•

Constance's recurring nightmares, which give us a fragmented sense of the past she forgets, intersperse with a series of flash-forwards to the future; thus the viewer is processing bits of past, present, and future all at once—another indication of this production's focus on time and a provocation to consider its engagement with Jacques Derrida's insistence upon the "noncontemporaneity with itself of the living present."[7] The time of this tale is "out of joint" not only because it is asynchronous and centered on a time never consciously present but also because it invites us to see its present as haunted by centuries of victims to senseless violence. The flash-forwards begin the moment Constance makes an emotional connection to Alan King (this tale's version of Chaucer's King Alla, played by Andrew Lincoln), an employee of Mark who has been staying with his domineering, racist mother, Leila, in the large country house she declares his "birthright." Unlike Chaucer's tale, which does not introduce King Alla until Custance's trial for the murder of Hermengyld, the BBC production introduces Alan on the day of Constance's arrival. He stops by to pick up Mark and sees her as she, curious, gazes down at him from a window, quickly withdrawing when she's seen. Thus a charming, quite courtly romance begins, in sharp contrast to Terry's menacing pursuit.

At a dinner party arranged by Leila, the couple engages in their first conversation, light and playful. Only with Alan does Constance smile. Nicky snaps a photo of the pair. The tale then flashes forward to the British embassy

---

7. Jacques Derrida, *Specters of Marx: The State of the Debt, the Work of Mourning, and the New International* (New York: Routledge, 1994), xix.

in Nigeria, where Alan, tattered photo in hand, is desperately trying to find Constance. We learn that she had gone there with "papers" but reported a robbery and, paperless, was handed over to the Nigerian police. From that point we toggle back and forth between this search and the developing romance between Constance and Alan, as well as the resistance to it by Leila and by Terry. Connections with Alan always take us to the future and to his quest; connections with Terry provoke an upsurge of the repressed, violent past. Likewise, the narrative dances between Alan's courtship of Constance, usually on the sunny open sea as he teaches her to sail (thus answering Chaucer's many references to her "steerless" ship), and Terry's lascivious pursuit, always in dimly lit, religious settings. Nicky is a steady presence, a facilitator for Alan and Constance, and an object of Terry's growing jealousy.

Unlike Chaucer's lustful knight, who carefully plots his murder of Hermengyld to frame Custance after she spurns his advances, Terry is compulsive and confused. Arriving unannounced one evening after Constance has been out sailing with Alan and the couple has exchanged their first kiss, Terry finds Constance alone in the kitchen. He addresses her at first with questions and pleas but quickly escalates to a state of violent, erotic rage, intensified by his jealousy of both Nicky and Alan. Misrecognizing Constance's "sign of peace" in church as a sign of sexual desire, he insists she "liked it in church" and begins his physical assault as he accuses her of "messing with my head . . . I pray, but all I see is you. . . . I get these thoughts . . . ." Hearing Constance scream, Nicky arrives and intervenes. The viewer never sees the raised knife that triggers Constance's return to the traumatic scene of her mother's death, and in her vision, as well as the viewer's, Terry's attack and his murder of Nicky is exchanged with the attack and murder of Constance's mother. If Terry's confusion and mania signal the proximity of sexuality and spirituality, then his violence—perhaps "psychopathic desire" on the level of the individual, as Kathleen Forni suggests[8]—also signals the mass violence that can be unleashed in the name of religion. Once again, the past persists, and is simultaneous with, the present. When Mark returns home, he finds Constance cradling and rocking Nicky's blood-soaked body, remembering nothing.

Constance is charged with murder and is thus plunged into the legal and political system that Nicky had held at bay. When Alan visits her in prison, he becomes frustrated by her steadfast faith and insistence upon God's purpose. The difference between their religious positions and its relationship to sex was clear from their first exchange. In contrast to Terry's unchecked spiritual/

---

8. Kathleen Forni, "Popular Chaucer: The BBC's *Canterbury Tales*," *Parergon* 25.1 (2008): 171–89, 182.

erotic desire, Alan expressed his agnosticism with humor: "Me and God we practice safe religion. Kind of like safe sex, but not as fun." Constance recognizes that he is "joking," and it is this space of difference—between signifiers and meaning, between religious/sexual passion and agnosticism/restraint (safe sex)—that holds intensity in check and gives this interracial, intercultural relationship room to breathe.

With Terry's murder of Nicky this opening seems to collapse. Alan, as had Mark before him, now demands that Constance explain what happened—to deliver the past—and thereby save herself. He thus works within the conception of the "time of history" that Bevernage analyzes as associated with state authority—the very authority that incarcerates Constance. Positioned as the perpetrator of injustice, she must turn the past into evidence. Her temporal dilemma is thus aligned with Bevernage's observation that "the disjointedness of time can be a feature of injustice, but it also conditions the very possibility of justice."[9] Constance, however, can only proclaim that she cannot remember and that Jesus will save her, a belief that defies her experience: "My God is a jealous God," she cries, "the ones I love, they die." At this point, the uncompromising changelessness of "constancy" appears desolate and destructive, dedicated to a closed system that is by definition self-annihilating. The connection between God's and Terry's jealousy, linked to the violence of Constance's past, is inescapable and points to the violent potential of "extremism." On the other hand, Constance's changelessness and unswerving faith interchanges with the imperative of guarding the "eternal contemporaneity" of the past, even though in this case it is a past that, for reasons of state, Constance cannot remember. Her eventual recollection of this past will alter, but not eliminate, the political dilemma inherent in this relation of change and changelessness, history and memory, as we will see.

In a sense Jesus does save Constance through Terry's own belief, which becomes the mechanism of his self-condemnation. In Chaucer's trial scene, the lustful knight self-accuses when his body betrays him: he swears falsely upon the Bible, a supernatural hand strikes him, and his eyes burst from his head. In the BBC version, Terry likewise swears falsely, and Constance, stunned by this behavior, can only insist to her lawyer: "He is a Christian. He believes in God. . . . He swore an oath on the bible." The lawyer takes the point, and with Terry on the stand she presses him about his jealousy and about his oath: "You understand that perjury is not only a criminal offense, but breaking the oath you swore on the Bible." He quickly dissolves, unable to sustain the self-difference of his lie. Here, for the last time in this BBC tale, spiritual desire

---

9. Bevernage, *History,* 144.

aligns with destruction—this time self-destruction. Moreover, with Terry's exit we never again see a flashback to Constance's repressed past; when we next see and hear of this past, it will be in her own words.

Meanwhile, the flash-forwards show Alan going deeper into rural Nigeria and its bubbling hostilities. From here on, the tale tightens these present and future narrative threads until they converge in Nigeria. We learn that after being exonerated, Constance must nonetheless be deported as an illegal alien, with the only recourse being marriage to a citizen. Alan enthusiastically proposes, over Leila's objections: "think of all the differences" she pleads, echoing her earlier racist comment about Nicky. Over her objections the couple marries, and like Chaucer's Donegild (King Alla's mother), Leila becomes the new villain. Thus this version makes no attempt to reconfigure the tale's misogynistic trope of the evil mother-in-law present in Chaucer's tale. Leila's opportunity arises when the couple must temporarily separate. Whereas in Chaucer's tale King Alla departs on a military sojourn shortly after marrying and impregnating Custance, here it is Constance who must travel to Nigeria to claim her visa and then return as a legal citizen. In both cases, then, the separation is due to reasons of state. From the flash-forwards we discover that the pregnant Constance was treated brutally by Nigerian authorities but, rescued by a priest, safely delivered a boy.

The narrative of Constance's abuse interchanges with that of Leila's manipulation and lies. We learn that, when under arrest in Nigeria, Constance twice tries to phone Alan, once through the mediation of a Nigerian official and once directly. However, Leila intercepts the calls, denying the marriage and telling Constance that Alan "doesn't wish you to speak to him. It's all a mistake." Again like Donegild, as Alan learns from Mark nearly a year later, Leila forges a letter—in this case an email purportedly from Constance to Alan stating that she had planned her return to Nigeria all along and did not wish him to pursue her. Upon Alan's discovery of the truth, the narrative reduces to a single temporal thread: Alan standing face to face with Constance as she finally tells her story in full.

The question of difference, whether linguistic (metaphors, jokes, lies, broken oaths), temporal disjunction, physical separation, cultural/racial difference, or British wealth/Nigerian poverty, jostles throughout this tale with that of sameness—truth, "constancy," synchrony, identity. Their relations function both with respect to Constance's story of twenty-first-century violence and to the repetition/persistence of such violence over the centuries—constantly reimported, as it were, over the waves of time. In the resolution of her story, Constance gains some control of the past that had haunted her and marked both her asynchronous existence and her political dilemma. The specter of her unremembered past, to cite Bevernage, "is not just a piece of 'traumatic' past popping up into the present; rather, its logic questions the entire traditional relationship among past, present, and future."[10] What would it mean to exorcise the specter?

In an important sense, Constance does exorcise the specter, in a manner that accords precisely with Dinshaw's points that "patriarchal reproduction enacts temporal progress" and "the birth of sons is the proper measure of time's passing."[11] Sure enough, at the very moment that Constance delivers a son, the queerness of her asynchronicity disappears, and time is straightened out. When they reunite, Constance explains to Alan that at the instant of her son's birth, her memory returned: "When he was born, I remembered. It was a blessing from God to give me back my past." She tells (and we see) the story of her father's and mother's murders in its full context of religious conflict and unchecked violence. Thus she finally "delivers" the past, sets it within chronology, and as such consigns it *to* the past. In her analysis of patriarchal time, Dinshaw suggests that the "spectacular asynchrony interposed by the divine" often resides in the "image of a pregnant woman."[12] In this BBC tale, such divine interposition interchanges with state violence, and Constance suffered asynchrony as she carried the weight of its disjunction from the authoritative "time of history." At no point in the tale is she able to challenge this time of history, to confront it with a memory that, in Bevenage's terms, is also a living present. Even more emphatically than Chaucer's version of this tale, then, the BBC production repositions Constance within the logic of historical reproduction, upon which her happy life in the British metropole with Alan will depend.

In this sense, the outcome of Constance's tale is not in the spirit of Dinshaw's project, which seeks to recuperate the asynchronous in a more celebratory way than is possible in a study of temporality linked with historical violence. Indeed, given Dinshaw's points about the gendered and sexed character of *straight* time, it could hardly work otherwise for Constance, the very carrier of this historical, reproductive time. Her only respite was the amnesia brought on by trauma, the ironic potential of which is signaled by her relationship with Nicky, unencumbered by the demand to recount the past as state evidence. Nonetheless, the possibilities of thinking Dinshaw's "heterogeneous *now* in which the divide between living and dead, material and immaterial,

---

10. Bevernage, *History*, 142–43.
11. Dinshaw, *How Soon*, 48.
12. Dinshaw, *How Soon*, 56.

reality and fiction, text and spirit, present and past is unsettled,"[13] is precisely what is at stake in this tale, if not all the tales, in this BBC series. Reminding us that the conditions of temporal disjunction, spectrality, and asynchronicity are themselves always historically specific yet also the conditions of history, these tales tap into Chaucer's pained and perhaps bewildered engagement with temporality, with the impossibility of a present that is contemporaneous with itself.

---

13. Dinshaw, *How Soon*, 37.

PART V
ABSENT PRESENCE

CHAPTER 17

MARKETING CHAUCER
Mad Men *and the* Wife of Bath

LAURIE FINKE and MARTIN B. SHICHTMAN

IT IS NEARLY impossible to conjure up again the gleeful horror with which we watched the initial episodes of *Mad Men* (2007–15) for the first time. For those of us old enough to be children of the 1950s, there was a breathtaking audacity in scenes depicting ten-year-old Sally (Kiernan Shipka) playing "spaceman" with a plastic dry cleaning bag on her head or mixing martinis for family guests, or Anne Dudek playing a hugely pregnant suburban housewife, Francine Hanson, puffing away on a cigarette and swilling a cocktail. It was as if our ids were given permission by proxy to indulge in all the things today we are too well-socialized to do, activating a "spiky nostalgia" that hit just the right tension "between longing and disavowal."[1] This was not history; this was *zeitgeist*. Scenes like these hooked us on the show. Slavoj Žižek reminds us that "in the fantasy-scene, the desire is not fulfilled, 'satisfied,' but constituted (given its objects, and so on)." He suggests that fantasy is the frame, the "window," through which the desired object is both realized and revealed, through which *"we learn 'how to desire.'"*[2] Even as entire cable television networks

---

1. The term *spiky nostalgia* comes from Jerome de Groot, "Perpetually Dividing and Suturing the Past and Present: *Mad Men* and the Illusions of History," *Rethinking History* 15 (2011): 269–85, 276. Also see Aviva Dove-Viebahn, "Mourning Becomes the *Mad Men*," *InVisible Culture* 17 (2012), ivc.lib.rochester.edu.

2. Slavoj Žižek, *The Sublime Object of Ideology* (New York: Verso, 1989), 118; italics in original.

251

like TV Land offered constant reruns of 1950s situation comedies, AMC's *Mad Men* allowed the television screen to reframe the fantasy of that decade, teaching us not to long for the America of *Leave It to Beaver, The Adventures of Ozzie and Harriet,* and *I Love Lucy* but rather to desire the strangely erotic dream of family and workplace dysfunction, where fathers drink heavily and womanize, while stay-at-home moms pop diet pills and share malignant gossip about too-pretty neighbors. The raw power of the male gaze was never so blatant as the scene in Episode Six ("Babylon") in which the office secretaries apply lipstick while their bosses watch behind one-way glass, drinking and wisecracking at the midday entertainment. Here was not merely a binary system of unequal gender relations, or even sexism, but egregious and brazen misogyny, openly and joyfully let loose to play among the characters and storylines—a misogyny so atavistic, it seems almost, well, medieval. These episodes were a win-win scenario for viewers. Closet misogynists could revel nostalgically in a time when men were men and women shut up and looked sexy. Feminists and postfeminists alike could take solace in what a long way we have come, baby, secure that sexism has been swept away with the other detritus of the period, perhaps through warning labels like those that now come with dry cleaning bags, cigarettes, and booze.[3]

Concomitant with its predilection for flouting social pieties, *Mad Men* was one of a number of hour-long dramas produced by cable networks that turned conventional network televisual narrative on its head. *Mad Men* has never been either a serial or a series but an innovative hybrid of the two styles.[4] Like soap operas, it presents often season-long arcs for its characters, the end of an episode never quite coinciding with the end of a storyline. But it also contains elements of the series in which each episode is a self-contained narrative. Despite continuity of character and setting, the series stresses discontinuities from episode to episode. Just as it has its nostalgia and critiques it, *Mad Men* has its narrative cake and eats it too, juggling forty-three-minute storytelling with narratives that spill out of this temporal container.

---

3. We demur from Scott Stoddart's argument that the show "de-romanticizes the era" ("Camelot Regained," *Analyzing* Mad Men: *Critical Essays on the Television Series,* ed. Scott Stoddart [Jefferson, NC: MacFarland, 2011], 207–33, 220). While later seasons show Don Draper, his marriage, and his work life spiraling out of control, the early episodes we examine unfold in a kind of romantic haze that often colors recreations of the 1950s. On *Mad Men's* postfeminist politics, see Katixa Agirre, "'Whenever a Man Takes You to Lunch around Here': Tracing Post-Feminist Sensibility in *Mad Men*," *Catalan Journal of Communication and Cultural Studies* 4 (2012): 155–69.

4. Monique Miggelbrink, "Serializing the Past: Re-evaluating History in *Mad Men*," *InVisible Culture* 17 (2012), ivc.lib.rochester.edu.

The show's narrative innovations allow us the liberty to break off a chunk of text for analysis that coincides with neither the episode nor the season. The first three episodes of *Mad Men* offer a meditation on the creativity of the advertising industry: the show is about the rise of the great Madison Avenue publicity houses during the late 1950s.[5] They also open up the prospect of the 1950s as a time of radical self-fashioning, introducing the range of opportunities offered—and just as often taken away—by an American society in flux, where class and financial status, sexual and racial politics, are all beginning to unravel. We propose to examine a minor arc that develops in these episodes that we believe remediates—adapts—a decidedly Chaucerian subplot. Haunting the episodes that introduce the show's hero, Don Draper (Jon Hamm), are—perhaps—subtle allusions to Chaucer and his Wife of Bath. The first three episodes of the series play with the figure of Chaucer's Wife of Bath, herself an "adapted" text made up of references and allusions to a plethora of classical, biblical, and medieval misogynist texts that delimit how she can imagine herself and how she is imagined by others. What *Mad Men* and The Wife of Bath's Prologue and Tale might have in common are the ways in which they explore the various publicities that can and will be attached to women, reflecting on who is empowered to create these publicities in times of social, political, and economic change. By publicities we are referring to discourses that manage the public's perception of a subject—in this case, women. In the fourteenth century, these fantasy frames were created by clerics; in the twentieth, by ad men.

The suggestion that *Mad Men* might be surreptitiously adapting a medieval literary text is not as mad as it may first appear. Critics agree that the show is a tissue of allusions and references to both popular and literate cultures. The essays in Scott Stoddart's 2011 collection, *Analyzing* Mad Men: *Critical Essays on the Television Series*, demonstrate how *Mad Men* constructs its sense of the time by citing other texts, "riffing off of famous contemporary films and books."[6] *Mad Men* "is a copy of a copy, a media text based not . . . on history

---

5. Technically, the show begins in 1960, but as McDonald notes "the fifties" are not bound by a set of beginning and end dates. While later seasons of the series evoke '60s tropes (drugs, rock 'n roll, the Kennedy assassination, civil rights), *Mad Men* begins by invoking the 1950s; see Tamar Jeffers McDonald, "Mad Men and Career Women: The Best of Everything?" *Analyzing* Mad Men," 117–35, 117.

6. The volume's essays describe the show's many intertexts, although essays focus primarily on the popular culture of the 1950s and '60s. *The Man in the Gray Flannel Suit* (both book and film; see Stoddart, *Analyzing* Mad Men, 211–15); '50s bestsellers like *The Organization Man* and the *Lonely Crowd* (see Maura Grady, "The Fall of the Organization Man: Loyalty and Conflict in the First Season," 45–63); the "Camelot myth" of the Kennedy administration (see Stoddart, *Analyzing*, 215–20); Rona Jaffe's *The Best of Everything* (again both book and film;

but on other media texts."[7] For a show devoted to the loving recreation of a particular modern period, references to a medieval poet might seem anachronistic. But the show's executive producer and head writer, Matthew Weiner, isn't averse to the occasional medieval literary reference, as season six opens with Draper reading from John Ciardi's translation of Dante's *Inferno*, first published in 1954, and meditating on the dark wood of middle age in which he finds himself. Aranye Fradenburg notes that the Wife of Bath has frequently been characterized as so lively and realistic that she seems more "modern" than any of Chaucer's other pilgrims and wonders why that characterization is so often linked to "the Wife's pursuit of carnal pleasure" and wealth.[8] If the Wife's Prologue presents us with an upwardly mobile, thoroughly modern Alisoun, her tale engages us with the nostalgic fantasy of metamorphosis, the dream of transforming old age into youth, beauty, and wealth. However much *Mad Men* strives for verisimilitude in recreating a bygone American era, it also engages us in these transformative fantasies. Its success is as much dependent on arousing romance, nostalgia, and pleasure as it is on its realistic recreation of Madison Avenue in 1960. The Wife of Bath's Prologue and Tale provides one way of exploring the fantasies of transformation, metamorphosis, and self-fashioning that both reinforce and challenge class and gender hierarchies in the show.

Let us not think of the Chaucerian allusions we uncover as adaptation, as direct quotation or traditional intertextual reference, so much as a ghostly presence that haunts the first three episodes, there and not there at one and the same time, a kind of spectral remediation.[9] With a wink and a smile, they

---

see McDonald, "Mad Men," 118–27); and Douglas Sirk melodramas (see Brenda Cromb, "'The Good Place' and 'The Place That Cannot Be': Politics, Melodrama, and Utopia," 67–78) are all cited as intertexts that both impart verisimilitude to the show's recreation of the era and sketch out its characters. Even Betty Friedan's *Feminine Mystique* lies in wait to explain Betty Draper's neurotic depression. Don Draper has been compared to such luminaries of the American literary canon as Natty Bumpo, Huck Finn, and Jay Gatsby, perhaps because of his ability to reinvent himself. On Draper's relationship to the great white male heroes of American literature, see Melanie Hernandez and David Holmberg, "'We'll Start Over like Adam and Eve': The Subversion of Classic American Mythology," 15–44.

7. McDonald, "Mad Men," 118.

8. Aranye [Louise O.] Fradenburg, "'Fulfild of fairye': The Social Meaning of Fantasy in The Wife of Bath's Prologue and Tale," *The Wife of Bath*, ed. Peter Beidler (Boston: Bedford, 1996), 205–20, 205.

9. On the state of adaptation studies today, see Linda Hutcheon, *A Theory of Adaptation*, 2nd ed. (New York: Routledge, 2006); Thomas Leitch, "Twelve Fallacies in Contemporary Adaptation Theory," *Criticism* 45.2 (2003): 149–71, and "Adaptation Studies at a Crossroads," *Adaptation* 1 (2008): 63–77. On remediation as "the formal logic by which new media refashion prior media forms," see Jay David Bolter and Richard Grusin, *Remediation: Understanding New*

appear, offering the viewer a quick instant of recognition—the feeling that some connection has been made, understanding has been reached—only to withdraw just as suddenly, leaving behind uncertainty. The references create a fuzziness that both assures and subverts; they promise inclusion—to join the cognoscenti who get the reference, the "in" joke—even as they lead only to another puzzle and another bit of puzzlement. Certainly neither Chaucer nor any of his texts or characters are ever directly referred to in the three episodes we examine. We have no evidence that Weiner ever intended a reference to Chaucer; we need not attribute them to an "authorial intention." So how do we think we know these Chaucerian allusions are "there"?

First, we know through visual cues that allow us to make the connection, but because episodic viewing, like reading, is a recursive process, perhaps only retrospectively. In one of the most inspired turns of the opening episodes, Weiner has his hero, Don Draper, butt heads with Jewish department store heiress Rachel Menken (played by Maggie Siff), an entrepreneurial woman, like Chaucer's Wife of Bath, in the "rag business": "Of clooth-makyng she hadde swich an haunt" (1.447).[10] Let us consider a screen shot of Menken from Episode Three, "The Marriage of Figaro," in which she leaves the office after her second meeting with the Sterling Cooper ad agency. As we have frozen a moment of screen time, let us look at this image through Roland Barthes's distinction between *studium* and *punctum* in the photographic image.[11] The *studium* is the whole interpretation of the image, its cultural and linguistic context. This image's *studium* both challenges and reinforces the kinds of class and gender roles that have been put in place through the first three episodes of the series. This image gives us a particular view of Rachel Menken. She appears for this meeting wearing a stunning and highly sexualizing red dress, an outlandish feathery hat "as brood as is a bokeler or a targe" (1.471), and expensive-looking shoes "ful moyste and newe" (1.457). Like the Wife, Menken is the woman in red—"hir hosen weren of fyn scarlet reed" (1.456)—with the striking hat.

This shot is one of several countershots that neutralize Menken's aggressive (perhaps compensatory) confidence by sexualizing her. She is exotic and erotic—at least in part erotic because she is exotic. Men cannot take their eyes off her. She is constantly being followed. Menken is characteristically shot

---

Media (Cambridge: MIT Press, 1998), 273. Werner Wolf has coined the term *intermediality* to describe much the same phenomena.

10. Quotations of Chaucer are taken from *The Riverside Chaucer*, ed. Larry D. Benson, 3rd ed. (Boston: Houghton Mifflin, 1987), and cited parenthetically.

11. Roland Barthes, "Extracts from *Camera Lucida*," *The Photography Reader*, ed. Liz Wells (New York: Routledge, 2003), 19–39, 25.

in close-up, followed by a reverse shot that shows her from behind, usually with a man behind her. Men (and the viewer) are always looking at her from behind, just as they are always looking at her behind. Menken is a creation of the male gaze.[12] In this shot, a character from another subplot, a complete stranger, casually fixes her with his gaze as she exits the office, his attitude suggesting that this is nothing more than his right. This gaze is one of the ways in which the businessmen who constantly surround Menken attempt to put her back into her properly gendered place, the place for women that the show has carefully constructed through these first episodes (at home, in the kitchen or bedroom; behind the typewriter, supporting the working man). Menken's "power" outfit, the flamboyance of which marks her as a *parvenue* and signals her membership in a newly wealthy merchant class, is turned against her at Sterling Cooper. For the old-monied, university-educated men there (among whom Don Draper uncomfortably moves as an imposter), Menken's display of conspicuous consumption makes her simultaneously desirable and an object of derision. Like the Wife, whom The General Prologue describes as wearing the ostentatious clothing of the *nouveau riche,* Menken's presentation is outlandish rather than understated, and the effect is sexy rather than elegant or businesslike. The red stands out in a world of gray flannel suits. This is the dress of someone who wants to be noticed. Menken presents herself for the gaze, performs for it. Her performance links her visually to the secretaries who are expected, even instructed, to provide colorful decoration in this dull gray business world. If Menken relishes and clings to her independence, she also desperately desires inclusion among the wealthy and powerful who do not need to flash their money to exercise influence (the clients of Sterling Cooper). But she does not know how to perform old, Christian money. She is both admirable and pitiable—strong, self-confident, assertive (even aggressive) but also an object of mockery and haunted by her marginalization because she is Jewish and a woman. If the dress indicates her unwillingness to be controlled and her desire to assert herself as a woman, a Jew, a member of the bourgeoisie, it also kick-starts the very forces of domination and hierarchy that have put patrician institutions like Sterling Cooper in place to begin with.

The rooster is the *punctum* that pierces or pricks this image that so effortlessly recapitulates an objectifying male gaze[13] (see figure 17.1). It is a sight gag

---

12. Arguably this is true of most of *Mad Men*'s women—Elizabeth Moss's Peggy Olson is an interesting exception—but seems particularly true for Menken and Christina Hendrick's Joan, both of whom consistently perform for the male gaze.

13. As Barthes states, "A photograph's punctum is that accident which pricks me (but also bruises me, is poignant to me)" ("Extracts," 25).

FIGURE 17.1. The rooster.

that could be explained through an unrelated subplot but here is slipped into the *mise-en-scène* without comment.[14] What is a barnyard animal doing in this modern office? It is an anachronistic detail that points back to an older, more primitive time when humans and animals occupied space together. Is it Chauntecleer (or his ghost) from The Nun's Priest's Tale silently strutting through the shot, the atavistic Chaucerian Middle Ages erupting into the sleek modernity of Matthew Weiner's lovingly built 1950s set? At the same time, it is the very essence of the "strutting" white, masculine culture at Sterling Cooper—preposterous, out-of-date, and yet unwilling, or unable, to see that its time has passed. "A new junior exec," Draper quips. The rooster is somehow indifferent to the steel, concrete, and glass surrounding it, incapable of understanding that modernity has arrived. Rachel Menken is the now, the new woman, the new Jew, the new merchant class. The men staring at her posterior—and the viewers doing the same—like the rooster, just haven't heard the news.

---

14. The rooster is a leftover from a racist prank that coworkers play on Pete Campbell on his return from his honeymoon.

What might the ghostly presence of a Chaucerian narrative contribute to the class and gender politics of *Mad Men*? Chaucer's Wife, a career woman who, nevertheless, has gained most of her wealth through multiple marriages to rich old men, initially holds up women's "experience" in opposition to the monolithic power of medieval misogynist literature, seeking to recast authoritative beliefs about feminine virtue and vice that structure her social identity. Ultimately, she engages in a battle of books, staking out positions, like the clerics she so despises, by commenting on literary precedent. She argues that, by a set of criteria different from that offered by, say, her fifth husband's "book of wikked wyves" (3.685), instead of being regarded as a gold-digging strumpet, she might be understood as a lady, perhaps even a patroness:

By God, if wommen hadde writen stories,
As clerkes han withinne hire oratories,
They wolde han writen of men moore wikkednesse
Than al the mark of Adam may redresse. (3.693–96)

If fourteenth-century women controlled the means to produce publicity, the Wife insists, they would award themselves exceptional reputations.

Perhaps in the twentieth-century they do. Menken is also looking for a reputation makeover, for some assistance in extricating herself from the oppressions of patriarchy; she is seeking a way to refashion herself by reimagining her father's department store—the second home that has largely structured her identity. Because she is a "modern" woman, she hires an advertising agency to facilitate her transformation from Jewish, middle-of-the-road merchant to proprietor of an exclusive shop in the same league as Saks and Tiffany, with whom her store shares a wall. Mired in a kind of self-hatred that touches on class, gender, religion, and perhaps even race, Menken commissions Draper's firm, Sterling Cooper, a bastion of Christian, white, male entitlement. When asked if Sterling Cooper employs any Jews, Draper counters, "Not on my watch"—because, after all, this is where real power resides. Like the Wife, Menken believes that she can turn both the organizations and the discourses that have subjugated women to her advantage, even if the game is stacked against her. Unlike most of the women introduced in the series' opening episodes, who function as supports for men's egos, Menken expects that men will pay attention to what she says ("What I think matters most now"). She has both the experience and the money—she can pay men to pay attention—to back up her demands. Men find her repulsive, however, not only because she challenges their sexism but also because Weiner fills the dialogue with anti-Semitic commentary. In the world of Sterling Cooper, "Jewish guys" only work for Jewish firms selling Jewish products to Jewish people. Menken's Jewishness replaces the Wife's advanced age as a sign of her failure to conform to normative gender; it makes her doubly an outsider. It also marks her as part of a money economy—fulfilling the stereotype of the Jew. She talks about money while other characters talk about the product.

In what we might read as an updated version of the Wife of Bath's parody of Western misogynist tropes in her Prologue, the casual misogyny of the Sterling Cooper offices is clearly established before Menken appears through a series of brief scenes: the sexy Joan introducing the dowdy Peggy Olsen to the sexual politics of the office; the banter about Pete Campbell's bachelor party; the awkward sexual jokes that pass between Don and the closeted Salvatore; Don's contemptuous dismissal of the repressed German psychologist's research, tossing her report in the trash can;[15] and Pete's criticisms of Peggy's appearance. Unsurprisingly, Menken's first meeting with Draper does not go well. "You were expecting me to be a man. My father was too," she says, citing an age-old trope for women's independence—the failure of the father to produce a male heir. She has inherited her wealth rather than marrying it as the Wife of Bath does. Draper, a habitual womanizer, finds her repellent—although that does not prevent him from eventually sleeping with her. Incensed by her demands, he storms out of the meeting because she has the audacity to question the conventional advertising strategy he lays out for her; he suggests appealing to the frugality of her customers by offering coupons (selling Jewish product to Jewish people). She has hired Sterling Cooper to attract a more blue-blooded clientele. "I want your kind of people, Mr. Draper, people who don't care about coupons, who come to the store because it is expensive," a strategy he declares "silly." When she insists, he tells her she is "out of line": "I'm not going to let a woman talk to me like this. This meeting is over."

Why does Draper react with such extraordinary revulsion for Menken? Why is he so ready to dismiss a well-heeled, if socially problematic, client worth, we are told, three million dollars? How is it even possible that an advertising man who happily sells cigarettes, knowing full well their carcinogenic attributes, will walk away from what would appear a simple and straightforward assignment, the opportunity to change a department store's image? Draper's response seems gratuitous, his failure perhaps associated with his unwillingness to subvert the authority of the white male gaze that structures his own identity—or, at very least, the identity he struggles to maintain. This

---

15. Is Draper's criticism of psychoanalysis (the "Jewish science")—"I find your whole approach perverse"—an outgrowth of his anti-Semitism?

woman gets under his skin. Draper hates her—she makes him nervous—and yet he is undeniably attracted to her. His coworkers readily acknowledge by their knowing glances that sparks are flying. The Wife of Bath is also the creation of a combined white male gaze—Chaucer's and the reader's. She is the product of a misogyny that responds to her alternating gestures of resistance and submission with anxiety and desire. On the one hand, Chaucer represents the Wife as the tough, dominating mistress whose arguments with authority are visually on display: she carries a whip and, likely, rides like a man, wearing spurs, which would make side-saddle travel difficult if not impossible (1.473). She is all business. Even her sexual encounters with her first three husbands involve financial transactions. On the other hand, she is the always already available woman, welcoming the prospect that husband number six will swing by and sweep her off her feet (3.45). She acknowledges her hypersexuality and is vulnerable to men who can please her. She knows what she wants and is desperately waiting for the men around her to figure it out. Both Menken and the Wife are hard-as-nails romantics, puzzles to themselves and mysteries to the men around them.

Menken never exists apart from Draper's gaze. She is always being fashioned by his misogyny and his lust—and therefore ours as well, since Draper is the character with whom the viewer is sympathetically identified by both the narrative and the camera. But Draper, too, becomes fixed by a hegemonic gaze. We understand that both Menken and Draper are posturing—pretending that they are, or, at very least, that they can become, what they are not: members of a white, male, entitled, Christian, old-moneyed elite. Can it be that each initially detests and desires the other for the weaknesses they see, for not living up to the fantasy of American privilege? After Roger—eager for her business—asks Don to patch it up with Rachel Menken, the two have dinner together. In this scene, Draper encounters in Menken a mix of hardness and coquettish sweetness. She is like the Wife of Bath, simultaneously meeting the expectations of the male gaze and yet also somehow bewildering. Just what is it that this woman wants? Draper thinks he knows—in his mind, he does after all create women's desire—but also worries that he does not. Apologizing for his earlier rudeness, he then asks a "personal question" that attempts quite literally to put her in her place, a social location he can understand: "Why aren't you married? Wouldn't getting married make you happier than being a beautiful educated woman?" Rachel's answer suggests that she shares the Wife's disdain for the "wo that is in mariage" (3.3), though she has rather less experience of it. Like Alisoun of Bath she wants to turn the tables on representational strategies that naturalize women's subordination. "If I weren't a woman," Menken tells Draper, "I would be allowed to ask you the same question. I wouldn't have to choose between putting on an apron and the thrill of making my father's store what I always thought it should be." Like the Wife of Bath, she asks, "Who peyntede the leon, tel me who?" (3.692). But clerks have been replaced by ad men who now tell women who they are and what they want. When Menken tells Draper that she has never married because she's never been in love, Don dismisses love as just another advertising slogan. She counters, "For a lot of people love isn't just a slogan." He parries, "What you call love was invented by guys like me to sell nylons."

Menken is unimpressed with Draper's cynicism, the social comfort he locates in his insistence that everything serves the interests of commerce. Nor is she sold on his modern-day, "new man" status. Excluded because of her gender, her social class, and her religion—all aspects that Draper, in his white male self-satisfaction, reminds her to consider—she also recognizes in him a similar alienation: "Mr. Draper. I don't know what you really believe in, but I do know what it feels like to be out of place, to be disconnected, to see the whole world laid out in front of you the way other people live it. There is something about you that tells me you know it, too." And, as we find out in later episodes, he does indeed know his world from the perspective of the outsider.

Thus if Menken is Chaucer's Wife of Bath, Draper is at once Weiner's Chaucer, the knight of her tale, and the transformed hag. Played to perfection by Hamm, Don Draper, the handsome, brilliant, philandering, creative director of the Sterling Cooper advertising agency, stands at the center of *Mad Men*. The subplot that develops around Mencken reconfigures Don Draper's Chaucer as a media-savvy manipulator of public desire. Remarking this equivalency requires us to think of Chaucer not as the "Father of English Literature" but instead as the grandson and son of vintners, a member of the merchant class, who, through his ability to influence technologies of culture and governance—in particular, his ability to deploy language—ingratiated himself into the court of Edward III. This Geoffrey Chaucer is the talented outsider, always in close proximity to the elite but never quite able to sit at the table of power, authority, wealth, or title. We like to think that Weiner might delight in the play of Chaucer's language when he calls himself a "servant of the servants of love"—"For I, that God of Loves servantz serve" (*Troilus and Criseyde* 1.15). On the one hand, the poet emphasizes his subjugation, his inability to participate in the games of his aristocratic masters, his always excluded position in all things important. On the other hand, he paraphrases the title, *Servus Servorum Dei*, Servant of the Servants of God, first used in the sixth century by Pope Gregory I to refer to the role of the papacy, a title suggesting the superiority of its holder to all others. We might see in this play of language Chaucer's capacity to remake himself, to rebrand his identity, to spring from his own platonic conception of himself. We might see a space where the patronage economy of late medieval England fleetingly intersects with the capitalism of late twentieth- and twenty-first-century Hollywood.

If Draper is Chaucer, he is also the knight in somewhat tarnished armor—if not a rapist, at least a persistent womanizer. Episode Two, "Ladies Room," presents the most sustained Chaucerian riff on the repeated question, posed by Draper, "What do women want?" Although Menken does not appear in this episode, she has challenged his smug worldview. In a neat twist, this episode refashions Draper as the knight from The Wife of Bath's Tale, with Draper taking up the quest Menken lays on him: to discover what women want, but not "in some bullshit research psychology way." Draper raises this question in three different sequences in the episode. About halfway through the episode, as his creative team pitches Right Guard ads, Draper muses on the fact that even though he has spent his life manipulating media to sell products to women, he has never really thought about their desires: "You think they want a cowboy? He's quiet and strong. He always brings the cattle home safe. You watch TV. What if they want something else? Inside, some . . . mysterious wish that we're ignoring."[16] But his colleagues are no help; they just don't care. They can only parrot misogynist tropes: "Well, I've stopped trying to figure out what they think"; "I always thought women liked the way we smell." They stare blankly at him.

A few minutes later in a sequence with Roger Sterling, Draper repeats the question. Roger responds with the same indifference—"Who cares"—and the misogynist commonplace that women are greedy spendthrifts ("al is for to selle" [1.414]): "Jesus, you know what they want? Everything, especially if the other girls have it." They banter about the efficacy of psychiatry. Draper's wife is visiting a psychiatrist because of hysterical symptoms—her hand keeps going numb. He cannot understand how she could possibly be unhappy: "Who could not be happy with all this?" Who wouldn't be happy with a knight—or a cowboy—like Don Draper? In his own weird mixture of confidence and insecurity, he cannot understand her pain at living what should be the dream of domestic bliss. What more could women want? His boss cannot answer his question either.

Unlike the Wife of Bath's knight, Draper never asks any woman what she wants—at least not in any serious way. The third time the question is repeated (in good fairy-tale fashion), he asks his mistress, Midge Daniels (Rosemarie

---

16. Since the cowboy is little more than America's reimagining of the medieval knight in shining armor, perhaps Draper's question puts his own masculinity in doubt.

Dewitt), a greeting-card illustrator. She tells him that women want "not being asked something like that." Her response reminds us of Shoshana Felman's analysis of Freud's version of the question, which demonstrates that Freud's question must really be asking "What is femininity—for men" and, in doing so, raises the further question, "What does the question—what is femininity—*for men?*—mean *for women?*"[17] Midge's response to Draper's question disrupts "the transparency and misleadingly self-evident universality of its male enunciation," calling attention not only to a reading of sexual difference but also to "the intervention of sexual difference in the very act of reading."[18] This difference is evoked, however, only to be deflected. Draper has no real need to listen to his wife, his mistress, or even Menken. Although his conversations with his creative team and his boss seem pensive, even serious, the storyline ends with an easy joke. In bed with his mistress, he finally gets his inspiration—"What do women want? Any excuse to get closer." His mistress laughs at him: "Thank God. There's that ego people pay to see." Whereas the Wife of Bath's knight seems educable, Draper is not. Draper never gets that he has missed the point. He has his tagline.

Just in case viewers miss the literary reference, or think this quest to discover what women want is such a commonplace that it may be considered apart from Chaucer's Wife of Bath's Tale, in Episode Three, Menken reinforces the allusion by giving Draper a gift, a set of cuff links depicting a medieval knight, rebranding him with a twentieth-century heraldic sign. With this small gesture, Menken supplies Draper with markers of genealogical transmission and legitimation, completing the perhaps tongue-in-cheek transformation of the businessman into fairy-tale knight. Draper's transformation would seem to suggest that his quest has ended, though perhaps with less enlightenment than the knight of the Wife's tale receives. But the episode makes some notable changes in the story—remediating it—reminding viewers that white men have gained, not lost, privilege since the Middle Ages.

Even in his triumph, Draper is not all that he seems. The joke points to Draper's insecurities about his transformation into the "ego people pay to see." The kernel of the Real around which *Mad Men* is structured,[19] around which its fantasy of social mobility coalesces, is the absent and dead Don

---

17. Shoshana Felman, "Rereading Femininity," *Yale French Studies* 62 (1981): 19–44, 21; italics in original.

18. Felman, "Rereading," 21.

19. As Slavoj Žižek explains, "The kernel of reality is horror, horror of the Real, and what constitutes reality is the minimum of idealization the subject needs in order to be able to sustain the Real" ("The Abyss of Freedom," *The Abyss of Freedom / Ages of the World,* Slavoj Žižek and F. W. J. Von Schelling [Ann Arbor: University of Michigan Press, 1997], 3–10, 22).

Draper—killed by a mortar shell during the Korean War—the one whose life Dick Whitman has stolen, allowing him to transform himself from the bastard son of a prostitute into the suave creative director of the classy Sterling Cooper agency, whose name drips old money (sterling). Chaucer's Wife of Bath's Tale, with its transformation of the old hag into the beautiful young wife, provides support to the fantasy of a metamorphosis that will gain Draper access to the good life, the American Dream of upward mobility. Like a handsomer version of Chaucer, who, at various times, disappears from the historical record,[20] Weiner presents Draper as a man without a past, a man who has invented himself, who believes in the copy he produces and yet cynically thinks the copy he produces is empty: "Advertising is based on one thing, happiness. And you know what happiness is. . . . It's a billboard on the side of the road that screams with reassurance that whatever you're doing . . . it's ok." He is a pretender, surrounded by the privileged graduates of elite colleges and universities and people who made their money "the old fashioned way," by inheriting it; he fits in, but never comfortably. He looks right, sounds right, performs all the culturally correct ceremonies of his peers, but retains the critical eye of the outsider—and with it a degree of awkward distance. This remediated Chaucer—who, like his predecessor, happens to be a media professional—requires us to rethink the mechanisms of upward mobility both in the Middle Ages and at the beginning of the twenty-first century.

Draper's quest points to the impossibility of the happy ending, exposes the lie of the domestic bliss in which Draper has wrapped himself, forgetting that this too is a slogan he has created to sell cleaning products. The Wife of Bath concludes her tale with a series of transformations that seem to lead to domestic harmony. The hag who schooled the knight in "gentillesse" (3.1109–212) has demanded that he not only marry her but also accede to her authority. Her knight, properly chastised, has shown his willingness to hand over sovereignty, to relinquish the role of dominant male. He is transformed from a rapist to a receptive husband. But suddenly there is a re-inscription of the medieval status quo. Another metamorphosis takes place unremarked in which the old hag becomes young, beautiful, and submissive to her husband, handing back the very sovereignty she desired. The fairy-tale ending provides a frame, a fantasy frame that is "the support that gives consistency to what we call 'reality,'"[21] in this case the reality of medieval marriage, the subject of the Wife's performance. The metamorphosis covers over and coalesces around the

---

20. We discuss Chaucer's self-fashioning in our analysis of another Chaucerian film, Brian Helgeland's *A Knight's Tale*, in *Cinematic Illuminations: The Middle Ages on Film* (Baltimore, MD: Johns Hopkins University Press, 2010), 347–48.

21. Žižek, *Sublime*, 44.

Real of aging and death. In the last shot of the first episode of *Mad Men,* the camera settles on a different domestic tableau, a voyeuristic shot through the window of a suburban home. As the camera zooms back, the Vic Damone and Percy Faith version of "The Street Where You Live" plays. Don Draper's domestic bliss is momentarily framed by the house window. This fantasy frame of domesticity is forged from a host of transformations, all of which are dependent on the advertising industry that after World War II sold the American dream of consumerism. If, as Žižek argues, "what we experience as 'reality' is structured by fantasy, and if fantasy [of, say, domestic bliss] serves as the screen that protects us from being directly overwhelmed by the raw Real, then reality itself can function as an escape from encountering the Real."[22] This image, then, has to be read ironically, as suggesting that we never, ever, fit comfortably into the fantasy frame, into the skins of new identities, however magical the metamorphosis. Chaucer and his Wife of Bath, along with Don Draper, have sold us a bill of goods.

---

22. Slavoj Žižek, "From Che vuoi? to Fantasy: Lacan with *Eyes Wide Shut,*" *How To Read Lacan,* Web, 4 Jul. 2009, www.lacan.com/essays/?p=146.

CONTRIBUTORS

LYNN ARNER, associate professor of English at Brock University in Canada, is the author of *Chaucer, Gower, and the Vernacular Rising: Poetry and the Problem of the Populace after 1381*. She has published articles on various late medieval English texts and on gender and class in the current American professoriate. She has also guest-edited a special issue of *Exemplaria: A Journal of Theory in Medieval and Renaissance Studies*.

SUSAN ARONSTEIN, professor of English at the University of Wyoming, is the author of *Hollywood Knights: Arthurian Cinema and the Politics of Nostalgia* and the coeditor of *The Disney Middle Ages: A Fairy-Tale and Fantasy Past*. She has also published several articles on medievalism and popular culture, addressing such topics as Disneyland, Excalibur Hotel, *Monty Python and the Holy Grail*, and *The Da Vinci Code*.

ARTHUR BAHR is associate professor in the Literature Faculty of the Massachusetts Institute of Technology. He is the author of *Fragments and Assemblages: Forming Compilations of Medieval London* and, with Alexandra Gillespie, coeditor of *Medieval English Manuscripts: Form, Aesthetics, and the Literary Text*, a special issue of *The Chaucer Review* that appeared in April 2013. His current book project is on the *Pearl* manuscript.

CANDACE BARRINGTON, professor of English at Central Connecticut State University, has long-term interests in Chaucer's reception. She has supplemented her *American Chaucers* with articles examining Chaucerian appropriations in children's literature and historical fiction; on YouTube and Louisiana Mardi Gras parade routes; and by African-American poets and American Civil War veterans. With

Jonathan Hsy, she directs *Global Chaucers,* a project examining post-1945, non-Anglophone adaptations and translations of the *Canterbury Tales.*

LOUISE D'ARCENS is professor in the English Literatures Program at Macquarie University and holds a Future Fellowship from the Australian Research Council. Her PhD and BA (Honors) are from the University of Sydney. Her publications include *Old Songs in the Timeless Land: Medievalism in Australian Literature 1840–1910, Laughing at the Middle Ages: Comic Medievalism,* and the edited volumes *International Medievalism and Popular Culture* and *Maistresse of My Wit: Medieval Women, Modern Scholars.*

KATHLEEN DAVIS, professor of English at the University of Rhode Island, is the author of *Periodization and Sovereignty: How Ideas of Feudalism and Secularization Govern the Politics of Time* and editor, with Nadia Altschul, of *Medievalisms in the Postcolonial World: The Idea of "The Middle Ages" Outside Europe.* She has published widely in the fields of Old English literature, Chaucer studies, translation theory, and the historiography of the Middle Ages.

SIÂN ECHARD is professor of English and Distinguished University Scholar at the University of British Columbia. Her research areas include Anglo Latin, John Gower, book history, and Arthurian literature (especially Geoffrey of Monmouth), on which she has published such books as *Arthurian Narrative in the Latin Tradition, The Book Unbound: Editing and Reading Medieval Manuscripts and Texts,* and *The Latin Verses in the* Confessio Amantis: *An Annotated Translation.* Her work on the postmedieval reception of medieval literature includes *Printing the Middle Ages.*

STEVE ELLIS is professor of English Literature at the University of Birmingham and author of several books and articles on the modern reception of medieval writers, principally *Dante and English Poetry: Shelley to T. S. Eliot* and *Chaucer at Large: The Poet in the Modern Imagination.* He is also the editor of *Chaucer: An Oxford Guide.*

LAURIE FINKE, professor of Women's and Gender Studies at Kenyon College, has published seven books, including her most recent, *Cinematic Illuminations: The Middle Ages on Film,* with her frequent collaborator Martin B. Shichtman. Her articles have appeared in *Theatre Survey, Signs, Theatre Journal, Exemplaria, Arthuriana,* and other journals. She is currently the medieval editor of the *Norton Anthology of Criticism and Theory.*

KATHLEEN FORNI is professor of English at Loyola University Maryland. Her primary research interest focuses on Chaucer's canonization and reception, as evident in her books examining appropriations both past (*The Chaucerian Apocrypha: A Counterfeit Canon*) and present (*Chaucer's Afterlife: Adaptations in Recent Popular*

Culture). She also edited *The Chaucerian Apocrypha: A Selection*, as part of the Teaching the Middle Ages series.

TERRY JONES is a founding member of the comedy ensemble, Monty Python, and has filmed the Middle Ages with such works as *Monty Python and the Holy Grail* and *Erik the Viking*. His medieval scholarship includes *Chaucer's Knight: The Portrait of a Medieval Mercenary* and *Who Murdered Chaucer? A Medieval Mystery*.

KATHLEEN COYNE KELLY is professor of English at Northeastern University. She is coeditor (with Marina Leslie) of *Menacing Virgins: Representing Virginity in the Middle Ages and Renaissance*, coeditor (with Tison Pugh) of *Queer Movie Medievalisms*, and author of *A. S. Byatt* and *Performing Virginity and Testing Chastity in the Middle Ages*.

KATHRYN L. LYNCH, dean of faculty affairs and Katharine Lee Bates and Sophie Chantal Hart Professor of English at Wellesley College, specializes in medieval English literature. She is the author of two books—*The High Medieval Dream Vision: Poetry, Philosophy, and Literary Form* and *Chaucer's Philosophical Visions*—and the editor of two others, *Chaucer's Cultural Geography* and a Norton Critical Edition of Chaucer's dream poetry, *Dream Visions and Other Poems*.

PETER PAROLIN is associate professor of English at the University of Wyoming. His publications include *Women Players in Early Modern England, 1500–1660: Beyond the "All-Male" Stage*, which he coedited with Pamela Allen Brown.

TISON PUGH is professor of English at the University of Central Florida and is the author of *Queering Medieval Genres; An Introduction to Geoffrey Chaucer*; and *Chaucer's (Anti-) Eroticisms and the Queer Middle Ages*. He has also coedited such Chaucerian essay collections as *Approaches to Teaching Chaucer's* Troilus and Criseyde *and the Shorter Poems* (with Angela Jane Weisl) and *Men and Masculinities in Chaucer's* Troilus and Criseyde (with Marcia Smith Marzec).

ELIZABETH SCALA is professor of English at the University of Texas at Austin. She has published essays on Chaucer, Arthurian literature, and medieval romance in *Chaucer Review, Studies in the Age of Chaucer, Word & Image, Philological Quarterly*, and *Studies in Philology*. Her books include *Desire in the* Canterbury Tales, *Absent Narratives: Manuscript Textuality and Literary Structure in Late Medieval England*, and *The Post-Historical Middle Ages*.

LARRY SCANLON is associate professor of English at Rutgers University, New Brunswick. He is the author of *Narrative, Authority, and Power: The Medieval Exemplum and the Chaucerian Tradition*. He has edited *Studies in the Age of Chaucer* as well as two critical anthologies, *John Lydgate: Poetry, Culture, and Lancastrian England* (with James Simpson) and *The Cambridge Companion to Medieval English Literature, 1050–1500*. He is currently completing a study on homoeroticism and medieval culture, titled *At Sodom's Gate: The Sin against Nature and Middle English Poetry*.

MARTIN B. SHICHTMAN is director of Jewish studies and professor of English at Eastern Michigan University. His books include *Cinematic Illuminations: The Middle Ages on Film* and *King Arthur and the Myth of History*, both cowritten with Laurie Finke; and *Culture and the King: The Social Implications of the Arthurian Legend*, cowritten with James P. Carley.

GEORGE SHUFFELTON is professor of English and associate dean at Carleton College. He has published work on *Piers Plowman*, Chaucer, Gower, the representation of minstrels, and an edition of Codex Ashmole 61, a late medieval collection of popular verse. He is currently studying book exchanges and friendships among medieval university alumni.

SARAH STANBURY is Distinguished Professor in the Arts and Humanities at the College of the Holy Cross. She is the author of *The Visual Object of Desire in Late Medieval England* and *Seeing the Gawain-Poet: Description and the Act of Perception*. She is also the editor of *Women's Space: Place, Patronage and Gender in the Medieval Church* (with Virginia Raguin), *Feminist Approaches to the Body in Medieval Literature* (with Linda Lomperis), *Writing on the Body: Female Embodiment and Feminist Theory* (with Katie Conboy and Nadia Medina), and an edition of *Pearl*.

SELECTED BIBLIOGRAPHY

This selected bibliography compiles the major works on Chaucer, Chaucer on screen, theory, and film theory cited in this volume. See each essay for articles, reviews, and additional sources specific to the film, television episode, or critical intervention that it addresses.

Aberth, John. *A Knight at the Movies: Medieval History on Film*. New York: Routledge, 2003.

Allman, W. W., and D. Thomas Hanks. "Rough Love: Towards an Erotics of the *Canterbury Tales*." *Chaucer Review* 38 (2003): 36–65.

Ashton, Gail, ed. *Medieval Afterlives in Contemporary Culture*. London: Bloomsbury Academic, 2015.

Bakhtin, Mikhail. *Rabelais and His World*. Trans. Helene Iswolsky. Bloomington: Indiana University Press, 1984.

———. "Response to a Question from the *Novy Mir* Editorial Staff." *Speech Genres and Other Late Essays*. Trans. Vern McGee. Ed. Caryl Emerson and Michael Holquist. Austin: University of Texas Press, 1986. 1–9.

Bal, Mieke. *Narratology: Introduction to the Theory of Narrative*. 2nd ed. Toronto: University of Toronto Press, 1997.

Barr, Charles, ed. *All Our Yesterdays: Ninety Years of British Cinema*. London: British Film Institute, 1986.

Barrington, Candace. *American Chaucers*. New York: Palgrave Macmillan, 2007.

———. "'Forget What You Have Learned': The Mistick Krewe's 1914 Mardi Gras Chaucer." *American Literary History* 22.4 (2010): 806–30.

———. "Re-Telling Chaucer for Modern Children: Picture Books, the Marketplace, and Evolving Feminism." *Sex and Sexuality in a Feminist World*. Ed. Katherine Hermes and Karen Ritzenhoff. Newcastle upon Tyne: Cambridge Scholars, 2009. 18–31.

Barthes, Roland. "Extracts from *Camera Lucida*." *The Photography Reader*. Ed. Liz Wells. New York: Routledge, 2003. 19–39.

Baudrillard, Jean. *Selected Writings*. Ed. Mark Poster. Stanford: Stanford University Press, 1998.

Beers, Henry A. *From Chaucer to Tennyson: With Twenty-Nine Portraits and Selections from Thirty Authors*. Meadville, PA: Flood and Vincent, 1894.

Beidler, Peter. "Just Say Yes, Chaucer Knew the *Decameron*: Or, Bringing The Shipman's Tale Out of Limbo." *The* Decameron *and the* Canterbury Tales*: New Essays on an Old Question*. Ed. Leonard Koff and Brenda Deen Schildgen. Madison, NJ: Fairleigh Dickinson University Press, 2000. 25–46.

———. *The Lives of the* Miller's Tale*: The Roots, Composition, and Retellings of Chaucer's Bawdy Story*. Jefferson, NC: McFarland, 2013.

Bennett, Tony. "The Politics of 'the Popular' and Popular Culture." *Popular Culture and Social Relations*. Ed. Tony Bennett, Colin Mercer, and Janet Woollacott. Philadelphia: Open University Press, 1986. 6–21.

Benson, C. David. *Chaucer's Drama of Style: Poetic Variety and Contrast in the* Canterbury Tales. Chapel Hill: University of North Carolina Press, 1988.

Bernau, Anke, and Bettina Bildhauer, eds. *Medieval Film*. Manchester: Manchester University Press, 2009.

Bevernage, Berber. *History, Memory, and State-Sponsored Violence*. New York: Routledge, 2012.

Biddick, Kathleen. *The Shock of Medievalism*. Durham: Duke University Press, 1998.

Bildhauer, Bettina. *Filming the Middle Ages*. London: Reaktion, 2011.

Blandeau, Agnès. *Pasolini, Chaucer, and Boccaccio: Two Medieval Texts and Their Translation to Film*. Jefferson, NC: McFarland, 2006.

Bluestone, George. *Novels into Film*. 1957. Baltimore, MD: Johns Hopkins University Press, 2003.

Bolter, Jay David, and Richard Grusin. *Remediation: Understanding New Media*. Cambridge: MIT Press, 1998.

Bordwell, David. *Narration in the Fiction Film*. Madison: University of Wisconsin Press, 1985.

Brown, Catherine. "In the Middle." *Journal of Medieval and Early Modern Studies* 30.3 (2000): 547–74.

Brown, Peter. *Geoffrey Chaucer*. Oxford: Oxford University Press, 2011.

Burt, Richard. *Unspeakable ShaXXXpeares: Queer Theory and American Kiddie Culture*. New York: St. Martin's, 1998.

Calasanti, Toni M., and Kathleen F. Slevin, eds. *Age Matters: Realigning Feminist Thinking*. New York: Routledge, 2006.

Cannon, Christopher. *The Making of Chaucer's English: A Study of Words*. Cambridge: Cambridge University Press, 1998.

Cartmell, Deborah, and Imelda Whelehan. *Screen Adaptation: Impure Cinema*. Basingstoke, Hampshire: Palgrave Macmillan, 2010.

———, and I. Q. Hunter, eds. *Retrovisions: Reinventing the Past in Film and Fiction*. London: Pluto, 2001.

Casetti, Francesco. "Adaptation and Mis-Adaptations: Film, Literature, and Social Discourses." *A Companion to Literature and Film*. Ed. Robert Stam and Alessandra Raengo. Oxford: Blackwell, 2004. 81–91.

Chaucer, Geoffrey. *The Riverside Chaucer*. Ed. Larry D. Benson. 3rd ed. Boston: Houghton Mifflin, 1987.

Coffman, George R. "Old Age from Horace to Chaucer: Some Literary Affinities and Adventures of an Idea." *Speculum* 9 (1935): 249–77.

Correale, Robert M., and Mary Hamel, eds. *Sources and Analogues of the* Canterbury Tales. 2 vols. Cambridge: Brewer, 2002 and 2005.

Cowart, David. *Literary Symbiosis: The Reconfigured Text in Twentieth-Century Writing.* Athens: University of Georgia Press, 1993.

D'Arcens, Louise. "Deconstruction and the Medieval Indefinite Article: The Undecidable Medievalism of Brian Helgeland's *A Knight's Tale*." *Parergon* 25.2 (2008): 80–98.

David, Alfred. "Old, New, and Yong in Chaucer." *Studies in the Age of Chaucer* 15 (1993): 5–21.

de Groot, Jerome. "Perpetually Dividing and Suturing the Past and Present: *Mad Men* and the Illusions of History." *Rethinking History* 15 (2011): 269–85.

Delony, Mikee Chisholm. "From Textual Interpretation to Film Adaptation: The Narratorial, Readerly, and Directorial Gaze at the 'Joly Body' of Geoffrey Chaucer's Wife of Bath." University of Houston, PhD dissertation, 2007.

Derrida, Jacques. *Archive Fever: A Freudian Impression.* Trans. Eric Prenowitz. Chicago: University of Chicago Press, 1995.

———. *Specters of Marx: The State of the Debt, the Work of Mourning, and the New International.* New York: Routledge, 1994.

Dimock, Wai Chee. "A Theory of Resonance." *PMLA* 112 (1997): 1060.

Dinshaw, Carolyn. *Chaucer's Sexual Poetics.* Madison: University of Wisconsin Press, 1990.

———. *Getting Medieval: Sexualities and Communities, Pre- and Postmodern.* Durham: Duke University Press, 1999.

———. *How Soon Is Now? Medieval Texts, Amateur Readers, and the Queerness of Time.* Durham: Duke University Press, 2012.

Donaldson, E. Talbot. *Speaking of Chaucer.* New York: Norton, 1970.

Echard, Siân. *Printing the Middle Ages.* Philadelphia: University of Pennsylvania Press, 2008.

Edelman, Lee. *No Future: Queer Theory and the Death Drive.* Durham: Duke University Press, 2004.

Edmondson, George. "Naked Chaucer." *The Post-Historical Middle Ages.* Ed. Elizabeth Scala and Sylvia Federico. New York: Palgrave Macmillan, 2010. 139–60.

Eldridge, David. *Hollywood's Historical Films.* London: Tauris, 2006.

Eliot, T. S. *The Sacred Wood: Essays on Poetry and Criticism.* London: Methuen, 1920.

Ellis, Steve. *Chaucer at Large: The Poet in the Modern Imagination.* Minneapolis: University of Minnesota Press, 2000.

———. ed. *Chaucer: An Oxford Guide.* Oxford: Oxford University Press, 2005.

Evans, Ruth. "Chaucer in Cyberspace: Medieval Technologies of Memory and the *House of Fame.*" *Studies in the Age of Chaucer* 23 (2001): 43–69.

Fein, Susanna, and David Raybin, eds. *Chaucer: Contemporary Approaches.* University Park: Pennsylvania State University Press, 2010.

Felman, Shoshana. "Rereading Femininity." *Yale French Studies* 62 (1981): 19–44.

Ferris, Susanne, and Mallory Young, eds. *Chick Flicks: Contemporary Women at the Movies.* New York: Routledge, 2008.

Finke, Laurie, and Martin B. Shichtman. *Cinematic Illuminations: The Middle Ages on Film.* Baltimore: Johns Hopkins University Press, 2010.

Fisher, Sheila, trans. *The Selected Canterbury Tales: A New Verse Translation.* New York: Norton, 2012.

Forni, Kathleen. *The Chaucerian Apocrypha: A Counterfeit Canon.* Gainesville: University of Florida Press, 2001.

———. *The Chaucerian Apocrypha: A Selection.* Kalamazoo, MI: Medieval Institute Publications, 2005.

———. *Chaucer's Afterlife: Adaptations in Recent Popular Culture.* Jefferson, NC: McFarland, 2013.

———. "Reinventing Chaucer: *A Knight's Tale. Chaucer Review* 37 (2003): 253–64.

Ganim, John. *Chaucerian Theatricality.* Princeton: Princeton University Press, 1990.

Grindon, Leger. *Shadows on the Past: Studies in Historical Fiction Film.* Philadelphia: Temple University Press, 1994.

Hansen, Elaine Tuttle. *Chaucer and the Fictions of Gender.* Berkeley: University of California Press, 1992.

Harty, Kevin. "Chaucer for a New Millennium: The BBC *Canterbury Tales.*" *Mass Market Medieval: Essays on the Middle Ages in Popular Culture.* Ed. David Marshall. Jefferson, NC: McFarland, 2007. 13–27.

———. *Cinema Arthuriana: Twenty Essays.* Rev. ed. Jefferson, NC: McFarland, 2010.

———. *The Reel Middle Ages: Films about Medieval Europe.* Jefferson, NC: McFarland, 1999.

Haweis, Mary Eliza Joy. *Chaucer for Children: A Golden Key.* London: Chatto and Windus, 1877.

Haydock, Nickolas. *Movie Medievalism: The Imaginary Middle Ages.* Jefferson, NC: McFarland, 2008.

Hellekson, Karen, and Kristian Busse, eds. *Fan Fiction and Fan Communities in the Age of the Internet: New Essays.* Jefferson, NC: McFarland, 2006.

Howard, Donald. *Chaucer: His Life, His Works, His World.* New York: Dutton, 1987.

Hutcheon, Linda. *A Theory of Adaptation.* 2nd ed. London: Routledge, 2006.

Jenkins, Henry. *Convergence Culture: Where Old and New Media Collide.* New York: New York University Press, 2008.

Keen, Maurice. *Chivalry.* New Haven: Yale University Press, 1984.

Kelly, Kathleen Coyne. "The BBC *Canterbury Tales* (2003)." *Medieval Afterlives in Contemporary Culture.* Ed. Gail Ashton. London: Bloomsbury Academic, 2015. 134–43.

Kipnis, Laura. "Pornography." *Film Studies: Critical Approaches.* Ed. John Hill and Pamela Church Gibson. Oxford: Oxford University Press, 2000. 151–55.

Kittredge, George Lyman. *Chaucer and His Poetry.* Cambridge: Harvard University Press, 1915.

Kolve, V. A. *Chaucer and the Imagery of Narrative: The First Five* Canterbury Tales. Stanford: Stanford University Press, 1984.

Kracauer, Siegfried. *Theory of Film: The Redemption of Physical Reality.* Princeton: Princeton University Press, 1997.

Lange, John. "The Argument from Silence." *History and Theory* 5 (1966): 288–301.

Lee, Hyapatia. *The Secret Lives of Hyapatia Lee.* 1st Book Library, 2000.

Lehman, Peter, ed. *Pornography: Film and Culture.* New Brunswick: Rutgers University Press, 2006.

Lehrer, Seth, ed. *The Yale Companion to Chaucer.* New Haven: Yale University Press, 2006.

Leitch, Thomas M. "Adaptation Studies at a Crossroads." *Adaptation* 1 (2008): 63–77.

———. "Adaptation, the Genre." *Adaptation* 1.2 (2008): 106–20.

———. "Twelve Fallacies in Contemporary Adaptation Theory." *Criticism* 45.2 (2003): 149–71.

Lochrie, Karma. "Women's 'Pryvetees' and Fabliau Politics in The Miller's Tale." *Exemplaria* 6 (1994): 287–304.

Marlow, John Robert. *Make Your Story a Movie.* New York: St. Martins, 2012.

Matthews, David. "Infantilizing the Father: Chaucer Translations and Moral Regulation." *Studies in the Age of Chaucer* 22 (2000): 93–114.

———. *The Making of Middle English, 1765–1910.* Minneapolis: University of Minnesota Press, 1999.

McNeil, Alex. *Total Television: The Comprehensive Guide to Programming from 1948 to the Present.* 4th ed. New York: Penguin, 1996.

Palmer, Paulina. *The Queer Uncanny: New Perspectives on the Gothic.* Aberystwyth: University of Wales Press, 2012.

Pasolini, Pier Paolo. *Lutheran Letters.* Trans. Stuart Hood. Manchester: Carcanet New Press, 1983.

Patterson, Lee. "Chaucer's Pardoner on the Couch: Psyche and Clio in Medieval Literary Studies." *Speculum* 76 (2001): 638–80.

Paxson, James. "The Anachronism of Imagining Film in the Middle Ages: Wegener's *Der Golem* and Chaucer's *Knight's Tale.*" *Exemplaria* 19.2 (2007): 290–309.

Phelan, Peggy. *Unmarked: The Politics of Performance.* New York: Routledge, 1993.

Polan, Dana. *Scenes of Instruction: The Beginnings of the U.S. Study of Film.* Berkeley: University of California Press, 2007.

Powell, Michael. *A Life in Movies: An Autobiography.* New York: Knopf, 1987.

———. *Million-Dollar Movie.* New York: Random House, 1992.

Prendergast, Thomas, and Stephanie Trigg. "What Is Happening to the Middle Ages?" *New Medieval Literatures* 9 (2007): 215–29.

Pugh, Tison, and Angela Jane Weisl. *Medievalisms: Making the Past in the Present.* London: Routledge, 2013.

Richmond, Velma Bourgeois. *Chaucer as Children's Literature.* Jefferson, NC: McFarland, 2004.

Roach, Joseph. *It.* Ann Arbor: University of Michigan Press, 2007.

Rogerson, Margaret. "Prime-Time Drama: *Canterbury Tales* for the Small Screen." *Sydney Studies in English* 32 (2006): 45–63.

Rohdie, Sam. *The Passion of Pier Paolo Pasolini.* Indianapolis: Indiana University Press, 1995.

Roman, James. *From Daytime to Primetime: The History of American Television Programs.* Westport, CT: Greenwood, 2005.

Rothwell, Kenneth. *A History of Shakespeare on Film: A Century of Film and Television.* 2nd ed. Cambridge: Cambridge University Press, 2004.

Rumble, Patrick. *Allegories of Contamination: Pier Paolo Pasolini's Trilogy of Life.* Toronto: University of Toronto Press, 1996.

Rupp, Katrin. "Getting Modern on Alisoun's Ass: The BBC and Chaucer's Miller's Tale." *Neophilologus* 98 (2014): 343–52.

Salda, Michael N. *Arthurian Animation.* Jefferson, NC: McFarland, 2013.

Salwolke, Scott. *The Films of Michael Powell and the Archers.* Lanham, MD: Scarecrow, 1997.

Scala, Elizabeth. "Yeoman Services: Chaucer's Knight, His Critics, and the Pleasures of Historicism." *Chaucer Review* 45.2 (2010): 194–221.

Sedgwick, Eve Kosofsky. *Epistemology of the Closet.* Berkeley: University of California Press, 1990.

Shakespeare, William. *The Riverside Shakespeare.* Ed. G. Blakemore Evans. 2nd ed. Boston: Houghton Mifflin, 1997.

Shuffelton, George. "Chaucer's Obscenity in the Court of Public Opinion." *Chaucer Review* 47 (2012): 1–24.

Snyder, Stephen. *Pier Paolo Pasolini.* Boston: Twayne, 1980.

Spargo, J. W. "Chaucer's Shipman's Tale: The Lover's Gift Regained." *FF [Folklore Fellows] Communications* 91 (1930): 5–70.

Spearing, A. C. *Medieval Autographies: The "I" of the Text.* Notre Dame: University of Notre Dame Press, 2012.

Staiger, Janet. *Perverse Spectators: The Practices of Film Reception.* New York: New York University Press, 2000.

Stoddart, Scott, ed. *Analyzing* Mad Men: *Critical Essays on the Television Series.* Jefferson, NC: McFarland, 2011.

Summit, Jennifer. *Lost Property: The Woman Writer and English Literary History, 1380–1589.* Chicago: University of Chicago Press, 2000.

Trigg, Stephanie. "Chaucer's Influence and Reception." *The Yale Companion to Chaucer.* Ed. Seth Lerer. New Haven: Yale University Press, 2006. 297–323.

———. *Congenial Souls: Reading Chaucer from Medieval to Postmodern.* Minneapolis: University of Minnesota Press, 2002.

van Es, Bart. *Shakespeare in Company.* Oxford: Oxford University Press, 2013.

Viano, Maurizio. *A Certain Realism: Making Use of Pasolini's Film Theory and Practice.* Berkeley: University of California Press, 1993.

Watson, Nicholas. "The Phantasmal Past: Time, History, and the Recombinative Imagination." *Studies in the Age of Chaucer* 32 (2010): 1–37.

Welsh, James. "Issues of Screen Adaptation: What Is Truth?" *The Literature/Film Reader: Issues of Adaptation.* Ed. James Welsh and Peter Lev. Lanham, MD: Scarecrow, 2007. xiii–xxviiii.

Willemen, Paul, ed. *Pier Paolo Pasolini.* London: British Film Institute, 1977.

Williams, Linda. *Hard Core: Power, Pleasure, and the "Frenzy of the Visible."* Berkeley: University of California Press, 1989.

Wilson, R. W. *The Lost Literature of Medieval England.* London: Methuen, 1952.

Wimsatt, W. K., and Monroe Beardsley. "The Intentional Fallacy." *The Verbal Icon: Studies in the Meaning of Poetry.* Lexington: University of Kentucky Press, 1954. 3–18.

Žižek, Slavoj. *Looking Awry: An Introduction to Jacques Lacan through Popular Culture.* Cambridge: MIT Press, 1991.

———. *The Plague of Fantasies.* London: Verso, 1997.

———. *The Sublime Object of Ideology*. New York: Verso, 1989.

———. *Welcome to the Desert of the Real: Five Essays on September 11 and Related Dates*. London: Verso, 2012.

———, and F. W. J. Schelling. *The Abyss of Freedom / Ages of the World*. Ann Arbor: University of Michigan Press, 1997.

INDEX

Abel, Richard, 74–75
Academy of Motion Picture Arts and Sciences, 69
actors, acting, 20, 23, 24, 26–29, 37–41, 59, 65, 74, 93, 94, 101, 117, 152, 154, 162–64, 178, 188, 190, 204, 213, 215, 233
Adam Scriveyn, 20
adaptation, theory, 1–16, 35–43, 52–54, 209, 213, 219, 222–23; marketability, 57–63
aesthetics, 2, 4, 5, 10, 29, 53–56, 61, 63, 65, 74, 75, 86, 114, 123, 157, 176, 177, 219, 221–22
aging, 199, 200–202, 204, 205, 240, 265; cougar, 199, 200, 203; middle-age(d), 162, 203, 204, 207; old age, 164, 199, 200, 201, 202n16, 254
AIDS, 155, 236
Alighieri, Dante. *See* Dante
Almereyda, Michael, 38–40
Amuka-Bird, Nikki, 239
anachronism, 4n11, 21n4, 169n3, 171n5, 177, 181, 201, 201n14, 202, 202n15, 203, 205, 206
Anderson, Anne, 173 fig. 10.2, 174
Aquinas, St. Thomas, 48
archive, 3, 9, 13, 37, 38–39, 43, 44, 89–94, 97, 101, 106, 107; archontic literature, 37, 37n10
Asbury, Kelly, 29

asynchrony, 156, 241, 243, 247
auctor, auctorite, 33, 34, 43, 102, 158. *See also* authority
Auerbach, Erich, 3
Austen, Jane, 13, 49, 49n9, 50n10, 52, 53, 53n16, 54, 56
authority, 20, 103, 142, 143, 158, 164, 193, 199, 204, 229, 260, 261, 264; Chaucer and, 14, 43, 157, 161, 162, 164, 165; Church and, 193; male/patriarchal, 14, 149, 159, 164, 165, 192, 259; state and, 241, 242, 245; textual, 34, 38. *See also auctor, auctorite*

Bakhtin, Mikhail, 7, 144, 192–93, 229
Bal, Mieke, 51
Bally, Charles, 52
Barrington, Candace, 1n1, 13, 74, 79, 80, 81–82, 83, 84, 85n69, 95n29, 177, 181n17
Barthes, Roland, 113, 255, 255n13
Baudrillard, Jean, 13, 45–48, 51, 55
bawdy, 61, 128, 148, 149, 153, 153–54n9, 161, 162, 188, 196, 207
BBC, 11, 11n30, 15, 42n16, 60, 62, 64, 152
BBC *Canterbury Tales,* xi, 1, 5, 10, 11, 11n30, 14, 15, 42, 57, 62, 187–248
Becket (film), 73
Becket, Thomas, 71
Beidler, Peter, 7, 10n28, 227, 254n8

279

280 INDEX

Benson, C. David, 22n5, 147–48n36
Berber, Bevernage, 242, 245, 247
Bettany, Paul, 20, 22, 167n2, 178, 180, 182, 183n20
Birds of a Feather (television), 203
Blaché, Alice Guy, 76
Black Knight, The (1954 film), 103n43
Black Knight (2001 film), 154
Blundell, Graeme, 212–13
Boccaccio, Giovanni, 10, 60, 73, 74, 74n20, 131, 132, 137, 139n19, 142n22; *Decameron*, 74, 130, 137n16, 226–27; *Teseida*, 169, 216
Boethius, 169
Bolter, Jay David, and Richard Grusin, 10n27, 219, 254n9
Bonaventure, St. (*Meditationes Vitae Christi*), 49
Boogie Nights (film), 155
Bordwell, David, 54
Bosch, Hieronymous, 141
Bradbury, Nancy, 7–8
Bradshaw, Peter, 177, 182
Branagh, Kenneth, 19, 39, 40, 40n14, 41
Braswell, Mary Flowers, 173n7
Brueghel, Pieter (the Elder), 133, 134, 135, 147
Brut, The, 223, 223n8
Burger, Glenn, 160n27, 230–31n1
Burt, Richard, 21n4, 29n14, 60n11, 64n27, 152n5, 157

Camelot (film), 154
Canby, Victor, 131, 131nn3–4
Canterbury Pilgrimage (film), 71
Canterbury Tale, A (film), 5, 13, 19n1, 111–29, 157
Canterbury Tales, 6, 8, 12, 14, 16, 19n1, 21, 22, 30, 31, 56, 57–58, 59, 60, 61, 62, 65, 66, 74, 82, 85, 102, 106, 108, 111, 114, 116, 119, 128, 130, 132, 136–38, 141, 142, 151, 152, 157, 159, 161, 162, 165, 167–68, 172, 179, 182, 188, 213, 215, 218, 219, 227–28, 232, 237; The Clerk's Tale, 65, 71, 76, 174; The Cook's Tale, 138, 142, 144; The Friar's Tale, 142; General Prologue, 11, 21, 22, 30, 50, 51, 58, 116, 117, 162, 167, 180, 187, 213, 220, 256; Harry Bailly, 12, 14, 178, 234; The Knight's Tale, 4, 14, 20, 22, 43, 76, 102, 142, 168, 169, 171–74, 177, 187, 192, 212, 215–16, 218; The Manciple's Tale, 228; The Man of Law's Tale, 16, 76, 136, 147n36; The Merchant's Tale, 76, 133, 142, 161–62, 191–92, 218; The Miller's Prologue and Tale, 76, 102, 142, 162, 179, 182, 188, 189, 190–93; The Pardoner's Prologue and Tale, 8, 15, 51, 71, 139, 140, 142, 230–37; The Parson's Tale, 8, 142; The Reeve's Tale, 61, 133–34, 142, 151, 161, 163; Retraction, 128, 136, 139n19, 142; The Shipman's Tale, 15, 218–20, 225, 229; Sir Thopas, The Prologue and Tale of, 136, 178; The Summoner's Tale, 133, 135, 139–40, 142; The Wife of Bath's Prologue and Tale, 14, 15, 62, 94–97, 100–104, 107, 136, 142, 160–61, 164, 188–89, 197–200, 204, 205, 207, 253, 254, 259, 262–64
Canterbury Tales, The (BBC animated film), 10, 11, 12, 43, 57, 61, 63n21, 157, 213, 214, 216. *See also* Jonathan Myerson
Cattrall, Kim, 201
celebrity culture, 15, 199, 203, 204
Chandler, Raymond, 101–2
Chaplin, Charlie, 144
Chaplin, Geraldine, 144
character(s), 7, 47, 51, 54, 58, 64, 75, 115, 119, 120, 123n21, 126, 130, 143n25, 148, 203, 221, 222, 231, 252, 253–54n6, 256, 259, 260; Chaucer, as adapted, 12, 13, 20, 21, 22, 29, 32, 63n21, 70, 71, 82, 95, 96, 133, 138, 143, 144, 147, 154, 158–60, 162, 174, 178, 188, 197, 204, 205, 209, 215, 216, 220–22, 224, 231, 232, 234, 240, 255; claymation, 10; Shakespeare, as adapted, 20, 22, 23, 28, 32
Chaucer, Geoffrey. *Book of the Duchess*, 29, 30, 102, 179, 182, 232, 237; *House of Fame*, 30, 45, 46, 47, 102, 105n54, 138; *Legend of Good Women*, 76; *Troilus and Criseyde*, 12, 20, 33, 35 fig. 2.1, 65, 76, 261; as character, 23–24, 32–24, 41–42, 43, 44, 148–50, 190–92; as pilgrim, 23, 180. *See also Canterbury Tales*
Chaucerian apocrypha, 1
Chesterton, G. K., 82, 87
Ciardi, John, 254

class, 2, 15, 32, 60, 63–64, 65, 85, 87, 143n24, 147, 152, 200, 222, 231, 253–56, 258, 261; working class(es), 75, 79, 85
Coghill, Neville, 84
Coke, Cyril, 53
Collette, Carolyn P., 8–9
commodity, commodification, 57, 92, 161, 222
Connecticut Yankee in King Arthur's Court, A (films), 73n16, 77–78
consumers, consumerism, 2, 20, 26, 36, 42, 153, 224, 265
convergence culture, 34–36
cougar. *See* aging
Cowart, David, 228
crone, 62, 95, 198, 199, 203, 205
Crusades, 73
Curtis, Scott, 86n74, 87

Dante (Alighieri), 46, 47, 70, 71, 73, 74, 78, 79, 82, 131, 132, 254; film adaptations of his literature, 73–74, 78, 79, 82; *Inferno*, 70–71, 254; *Paradiso*, 46
D'Arcens, Louise, 15, 177, 181n17, 216n26
Davoli, Ninetto, 146
"Deadly Riddle, The," 13, 88–107
Derrida, Jacques, 7, 37, 44, 107n55, 177n12, 243
desire, 14, 15, 27, 28, 38, 57, 95, 103, 106, 115, 119, 120, 122, 125–26, 161, 164, 177, 191, 197–99, 202–5, 211, 216, 226, 242–45, 251, 252, 256, 260–62, 264
detective fiction, 94, 100, 101–2, 106
de Witt, Johannes, 33
digital restoration, 133
Dimock, Wai Chee, 231n2, 236
Dinshaw, Carolyn, 113, 156n16, 207n22, 230–31n1, 239, 241, 242, 247, 248n13
Donaldson, E. Talbot, 50–51
dramatic principle, 22
dreams, 28, 58, 120, 148, 189, 190, 192, 252; American dream, 57, 65, 264, 265; dream, dreamer (Chaucer), 12, 20, 30–31, 45, 46, 47, 102, 138; dream vision, 30, 138
Dryden, John, 214
DVD, 52, 53n16, 60, 90, 92–93n17, 133, 149, 175

Dworkin, Andrea, 160

Echard, Siân, 14, 23, 77n30, 83
Edelman, Lee, 76
Edmondson, George, 30n18
education, educational films, 2, 11, 33, 42, 58, 60, 62, 69–70, 83n59, 84–86, 194, 209–10, 212–13, 216, 217
Ejiofor, Chiwetel, 208
Eliot, T. S., 218
Ellis, Steve, 10n28, 14, 57–58, 58n3, 64n25, 77n30, 80, 81n53, 82, 83, 84, 87, 90n9, 142n23, 149n1, 177, 194n21, 230
Emmerich, Roland, 20

fabliau, 59, 161, 219, 220
Fairbanks, Douglas, 69–70, 73n14, 86–87. *See also Robin Hood* (films)
Fair Unknown romance, 31
fans, 6, 89, 90, 189; fan fiction, 36, 37n10, 43, 43n17; fan magazines, 75, 81, 86 fig. 5.2
fantasy, 21, 29, 31, 32, 61, 86 fig. 5.2, 87, 97, 97n33, 98, 107, 114, 119, 121n18, 146, 154, 156, 157, 168, 190, 251–54, 254n8, 260, 263–64; fantasist, 59; male, 159, 163, 165
Ferguson, Frances, 50
Ferrante, Elena, 132
Fiennes, Joseph, 20, 40
film elements, 89–94, 97, 100–101
film noir, 62, 97, 101–2, 105, 201, 221–23, 225; medieval noir, 102, 105nn44–45
Fincher, David, 8
Finke, Laurie, and Martin B. Shichtman, 2n4, 97, 155n13
Fisher, Sheila, 56, 64
Flaubert, Gustave, 50, 52
Flint, Sir William Russell, 174
Ford, John, 8
Forni, Kathleen, 10n28, 13, 29n15, 90n9, 102, 131n4, 153n6, 176, 177, 181n17, 188, 189n7, 198n4, 198n6, 200n8, 209n4, 210, 215, 220n4, 244
free indirect discourse/*style indirect libre*, xi, 13, 50–54, 141n21, 143
Freidan, Betty, 105

Game of Thrones (television), 19
Ganatra, Nitin, 220
Ganim, John, 22n5, 102, 103nn44–45
Gibson, Mel, 38
Giotto, 132, 132n8, 140, 144
Goble, Warwick, 174
Golem, Der (film), 4
Gower, John, 97n32, 102
Greenaway, Peter, 40
Griffith, D. W., 77, 77n31
Griffith, Hugh, 143

Hamlet (play and films), 38, 40, 41, 42
Hamm, Jon, 253, 61
Hansen, Elaine Tuttle, 159, 160, 190n10
Harry Potter (films), 19, 42, 204
Harty, Kevin J., 5n15, 71n9, 154n11, 209n4, 220n4
Haweis, Mary Eliza Joy, 173 fig. 10.1, 173
Hawes, Keeley, 208
Haydock, Nickolas, 2n4, 19n1, 23n9, 25n10, 176, 177
Helgeland, Brian, 8, 13, 14, 20, 21n4, 31–32, 43–44, 57, 65, 167–83, 264n20. See also *A Knight's Tale*
heteronormativity, 76, 152, 157
Hetreed, Olivia, 238, 240
historicism, 30n17
Hoggart, Paul, 193–94
Hollywood, 13, 27, 29, 40, 41, 54, 57, 60n11, 61n13, 71, 73, 75–78, 81, 85, 93, 94n27, 101, 102, 112n3, 154, 157, 177n14, 181, 201, 203, 262
Holsinger, Bruce, 102
Homer, 46–47, 216
Howard, Donald, 65, 115n11, 238n9
Huggins, Roy, 93, 94, 100, 101–2
Hutcheon, Linda, 6, 35, 36n3, 37nn8–9, 38–39, 42, 59n6, 66n31, 254n9

illustration, 173–75
immigrants and immigration, 62, 74, 79, 240–42

intertexts, intertextuality, 7, 8, 38, 91, 97, 106, 138, 198, 254–55n6, 255
In the Days of Chivalry (film), 69–70, 73, 83, 87
Islam, 239, 240, 242n4

Jacobs, Lea, 72, 75, 76, 85, 86
Jenkins, Henry, 36
Joan the Woman (film), 73
Junger, Gil, 40

Keen, Maurice, 23n9
Kelly, Kathleen Coyne, 11n30, 42n16, 224n8, 237n8
Kelman, Janet Harvey, 174, 174n9, 175 fig. 10.3
Kelmscott Chaucer, 77, 80n41
King Arthur, 13, 73, 95–97, 154n11
Kingsley-Smith, Jane, 25n11
Kittredge, George Lyman, 21, 22n5
Knight's Tale, A (film), xi, 5, 8, 13, 14, 20, 21–24, 25n10, 29–32, 43–44, 57, 65, 154, 167–83, 216n26, 264n20. See also Helgeland, Brian
Koff, Leonard, 227
Kolve, V. A., 169, 192
Krishna, 223, 224
Kurosawa, Akira, 39–40
Kyng Alisaunder, 223

Lange, John, 49n8
lantern slides, 84, 85n69
Ledger, Heath, 167n2, 182
Lee, Bud, 13, 60, 150, 154, 159, 165
Lee, Hyapatia (Victoria Lynch), 14, 149–66
Leitch, Thomas, 4–5, 6n19, 254n9
Lincoln, Andrew, 243
literacy, 65, 208–12, 216
Logan, Joshua, 154
London, 23, 24 fig. 1.1A, 24 fig. 1.1B, 30, 123, 127, 170, 190, 198; London Bridge, 23; London Eye, 181; medieval, 171, 181; theatre, 23, 33; Wandsworth Prison, 208
Lord of the Rings (films), 19

"The Lover's Gift Regained" (*Le bouchier d'Abevile*), 225–26, 228
Lubbock, Percy, 52–53
Luhrmann, Baz, 38
Luthra, Avie, 220–29

MacDonald, David, 113
MacKaye, Percy, 85
MacKinnon, Catherine, 160, 161n29
Madden, John, 20, 40
Mad Men (television), 251–65
manuscript, 3n7, 33, 36, 78, 80, 80n44, 82, 83, 89, 119, 218, 219, 226; culture, 89; illuminations, 169
Marchant, Tony, 15, 187n1, 208–17
marketing and marketability, 8, 8n24, 42–44, 57, 58n5, 60, 61, 62, 54, 74 fig. 5.1, 74, 75, 84, 86 fig. 5.2, 91, 95n29, 121, 153, 153n8, 166, 188, 194, 202, 211–12n4, 228, 251ff.
Marlowe, Christopher (Kit), 25
Matthews, David, 21n4, 82n55, 173n7
McDermott, Marc, 72 fig. 5.1, 73
McKay, John, 180, 219, 222, 223
McLuhan, Marshall, 219
medievalism, neomedievalism, 2–4, 19n1, 57, 64, 77, 100, 102n42, 103n43, 106, 113, 119, 154–55, 157, 176n11, 177, 216n26
Meditations on the Supper of Our Lord and the Hours of the Passion, 49
memory, 41, 41, 107, 107n54, 138, 165, 213, 236, 239ff.
Merritt, Stephanie, 213–14
metanarrative, 11, 25n10, 111, 124, 129, 147, 254
middle age(d). *See* aging
Middle English, as impediment to adaptation, 58, 64, 75, 152, 154, 213
Miller, Jonny Lee, 231
mise-en-scène, 6, 23, 257
modern (versus medieval), 12, 13, 14, 16, 20, 21, 23, 26, 29, 30, 32, 34, 36, 40, 41, 45–46, 49–52, 55, 62n20, 65, 74–75, 77–79, 81, 82, 100, 104, 106, 107, 111, 117, 119, 126, 129, 132, 139, 147, 149, 152, 154, 156, 161, 166, 170, 175, 177–79, 181, 188, 190–91, 193, 198, 209, 212–13, 218, 229, 231, 235, 254, 257, 261; modernity, modernist, 1, 46, 48, 49, 78, 99, 112, 257; modernize(d)(s), modernization, modernizers, modernizing, 12, 42, 189, 194, 198, 213, 214, 216, 217, 219, 222, 257; early modern, 34, 36, 40; postmodern(ity)(ist), 7, 8, 25, 25n10, 45, 46, 47, 51, 65, 176; premodern(ity), 48, 65, 154, 161, 166, 207, 216
Morris, William, 77, 77n29, 81n53
Myerson, Jonathan, 10–12, 61, 63n21, 213–14, 216
My Own Private Idaho (film), 38

narrative(s), 3, 4, 6, 7, 12, 14, 20, 22n7, 23, 25–27, 29, 31–32, 46, 47, 49, 50–54, 62, 75, 85, 96, 97, 103, 107, 111–12, 114, 122, 128–29, 136–37, 139–40, 142–44, 147–48, 151–52, 155–58, 164, 165, 168–72, 176, 187, 188, 192, 202, 204, 205, 208–11, 214–15, 227, 228, 230, 231, 235, 237, 244, 246, 252–53, 258, 260; frame narrative, 10, 151; metanarrative, 11, 25n10, 111, 124, 129, 147, 176; narrating, 21, 53, 137, 175; narration, 29, 43, 54, 76, 116, 117, 121, 147; narrative distancing, 29; narrator(s), 2, 12, 20, 22, 32, 51, 107, 138, 143n25, 147–48n36, 158, 162, 187, 230; narratorial, narratological, narratively, 51, 106, 147n36, 153n9, 188, 206
nationalism, American, 75; British, 64, 64n28, 227, 232
naturalism, 75, 85, 138
Nelson, Tim Blake, 40
Nesbitt, James, 189–90
Nicholls, Paul, 196
Nichols, Stephen G., 3
nostalgia, 2, 112, 155, 157, 251, 252

old age. *See* aging
Olivier, Laurence, 38, 40, 113
On Borrowed Time (film), 71, 76, 78
Ovid, 199, 214

Pacino, Al, 40
Palmer, Paulina, 230n1
Paltrow, Gwyneth, 27
Pasolini, Pier Paolo, 13, 14, 57, 59, 60, 63, 130–48, 153, 158; *Il Decameron*, 59, 131,

137; *Il fiore delle mille e una notte,* 137, 148; *I racconti di Canterbury,* 14, 19, 57, 59, 130–48, 153, 158; *Trilogia della vita,* 59, 60, 130–32, 137, 147
pastiche, 23n9, 25, 176, 177, 181
patriarchy, patriarchal, 63, 160, 163, 165, 192, 241, 242, 247, 258
Patterson, Lee, 233n5
Paxson, James J., 4, 5, 169n3, 171n5
Pearsall, Derek, 135
performance(s), 14, 20, 20n2, 22n7, 24, 26–27, 34, 38–41, 79, 85, 119, 135, 177, 178, 180, 189, 202, 203n18, 204, 256, 264
Photoplay, 81
Picture Play Magazine, 81
Pile, Stephen, 187n1, 194n22, 216n24, 222nn6–7, 240n2
Pilgrimage to Canterbury, A (film), 71
Piper, Billie, 189
playhouse(s), 21, 23, 25, 33
Polan, Dana, 83
pornography, 14, 57, 59, 149–66
Powell, Michael, and Emeric Pressburger, 13, 19n1, 111–29, 157
Pride and Prejudice (BBC), 53
prisons, prisoners, 145, 169, 170, 173–74, 178, 193, 208, 209–13, 215, 217, 244
Prospero's Books (film), 40
proverbs, 7n22, 133, 134
psychology, 25, 29, 30, 30n16, 31, 38, 65, 105, 198, 209, 259, 262
Puri, Om, 220

queer(ness), 15, 76n27, 113, 152n5, 156n16, 160, 170, 207, 230, 230–31n1, 234–37; time, 239n1, 241, 247. *See also* straight time

Raimi, Sam, 8
rape, 61, 62, 65, 84, 103, 115, 159, 160, 163, 165, 197, 233, 234
realism, realist, realistic, 11, 48, 50, 51, 52, 54, 57, 58, 61, 74, 75, 210, 215, 254; neorealist, 59; pseudo-realism, 154
Reed, Carol, 113

remediation, 10n27, 35, 37, 39, 41, 43, 172, 219, 222, 254, 254n9
resonance(s), 14, 15, 168, 182, 189n7, 226, 231–32, 236–38
Ribald Tales of Canterbury (film), xi, 5, 13, 14, 60, 149–66
Richardson, Samuel, 50
Richmond, Velma Bourgeois, 74, 77n30, 79, 81n53, 83, 84n64, 172n6
Riffaterre, Michael, 6
Roach, Joseph, 198, 203
Robin Hood, 13, 70, 86, 103
Robin Hood (films), 70, 73, 87, 153
Robinson, Heath, 174, 175 fig. 10.3
Rumble, Patrick, 133–34, 137, 139n19

Savada, Elias, 183n20
Scala, Elizabeth, 30n18
screenplay, 20, 25, 132n8, 136, 137, 142
Sedgwick, Eve Kosofsky, 236
Seinfeld (television), 205
Sernas, Jacques, 94, 96–97, 99
Se7en (film), 8
sex, sexuality, sexiness, 14, 15, 59, 60, 61, 64, 65, 95n29, 113n6, 115, 119, 120, 124–27, 134, 143, 147, 151–57, 160, 160n27, 161, 163–66, 188, 189, 192, 196, 198, 199, 200–204, 207, 207n22, 216, 218–20, 223, 226, 230–35, 240, 243, 244, 245, 247, 252–53, 255, 256; sexism, 160, 252, 258, 259, 260, 263
Sex and the City 2 (film), 201
Shakespeare, William, film adaptations, 38, 40–43, 57, 60, 72, 73, 79; *Gnomeo and Juliet* (Asbury), 39; *Hamlet* (Almereyda), 40; *Hamlet* (Zeffirelli), 38; *Henry V* (Branagh), 40; *Henry V* (Olivier), 40; *Love's Labour's Lost* (Branagh), 40; *Macbeth* (Kurtzel), 19; *Merchant of Venice* (Radford), 40; *A Midwinter's Tale* (Branagh), 40; *Much Ado about Nothing* (Whedon), 19, 38; *O* (Nelson), 40; *Prospero's Books* (Greenaway), 40; *Ran* (Kurosawa), 40; *Romeo and Juliet* (Zeffirelli), 38; *Ten Things I Hate about You* (Junger), 40; plays, *Hamlet,* 41; *King Lear,* 41; *Macbeth,* 22; *A Midsummer Night's Dream,* 22; *Richard II,* 231;

Romeo and Juliet, 24–25, 26, 27–28, 29, 32, 41; *Titus Andronicus*, 25; *Troilus and Cressida*, 22; *Two Gentlemen of Verona*, 27; *Two Noble Kinsmen* (with John Fletcher), 22, 22n6; pornographic, 152, 157; use of Chaucer, 22

Shakespeare in Love (film), 19, 21–28, 31, 32, 44

shot/reverse shot, 54

Siff, Maggie, 255

Simms, John, 208, 215

Simple Plan, A (film), 8

Sir Gawain and Dame Ragnelle, 97

Skura, Meredith, 22n7, 26

Smoodin, Eric, 83

Spargo, J. W., 83n59

Spearing, A. C., 197

spectacle, 14, 23, 26, 117, 168, 172, 197, 247

spectators, spectatorship, 8, 27, 33, 43, 71, 121, 153, 156, 164, 165, 168

Spitzer, Leo, 3

state authority. *See* authority

Stern, Seymour, 77

Stoppard, Tom, and Marc Norman, 24–25

straight time, 247

Studlar, Gaylyn, 86, 87, 122

Śukasaptati (*Seventy Tales of the Parrot*), 15, 225, 227, 228

Sunset Boulevard (film), 201

Swanson, Gloria, 201

Swan Theater, 33, 34, 34n1, 35 fig. 2.2

Taymor, Julie, 39–40

television, 1, 5, 8, 10, 11, 13, 16, 34, 52, 54, 54n18, 60, 64, 188–91, 193, 196, 211, 213, 217, 219, 221–22, 224; American, 89–95, 99, 100, 102, 105, 106, 251, 252; TV set, 140, 141n21. *See also* BBC

theater, 10, 11, 20–26, 28 fig. 1.2, 29, 33, 34, 38, 66, 78, 93, 94, 122–24, 126, 164, 171, 172; metatheatrical, 172; theatrical (movie house), 57, 124; theatricality, 20, 21, 22, 22n5, 32, 36, 40, 69nn1–2, 78n33, 140, 196, 200. *See also* Swan Theatre

This England (film), 113

Thousand and One Nights, A, 130

trauma, 3, 47, 164–65, 240, 241, 244, 247

Treasure of the Sierra Madre, The (film), 8

Trigg, Stephanie, 81n53, 83, 177n12, 227n16

Twain, Mark, 78

uncanny, 230n1, 234

Underdown, Emily, 173 fig. 10.2, 174n8

updaptation, 219, 220, 222, 226

Uricchio, William, and Roberta E. Pearson, 72, 73n13, 79

Urry, John, 72 fig. 5.1

Usk, Thomas, 237

Van Es, Bart, 20n2

van Sant, Gus, 38–39

Variety, 71, 85

Varma, Indira, 220

Vergil, 46–47

vernacular, vernacularity, 34, 75, 152

VHS, 133, 133n11, 153, 155

Viano, Maurizio, 131, 143n21, 147

Victorians, Victorian era, 77, 83, 174, 208

videotape, 89, 89n7, 91

la Vieille, 199

Villon, François, 73, 74

Wainwright, Sally, 197, 198, 200, 203, 204, 205, 207

Walters, Julie, 196, 204

Warner Brothers, 90n9, 93, 94, 101, 103; *Warner Brothers Presents*, 92, 93, 93n19, 93n21, 94, 94n27, 95, 97, 101, 106

Warren, Renee, 49n9

Watkin, Lawrence Edward, 71

Watson, Nicholas, 88

Wegener, Paul, 4

Weiner, Matthew, 254–55, 257–58, 261, 264

Weldon, Fay, 53

Welles, Orson, 39

Welsh, James, 58

Whedon, Joss, 19, 40, 41; *Much Ado about Nothing* (film), 41

Wilde, Oscar, 237

Williams, Linda, 162
Wimsatt, W. K., and Monroe Beardsley, 228
Wood, Natalie, 13, 89–92, 94, 96–97, 99 fig. 6.3
Wright, David, 209n2, 219

Young Mr. Pitt, The (film), 113

Zeffirelli, Franco, 38
Žižek, Slavoj, 13, 45, 46, 47, 48, 51, 55, 97n33, 100, 105, 106, 251, 263n19, 264n21, 265n22

INTERVENTIONS: NEW STUDIES IN MEDIEVAL CULTURE
Ethan Knapp, Series Editor

Interventions: New Studies in Medieval Culture publishes theoretically informed work in medieval literary and cultural studies. We are interested both in studies of medieval culture and in work on the continuing importance of medieval tropes and topics in contemporary intellectual life.

Chaucer on Screen: Absence, Presence, and Adapting the Canterbury Tales
EDITED BY KATHLEEN COYNE KELLY AND TISON PUGH

Chaucer, Gower, and the Affect of Invention
STEELE NOWLIN

Fragments for a History of a Vanishing Humanism
EDITED BY MYRA SEAMAN AND EILEEN A. JOY

The Medieval Risk-Reward Society: Courts, Adventure, and Love in the European Middle Ages
WILL HASTY

The Politics of Ecology: Land, Life, and Law in Medieval Britain
EDITED BY RANDY P. SCHIFF AND JOSEPH TAYLOR

The Art of Vision: Ekphrasis in Medieval Literature and Culture
EDITED BY ANDREW JAMES JOHNSTON, ETHAN KNAPP, AND MARGITTA ROUSE

Desire in the Canterbury Tales
ELIZABETH SCALA

Imagining the Parish in Late Medieval England
ELLEN K. RENTZ

Truth and Tales: Cultural Mobility and Medieval Media
EDITED BY FIONA SOMERSET AND NICHOLAS WATSON

Eschatological Subjects: Divine and Literary Judgment in Fourteenth-Century French Poetry
J. M. MOREAU

Chaucer's (Anti-)Eroticisms and the Queer Middle Ages
TISON PUGH

Trading Tongues: Merchants, Multilingualism, and Medieval Literature
JONATHAN HSY

Translating Troy: Provincial Politics in Alliterative Romance
ALEX MUELLER

Fictions of Evidence: Witnessing, Literature, and Community in the Late Middle Ages
JAMIE K. TAYLOR

Answerable Style: The Idea of the Literary in Medieval England
EDITED BY FRANK GRADY AND ANDREW GALLOWAY

Scribal Authorship and the Writing of History in Medieval England
MATTHEW FISHER

Fashioning Change: The Trope of Clothing in High- and Late-Medieval England
ANDREA DENNY-BROWN

Form and Reform: Reading across the Fifteenth Century
EDITED BY SHANNON GAYK AND KATHLEEN TONRY

How to Make a Human: Animals and Violence in the Middle Ages
KARL STEEL

Revivalist Fantasy: Alliterative Verse and Nationalist Literary History
RANDY P. SCHIFF

Inventing Womanhood: Gender and Language in Later Middle English Writing
TARA WILLIAMS

Body Against Soul: Gender and Sowlehele *in Middle English Allegory*
MASHA RASKOLNIKOV

www.ingramcontent.com/pod-product-compliance
Lightning Source LLC
Chambersburg PA
CBHW030130240426
43672CB00005B/88